GUIDE TO THE SOUTH SLAVONIC LANGUAGES

GUIDE TO THE SOUTH SLAVONIC LANGUAGES

(Guide To The Slavonic Languages,
Third Edition, Revised And Expanded, Part 1)

by

R. G. A. de Bray

Emeritus Professor of Russian,
The Australian National
University, Canberra

1980

Slavica Publishers, Inc.

For a list of some other books from Slavica, see the last pages of this book. For a complete catalog with prices and ordering information, write to: Slavica Publishers, Inc.
P.O. Box 14388
Columbus, Ohio 43214

Published with the financial assistance of the United Nations Educational, Scientific, and Cultural Organization (UNESCO). The opinions expressed in this book are those of the author, and not necessarily those of either the publisher or UNESCO.

ISBN: 0-89357-060-5.

Copyright © 1951 by J. M. Dent & Sons Ltd., London; revisions copyright © 1969 and 1980 by R. G. A. de Bray. All rights reserved.

Printed in the United States of America.

To the memory of
Robert Auty
Colleague, counsellor,
and friend

CONTENTS

PUBLISHER'S NOTE................................ 7
PREFACE... 9
LIST OF ABBREVIATIONS USED...................... 13

INTRODUCTION

THE PURPOSE OF THIS BOOK........................ 15
THE PLAN AND ARRANGEMENT OF THIS BOOK........... 16
THE METHOD OF USING THIS BOOK................... 18
THE DISTRIBUTION OF THE SLAVONIC LANGUAGES...... 20
CHARACTERISTICS OF THE SLAVONIC LANGUAGES....... 22
THE IMPORTANCE OF OLD SLAVONIC.................. 23

BIBLIOGRAPHY

OLD SLAVONIC.................................... 25
BULGARIAN....................................... 27
MACEDONIAN...................................... 28
SERBOCROATIAN................................... 29
SLOVENIAN....................................... 31
THE SLAVONIC GROUP.............................. 33

Section 1.
OLD SLAVONIC (OLD BULGARIAN)

INTRODUCTION.................................... 35
ALPHABET.. 36
INDO-EUROPEAN RELATIONSHIP...................... 39
FEATURES CHARACTERISTIC OF OLD SLAVONIC......... 40
MORPHOLOGY...................................... 44
    Declensions of—
      nouns....................................... 44
      indefinite adjectives and participles........ 47
      active participles........................... 49
      comparative adjectives and their formation... 50
      numerals..................................... 52
      pronouns..................................... 53
      definite adjectives.......................... 56
      definite comparative adjectives.............. 57
      the definite form of participles............. 58
      personal pronouns............................ 59
    Adverbs... 60
    Conjunctions.................................... 60
    Prepositions.................................... 61
    Conjugation of Verbs............................ 61
      Voices and tenses............................ 61
      Classification............................... 62
      Personal endings............................. 63
      Participles, Verbal Nouns.................... 64
      Simple tenses, examples...................... 65

CONTENTS

    Irregular verbs......................................70
    Compound tenses.....................................71
    Aspects...72
TEXTS...73

Section 2.
BULGARIAN

INTRODUCTION..77
NOTE ON THE LATEST SPELLING REFORMS.....................80
ALPHABET..81
PRONUNCIATION...82
DIALECTS..87
VOWEL GRADATION AND VOWEL LENGTHENING...................89
SLAVONIC CHARACTERISTICS................................89
FEATURES CHARACTERISTIC OF BULGARIAN....................92
MORPHOLOGY..95
    Treatment of Nouns..................................96
    Definite Article...................................101
    Adjectives...102
    Numerals...104
    Pronouns...106
    Adverbs..109
    Conjunctions.......................................110
    Prepositions.......................................110
    Conjugation of Verbs...............................113
        Voices and tenses..............................113
        Classification.................................115
        Present tense..................................116
        Aorist...116
        Imperfect......................................117
        Imperative.....................................118
        Infinitive.....................................119
        Gerund and Participles.........................119
      Compound tenses:
    Future...122
    Future of Renarration..............................122
    Future Perfect.....................................122
    Compound Past (Perfect)............................123
    Compound Past in Renarration.......................124
    Pluperfects..124
    Pluperfects of Renarration.........................124
    Conditional..124
    Past Conditional...................................124
    Past Conditional of Renarration....................125
    Conjugation, examples: See separate tenses
    Irregular verbs....................................125
    Verbs of going and conveying.......................127
    Aspects..128
WORD ORDER WITH ENCLITICS..............................129
TEXTS..132

CONTENTS

Section 3.
MACEDONIAN

INTRODUCTION	137
ALPHABET	143
PRONUNCIATION	144
DIALECTS	153
VOWEL GRADATION AND VOWEL LENGTHENING	155
SLAVONIC CHARACTERISTICS	155
FEATURES CHARACTERISTIC OF MACEDONIAN	160
FEATURES CHARACTERISTIC OF MACEDONIAN AND BULGARIAN	162
FEATURES CHARACTERISTIC OF MACEDONIAN AND SERBOCROATIAN	163
FEATURES CHARACTERISTIC OF ALL SOUTH SLAV LANGUAGES	163
OTHER FEATURES	164
MORPHOLOGY	164
Treatment of Nouns	164
The Articles	171
Adjectives	174
Adjectives (Comparison)	175
Numerals	176
Pronouns	180
Adverbs	186
Conjunctions	192
Prepositions	194
Conjugation of Verbs	197
Voices and tenses	197
Present tense	199
Classification	200
Aorist	201
Imperfect	203
Imperative	204
Present Gerund	205
Participles	206
Verbal nouns	208
Compound tenses:	
Future	209
Reported Future	209
Compound Past	210
Past Definite (Perfect)	212
Pluperfect	212
Conditional	213
Past Conditional	214
Conjugation, examples: See separate tenses	
Irregular and noteworthy verbs	216
Verbs of going and conveying	218
Aspects	220
WORD ORDER WITH ENCLITICS	221
TEXTS	223

CONTENTS

Section 4.
SERBOCROATIAN

INTRODUCTION..233
ALPHABETS (CYRILLIC AND LATIN).....................237
PRONUNCIATION...238
ACCENTS...240
DIALECTS..242
VOWEL GRADATION AND VOWEL LENGTHENING..............243
SLAVONIC CHARACTERISTICS............................244
FEATURES CHARACTERISTIC OF SERBOCROATIAN...........246
MORPHOLOGY..250
    Declensions of—
        nouns..253
        numerals.......................................260
        pronouns.......................................263
        personal pronouns..............................269
        adjectives.....................................269
    Adjectives (Comparison).........................273
    Adverbs...276
    Conjunctions....................................279
    Prepositions....................................280
    Conjugation of Verbs............................282
        Voices and tenses..............................282
        Classification.................................283
        Tense and mood endings and formation.........284
        Conjugation, examples of the simple tenses...289
        Irregular verbs................................290
        Verbs of going and conveying.................294
        Aspects..296
WORD ORDER WITH ENCLITICS..........................296
TEXTS...299

Section 5.
SLOVENIAN

INTRODUCTION..309
ALPHABET..316
SYSTEM OF ACCENTUATION..............................318
PRONUNCIATION...319
ACCENTS...326
COMPARISON OF SLOVENIAN AND SERBOCROATIAN ACCENTS..328
DIALECTS..330
VOWEL GRADATION AND VOWEL LENGTHENING..............331
SLAVONIC CHARACTERISTICS............................331
FEATURES CHARACTERISTIC OF SLOVENIAN...............334
MORPHOLOGY..338
    Declensions of—
        nouns..339
        indefinite adjectives (note on).............348

CONTENTS

```
            numerals...............................349
            pronouns...............................352
            adjectives.............................359
      Adjectives (Comparison).......................362
      Adverbs.......................................365
      Conjunctions..................................369
      Prepositions..................................370
      Conjugation of Verbs..........................373
            Voices and tenses......................373
            Classification.........................376
            Tense and mood endings and formation...378
            Infinitive, Supine.....................380
            Gerunds and Participles................380
            Verbal Nouns...........................382
            Conjugation, examples..................382
            Irregular verbs........................387
            Verbs of going and conveying...........390
            Aspects................................391
WORD ORDER WITH ENCLITICS.........................392
TEXTS.............................................395
```

PUBLISHER'S NOTE

   Slavica is very pleased to be able to make available this Third, revised and expanded edition of Professor de Bray's work, which has been a standard reference for nearly thirty years. Eight of the twelve sections have been substantially revised for this edition, and considerable new material has been included.
   In order to make the work even more useful, the author has recorded native speakers reading the texts at the end of each section. These recordings are available on cassettes or open-reel tapes from the publisher. For information and prices, please write directly to Slavica at P.O. Box 14388, Columbus, Ohio 43214.
   Another innovation in the Third Edition is that the book has been split into three more manageable parts, each of which can be used individually, instead of a single book of over 1100 pages. One part is devoted to the South Slavic languages, a second to the West Slavic languages, and the third to the East Slavic languages. Since the parts are sold separately, students taking such commonly-taught courses as "Introduction to the South (West, East) Slavic Languages" will be able to use the appropriate volume, without having to buy and carry around the entire work.
   Because the academic recession of the 1970's has so strongly depressed the market for scholarly books, it has been necessary to set this edition in more economical cold type, instead of the more elegant hot type with justified right margins which was used in the previous two editions. Slavica is grateful to UNESCO for a subvention which has met part of the costs of resetting the book. We are even more grateful to the typists who have done such a good job of coping with very difficult material. Eleanor B. Sapp typed the sections on Czech, Lusatian, Polish, and Slovenian. Karen L. Black typed the sections on Belorussian, Serbo-Croatian, Ukrainian, and much of the section on Old Church Slavonic. Debra E. Barco typed Bulgarian and Macedonian; Marcia Gauntt typed Slovak; David Birnbaum and Patricia Hansen typed Russian, and Joel and Monica Wilkinson typed part of the section on Old Church Slavonic. Dr. Black took overall responsibility for paginating, cross-referencing, checking corrections, and typing the Introduction and

Bibliography. I wish to thank her here for a complex job well done. Don D. Smith was in charge of checking the corrections from the second proofs and of making various other small but important corrections and improvements in the final camera-ready copy. I am grateful to him for careful attention to tedious and time-consuming work.

We have tried hard, by a system of double and even triple checking, to eliminate misprints, but some are bound to creep into a work of this complexity. Readers who find misprints are asked to send a list of them to the publisher at P.O. Box 14388, Columbus, Ohio 43214. A year or two after the publication of this work, we will publish a list of misprints in our journal, *Folia Slavica*, so that both individuals and libraries may correct their copies.

Columbus, Ohio
May 17, 1980

Charles E. Gribble
President and Editor

PREFACE TO THE FIRST EDITION

It is my pleasant duty to acknowledge with gratitude here the many useful suggestions and the generous encouragement of Professor N. B. Jopson, M.A., Professor of Comparative Philology in the University of Cambridge, Professor W. J. Rose, M.A., Ph.D., former Professor of Polish Literature and History and Director of the School of Slavonic and East European Studies, University of London, and Dr. W. A. Morison, B.A., Ph.D., formerly Lecturer in Comparative Slavonic Philology in the same institution. My sincere thanks are also due to Professor Sir Ellis Minns, Litt.D., F.B.A., of Cambridge, for looking through the first part of this text and making many valuable suggestions, especially as regards presentation, and also for his initial encouragement, without which this book might never have been offered for publication.

I also here express my sincere thanks to my numerous colleagues and friends for their invaluable help and advice with regard to the separate sections of this book: Professor G. Nandriş, Ph.D., Mr. A. Oleynyk, Professor S. Świaniewicz, Professor F. Ramovš, Miss Boža Anžič, Mr. Krum Tošev, Mr. Kiro Petrovski, Mr. D. M. Pavlović, Mr. A. Poberaj, Miss V. Jukova, Mr. K. Naumov, Mr. V. de S. Pinto, Mr. M. Kusseff, Dr. J. Pietrkiewicz, Dr. O. Kolman, Dr. V. Polák, Mrs. E. V. de Bray, Miss T. Ruppeldtová, Dr. E. M. Cyžowa, Dr. J. Rjenč, Rev. Dr. Č. Sipovič, and many others.

It gives me pleasure also specially to mention the tireless help, encouragement, and expert criticism of my wife, who also performed the stupendous feat of typing the entire work in preparation for printing. Her knowledge of several Slavonic languages and her understanding and sympathy with the aims of my work enabled her to make many valuable suggestions in shaping the book.

I would also like to thank my publishers, Messrs. J. M. Dent and Sons, Ltd., for their endless patience and unfailing encouragement in the writing of this work over a period of seven years and under various difficult circumstances.

Finally I warmly thank my printers, Messrs. Stephen Austin and Sons, Ltd., for their untiring perseverance and unfailing courtesy during the printing of my technically extremely difficult text and for the production of such excellent work.

PREFACE

The brief bibliography also serves the purpose of expressing my acknowledgments of indebtedness to the authors of the many valuable works which I have consulted. The list is not intended to be an exhaustive bibliography, but rather a guide to the student who wishes to start delving deeper for treasures which I here only indicate. (The purpose, plan, and method of using this book are explained in the following Introduction.)

Chalfont St. Giles
15. iv. 1950

PREFACE TO THE SECOND EDITION

In this edition the sections on Bulgarian, Czech and Polish have been corrected, revised and slightly expanded, where necessary. The section on Byelorussian has been fully revised and brought up to date in accordance with the new authoritative grammar of Byelorussian published by the Institute of Linguistics of the Byelorussian Academy of Sciences in Minsk. Some misprints have also been corrected in the section on Slovak.

A selection of the most important new practical works published since 1951 have been added to the bibliography.

I would like to express my warmest thanks to Dr. Václav Polák, Professor Ivan Duridanov, and Professor M. R. Sudnik and his colleagues in the Institute of Linguistics of the Byelorussian Academy of Sciences, Minsk, and to all my reviewers for their many helpful suggestions and criticisms.

New Barnet
11. x. 1968

PREFACE TO THE THIRD EDITION

For this edition the author has attempted to revise and bring up to date all the chapters that had not been thoroughly revised for the second edition, namely the chapters on Old Slavonic, Russian, Ukrainian, Macedonian, Serbo-Croätian, Slovenian, Slovak and Lusatian (Sorbian). A number of new grammatical tables have been added, especially in the chapters on Old Slavonic and Serbo-Croätian, and the introduction to the chapter on Russian has been considerably expanded. In the chapter on Ukrainian a more modern approach to the subdivision of the dialects has been adopted on lines suggested by Professor F. T. Zhylkó of the Institute of Dialectology in Kiev. The chapters on Macedonian, Slovak and Lusatian in particular have been revised so as to comply with modern orthographical and grammatical norms. The chapters on Byelorussian, Bulgarian, Czech and Polish, which were revised for the second edition, have only been lightly revised, where necessary.

It is my pleasant duty to thank all my colleagues and friends who have helped me with advice, opinions and information in connection with my work for this edition, and in particular Professor R. I. Avanesov, Professor V. A. Artemov, Professor O. S. Akhmanova, Dr. E. A. Bryzgunova, Mr. B. K. Yoondin, Dr. I. Miloslavsky, Professor A. M. Babkin, Professor L. R. Zinder, Mr. V. Swoboda, Professor F. T. Zhylkó (mentioned above), Professor M. Zhovtobriuch and other colleagues at the Institute of Linguistics of the Ukrainian Academy of Sciences in Kiev, Academic B. Koneski, Academic H. Polenakoviḱ, the late Professor Krum Toshev, Professor T. Stamatoski, Professor T. Dimitrovski, Professor B. Korubin and other colleagues at the Krste Misirkov Institute of the Macedonian Language, Skopje, Professor B. Vidoeski, Miss Olga Spirkoska, Professor M. Stevanović, the late Dr. B. Nikolić, Professor P. Ivić, Professor M. Ivić, Dr. I. Grickat-Radulović, Dr. O. Banković-Todorović and other colleagues of the Serbo-Croatian Language Institute of the Serbian Academy of Sciences, Academic L. Jonke, Dr. B. Finka, Dr. V. Putanec, Dr. D. Alerić and other colleagues of the Language Institute of the Yugoslav Academy of Sciences and Arts, Zagreb, Professor J. Jurančič, Dr. J. Rigler, Professor A. Bajec, Professor M. Tomšič, Dr. L. Legiša, and other colleagues of the Slovenian Language Institute of the Slovenian Academy of Sciences and Arts, Ljubljana, Professor J. Toporišič, Professor J. Zor, Professor J. Ružička, Professor L. Dvonč, and Professor V. Blanár of the L'udevit Štúr Institute of the Slovak Language of the Slovak Academy of Sciences, Miss Eva Ružičková, Dr. R. Pynsent, Dr. M. Corbridge-Patkaniowska, Professor H. Schuster-Šewc, Dr. L. Hajnec, Professor P. Nowotny, and Mr. J. Rjenč.

It is my pleasure also to acknowledge with sincere thanks the material help proffered by the Central Research Fund of the University of London and also by the Australian National University. Both generously helped me to make numerous visits to the Slavonic-speaking countries of Eastern Europe in pursuit of my research. I also express my gratitude to the then

Director of the School of Slavonic and East European Studies, University of London, Dr. G. Bolsover, to the Vice-Chancellor of the Australian National University in Canberra, Professor D. A. Low, and to the Dean of the Faculty of Arts, Dr. W. S. Ramson, for granting me study leave for research purposes between 1968 and 1976, without which I would not have had the opportunity to collect the necessary material for the completion of this work. To all the abovementioned, to my secretary of the Department of Slavonic Languages, the Australian National University, Ms. K. North, and to my publishers for their interest and continual support, I offer my most heartfelt thanks.

Finally, I wish to express my deep gratitude to the Slav Studies project of UNESCO, under the able guidance of Professor V. Tiourine, for their subsidy which enabled the project of the publication of this work to be realized.

If this work will in any way help its readers the better to understand the Slavonic languages, literatures and culture, and the peoples who have created them, it will have achieved its modest purpose.

     молю же вьсѣхъ почитаѭштихъ· не
     можете клати, нъ исправльше почитаите.
     тако бо и стꙑи апл҃ъ паѵлъ гл҃еть·
     бл҃те, а не кльнѣте. амин҃ъ.

Canberra
1 July 1977

ABBREVIATIONS

A., Acc.	Accusative	g., gend.	genders
Act.	Active	G., Gen.	Genitive
adj.	adjective	Germ.	German
adv.	adverb	Gk.	Greek
an.	animate		
Aor.	Aorist	I., Instr.	Instrumental
approx.	approximate	I.E.	Indo-European
arch.	archaic	Imper.,	
art.	article	Imperat.	Imperative
aux.	auxiliary	Imperf.	Imperfect
		impers.	impersonal
b.	born	Impfve.	Imperfective
B-r.,		inan.	inanimate
Byelor.	Byelorussian	Ind.	Indicative
Bulg.	Bulgarian	indef.	indefinite
		Infin.	Infinitive
Card.	Cardinal	interrog.	interrogative
cf.	compare	intrans.	intransitive
Cl.	class	irreg.	irregular
coll.	collective	irr. vb.	irregular verb
colloq.	colloquial	Iter.	Iterative
Comp.	Comparative		
Comp. Past	Compound Past	L., Loc.	Locative
Cond.	Conditional		(= Prepositional)
conj.	conjunction	Lat.	Latin
cons.	consonant	L.L.,	
Cr.	Croätian	Lower L.	Lower Lusatian
C.S.	Common Slav	lit.	literally
Cyr.	Cyrillic	lit. lang.	literary language
Cz.	Czech	Lus.	Lusatian
d.	died	m., masc.	masculine
D., Dat.	Dative	Mac.	Macedonian
Demonstr.	Demonstrative	m. impers.	masculine impersonal
def.	definite	m. pers.	masculine personal
dial.	dialect	Mod. Gk.	Modern Greek
Distrib.	Distributive		
du.	dual	n., neut.	neuter
		N., Nom.	Nominative
ed.	edition	neg.	negative
encl.	enclitic	num.	numeral
Eng.	English		
		Obl.	Oblique (case)
fam.	familiar	Opt.	Optative
f., fem.	feminine	Ord.	Ordinal
Fr.	French	O.S.	Old (Church) Slavonic
Freq.	Frequentative		
Fut.	Future	p.	page

ABBREVIATIONS

p., pers.	person, personal	vol.	volume
pal.	palatal		
Part., Partic.	Participle	Zogr.	Codex Zographensis
Pass.	Passive	=	equals (translation)
Past Ger.	Past Gerund	>	into, becomes
Perf.	Perfect	<	from, derived from
Pers. Pron.	Personal Pronoun	><	as opposed to
Pfve.	Perfective	*	indicates a supposed, deduced form
phon.	phonetic script		
pl., plur.	plural		
Plup.	Pluperfect		
poet.	poetical		
Pol.	Polish		
Pos.	Positive		
Poss. Pron.	Possessive Pronoun		
P.P.A.	Past Participle Active		
P.P.P.	Past Participle Passive		
prep.	preposition		
Pres.	Present		
Pres. Ger.	Present Gerund		
pron.	pronounce(d)		
R., Russ.	Russian		
Reflex.	Reflexive		
reg.	regular		
Rel. Pron.	Relative Pronoun		
s., sg., sing.	singular		
Sb.	Serbian		
Sbcr., Serbocr.	Serbocroätian		
Slk.	Slovak		
Sln.	Slovenian		
Span.	Spanish		
st.	stem		
subst.	substantive		
Sup.	Superlative		
trans.	transitive		
Ukr.	Ukrainian		
U.L., Upper L.	Upper Lusatian		
V., Voc.	Vocative		
vb.	verb		
V.N.	Verbal Noun		

INTRODUCTION
The Purpose of this Book

This book is an attempt to simplify the task of learning the Slav languages as a group for those who know one of them already. It was originally conceived during the 1939-1945 war with a more limited programme.[1] It has a scientific, philological basis. But as it is not intended exclusively for philologists and university students it is written on as nearly "popular" lines as such a subject permits, with a minimum of specialized terminology. It is intentionally an effort at popularization, as the writer believes that all those knowing any one Slavonic language can with profit widen their linguistic horizon by the relatively easy method of learning other Slavonic languages. Those knowing Russian should interest themselves in the Balkans and/or Central Europe, and *vice versa*. A consciousness would thus grow up of the unity of Europe and the continuity, both geographical and cultural, of Russia with Western Europe by way of the intervening central region of Eastern Europe.

It has been the writer's experience that many officials and workers in various fields and even teachers and examiners are given the task of dealing with material in the Slav languages as a group on the strength of their knowledge of only one of them. It is to help this class of language worker, among others, that this work aims. It should be equally useful to the student (whether academic or not) of any of the Slav languages (even if he is a beginner), when his curiosity drives him to "look over the fence" and find out something about the other Slavonic languages beyond.

It is thus also an introduction to the comparative study of the modern Slavonic languages. In these three volumes we give a summary of every language of the group, including Old Slavonic—a synthesis of a very extensive field of knowledge, difficult to master just because of the closeness of one Slav language to another. For every language we try to give a list of its most characteristic phonetic and morphological features, thus showing where the main differences and similarities should be expected and observed.

---

[1] See p. 18.

INTRODUCTION

The Plan and Arrangement of this Book

For the sake of clarity and simplicity each language is treated in a separate section, giving the student a complete conspectus of a clearly defined subject—a single language. This is a new method of approach in dealing with comparative Slavonic grammar, calculated to suit the English beginner with only a modest experience in the Slavonic field. Many a student has found learned works from the Continent forbidding and confusing as an introduction to the comparative philology of the Slavonic languages, for these give as examples of the points they are illustrating rare and archaic words by the side of common words, words from obscure dialects by the side of words from the modern literary and conversational languages. From such works it is impossible to get a clear, working knowledge of any separate modern Slavonic literary or spoken language, for that is not what such books intend to impart. But the English student is often of a practical turn of mind and his needs may rightly be satisfied.

This book starts with a brief summary of the phonetics and grammar of Old Slavonic (also called Old Bulgarian). A knowledge of this dead language casts a great deal of light on the kinship of the modern Slavonic languages, just as a knowledge of Latin helps one to understand the Romance group of languages as a whole. But it must be borne in mind that Old Slavonic is not a "parent language," but rather an "elder sister" language of the *South* Slav group, preserved exclusively in Orthodox ecclesiastical texts. (The South Slav group also includes modern Bulgarian, Macedonian, Serbocroätian, and Slovenian.) Old Slavonic is the nearest we have today to "Common Slav," the "reconstructed" and supposed parent language of all three groups. The East Slav group consists of Russian, Ukrainian, and Byelorussian, while the Western group comprises Czech, Slovak, Polish, and Lusatian or Wendish. Old Slavonic differs from "Common Slav" in a number of important features, e.g. in the combinations of vowels and liquids. But on the whole it is sufficiently close to Common Slav to be used by the student as the essential pivot for passing from one Slavonic language to another.

Each section is built on the same plan:—
1. a brief history of the development of the language together with references to its main writers;

INTRODUCTION

2. a more detailed section on its script and sounds (orthography and descriptive phonetics);
3. a summary of its characteristic features, presented in historical perspective, i.e. compared with Old Slavonic or Common Slav and/or the closely related modern Slav languages—perhaps the most important part of each section. This is either preceded or followed by:
4. a brief summary of the main dialects. These are dealt with mainly from the point of view of their contributions to the formation of the literary language. They are not regarded as "languages" in their own right and of equal status to the generally recognized literary languages. The existence of a literature in a given language and the acceptance and use of the language in a cultured society have been taken as the criteria for dividing off languages from dialects;
5. a concise summary of the "grammar" of the language (its morphology).
6. a special section, where necessary, on word order with enclitics. This subject is always a stumbling block in the mastery of an *active* knowledge of those languages which have enclitics (i.e. South and West Slav here);
7. a few pages of selected texts (without any commentary) as samples of the language as it is printed for the native (i.e. without stress accents) to serve as illustration and reading practice for the student.

Each section also adheres as rigidly as possible to the same scheme and order of explaining the details in the above parts, so as to render the comparison of these details between any two or more of these languages as easy as possible. A minimum of directly comparative tables is included, thereby leaving the student to compare *any* language he likes of the group with any other. This overcomes the difficulty of different people starting out from a knowledge of different single languages.

For Old Slavonic, Byelorussian, Slovenian, and Macedonian till late there have been no text-books at all in English, while for Ukrainian, Bulgarian, and Slovak until recently aids have been only inadequate. For these languages, therefore, fresh material is presented to the English reader; but at the same time it is put *in perspective* and connected with knowledge previously available. The section on the recently recognized Macedonian language is an entirely new contribution to Slavonic studies in any West European language.

It will be seen, therefore, that this work also attempts to fill gaps in the knowledge of the English student, rather than cover familiar ground over again. For this reason less space is given to Russian (as already extensively treated and studied) and Serbocroätian for which grammars, similar to those for Russian, have been available. But Czech and Polish, owing to their complex morphology and the different arrangement of their grammars in the better works, have been rather more fully dealt with here to show their close connection with the other Slavonic languages. Relatively more space, therefore, is devoted to them and the languages named above for which material has so far been unavailable or only inadequate in English.

Any other disparities of length under the separate headings in each section are due to (a) the not sufficiently known lack of adequate material in this country, especially on the more obscure languages of this group; (b) the fact that the original wartime conception of the book covered only Old Slavonic, Russian, Serbocroätian, and Bulgarian, and that the greatest possible brevity for these was required.[1] The sections on these last-named languages have subsequently been revised and brought up to date, but not expanded to the length of the other sections, for the reasons given above.

As this book is mainly concerned with showing the general principles of phonetic and grammatical structure of each language rather than with the study of individual words, a word index has been deliberately omitted. In compensation, the contents have been tabulated as fully as possible to facilitate prompt comparison between the sections. Thus, for example, it is very easy to compare the behaviour of the adjectives in all the languages given by simply looking under the heading "The (Declension of the) Adjectives" under "Morphology" in the Contents List for each language.

The Method of Using this Book

The student should be warned that, as this book attempts a synthesis of a very vast field, the material given is necessarily very condensed. The student, therefore, and especially the beginner, should not attempt to absorb too much at a time. If he bites off

---

[1] See also p. 15.

a little at a time, he will more easily avoid mental indigestion.

As a general word of advice one may say that a person knowing one Slavonic language and approaching another for the first time is well advised to assume in the first place that he *knows* the new language in *outline*; and then—far more important and difficult—carefully and continuously to note and study all differences of phonetics, form, grammar, syntax, and meaning. He must always bear in mind that he is dealing with a really different language with different sounds, intonations, rhythms, and a different historical and sociological background, and different neighbouring influences. In the Slavonic field these languages are different and yet very similar and closely interlinked by linguistic, social and spiritual ties. Their literary vocabularies differ more than those in the Romance languages, and the "speech habits" in the conversational languages of the various Slavs are also very distinct. But the basic vocabulary for the ordinary things of everyday life is strikingly similar—a phenomenon which reminds one of the broad similarities of outlook and attitude to life which undoubtedly exist among the Slavs.

For the Englishman each Slavonic language presents its own difficulties and it would be fruitless to discuss which is the most difficult for him to master. But the difficulties to be met with can all be mastered in time by interest and enthusiasm, because the Slavs are, after all, distant cousins of the British, and often large passages of their languages can be translated literally and in almost the same word order and still make sense! This is impossible with more remote languages.

The importance also of using the brief section on Old Slavonic as a basis for learning another Slavonic language or for studying the whole group cannot be over-emphasized. The trouble of doing this will certainly be repaid and the task greatly facilitated. The student who takes this trouble will see in true perspective the relationship of one Slavonic language to another and gain a real mastery of several languages with an ease that will surprise him or her and give deep satisfaction.

Finally, the student is advised to make a careful study of the sound laws that can be inferred from the sections dealing with the characteristics of each language. Besides bringing out the salient differences of each tongue, these will explain many apparent irregularities and changes in the declensions and conjugations, etc. The importance of a patient study of the phonology (Lautlehre, or historical phonetics) can hardly be overstressed.

For a more detailed description of the languages and for adequate exercises the student is referred to the special grammars of the languages concerned, a list of which is appended in the brief bibliography which precedes each of the three main language groups. Complete lists, e.g. of exceptions, details of syntax, etc., have purposely been often omitted for the sake of brevity, as has all such information as, e.g., the names of the days and months, which can be found in dictionaries.

Each section is furnished with a short appendix of texts on which the student is urged to try his skill with the knowledge he acquires from the study of the preceding pages. He will find he has embarked on a journey of endless fascination.

* * *

The ultimate aim of this work is to enable a direct and reliable approach to be made to the wider issues reflected in the Slavonic literatures and their background, through an accurate knowledge of the Slavonic languages, and so help to create true understanding and friendship between the Slav peoples, great and small, and the English-speaking world. The student is urged always to have these "wider issues" in view and to remember that even an *accurate* translation, if it is torn from its context and background, can be totally misleading and distort the truth. To know the reality, truth, and beauty of the Slavonic world is an unforgettable experience. It enriches and brings hope.

ὄναρ ἀντ' ὀνειράτων
πολλῶν τε καὶ καλῶν

The Distribution of the Slavonic Languages

The greater part of Eastern Europe between Germany and the Urals is inhabited by Slavs. In the western part of this area Polish, Czech, and Slovak are spoken, as well as Lusatian, or Wendish, in a small linguistic island south-east of Berlin round the towns of Cottbus and Bautzen. Together these four languages form the West Slav group.

Adjoining these areas, to the east, Byelorussian —or White Russian—and Ukrainian are spoken, which

INTRODUCTION 21

together with Great Russian form the East Slav group. These linguistic areas are now in the U.S.S.R., but prior to 1939 they extended in the west to inside the frontiers of Poland for both languages, and into Czechoslovakia for Ukrainian only.

The Ukrainian language is essentially a unity, though in the west, in Galicia, it is naturally more influenced by Polish. The name Ruthenian came into English via German from non-classical Latin, being a corruption of the word "Rusin," meaning vaguely a Russian, more specifically a Ukrainian or "Little Russian," as they used to be called. This curious corruption of their name was a convenient cloak under the Austro-Hungarian Empire for disguising the essentially East Slav, or "Russian," character of their Ukrainian subjects (the name Russian really covers all three branches of the East Slav group, the people whom we know popularly as Russians being more precisely Great Russians). All Ukrainians now prefer the fairly modern name, Ukrainian. In more recent times "Ruthenian" came specifically to refer to Subcarpathian Russia, later called Transcarpathian Ukraine, at the extreme eastern end of pre-1939 Czechoslovakia and now incorporated into the Ukrainian S.S.R.—a convenient, but illogical, restriction of its meaning.

Byelorussian, a language even more akin to Great Russian than Ukrainian is to Great Russian, and with a very phonetic spelling, is even younger as a literary language and has also been called in some books White Ruthenian. In Polish the word "ruski" now means only Ruthenian or Ukrainian, whereas in Russian it means (Great) Russian. Owing to the political associations of the name "White Russian," Soviet authorities have also called it "Byelorussian," preserving the Russian word for "white".

North-east and east of the Byelorussian and Ukrainian speaking areas we find the Great Russian area, the language generally known loosely in English as Russian, the language of such great writers as Pushkin, Tolstoy, Dostoyevsky, etc. Geographically one might say that, whereas the Dniepr is the great river of the Ukraine, the Volga with its tributaries forms the chief artery of the Great Russian speaking area, but in its lower reaches it flows through territory peopled by many other nationalities besides the Great Russians. The Great Russian language spread across a sparsely populated Siberia from the seventeenth century onwards with the comparatively peaceful expansion of the Russian Empire across Northern Asia.

South of Austria, Hungary, and Romania, we have the area of the third, Southern, group of Slav tongues.

In the very north-west corner of it, Slovenian, or Slovene, is spoken by not quite two million people, still not all included in Yugoslavia. East and south of this area we have the Serbocroätian speaking region, corresponding roughly with Yugoslavia's northern, eastern, and south-western frontiers. By the Catholics of Croätia, Dalmatia, etc., and the Moslems of Bosnia, Serbocroätian is generally written in the Latin alphabet, whereas in Serbia the Cyrillic alphabet is prevalent; but as explained later, these and dialectical differences cannot be regarded as forming either racial or linguistic boundaries (the different alphabets are only an indication of a difference of religion), as the language is essentially one, i.e. mutually intelligible without previous study. This cannot truthfully be said of any other two Slav languages considered together except "Serbian" and "Croätian". In Southern Yugoslavia, Northern Greece and South-Western Bulgaria, the Macedonian dialects are prevalent. Linguistically they are somewhat more than a transitional stage to Bulgarian. Since 1944 the Macedonian literary language has been officially recognized for all purposes in the territory of the federative Macedonian People's Republic in Yugoslavia. Bulgarian is the fourth separate literary language of this (South Slav) group, spoken over an area pretty well corresponding to Bulgaria's political frontiers; and, owing to its greater divergence from Serbocroätian, it is classed by some (with Macedonian) as East South Slav as opposed to West South Slav.

Characteristics of the Slavonic Languages

Apart from the Cyrillic and the adapted Latin scripts which are purely superficial characteristics, the main features of the Slavonic languages are:—

Pronunciation:—

1. Varying degrees of "palatalization," i.e. variants of the consonants obtained by using the palate to alter their quality.
2. Few true diphthongs.
3. Agglomerations of consonants (but no aspirated consonants).

Grammar:—

4. A high degree of inflection in nouns, pronouns, adjectives, and verbs, comparable to Latin in their complexity.

5. "Aspects" in verbs, a duality of forms presenting an action regarded as either completed or not, or else as single or habitual.

Sentence construction:—

6. Frequent inversion of sentence order, i.e. verb first and subject later, as in Spanish. In Slavonic, owing to the inflections, the word order is much more elastic and variable than in English, French, or German.

The Importance of Old Slavonic

The necessity of knowing Old Slavonic for acquiring a knowledge of the Slavonic group of languages is comparable to the need for knowing Latin for learning the Romance group. Old Slavonic is now a dead and purely ecclesiastical language, but its knowledge gives one an immense insight into, and understanding of, the reasons for the differences between the Slavonic languages. Hence it is very much worth while getting familiar with it, if one wishes to learn more than one language of the Slavonic group, or to study any of these languages at all seriously in its historical aspect, or again to study the group as a whole— a by no means impossible, even if exacting, task.

BIBLIOGRAPHY
(Aids to further study)

The following list is not intended to be an exhaustive bibliography of all the books written on every aspect of the Slavonic languages. In conformity with the introductory and descriptive character of this work, we give below under the headings for the separate languages a selected list of some of the best and most modern grammars, books on their orthography and phonetics, the easier historical grammars, and the most useful dictionaries for each language (in this order). Precedence is given to works in English, after which works in French and German follow—with works in the Slavonic languages themselves given last. This is done purely on the assumption that the English student will be, to start with, more at home in the West European languages, as is usually the case.

The author and title are given as in the original work except in the case of dictionaries, where the title is translated into English. The script of the author's name helps to indicate the origin of dictionaries published in the Slav countries and aiming primarily at assisting natives of those countries. Such works naturally do not contain all the information an English student needs, but can be very useful to him nevertheless.

For the sake of brevity we give preference to latest editions where advisable. We have excluded most works not completed at the time of our writing, and also very large works such as the average student would find inaccessible or beyond his means.

We conclude with a very brief list of the main works on the Slavonic languages as a group.

It will be seen that the student has at his command a very rich variety of aids, if works in the Slavonic languages are included.

OLD SLAVONIC

G. NANDRIŞ, R. AUTY. Handbook of Old Church Slavonic. 2 vols. London, 1959, 1960.
H. G. LUNT. Old Church Slavonic Grammar. 6th edition, The Hague-Paris, 1974.
W. R. SCHMALSTIEG. An Introduction to Old Church Slavic. Cambridge, Mass., 1976.
A. VAILLANT. Manuel du vieux slave (2 vols.). Paris, 1948.

ST. KUL'BAKIN. Le vieux slave. Paris, 1929.
A. LESKIEN. Handbuch der altbulgarischen Sprache. Heidelberg, 1922.
W. VONDRÁK. Altkirchenslavische Grammatik. Berlin, 1912.
P. DIELS. Altkirchenslavische Grammatik. Heidelberg, 1932.
N. VAN WIJK. Geschichte der altkirchenslavischen Sprache, I. Berlin-Leipzig, 1931.
J. J. MIKKOLA. Urslavische Grammatik, I. Heidelberg, 1913; II, 1942; III, 1950.
P. ARUMAA. Urslawische Grammatik, I. Heidelberg, 1964.
H. H. BIELEFELDT. Altslawische Grammatik. Halle, 1961.
B. ROSENKRANZ. Historische Laut- und Formenlehre des Altbulgarischen. Hague-Heidelberg, 1955.
Г. А. ХАБУРГАЕВ. Старославянский язык. Москва, 1974.
В. П. БЕСЕДИНА-НЕВЗОРОВА. Старославянский язык. Харьков, 1962.
Н. М. ЕЛКИНА. Старославянский язык. Москва, 1960.
Л. В. МАТВЕЕВА-ИСАЕВА. Лекции по старославянскому языку. Ленинград, 1958.
С. Д. НИКИФОРОВ. Старославянский язык. Москва, 1952.
А. М. СЕЛИЩЕВ. Старославянский язык, I, II. Москва, 1951, 1952.
А. И. СОБОЛЕВСКІЙ. Древній церковно-славянскій языкъ. Фонетика. Москва, 1891.
К. МИРЧЕВ. Старобългарски език. София, 1956.
J. HAMM. Staroslavenska Gramatika. Zagreb, 1958.
J. Łoś. Gramatyka starosłowiańska. Lwów-Warszawa-Kraków, 1922.
J. KURZ. Učebnice jazyka staroslověnského. Praha, 1966.
P. OLTEANU, G. MIHĂILĂ, L. DJAMO-DIACONIȚĂ, E. VRABIE, E. LINȚA, O. STOICOVICI, M. MITU. Slava veche și slavona românească. București, 1975.
M. WEINGART. Rukovět jazyka staroslověnského. Praha, 1937-1938.
W. VONDRÁK. Kirchenslavische Chrestomathie. Göttingen, 1910.
V. VONDRÁK. Církevněslovanská chrestomatie. Brno, 1925.

Dictionaries

T. A. LYSAGHT. Material towards the Compilation of a Concise Old Church Slavonic-English Dictionary. Wellington, 1978.
L. SADNIK, R. AITZETMÜLLER. Handwörterbuch zu den altkirchenslavischen Texten. The Hague, 1955.
FRANZ VON MIKLOSICH: Lexicon palaeoslovenico-graeco-latinum (reprint of 1862-1865 Vienna edition). Aalen, 1963.

BIBLIOGRAPHY 27

──. (Второе отдѣленіе Императорской Академіи наукъ). Словарь церковно-славянскаго и русскаго языка, I-III. С.-Петербургъ, 1867.
ЂУРО ДАНИЧИЋ. Рјечник из књижевних старина српских. Graz, 1962.
ed. J. KURZ et al. Slovník jazyka staroslověnského (А-П). Československá Akademie věd, Praha, 1966-1977.

BULGARIAN

A. B. LORD. Beginning Bulgarian. The Hague, 1962.
S. GHININA, Ts. NIKOLOVA, L. SAKASOVA. A Bulgarian textbook for foreigners. Sofia, 1965.
М. МАРИНОВА, М. ХУБЕНОВА, А. ДЖУМАДАНОВА. Български език, I (in English). Sofia, 1964.
L. BEAULIEUX. Grammaire de la langue bulgare. Paris, 1933.
Н. МАРКОВИЋ. Бугарска граматика. Београд, 1937.
П. С. КАЛКАНДЖИЕВЪ. Българска граматика. Пловдив-София, 1938.
Л. Д. АНДРЕЙЧИНЪ. Основна българска граматика. София, 1942.
Л. АНДРЕЙЧИН, Н. КОСТОВ, Е. НИКОЛОВ. Българска граматика. София, 1947.
Л. АНДРЕЙЧИН, Н. КОСТОВ, Е. НИКОЛОВ. Български език. София, 1960.
С. СТОЙКОВ. Граматика на българския книжовен език. София, 1964.
Л. АНДРЕЙЧИН, К. ПОПОВ, С. СТОЯНОВ. Граматика на българския език. София, 1977.
Правописен и правоговорен наръчник, edited by И. ХАДЖОВ, С.СТОЙКОВ, Л. АНДРЕЙЧИН. София, 1945.
С. СТОЙКОВ. Увод в българската фонетика. София, 1966.
Д. ТИЛКОВ, Т. БОЯДЖИЕВ. Българската фонетика. София, 1977.
S. MLADENOV. Geschichte der bulgarischen Sprache. Berlin-Leipzig, 1929.
Б. ЦОНЕВЪ. История на български езикъ. 3 vols. 1937-1940.
ХРИСТО ПЪРВЕВ. Очерк по история на българската граматика. София, 1975.

Dictionaries

М. МИНКОВ, and others. Bulgarian-English Dictionary. Sofia, 1958.
ed. М. МИНКОВ. English-Bulgarian Dictionary, vol. I. Sofia, 1973.
К. СТЕФАНОВЪ. Bulgarian-English Dictionary. Sofia, 1914.
К. СТЕФАНОВЪ. English-Bulgarian Dictionary. Sofia, 1929.

Г. ЧАКАЛОВ, И. ЛЯКОВ, З. СТАНКОВ. English-Bulgarian Dictionary. Sofia, 1961.
N. MARCOFF. Bulgarian-French Dictionary. Leipzig, 1912.
N. MARCOFF. French-Bulgarian Dictionary. Leipzig.
G. WEIGAND und A. DORITSCH. Bulgarian-German Dictionary. 6th edition. Leipzig, 1943.
С. Б. БЕРНШТЕЙН. Bulgarian-Russian Dictionary. Moscow, 1966.
С. МЛАДЕНОВЪ. Етимологически и правописенъ речникъ на българския книжовенъ езикъ. Sofia, 1941.
С. ЧУКАЛОВ. Russian-Bulgarian Dictionary. Sofia, 1951, or Moscow, 1962.
М. МЛАДЕНОВ. Bulgarian-Serbocroatian Dictionary. Belgrade, 1967.
М. МЛАДЕНОВ, Д. ЦРВЕНКОСКИ, Б. БЛАГОЕСКИ. Bulgarian-Macedonian Dictionary. Skopje-Belgrade, 1968.
Л. АНДРЕЙЧИН, and others. Български тълковен речник. Sofia, 1955.
Л. АНДРЕЙЧИН, and others. Правописен речник на българския книжовен език. Sofia, 1960.
П. ПАШОВ, Хр. ПЪРВЕВ. Правоговорен речник на българския език. София, 1975.
С. РОМАНСКИ, and others. Речник на съвременния български книжовен език. 3 vols. Sofia, 1955-1959.

MACEDONIAN

КРУМЕ КЕПЕСКИ. Македонска граматика. Скопје, 1946; 2nd edition. Скопје, 1950.
——. Македонски правопис. Скопје, 1945.
Б. КОНЕСКИ и К. ТОШЕВ. Македонски правопис со правописен речник. Скопје, 1950.
ed. К. ТОШЕВ et al. Правопис на македонскиот литературен јазик со правописен речник.* Скопје, 1970.
А. М. СЕЛИЩЕВ. Очерки по македонской диалектологии. 1918.
H. G. LUNT. Grammar of the Macedonian Literary Language. Skopje, 1952.
Б. КОНЕСКИ. Граматика на македонскиот литературен јазик. Скопје, vol. I, 1952, 1957; vol. II, 1954. 2nd edn. Parts I and II (1 vol.). Скопје, 1967.
Б. КОНЕСКИ. Историја на македонскиот јазик. Скопје-Београд, 1965.
K. TOŠEV, D. STEFANIJA. A Textbook of the Macedonian Language. Skopje, 1965.
R. PANOSKA, A. DŽUKESKI. A Handbook for the Study of the Macedonian Language (Beginner's Course). 2nd edition. Skopje, 1971.
*Accented dictionary.

BIBLIOGRAPHY

Dictionaries

Д. ЦРВЕНКОВСКИ, Б. ГРУИЌ. Macedonian-English Dictionary. Skopje-Cetinje, 1965.
Б. ГРУИЌ, Д. ЦРВЕНКОВСКИ. English-Macedonian Dictionary. Skopje, 1975.
Ѓ. МИЛОШЕВ, Б. ГРУИЌ et al. Serbo-Croatian-Macedonian Dictionary. Skopje-Cetinje, 1964.
Б. КОНЕСКИ, and others. Речник на македонскиот јазик со српскохрватски толкувања. 3 vols. Skopje, 1961, 1965, 1966.
Д. ТОЛОСКИ, В. М. ИЛЛИЧ-СВИТЫЧ, Н. И. ТОЛСТОЙ. Macedonian-Russian Dictionary. Moscow, 1963.
К. ГАВРИШ. Macedonian-Russian Dictionary. Skopje, 1969.
Б. ГРУИЌ, К. ГАВРИШ. Russian-Macedonian Dictionary. Skopje-Cetinje, 1966.

SERBOCROATIAN

V. JAVAREK, M. SUDJIĆ. Serbo-Croat. London, 1963.
T. F. MAGNER. Introduction to the Serbo-Croatian Language. Minneapolis, 1956.
A. B. LORD. Beginning Serbocroatian. The Hague, 1958.
M. PARTRIDGE. Serbo-Croat Practical Grammar and Reader. Beograd, 1972.
S. BABIĆ. SerboCroat for foreigners. Beograd, 1973.
D. SUBOTIĆ and N. FORBES. Serbian Grammar. Oxford, 1926.
J. D. PRINCE. Practical Grammar of the Serbo-Croatian Language. New York, 1928.
D. FRY and Ђ. KOSTIĆ. A Serbo-Croat Phonetic Reader. London, 1939.
A. MEILLET and A. VAILLANT. Grammaire de la langue serbo-croate. Paris, 1933.
M. REŠETAR. Elementar-Grammatik der kroatischen serbischen Sprache. 2nd edition. Zagreb, 1922.
И. В. АРБУЗОВА, П. А. ДМИТРИЕВ, Н. И. СОКАЛЬ. Сербохорватский язык. Ленинград, 1965.
А. БЕЛИЋ. Граматика српскохрватског језика за I-III разред средњих и стручних школа, Vols. I-III. Београд, 1933-4.
А. БЕЛИЋ. Савремени српскохрватски књижевни језик. 2 vols. Београд, 1951, 1949.
T. MARETIĆ. Gramatika i stilistika hrvatskoga ili srpskoga jezika. 2nd edition. Zagreb, 1931.
R. ALEKSIĆ i M. STEVANOVIĆ. Gramatika srpskoga ili hrvatskoga jezika za srednje škole. Sarajevo, 1947.
М. СТЕВАНОВИЋ. Граматика српскохрватског језика за више разреде гимназије. Београд, 1951.

BIBLIOGRAPHY

S. TEŽAK, S. BABIĆ. Pregled gramatike hrvatskosrpskog jezika. Zagreb, 1972.
I. BRABEC, M. HRASTE, S. ŽIVKOVIĆ. Gramatika hrvatskosrpskog jezika. Zagreb, 1968.
J. HAMM. Kratka gramatika hrvatskosrpskog književnog jezika za strance. Zagreb, 1967.
А. БЕЛИЋ. Правопис српскохрватског књижевног језика. 3rd edition. Београд, 1934.
Б. МИЛЕТИЋ. Основи фонетике српског језика. Београд, 1952.
———. Правопис српскохрватскога књижевног језика. Нови Сад. 1960.
———. Pravopis srpskohrvatskoga književnog jezika. Zagreb, 1960.
И. ЛАЛЕВИЋ. Синтакса српскохрватског језика за средње школе. Београд, 1936.
F. POLIANEC. Istorija srpskohrvatskog književnog jezika s pregledom naših dilekata i istorijskom čitankom. Beograd, 1931.
A. LESKIEN. Grammatik der serbokroatischen Sprache, I. Heidelberg, 1914.
P. IVIĆ. Die serbokroatische Dialekte, I. The Hague, 1958.

Dictionaries

*MORTON BENSON. Serbo-Croatian-English Dictionary. Belgrade, 1974.
B. GRUJIĆ. English-Serbocroatian Serbocroatian-English Dictionary. Belgrade-Cetinje, 1966.
S. RISTIĆ, Z. SIMIĆ, V. POPOVIĆ. English-Serbocroatian Dictionary. 2 vols. Belgrade, 1956.
И. М. ПЕТРОВИЋ. English-Serbian Dictionary. Belgrade, 1933.
R. FILIPOVIC et al. English-Croatian Dictionary. Zagreb, 1971.
ed. R. FILIPOVIC. English-Serbo-Croatian Dictionary. (Langenscheidt pocket dictionary. Pt. I.) Berlin-Zagreb, 1970.
Š. LOCHMER. English-Croatian Dictionary. Senj, 1906.
F. A. BOGADEK. English-Croatian, Croatian-English Dictionary. Pittsburgh, 1926; London, 1950.
M. DRVODELIĆ. Croatian-English Dictionary. Zagreb, 1953.
J. H. СТЕВОВИЋ. Serbian-French, French-Serbian Dictionary. Belgrade, 1930.
*C. РИСТИЋ и J. КАНГРГА. Serbian-German and German-Serbian Dictionary. 2 vols. Belgrade, 1928 (also in small edition).

*Accented dictionaries.

BIBLIOGRAPHY

*D. DAJIČIĆ a F. ŠOBRA. Serbian-Czech Dictionary. Prague.
*J. JURANČIČ. Serbo-Croatian—Slovenian Dictionary. Ljubljana, 1972.
*Л. А. МИЧА́ТЕКЪ. Дифференціальный сербско-русскій словарь. (Differential Serbian-Russian Dictionary.) St. Petersburg, 1903.
D. ĐUROVIC. Russian-Serbocroatian Dictionary. Belgrade, 1936.
*И. И. ТОЛСТОЙ. Serbo-Croatian-Russian Dictionary. Moscow, 1976.
*С. ИВАНОВИЧ, И. ПЕТРАНОВИЧ. Russian-Serbo-Croatian Dictionary. Moscow, 1976.
Л. БАКОТИЋ. Речник српскохрватског књижевног језика. Belgrade, 1936.
*F. IVEKOVIĆ i I. BROZ. Rječnik hrvatskoga jezika. Zagreb, 1901.
*ВУК СТЕФ. КАРАЏИЋ. Српски речник. (Serbian-German-Latin Dictionary.) 4th edition, Belgrade, 1935.

SLOVENIAN

M. GOBETZ, B. LONČAR. Slovenian Language Manual. Willoughby Hills, Ohio, 1976.
J. TOPORIŠIČ. Slovenski knjižni jezik. Maribor, vol. 1, 1968; vol. 2, 1966; vol. 3, 1967; vol. 4, 1970.
J. JURANČIČ. Slovenački jezik. Ljubljana, 1965.
A. BAJEC, R. KOLARIČ, M. RUPEL. Slovenska slovnica. Ljubljana, 1956.
(Uredniški Odbor). Slovenska gramatika. Državna založba Slovenije. Ljubljana, 1947.
A. BREZNIK. Slovenska slovnica za srednje šole. Celje, 1934.
C. PEČNIK. Praktisches Lehrbuch der slovenischen Sprache. 6th edition. Hartleben, Vienna-Leipzig. Very out of date.
M. RUPEL. Slovensko pravorečje. Ljubljana, 1946.
F. BEZLAJ. Oris slovenskega knjižnega izgovora. Ljubljana, 1939.
A. BREZNIK in F. RAMOVŠ. Slovenski pravopis (accented). Ljubljana, 1935.
A. BREZNIK in F. RAMOVŠ. Slovenski pravopis—mala izdaja (not accented). Ljubljana, 1937.
*F. RAMOVŠ, O. ZUPANČIČ (and others). Slovenski pravopis. Slovenska akademija znanosti in umetnosti. Ljubljana, 1950. A full orthographical *dictionary* as well as a treatise on orthography.

*Accented dictionaries.

BIBLIOGRAPHY

F. RAMOVŠ. Kratka zgodovina slovenskega jezika, I. Ljubljana, 1936.
F. RAMOVŠ. Historična gramatika slovenskega jezika. Vol. II. Ljubljana, 1924; Vol. VII, Ljubljana, 1936.
*――――. Slovenski pravopis. Ljubljana, 1962.
T. LOGAR. Slovenska narečja. Besedila (texts). Ljubljana, 1975.

Dictionaries

*J. KOTNIK. Slovenian-English Dictionary. Ljubljana, 1967.
R. ŠKERLJ. English-Slovenian Dictionary. Ljubljana, 1965.
A. GRAD, R. ŠKERLJ, N. VITOROVIČ. English-Slovenian Dictionary. Ljubljana, 1967.
*A. GRAD, R. ŠKERLJ, N. VITOROVIČ. Slovenian-English Dictionary. Ljubljana, 1967.
*F. BRADAČ. Slovenian-German Dictionary. Ljubljana, 1930.
F. TOMŠIČ. German-Slovenian Dictionary. Ljubljana, 1938.
*M. PLETERŠNIK. Slovenian-German Dictionary. 2 vols. Ljubljana, 1894. The only complete dictionary with full (tone) accentuation to date.
J. KOTNIK. Slovenian-French Dictionary. Ljubljana, 1937.
J. PRETNAR. French-Slovenian Dictionary. Ljubljana, 1932.
J. KOTNIK. Slovenian-Russian Dictionary. Ljubljana, 1967.
J. PRETNAR. Russian-Slovenian Dictionary. Ljubljana, 1947.
J. VESKIĆ. Slovenian-Serbocroätian (differential) Dictionary. Belgrade, 1932.
A. VILHAR. Slovenian-Serbocroätian Dictionary. Ljubljana, 1927.
*S. ŠKERLJ, R. ALEKSIĆ, V. LATKOVIĆ. Slovenian—Serbo-Croatian Dictionary. Belgrade-Ljubljana, 1974.
A. VILHAR. Serbocroätian-Slovenian Dictionary. Ljubljana, 1927.
A. ZAVADIL. Slovenian-Czech Dictionary. Prague.
*R. ŠKERLJ. Slovenian-Czech Dictionary. Ljubljana, 1967.
F. BRADAČ. Czech-Slovenian Dictionary. Ljubljana, 1967.

*Accented dictionaries.

BIBLIOGRAPHY

V. SMOLEJ. Slovak-Slovenian Dictionary. Ljubljana, 1976.
J. GLONAR. Slovar slovenskega jezika. 1936.
*(Inštitut za slovenski jezik SAZU.) Slovar slovenskega knjižnega jezika. I, II. Ljubljana, 1970, 1975.

THE SLAVONIC GROUP

W. J. ENTWISTLE and W. A. MORISON. Russian and the Slavonic Languages. London, 1964.
A. MEILLET. Le slave commun. 2nd edition. Paris, 1934.
A. VAILLANT. Grammaire comparée des langues slaves, I. Lyon, vol. I, 1950; vol. II, 1958; vol. III, 1966.
W. VONDRÁK. Vergleichende slavische Grammatik. 2 vols. Göttingen, 1924, 1928.
V. HRUBÝ. Vergleichende Grammatik der slavischen Sprachen. Hartleben, Vienna-Leipzig. Sketchy and out of date.
А. М. СЕЛИЩЕВ. Славянское языкознание, I: Западнославянские языки. Москва, 1941.
Н. КОНДРАШОВ. Славянские языки. Москва, 1956.
С. Б. БЕРНШТЕЙН. Очерк сравнительной грамматики славянских языков. Москва, 1961.
K. HORÁLEK. Úvod do studia slovanských jazyků. Praha, 1962.
T. LEHR-SPŁAWIŃSKI, W. KURASZKIEWICZ, F. SŁAWSKI. Przegląd i charakterystyka języków słowiańskich. Warszawa, 1954.
ed. W. WEINGART. Slovanské spisovné jazyky v době přítomné. Praha, 1937.
R. NAHTIGAL. Slovanski jeziki, I. Ljubljana, 1952.
O. BROCH. Slavische Phonetik. Heidelberg, 1911.
ed. T. LEHR-SPŁAWIŃSKI. Chrestomatia słowiańska. I (South Slav). Kraków, 1949; II (West Slav). Kraków, 1950.
E. BERNEKER. Slavische Chrestomathie. Trübner, Strasburg, 1902.
E. BERNEKER. Slavisches etymologisches Wörterbuch (to "morŭ" only). Heidelberg, 1908-1914.
F. MIKLOSICH. Dictionnaire abrégé de six langues slaves. 1885. Reprinted.

The attention of students is also drawn to the articles on the Slavonic languages in the various encyclopedias and, for samples of the spoken language, to the various series of records available in Great Britain and elsewhere.

*Accented dictionaries.

SECTION 1. OLD SLAVONIC (OLD BULGARIAN)
INTRODUCTION

The first writings in Old Slavonic are now generally considered by philologists to have been in the language of the Slavs of Macedonia of the second half of the ninth century. The Czech scholar, Abbé Josef Dobrovský (1753-1829), was the first to make a serious study of this language in his *Institutiones linguae slavicae dialecti veteris*, published in 1822. Franc Miklošič, the Slovene scholar, towards the middle of the nineteenth century advanced the theory that the language of these ancient manuscripts was the language of the Slavs of Pannonia (modern Hungary) and therefore maintained that the language was old Slovenian. Some later scholars, such as A. Leskien, a German, came to the conclusion on philological grounds that the language was really old Bulgarian; and one can agree that on the whole it is more similar to modern Bulgarian than to other modern Slavonic languages, though Bulgarian has developed striking characteristics peculiar to itself.

The Old Slavonic MSS. at present extant, however, probably do not date from earlier than the eleventh century. They therefore represent the language of a later period with an admixture of local dialectical characteristics and later developments. They are all ecclesiastical in content. The MSS. generally considered to be the two most complete, linguistically purest and oldest are the Slavonic versions of the four Gospels called Codex Zographensis and Codex Marianus, which the Croatian scholar Jagić transcribed into Cyrillic characters from the original Glagolitic. (The Glagolitic alphabet was an ancient Slavonic script, probably also invented by St. Cyril, which was gradually superseded by the clearer Cyrillic.) The majority of the ancient Slavonic MSS. are in the Glagolitic script, only the Sava Gospels and the Codex Suprasliensis being originally in Cyrillic.

It should be pointed out that the Slavonic language of the services, etc., of the Orthodox Church is not identical with the language of the most ancient Slavonic MSS. Owing to historical causes it is in fact a much Russianized version of Old Slavonic most conveniently called Church Slavonic. This applies to the Orthodox Church in Serbia and Bulgaria as well as Russia, where the word for "holy", for instance, is throughout in its later Russian form—svjatъ—and not in its original form, which is svętъ (with nasal vowel).

Nor yet can the language of these MSS. be regarded as Common (or proto-) Slav, i.e. the original Slavonic language from which the modern Slavonic languages directly derive. It possesses throughout certain *South* Slav features, as exemplified in the forms of the words for "castle, town" and "night": gradъ, noštь.

The Codex Zographensis (see texts) in most respects preserves the original form of the language the most accurately; for example, the nasal vowels ę (ᴀ) and ǫ (Ѫ) are consistently differentiated. But even here the letters ъ and ь are sometimes confused, as also are original ꙗ and ѣ by reason of the original script; ѥ is also not indicated.

THE OLD SLAVONIC ALPHABET

Cyrillic	Latin Transcription	Approximate English Equivalent
а	a	
Б	b	
В	v	
Г	g	
Д	d	
Є	e	
Ж	ž	[1]*zh*, Fr. *j*, *s* in "pleasure"
ѕ	dz	*1
З	z	
И, I, ι	i	2
ҕ	ǵ	§hard *g+y*
К	k	
Л	l	
М	m	
Н	n	
О	o	
П	p	
Р	r	
С	s	
Т	t	
ОУ	u	¶
Ф	f	
Х	ch *or* x	*ch* in "loch"
Ѡ	o	†(= ordinary Sl. *o*)
Щ *or* ШТ	št	¶[1]*sht*
Ц	c	[1]*ts* (pronounced together)
Ч	č	[1]*ch*
Ш	š	[1]*sh*

OLD SLAVONIC

THE OLD SLAVONIC ALPHABET

Cyrillic	Latin Transcription	Approximate English Equivalent
ъ	ъ	(neutral vowel, = a in "about")
ы	y	[3]similar to Russian ы
ь	ь	sign of palatalization, not wholly mute in earliest times, approx. = i in "bit"
ѣ	ě	ye in "yet", or vulg. Eng. "yeah"
ю	ju	= "you"
ꙗ	ja	¶= "yah"
ѥ	je	¶= "yes" without the s
ѧ	ę	‡Fr. *in*
ѫ	ǫ	‡Fr. *on*
ѩ	ję	‡Fr. *y + in*
ѭ	jǫ	‡Fr. *y + on*
ѕ	ks	†x
ѱ	ps	†
ѳ	f	†
ѵ (y)	i(ü)	†

[1] Palatal consonants.
[2] In the O.S. texts the ˘ (short mark) over и is not generally put in; but in grammars when и represents the semi-vowel "j" (<jь) after a vowel, ˘ may be put in to assist the student.
[3] Usually written ъı.
˘ or´= palatalization, "soft" consonants or yotation, e.g. мелетъ = мелѥтъ .
* ѕ changes to ꙃ in most MSS.; so Zogr.
† = Greek letters, mainly used in words directly borrowed from the Greek.
‡ = letter peculiar to O.S.
¶ = letter peculiar to O.S. in this form.
§ = letter peculiar to O.S. with this sound; occurs only in words of foreign origin.

Russian scholars will notice the absence of: ё, (й[2]), э, as well as the different order after ш (=o).
Serbian scholars will notice the absence of the letters introduced by Obradović and Vuk Karadžić (ѣ is put to a different use): ђ, ј, љ, њ, ћ, џ.
Bulgarian scholars will note that ѫ in O.S.

is a nasal vowel.
Ukrainian scholars will note the absence of:
ґ, є, ї (for phon. ji), and й.

The following vowels caused the preceding consonant to be palatalized: e (usually printed є), и, ь, ѣ, ѧ, and the j element, which had no separate letter in O.S., but appears in the letters ю, ıa, ıe, ıѧ, ıѫ, and in the composition of words and terminations.

In the palatalizations of the earliest periods, in the formative stage of Slavonic, these vowels actually caused the preceding consonants to change, thus producing word forms from common Indo-European roots which are peculiar to Slavonic, e.g. I.E. root *g^{w}enā "woman", Sl. žena "woman". In later periods the preceding consonant is supposed to have been merely "softened" or modified, as in Russian and also other non-Slavonic languages. This is a perfectly natural process, governed largely by the physical question of tongue position and convenience of enunciation. The degree of palatalization in the dead O.S. is entirely debatable and in reading can conveniently be ignored, except when indicated, rather on the lines of modern Serbian. The degree of palatalization[1] in early Slavonic doubtless depended on the dialects used. These were the modern Slavonic languages in embryo before the dispersal and migration of the Slavs from their original home, now supposed to be somewhere in the plains N.E. of the Carpathians in the Dniestr and Dniepr basins.

The basis of the pronunciation of the O.S. alphabet, it should be noted, is the Greek of the period, just as Greek clearly gave the models for the forms of most of the letters, e.g. г for g, п for p, etc. That is why в is used for v (β), н for i (η), etc. Additional letters for sounds not in Greek have been supposed to have been borrowed from Hebrew and other oriental languages such as Coptic, notably ш from the Hebrew ש, and supposedly ү, ц, ж, etc.

The position of the accent in the word, and even less the intonation, cannot be assumed with any certainty even from the collective evidence of Russian, Bulgarian, and the intonations of Serbocroătian and Slovenian. On the whole it is safest to follow the Russian model. Serbocroătian cannot be taken as a guide for position as all the "rising" accents have shifted one syllable nearer the beginning of the word and all final accents are excluded (see below).

[1] i.e. other than in the "1st, 2nd and 3rd Palatalizations of Velars" and with j.

INDO-EUROPEAN RELATIONSHIP

The studies made by Dobrovský, Šafárik, Kopitar, Karadžić, etc., of various aspects of the Slavonic languages were all part of the great revival of interest in language, which was one of the characteristics of the Romantic Movement at the beginning of the nineteenth century. Sir William Jones at the end of the eighteenth century in England first pointed to the relationship of the Western European languages, based on the comparison of Latin and Germanic and Greek, to Persian and Sanskrit. Slavonic, which with the Baltic languages (Lithuanian and Latvian), Armenian and Albanian, as well as Persian and Sanskrit, form the eastern or "satem" group of the Indo-European languages (as opposed to the western or "centum" group which also includes the Celtic languages), was first correlated with the other branches of the Indo-European group by the German scholar, Franz Bopp, at the beginning of the nineteenth century. These studies showed clearly the close relationship of Slavonic to West European languages, evident enough even to the layman in such examples as the Slavonic words for "three", три; "mother", матер-; "to give", дати, cf. Latin: *dare*; "new", новъ, cf. Latin: *novus*, English, "new." Slavonic was also found to share with other Indo-European languages certain linguistic phenomena or processes in word formation, such as vowel gradation or Ablaut (exemplified in the English verb paradigm "sing, sang, sung" and many similar verbs with vowel change in a regular alternating series), and vowel lengthening (as for example in the Latin verb paradigm *capio, cēpi, captum*).

Slavonic examples of vowel gradation or Ablaut:

ь — и — ѣ (e)	die	мьрѫ,	мрѣти
	count, read	уьтѫ,	уисти
	take	берѫ,	бьрати
ъ — оу	breathe; spirit	дъхнѫти;	доухъ
е — о	flow; course	текѫ;	токъ
ѣ — а	go out	изѣсти;	излазити
о — ъ	call	зовѫ,	зъвати
ѣ — и	garland; weave	вѣньць,	вити

Slavonic examples of vowel lengthening:

е — ѣ	oppress	оугнетѫ,	оугнѣтати
о — а	pierce	избости,	избадати
ь — и	collect	събьрати,	събирати
ъ — ы	breathe	дъхнѫти,	дыхати

FEATURES CHARACTERISTIC OF SLAVONIC

On the other hand, these scholars found that certain features were characteristic of Slavonic and corresponded regularly to different regularly recurring forms in the western "centum" languages, as well as in other Indo-European languages.

1. The Slavonic metathesis of vowel + *l* or *r*. Taking "*t*" to represent any consonant, the original syllables *tert*, *telt*, *tort*, *tolt*, in O.S. reversed the order of vowel and liquid, giving *trĕt*, *tlĕt*, *trat*, *tlat* with lengthening of the vowels. Compare:

Eng.	garden	O.S.	градъ	=city, castle
Germ.	Berg	O.S.	брѣгъ	=slope, bank
Gothic	valdan	O.S.	владѫ	=I rule
Eng.	milk	O.S.	млѣко	=milk

and, without an original initial consonant:

| Germ. | Arbeit | O.S. | работа | =slavery |

2. The influence of the "soft" or palatalized consonants on the subsequent vowels in terminations of words:

несомъ, знаѥмъ	being carried, being known	Present Participles Passive
водоѭ, доушеѭ	with water, soul	Instrumental singular feminine substantival declension.
водѣ, доуши	to the water, soul	Dative and Locative singular feminine substantival declension.
гробѣхъ, краихъ[1]	graves, edges	Locative plural masculine substantival declension.
водъ, доушь	of waters, souls	Genitive plural feminine substantival declension.
гробъі, краи[1]	with graves, edges	Instrumental plural masculine substantival declension.

[1] и after a vowel = *ji*.

OLD SLAVONIC

3. The "first palatalization" from the formative period of Slavonic. Here the vowels є, ь, ѧ, ѣ (when derived from $\bar{e}$), and и transformed the preceding velar consonants к, г or х into the then palatalized consonants ч, ж and ш respectively:

к/ч	say; speech	рєкѫ, рєчєши; рѣчь
	child	отрокъ, отрочѧ
г/ж	God	богъ, боже, Nominative, Vocative Sing.
х/ш	fright	страхъ, frightful страшьнъ, frighten страшити

but ск, зг changed to (palatalized) шт, жд, e.g.:

| board | дъска, (diminutive) дъштица |
| marrow | мозгъ, (adjective) мождань |

Similarly ц < к, and s, з < g become ч and ж respectively before the above vowels, e.g.:—

отьць = father, отьчє Voc. sing.
къназь = prince, кънаже Voc. sing.

The development of ц from k, and s, later з, from g is due to what is called the *third* palatalization of velars, in which these changes of the velars sometimes occur *after* (not before) front vowels when a back vowel (but not ы or ъ) follows.

Thus к, г and also х after ь, и (of non-diphthongal origin), ѧ and soft vocalic r' (рь or рь) become ц´, s´ > з´, с´ respectively, e.g.:—

отьць	from *otьkъ	=father
овьца	" *ovьka	=sheep
мѣсѧць	" *měsękъ	=month
срьдьцє	" *sŕdьko	=heart
лицє	" *liko	=face, cf. Russian Church Slavonic ликъ
дѣвица	" *děvika	=maiden, cf. O.S. дѣва
нарицати	(Impfve.)	=to call, name, cf. Imperative нарьци from Perfective Present нарєкѫ and Perfective Infinitive нарєшти
сиць	from *sikъ	=such, cf. такъ = such, какъ = of what kind?
стьза	" *stьga	=path, cf. Sbcr. стаза, Russian dialect стега
польза	" *polьga	=profit, advantage, cf. R. dial. польга
двизати	" *dvigati	=to move (Impfve.) cf.

къняsь from Old Germanic *kuningaz = prince Pfve. двигнѫти
растрѣзати (Impfve.) =to tear apart, also растрѣзгати, Pfve.: растрѣзгнѫти, Russ. растерзать
вьсь from *vьхъ =all (Nom. sing. masc.)

As will be seen from these examples, the third palatalization of velars does not affect the morphological flexions of Old Slavonic, but is of importance mainly in word formation, a subject outside the scope of this work.

4. The "second palatalization" from the formative period of Slavonic. Here before и and ѣ (when derived from *ai* or *oi*) the velars к, г, х changed to ц, s(з) and с respectively:

к/ц	course, current	токъ,	Nominative,
		тоцѣ	Locative sing.
	hand	рѫка,	Nominative,
		рѫцѣ	Dative/Locative sing.
	say	рекѫ,	Present 1st pers. sing.,
		рьци	Imperative 2nd pers. sing.,
		рьцѣмъ	1st pers. plural
х/с	breath, spirit	доухъ,	Nom., Loc.
		доусѣ, доуси	sing., Nom. pl.
г/s	God	богъ,	Nom., Loc. sing.
		возѣ	

while in this case ск, зг change to ст, зд: дъска board, Dat. Loc. sing. дъстѣ; дразга a wood, Dat. Loc. sing. драздѣ.

5. The influence of the *j* element. When consonantal word stems had endings beginning with *j* added, certain consonantal changes similar to the above palatalizations took place. Roots ending in vowels with the same endings added afford clear proof of the presence of the *j*. This appears in the terminations of the Past Participle Passive and of the Present tense, and also of some Comparative adjectives. This feature is called *yotation*.

Before *j*:—

			Infinitive/Present 1st p. sing.
к,г,х changed to ч,ж,ш		weep	плакати, плачѫ
		tell lies	лъгати, лъжѫ

OLD SLAVONIC

			Infin./Pres. 1st pers. sg.	
		breathe	дъхнѫти	доуша soul
т, д	changed to ⎫	throw	метати,	мештѫ
шт, жд	⎭	thirst	жадати,	жаждѫ
с, з	changed to ⎫	write	пьсати,	пишѫ
ш, ж	⎭	bind	вѧзати,	вѧжѫ
н, л, р changed to ⎫	drive	гонити,	гонѭ
н̂, л̂, р̂	⎭	order	велѣти,	велѭ
		plough	орати,	орѭ
п, б, insert л̂ ⎫	drown	потопити,	потоплѭ
в, м	⎭	love	любити,	люблѭ
		put	ставити,	ставлѭ
		feed	кръмити,	кръмлѭ
ст, зд changed to ⎫	announce	възвѣстити,	
шт (=щ)	⎬		възвѣщѫ	
жд	⎭	nail to	пригвоздити, пригвождѫ
ск, зг changed to ⎫	seek	искати, иштѫ
шт, жд	⎭	withy	розга collective:
				рождиѥ

6. Disappearance of consonants in roots before consonantal terminations and in word composition:—

sleep съпати, съ(п)нъ verb, noun
weave плетѫ, пле(т)лъ Pres. 1st p. sing., Past
                        Participle Active II

7. Epenthetic н, i.e. the insertion of н between two components:—

go into въ-н-ити Infinitive

8. The semivowels. It will be observed that in O.S. nearly all words end in a vowel or in the semivowels ъ or ь. These latter are "reduced vowels", i.e. shortened from original normal vowels in Indo-European. (Most final consonants of I.E. words are dropped.)

9. Common Slav vocalic $\mathring{l}$ and $\mathring{r}$ (hard) and $\mathring{l}'$ and $\mathring{r}'$ (soft) are rendered in O.S. indiscriminately: лъ, ль, ръ, рь, e.g. длъгъ = long, чръвь = worm. In a few words these same combinations represent true л+ъ, р+ь, etc., e.g. кръвь = blood, крьстъ = cross, плъть = flesh, сльза = tear.

OLD SLAVONIC

A BRIEF SUMMARY OF OLD SLAVONIC MORPHOLOGY
THE DECLENSIONS OF NOUNS

The declension of nouns in O.S. had seven cases—Nominative, Genitive, Dative, Accusative, Instrumental, Locative, and Vocative, for all three numbers, i.e. singular and plural and also dual (for two persons or things), and three genders—masculine, feminine, and neuter. For neuter nouns the Vocative singular is the same as the Nominative and Accusative singular.

There were six declensions, subdivided according to the basic feature of their stem:—
1. i-stems; 2. consonantal stems; 3. $\bar{u}$-stems; 4. $\breve{u}$-stems;
5. a-stems; 6. o-stems.

1. Examples of the declension of i-stem nouns. Masculines were few in number, feminines more numerous. (Cf. Latin *ovis*.)

пѫть = way (Masc.)

	Sing.	*Pl.*	*Dual*	
Nom.	пѫть	пѫтьѥ	пѫти	= N., A., V.
Gen.	пѫти	пѫтьй	пѫтью	= G., L.
Dat.	пѫти	пѫтьмъ	пѫтьма	= D., I.
Acc.	пѫть	пѫти		
Instr.	пѫтьмь	пѫтьми		
Loc.	пѫти	пѫтьхъ		
Voc.	пѫти			

кость = bone (Fem.)

Nom.	кость	кости	кости	= N., A., V.
Gen.	кости	костьй	костью	= G., L.
Dat.	кости	костьмъ	костьма	= D., I.
Acc.	кость	кости		
Instr.	костьѭ	костьми		
Loc.	кости	костьхъ		
Voc.	кости			

2. Consonantal stems in -n-, -s-, and -t- (masc. and neut.), and in -r- (two fem. nouns only). (Cf. Latin *nomen nominis, opus operis, caput capitis, mater matris*.)

камы = stone (Masc.)

	Sing.	*Plur.*	*Dual*	
Nom.	камы	камене	камени	= N., A., V.
Gen.	камене	каменъ	каменоу	= G., L.
Dat.	камени	каменьмъ	каменьма	= D., I.
Acc.	камень	камени		
Instr.	каменьмь	каменьми		
Loc.	камене	каменьхъ		

OLD SLAVONIC

има = name (Neut.)

	Sing.	Plur.	Dual	
Nom.	има	имена	именѣ	= N., A., V.
Gen.	имене	именъ	именоу	= G., L.
Dat.	имени	именьмъ	именьма	= D., I.
Acc.	има	имена		
Instr.	именьмь	имены		
Loc.	имене	именьхъ		

мати = mother (Fem.)

	Sing.	Plur.	Dual	
Nom.	мати	матери	матери	= N., A., V.
Gen.	матере	матеръ	материю	= G., L.
Dat.	матери	матерьмъ	матерьма	= D., I.
Acc.	матерь	матери		
Instr.	матерьѫ	матерьми		
Loc.	матери	матерьхъ		
Voc.	мати			

(So also the neuters: тѣло, тѣлесе = body, отроуа, отроуате = child, Acc.=Nom.)
Like камы except in Nom. sing. дьнь = day, Inst. pl. also дьны, Gen. Loc. dual also дьнью.

3. *ū*-stems, similar to consonantal stems, No. 2. Feminine only.

црькы = church

	Sing.	Pl.	Dual (wanting)
Nom.	црькы	црькъви	--
Gen.	црькъве	црькъвъ	--
Dat.	црькъви	црькъвамъ	--
Acc.	црькъвь	црькъви	--
Instr.	црькъвьѫ	црькъвами	--
Loc.	црькъве	црькъвахъ	--

So also: свекры = mother-in-law, боукы = letter, character, любы = love, смокы = fig, хорѫгы = flag, жрьны = millstone. Also кръвь = blood (originally Acc. sing. < Nom. sing. *kry).

4. *ŭ*-stems. I.E. *ŭ* changes to ъ in Slavonic. Masculines only. (Cf. Latin: *domus*)

съінъ = son

	Sing.	Pl.	Dual	
Nom.	съінъ	съінове	съіны	N.,A.,V.
Gen.	съіноу	съіновъ	съіновоу	G.,L.
Dat.	съінови	съінъмъ	съінъма	D.,I.
Acc.	съінъ	съіны		
Instr.	съінъмь	съінъми		
Loc.	съіноу	съінъхъ		
Voc.	съіноу			

So also: домъ = house, врьхъ = top, summit, медъ = honey, волъ = ox, ледъ = ice.

5. *a*-stems. These are actually subdivided into *a*- (hard) stems and *ja*- (soft) stems. The influence of the *j* has created what is apparently a different declension, but the changes are regular. To the *ja*-stems also belong the fem. nouns in -и and -ыни : ладии = boat, богыни = goddess. This entire group consists mostly of fem. nouns.

   A-STEM   JA-STEM
 жена = woman, wife; землга = earth, land

	Sing.		Pl.		Dual	
Nom.	жена	землга	жены	землѧ	женѣ	земли
Gen.	жены	землѧ	женъ	земль	женоу	землю
Dat.	женѣ	земли	женамъ	землгамъ	женама	землгама
Acc.	женѫ	землѭ	жены	землѧ		
Instr.	женоѭ	землеѭ	женами	землгами		
Loc.	женѣ	земли	женахъ	землгахъ		
Voc.	жено	земле				

6. *o*-stems. As in declension 5, these are subdivided into *o*-stems and *jo*-stems, hard and soft, with corresponding regular variations. There are both masculine and neuter versions of this declension.
   O-STEMS   JO-STEMS
 рабъ =slave; лѣто =year; конь =horse; полѥ =field

Sing.	Masc.	Neut.	Masc.	Neut.
Nom.	рабъ	лѣто	конь	полѥ
Gen.	раба	лѣта	конга	полга
Dat.	рабоу	лѣтоу	коню	полю
Acc.	рабъ	лѣто	конь	полѥ
Instr.	рабомь	лѣтомь	конѥмь	полѥмь
Loc.	рабѣ	лѣтѣ	кони	поли
Voc.	рабе		коню	

	Masc.	Neut.	Masc.	Neut.
Plur.				
Nom.	раби	лѣта	конӥ	полѩ
Gen.	рабъ	лѣтъ	конь̂	полъ̂
Dat.	рабомъ	лѣтомъ	конѥмъ	полѥмъ
Acc.	рабъı	лѣта	конѩ	полѩ
Instr.	рабъı	лѣтъı	конӥ	полӥ
Loc.	рабѣхъ	лѣтьхъ	конӥхъ	полӥхъ
Dual				
Nom.	раба	лѣтѣ	конѩ	полӥ
Gen.	рабоу	лѣтоу	коню	полю
Dat.	рабома	лѣтома	конѥма	полѥма

Mixed declensions:—

Already in Zogr. and other early MSS. we find a confusion of the *o*-stems with the *ŭ*-stems, e.g. богови (Dat. sing.), мѫжеви (Dat. sing.), дароу (Loc. sing.), and грѣховъ (Gen. plur.) (Codex Marianus).

Some *jo*-stems in -тель and -арь have Nom. and Gen. plur. according to the consonantal stem declension, e.g. мъıтаре = publicans, дѣлателе̂ = workers.

Nouns in -инъ decline like рабъ in the sing. and dual, but throughout the plural lose this final -инъ and have irregular Nom., Dat., Loc.: граждане, -немъ, -нехъ (Gen. -нъ, Acc., Inst. -нъı) = townsmen.

Words declined like o-stem and a-stem nouns:—

INDEFINITE ADJECTIVES AND PARTICIPLES

Into this category fall the *"indefinite"* adjectives, e.g. новъ "new", добль "brave" (e.g. новъ богъ = a new god, as opposed to новъıй богъ = the new god), also the following participles:—

Present Participle Passive:	несомъ	being carried
Past Participle Active II:	неслъ	carried, used only in Nom. with Perfect tense
Past Participle Passive :	несенъ	(having been) carried
	ѩтъ	taken

THE DECLENSION OF INDEFINITE ADJECTIVES

Hard stems:—

новъ = (a) new

Sing.	*Masc.*	*Neut.*	*Fem.*
Nom.	новъ	ново	нова
Gen.		нова	новъı

	Masc.		*Neut.*	*Fem.*
Dat.	НОВОУ			НОВѢ
Acc.	НОВЪ,	НОВА	НОВО	НОВѪ
Voc.	НОВЕ		НОВО	—
Instr.	НОВОМЬ			НОВОѬ
Loc.	НОВѢ			НОВѢ
Plur.				
Nom.	НОВИ		НОВА	НОВЪІ
Gen.	НОВЪ			НОВЪ
Dat.	НОВОМЪ			НОВАМЪ
Acc.	НОВЪІ		НОВА	НОВЪІ
Voc.	НОВИ		НОВА	НОВЪІ
Instr.	НОВЪІ			НОВАМИ
Loc.	НОВѢХЪ			НОВАХЪ
Dual				
N.A.V.	НОВА		НОВѢ	НОВѢ
G.L.	НОВОУ			НОВОУ
D.I.	НОВОМА			НОВАМА

Soft stems:—

БОУИ = (a) mad

Sing.	*Masc.*		*Neut.*	*Fem.*
Nom.	БОУИ		БОУѤ	БОУѨ
Gen.	БОУѨ			БОУѨ
Dat.	БОУЮ			БОУИ
Acc.	БОУИ,	БОУѨ	БОУѤ	БОУѪ
Voc.	—		БОУѤ	—
Instr.	БОУѤМЬ			БОУѤѪ
Loc.	БОУИ			БОУИ
Plur.				
Nom.	БОУИ		БОУѨ	БОУѨ
Gen.	БОУИ			БОУИ
Dat.	БОУѤМЪ			БОУѨМЪ
Acc.	БОУѨ		БОУѨ	БОУѨ
Voc.	БОУИ		БОУѨ	БОУѨ
Instr.	БОУИ			БОУѨМИ
Loc.	БОУИХЪ			БОУѨХЪ
Dual				
N.A.V.	БОУѨ		БОУИ	БОУИ
G.L.	БОУЮ			БОУЮ
D.I.	БОУѤМА			БОУѨМА

The spelling БОУИ in the Nom. and Acc. sing. masc. and in the Gen. plur. of all genders represents a form *bujь*. But in the Dat. sing. fem., the Loc. sing. of all genders, the Nom. and Voc. plur. masc., the Instr. plur. masc. and neut., and in the Nom., Acc. and Voc. dual neut. and fem. the same spelling represents a form *buji*.

ACTIVE PARTICIPLES

The Pres. Part. Act. is also thus declined except in the Nom. sing., masc., fem., and neut., and in the Nom. plur. masc., where it has the endings of the consonantal declension, viz.:—

несы = carrying

	Masc.	Neut.	Fem.
Sing.			
Nom.	несы	несы	несѫшти
Gen.	несѫшта		несѫштѦ
Dat.	несѫштоу		несѫшти
Acc.	несѫшть	несѫште	несѫштѫ
Instr.	несѫштемь		несѫштеѭ
Loc.	несѫшти		несѫшти
Plur.			
Nom.	несѫште	несѫшта	несѫштѦ
Gen.	несѫшть		несѫшть
Dat.	несѫштемъ		несѫштамъ
Acc.	несѫштѦ	несѫшта	несѫштѦ
Instr.	несѫшти		несѫштами
Loc.	несѫштихъ		несѫштахъ
Dual			
Nom.	несѫшта	несѫшти	несѫшти
Gen.	несѫштоу		несѫштоу
Dat.	несѫштема		несѫштама

So also:—
знаѩ, Gen. sing. masc.: знаѭшта
   (for *j* verbs) = knowing
хвалѧ, Gen. sing. masc.: хвалѩшта
   (for *i* verbs) = praising

The declension of the *Past Participle Active I* is similar:—

несъ = having carried

	Masc.	Neut.	Fem.
Sing.			
Nom.	несъ	несъ	несъши
Gen.	несъша		несъшѦ
Dat.	несъшоу		несъши
Acc.	несъшь	несъше	несъшѫ
Instr.	несъшемь		несъшеѭ
Loc.	несъши		несъши
Plur.			
Nom.	несъше	несъша	несъшѦ
Gen.	несъшь		несъшь
Dat.	несъшемъ		несъшамъ
Acc.	несъшѦ	несъша	несъшѦ
Instr.	несъши		несъшами

	Masc.	*Neut.*	*Fem.*
Loc.		несъшихъ		несъшахъ
Dual			
Nom.	несъша	несъши	несъши
Gen.		несъшоу		несъшоу
Dat.		несъшема		несъшама

So also:—

давъ Gen. sing. masc.: давъша = having given; and хвалъ Gen. sing. masc.: хвалъша = having praised.

THE COMPARISON OF ADJECTIVES

There are two sets of endings used for forming comparative adjectives:—

Nom. sing. masc. -jii, neut. -je, fem. -$j ь\check{s}i$, written respectively -ни, -є or -ю, -ьши, with yotation of the preceding consonant of the stem of the adjective, and more frequently the extended form with the ending enlarged by an initial -ѣ-, which causes the first palatalization of preceding velars:—

Nom. sing. masc. -$ěji$, neut. -$ěje$, fem. -$ěj ь\check{s}i$, written respectively -ѣи, -ѣю, -ѣиши.

The first set of endings is used for a small number of adjectives with consonantal stems, e.g.:—

		Masculine	*Neuter*	*Feminine*
гржбъ	= rough	гржблии	гржблю	гржблъши
драгъ	= dear	дражии	драже	дражьши
лихъ	= exceeding, excessive	лишии	лише	лишьши
лютъ	= violent	люштии	люште	люштьши
хоудъ	= bad, small, poor	хоуждии	хоужде	хоуждьши

The same endings are used for most adjectives ending in -ъкъ, -ькъ and -окъ, which lose this suffix in the comparative:—

		Masculine	*Neuter*	*Feminine*
высокъ	= high	выши	выше	вышьши
глжбокъ	= deep	глжблии	глжблю	глжблъши
сладъкъ	= sweet	слаждии	слажде	слаждьши
крѣпъкъ	= strong	крѣплии	крѣплю	крѣплъши

Most other adjectives use the second, extended set of endings, in which the characteristic -ѣ- changes to -а- or -ѩ- after palatalized consonants:—

OLD SLAVONIC

новъ	= new	M. новѣи	N. новѣѥ	F. новѣиши
старъ	= old	старѣи	старѣѥ	старѣиши
чистъ	= clean	чистѣи	чистѣѥ	чистѣиши
мъногъ	= many	мъножаи	мъножаѥ	мъножаиши
соухъ	= dry	соушаи	соушаѥ	соушаиши
добль	= valiant	добляи	добляѥ	добляиши

A few adjectives ending in -ъкъ, -ькъ retain this ending in forming the comparative; the -к- then undergoes the first palatalization, e.g.:—

		Masculine	*Neuter*	*Feminine*
горькъ	= bitter	горьчаи	*горьчаѥ	горьчаиши
тьнъкъ	= fine, tender	*тьнъчаи	тьнъчаѥ	*тьнъчаиши

Notice the irregular comparisons of the following common adjectives which have suppletive forms for the comparative degree formed from different roots from those of the positive degree:—

велии велнкъ	} = big	M. болии ваштии	N. болѥ ваште	F. больши=bigger, ваштьши=more, bigger
малъ	= small	мьнии	мьнѥ	мьньши=smaller, lesser
благъ добръ	} = good	лоучии оунии соулии соулѣи рауии	лоучѥ оунѥ оунѣѥ соулѥ соулѣѥ рауѥ	лоучьши оуньши соульши соулѣиши рауьши } better
зълъ	= bad	гории	горѥ	горьши = worse

Comparative adjectives have an indefinite (simple) and a definite (compound) declension like positive adjectives and all follow the *soft*-stem models. (See below). In the Nom. sing. masc. the indefinite and definite forms are identical.

Than = неже. The Genitive of comparison is also frequently used, e.g.: мъножаишѫ (Acc. pl. masc.) пръвыихъ = more numerous than the first.

The Superlative degree of *adjectives* is expressed by the comparative degree with вьсѣхъ = of all, e.g.: мьнии вьсѣхъ = the smallest (of all). Absolute Superlatives can be expressed with the adverb ѕѣло = very, e.g. ѕѣло глѫбокъ = extremely deep, the deepest; or with the prefix прѣ- , e.g.: прѣсвѧтъ = most holy.

The prefix наи- in Old Slavonic is only used with superlative adverbs: наивыше = highest, наипаче = most, the most. (See p.60.)

OLD SLAVONIC

ORDINAL NUMERALS

Ordinal numerals can follow the *o*- and *a*-stem nouns but are more often declined like the definite adjectives (see below):—

1	прѣвъ (-въıи)	8	осмъ
2	въторъ (-ръıи), etc.	9	девѧтъ
3	третьи	10	десѧтъ
4	четвръть	12	въторъ на десѧте
5	пѧтъ	20	дъвадесѧтьнъ
6	шестъ	100	сътьнъ
7	седмъ		

Also: ѥтеръ = a certain...

CARDINAL NUMERALS

1-4 are adjectival numerals, i.e. their case agrees with the noun they qualify. 5 onwards in O.S. govern the Gen. plur.:—

	Masc.	*Neut.*	*Fem.*	
1	ѥдинъ	ѥдино	ѥдина	pronominal declen., see тъ
2	дъва*	дъвѣ*	"	" " " тъ (du.)
3	трьѥ	три	declined like *i*-stems	
4	четъıре	четъıри	" " " , approx.	
5	пѧть		fem. *i*-stem	
6	шесть		" "	
7	седмь		" "	
8	осмь		" "	
9	девѧть		" "	
10	десѧть		mixed *i*- and consonantal	

11-19 ѥдинъ на десѧте, etc.   declension
20 два десѧти
30 три ѥ десѧте
40 четъıре десѧте
50-90 пѧть десѧтъ etc.
57 пѧть десѧтъ и седмь
100 съто   *o*-stem neuter
200 дъвѣ сътѣ
300 три съта
400 четъıри съта
500 пѧть сътъ etc.   * So also: оба, обѣ = both
1,000 тъıсѧшти or тъıсѫшти *ja*-stem fem.

COLLECTIVE NUMERALS

	Masculine	*Feminine*	*Neuter*	
2	дъвои	дъвоꙗ	дъвоѥ }	declined
	обои	обоꙗ	обоѥ }	like мои

	Masculine	Feminine	Neuter	
3	трои	троіѧ	троѥ } declined like мои
4	үетворъ	үетвора	үетворо declined
	үетверъ	үетвера	үетверо} like
5	пѧторъ	пѧтора	пѧторо o-
	пѧтеръ	пѧтера	пѧтеро } and
6	шесторъ	шестора	шесторо a-stem
7	седморъ	седмора	седморо nouns
8	осморъ	осмора	осморо "
9	деватъоръ	деватора	деваторо "
10	десѧторъ	десѧтора	десѧторо "

Collective numerals, expressing a number of persons or things as a group, are used in two ways in Old Slavonic: 1. in the plural, used adjectivally and agreeing with the noun in gender and case, including *pluralia tantum*, e.g. дъвоими веригами = with double chains, дъвои людьѥ = two *kinds* of people; 2. in the neuter singular with the noun following in the Genitive, e.g. десѧторо братриѩ = "(the) ten brothers.

Multiplicative numerals are expressed either with the cardinal numerals followed by the noun кратъ in the appropriate case, e.g. три краты = thrice, пѧть кратъ = five times, or with the suffix -шьди (= 'go'-s) attached to the cardinal numerals, e.g. дъвашьди = twice, тришьди = thrice, шестишьди = six times.

Notice also the *fractions*: полъ = half, третина = a third, үетврътъ = a quarter, and the *numeral nouns* дъвоица = a couple, третьница = a group of three, but троица = the Trinity, пѧторица = a group of five, седмица = a group of seven. These can be used adverbially in the Instrumental singular, e.g. съторицеѭ = a hundredfold.

DECLENSION OF PRONOUNS

The following categories of words fall into the pronominal declension, which has hard and soft stems like the nouns, but different endings from them:—

Demonstrative pronouns, e.g.: тъ that, овъ this
onъ that, сь this
Relative pronouns, e.g.: иже who
Interrogative pronouns, e.g.: къто who, үьто what
Indefinite pronouns, e.g.: нѣкъто someone
Negative pronouns, e.g.: никъто no one
Possessive pronouns, e.g.: мои my, нашь our
Definitive pronouns, e.g.: такъ such, вьсь all,
многъ many, самъ -self
Certain numerals: ѥдинъ 1, дъва 2, дъвои 2 each,

OLD SLAVONIC

инъ one, Lat. *alter*

Personal pronouns, e.g.: азъ I, ты thou, *и he (Nom. онъ)

Hard stems:—

тъ = that, *also* he

Sing.	*Masculine*		*Neuter*	*Feminine*
Nom.	тъ		то	та
Gen.		того		тоѩ
Dat.		томоу		тои
Acc.	тъ		то	тѫ
Instr.		тѣмь		тоѭ
Loc.		томь		тои
Plur.				
Nom.	ти		та	тꙑ
Gen.		тѣхъ		тѣхъ
Dat.		тѣмъ		тѣмъ
Acc.	тꙑ		та	тꙑ
Instr.		тѣми		тѣми
Loc.		тѣхъ		тѣхъ
Dual				
	та		тѣ	тѣ
		тою		тою
		тѣма		тѣма

Soft stems:—

онъ, она, оно = he, she, it (*и, *ꙗ, *ѥ)

	Masculine	*Neuter*	*Feminine*
Nom.	онъ (*и)	оно	она
Gen.	ѥго †		ѥѩ †
Dat.	ѥмоу		ѥи
Acc.	и°	ѥ	ѭ
Instr.	имь		ѥѭ
Loc.	ѥмь		ѥи
Nom.	они	она	онꙑ
Gen.	ихъ		ихъ
Dat.	имъ		имъ
Acc.	ѩ	ꙗ	ѩ
Instr.	ими		ими
Loc.	ихъ		ихъ
Nom.	она	онѣ	онѣ
Gen.	ѥю		ѥю
Dat.	има		има
Acc.	ꙗ	и	и

†Oblique cases of all genders and numbers are preceded by н after a governing preposition.

°Enclitic.

Soft stems:—

иже = who, which (Rel.)

	SING.			PLUR.			DUAL		
	Masc.	Neut.	Fem.	Masc.	Neut.	Fem.	Masc.	Neut.	Fem.
Nom.	иже	ѥже	ꙗже	иже	ꙗже	ѩже	ꙗже	иже	иже
Gen.	ѥгоже		ѥѩже	etc.			etc.		
Dat.	etc.								
Acc.	as онъ + же								
Instr.									
Loc.									

кыи = which?

	SING.			PLUR.			DUAL		
	Masc.	Neut.	Fem.	Masc.	Neut.	Fem.	Masc.	Neut.	Fem.
Nom.	кыи	коѥ	каꙗ	ции	каꙗ	кыѩ	—	—	—
Gen.	коѥго		коѥѩ	кыихъ		кыихъ	—	—	—
Dat.	коѥмоу		коѥи	кыимъ		кыимъ	—	—	—
Acc.	кыи	коѥ	коѭ	кыѩ	каꙗ	кыѩ			
Instr.	кыимь		коѥѭ	кыими		кыими			
Loc.	коѥмь		коѥи	кыихъ		кыихъ			

мои = my

	SING.			PLUR.			DUAL		
Nom.	мои	моѥ	моꙗ	мои	моꙗ	моѩ	моꙗ	мои	мои
Gen.	моѥго		моѥѩ	моихъ		моихъ	моѥю		моѥю
Dat.	моѥмоу		моѥи	моимъ		моимъ	моима		моима
Acc.	мои	моѥ	моѭ	моѩ	моꙗ	моѩ			
Instr	моимь		моѥѭ	моими		моими			
Loc.	моѥмь		моѥи	моихъ		моихъ			

сь = this

Sing.	Masculine	Neuter	Feminine
Nom.	сь	се	си
Gen.	сего		сеѩ
Dat.	семоу		сеи
Acc.	сь	се	сьѭ (сиѭ)
Instr.	симь		сеѭ
Loc.	семь		сеи
Plur.			
Nom.	сии (си)	си	сьѩ (сиѩ)
Gen.	сихъ		сихъ
Dat.	симъ		симъ
Acc.	сьѩ (сиѩ)	си	сьѩ (сиѩ)
Instr.	сими		сими
Loc.	сихъ		сихъ
Dual			
Nom.	сьꙗ (сиꙗ)	си	си
Gen.	сею		сею
Dat.	сима		сима

The words for "what", "who" and "all" had peculiar declensions:—

Sing.
Nom.	ҮЬТО (=what)	КЪТО (=who)
Gen.	ҮЕСО (ҮЬСО)	КОГО
Dat.	ҮЕСОМОУ (ҮЬСОМОУ)	КОМОУ
Acc.	ҮЬТО	КОГО
Instr.	ҮНМЬ	ЦѢМЬ
Loc.	ҮЕМЬ (ҮЕСОМЬ)	КОМЬ

Sing.	*Masculine*	*Neuter*	*Feminine*
Nom.	ВЬСЬ (=all)	ВЬСЕ	ВЬСА, ВЬСѢ (ѣ = ѧ)
Gen.	ВЬСЕГО		ВЬСЕѦ
Dat.	ВЬСЕМОУ		ВЬСЕИ
Acc.	ВЬСЬ	ВЬСЕ	ВЬСѪ
Instr.	ВЬСѢМЬ		ВЬСЕѪ
Loc.	ВЬСЕМЬ		ВЬСЕИ
Plur.			
Nom.	ВЬСИ	ВЬСА, ВЬСѢ (ѣ=ю)	ВЬСѦ
Gen.	ВЬСѢХЪ		ВЬСѢХЪ
Dat.	ВЬСѢМЪ		ВЬСѢМЪ
Acc.	ВЬСѦ	ВЬСА, -ѣ	ВЬСѦ
Instr.	ВЬСѢМИ		ВЬСѢМИ
Loc.	ВЬСѢХЪ		ВЬСѢХЪ

DEFINITE ADJECTIVES

The original declension of the *definite* adjectives was a composition of the substantival declensions (*o*- and *a*-stems) + the declension of *н added in the corresponding case. The two parts then started to coalesce. These contractions are already in full swing in all extant O.S. texts.

Hard stems:—

НОВЪЙ, НОВЪІЙ = the new

Sing.	*Masculine*	*Neuter*	*Feminine*
Nom.	НОВЪЙ, НОВЪІЙ	НОВОЮ	НОВАѦ
Gen.		НОВАЮГО	НОВЪІѦ
Dat.		НОВОУЮМОУ	НОВѢИ
Acc.	НОВЪЙ,НОВЪІЙ(or=Gen.)	НОВОЮ	НОВѪѪ
Instr.		НОВЪІИМЬ	НОВѪѪ, НОВОѪ
Loc.		НОВѢЮМЬ	НОВѢИ
Plur.			
Nom.	НОВИИ	НОВАѦ	НОВЪІѦ
Gen.		НОВЪІИХЪ	НОВЪІИХЪ
Dat.		НОВЪІИМЪ	НОВЪІИМЪ
Acc.	НОВЪІѦ	НОВАѦ	НОВЪІѦ
Instr.		НОВЪІИМИ	НОВЪІИМИ

OLD SLAVONIC

	Masculine	Neuter	Feminine
Plur. Loc.	новѣıихъ		новꙑихъ
Dual Nom.	новаꙗ	новѣи	новѣи
Gen.	новоую		новоую
Dat.	новꙑима		новꙑима

новъıи, новаего, Nom. and Gen. sing. masc. are regular, but новꙑимь, новꙑꙗ, Instr. sing. masc., Gen. sing. fem., новѣи, Dat. sing. fem., новѫѭ or новоѭ Instr. sing. fem., and новꙑихъ, Loc. Gen. plur., новꙑимъ, Dat. plur. show advanced contractions. вꙑшьнꙗи (-нии), "soft" adjective, вꙑшьниихъ Gen. plur., = the highest, and мьнѣи (-нии), definite Comparative adjective, Gen. sing. masc. neut. мьнѣшаего, = the lesser, show similar unexpected forms.

Soft-stems:—

вꙑшьнꙗи = (the) highest, supreme

Sing.	Masculine	Neuter	Feminine
Nom.	вꙑшьнꙗи, -нии	вꙑшьнєѥ	вꙑшьнꙗꙗ
Gen.	вꙑшьн-ꙗѥго, -ꙗаго, -ꙗго		вꙑшьнꙗꙗ
Dat.	вꙑшьн-юѥмоу, -юоумоу, -юмоу		вꙑшьнии
Acc.	= Nom. or Gen.	вꙑшьнєѥ	вꙑшьнѭѭ
Instr.	вꙑшьн-иимь, -имь		вꙑшьнѭѭ, -єѭ
Loc.	вꙑшьн-иѥмь*, -иимь, -имь		вꙑшьнии
Plur. Nom.	вꙑшьнии	вꙑшьнꙗꙗ	вꙑшьнꙗꙗ
Gen.		вꙑшьн-иихъ, -ихъ	
Dat.		вꙑшьн-иимъ, -имъ	
Acc.	вꙑшьнꙗꙗ	вꙑшьнꙗꙗ	вꙑшьнꙗꙗ
Instr.		вꙑшьн-ииӎи, -ими	
Loc.		вꙑшьн-иихъ, -ихъ	
Dual N.A.V.	вꙑшьнꙗꙗ	вꙑшьнии	вꙑшьнии
G.L.		вꙑшьнюю	
D.I.		вꙑшьн-иима, -има	

*Reconstructed form, not found in extant texts.

THE DECLENSION OF DEFINITE COMPARATIVE ADJECTIVES

мьнѣи = (the) lesser

Sing.	Masculine	Neuter	Feminine
Nom.	мьнѣи, -нии	мьнѣшєѥ or мьнѥѥ	мьнѣшиꙗ
Gen.		мьнѣшаего	мьнѣшаꙗ
Dat.		мьнѣшоуѥмоу	мьнѣшии
Acc.	= Nom. or Gen.	= Nom.	мьнѣшѫѭ
Instr.		мьнѣшиимь	мьнѣшѫѭ, -еѭ

OLD SLAVONIC

	Masculine	Neuter	Feminine
Sing.			
Loc.	мьнѣш-ИЄМЬ,*	-ИИМЬ	мьнѣшИИ
Plur.			
Nom.	мьнѣшИИ	мьнѣшаꙗ	мьнѣшАꙖ
Gen.		мьнѣшИИХЪ	
Dat.		мьнѣшИИМЪ	
Acc.	мьнѣшАꙖ	мьнѣшаꙗ	мьнѣшАꙖ
Instr.		мьнѣшИИМИ	
Loc.		мьнѣшИИХЪ	
Dual			
N.A.V.	мьнѣшаꙗ	мьнѣшИИ	мьнѣшИИ
G.L.		мьнѣшОУЮ	
D.I.		мьнѣш-ИИМа, -ИМа	

* Reconstructed form.

Comparative adjectives with a stem extended by -ѣ- are declined identically: Nom. sing. старѣи (masc.), старѣишеѥ or старѣѥ (neut.), старѣишиꙗ (fem.), Gen. sing. старѣишаѥго (masc., neut.), старѣишаꙗ (fem.), etc.

THE DECLENSION OF THE DEFINITE FORM OF PARTICIPLES

The declension of the definite form of the Present Participle Active and of the Past Participle Active I have unexpected forms in some of the Nominative and Accusative forms of all numbers, which should be noted. In the other cases they follow the declension of вꙑшьнйи above.

PRESENT PARTICIPLE ACTIVE
несꙑи = (he) who carries; знаꙗи = (he) who knows
молѧи = (he) who requests

	Masculine	Neuter	Feminine
SING.			
Nom.	несꙑи	несѫштеѥ	несѫштиꙗ
	знаꙗи	знаꙗштеѥ	знаꙗштиꙗ
	молѧи	молѧштеѥ	молѧштиꙗ
Acc.	несѫштьи, -ии	= Nom.	несѫштѫꙖ
	знаꙗштьи, -ии		знаꙗштѫꙖ
	молѧштьи, -ии		молѧштѫꙖ
PLUR.			
Nom.	несѫштеи, -ии	несѫштаꙗ	несѫштаꙗ
	знаꙗштеи, -ии	знаꙗштаꙗ	знаꙗштаꙗ
	молѧштеи, -ии	молѧштаꙗ	молѧштаꙗ
Acc.	несѫштаꙗ	= Nom.	= Nom.
	знаꙗштаꙗ		
	молѧштаꙗ		

OLD SLAVONIC

| DUAL
N. A. | *Masculine*
несѫштаѣ
знаѭштаѣ
молѩштаѣ | *Neuter and Feminine*
несѫштии
знаѭштии
молѩштии |

PAST PARTICIPLE ACTIVE

несъи, -ъіи = (he) who carried; знавъи, -ъіи = (he) who knew; моли̂и, -ии = (he) who requested

SING. Nom.	*Masculine* несъи, -ъіи знавъи, -ъіи моли̂и, -ии	*Neuter* несъшеѥ знавъшеѥ моли̂шеѥ	*Feminine* несъшиѣ знавъшиѣ моли̂шиѣ
Acc.	несъшьи, -ии знавъшьи, -ии моли̂шьи, -ии	= Nom.	несъшѫѭ знавъшѫѭ моли̂шѫѭ
PLUR. Nom.	несъшеи, -ии знавъшеи, -ии моли̂шеи, -ии	несъшаѣ знавъшаѣ моли̂шаѣ	несъшаѣ знавъшаѣ моли̂шаѣ
Acc.	несъшаѭ знавъшаѭ моли̂шаѭ	= Nom.	= Nom.

| DUAL
N. A. | несъшаѣ
знавъшаѣ
моли̂шаѣ | *Neuter and Feminine*
несъшии
знавъшии
моли̂шии |

The definite forms of the Present Participle Passive, e.g. несомъіи = who is being carried, and of the Past Participle Passive, e.g. несеиъіи = who was carried, follow the declension of definite hard stem adjectives, e.g. новъіи = the new.

The Past Participle Active II in -лъ, e.g. неслъ = carried, never occurs in the definite form. (It is only used in the Nominative in the composition of compound tenses and only changes (quite regularly) according to gender and number in agreement with the subject of the sentence. See pp. 64 and 71-72.)

PERSONAL PRONOUNS

The declension of the Personal Pronouns for "I", "we", "thou", "you", and of the Reflexive "self" (Acc.) is as follows:—

	I	we	we two	thou
Nom.	азъ	мъі	вѣ	тъі
Gen.	мене	насъ	наю	тебе

	I	we	we two	thou
Dat.	мн, мьнѣ	намъ	нама	ти, тебѣ
Acc.	мѧ, мене	нъі, насъ	на	тѧ, тебе
Instr.	мъноѭ	намн		тобоѭ
Loc.	мьнѣ	насъ		тебѣ

	you	you two	-self
Nom.	въі	ва	—
Gen.	васъ	ваю	себе
Dat.	вамъ	вама	сн, себѣ
Acc.	въі, васъ	(ва)	сѧ, себе
Instr.	вамн		собоѭ
Loc.	васъ		себѣ

Underlined forms are enclitic.

ADVERBS

Adverbs in O.S., as in other Slavonic languages, have a great variety of endings. Many are derived from adjectives, nouns, pronouns, particles, etc. To quote only a few examples:—

мало	(a) little	ѫтрь	inside
sѣло	very	вьнѣ	outside
болѥ	more	връхоу	up, above
сьде	here	латнньскъі	in Latin
паче	rather	дома	at home
лн	(interrogative particle)	ѥда	surely...not (interrogative particle)

Comparative adverbs have the form of the Nom. Acc. sing. neut. of indefinite Comparative adjectives, e.g. мьнѥ=less. нан- is prefixed for the Superlative.[1] Not = не, but "no" = нн, and "yes" = ѥн or еі, ен.

CONJUNCTIONS

Conjunctions, as in other I.E. languages, are of two categories, coördinating and subordinating. Owing to the fact that there is no subjunctive in Slavonic, the latter present little difficulty in their use. Examples:—

Coördinating: а and, but   нъ but   та and then
              н and   же[2] but   лн (нлн) or

Subordinating: аште if   ӕко   that
               ако   as, when   бо[2] for, as
               да   in order that, so that

[1] нанмьнѥ = least. See p. 51. [2] enclitic.

OLD SLAVONIC

PREPOSITIONS

Prepositions in O.S. govern the same case, in almost every instance, as in modern Slavonic languages. e.g.:—

без(ъ) (+Gen.) without   къ (+Dat.) to
изъ(ъ) (+Gen.) out of   въз(ъ) (+Acc.) up
о (объ) (+Loc.) round, about   до (+Gen.) up to, until
подъ (+Instr. for rest, +Acc. for motion to) under
за   (+Instr. for rest, +Acc. for motion) behind
надъ   "   "   "   "   "   "   above
прѣдъ   "   "   "   "   "   "   before
съ (+Instr.) with; (+Gen.) off
близъ (+Gen. or Dat.) near
кромѣ, вънѣ (+Gen.) outside
въ (+Loc. for rest, +Acc. for motion) in(to)
на " " " " " " on(to)
отъ (+Gen.) from   оу (+Gen.) by, at
при (+Loc.) by, near   междоу (+Instr.) between
дѣлꙗ*, ради* (+Gen.) for   прежде (+Gen.) before
по (+Dat.) over, according to; (+Acc.) over (motion) (+Loc.) after
противѫ, прѣмо (+Dat.) opposite, against
развѣ (+Gen.) except   сквозѣ (+Acc.) through
подлъгъ (+Acc.) along

    *These are also *post*positions.

    про- = through, прѣ- = over, раз(ъ)- = apart, are only used as verbal prefixes.

THE CONJUGATION OF VERBS

    Voice: Only the Active remains. The Passive is expressed by the Active verb + the Reflexive pronoun сѧ or periphrastically with the verb "to be" and the Present or Past Participle Passive.

    Tenses: Only the Present, Aorist, and Imperfect are not compound tenses. The others, such as the Imperfective Future and the Perfect, are expressed with the aid of auxiliary verbs, or in the case of the Future, by the use of the Present tense of the *Perfective* aspect of the verb in question.

    The meaning of the three past tenses, Aorist, Imperfect and Perfect, corresponds to that of the English tenses called usually the Simple Past (he did), Imperfect (he was doing) and Perfect (he has done). The Aorist (= unrestricted, or without limits, from the Greek ἀόριστος) denotes a single action in the past without reference to duration or limits, e.g. изиде = he went out. The Imperfect expresses the duration or repetition of an action in the past, e.g. сѣдѣаше = he was sitting, he used to sit, while the Perfect expresses an action in the past which has

some result in the present, e.g. оүмрьлъ нестъ = he has died (is dead).
Of the other MOODS, only the Imperative, the Conditional, the Infinitive and the Supine survive in Slavonic. The Infinitive ends in -ти as opposed to -тъ in the Supine. The Imperative is derived from the Indo-European Optative and is characterized by - и and -ѣ- (<-oi-) in its endings.
There are five PARTICIPLES in O.S., namely:—
Present Participle Active   ending in -ъі or -а
Past Participle Active I   "   " -ъ " -ь
Past Participle Active II   "   " -лъ
Present Participle Passive "   " -мъ
Past Participle Passive   "   " -нъ " -тъ

Classification of Old Slavonic verbs according to their Presents, with Subdivisions according to the Infinitives.

The verbs are most conveniently classified according to the endings of the Present tense, these being subdivided according to the form of the Infinitive, viz.:—

   3rd p. sg. Present   Infinitive

I. A (a) несетъ (=carry) нести[1]   the same consonantal stem in Present and Infinitive
     (b) пловетъ (=swim) плоүти   the same vowel stem in Present and Infinitive
   B (a) беретъ (=gather) бьрати   consonantal stem; Infinitive stem in -a-
     (b) ръветъ (=tear) ръвати   vowel stem; Infinitive stem in -a-

II.   двигнетъ
      (=move, lift, двигнѫти   "n" verbs: Pres. in -ne-,
      Pfve.)   Infin. in -nǫti, (consonantal stem)[2]

III. Pres. in -je-. 1. Primary verbs:—
  1. A (a) знаѥтъ(=know) знати   the same vowel stem in Pres. and Infin.
       (b) меліетъ(=grind) млѣти[3] the same consonantal stem in Pres. and Infin.
     B (a) таіетъ(=melt) таіати   vowel stem; Infin. stem in -a-
       (b) орѥтъ(=plough) орати   consonantal stem; Infin. in -a-

[1] Also: пеүетъ (=bake) 1st p. sing. Pres. пекѫ, пешти; мьретъ (=die) мрѣти (<*merti, cf. ftnt. #3); наүьнетъ (=begin, Pfve.) наүати.
[2] Vowel stem verbs also occur, e.g. минетъ (=pass by), минѫти.
[3] With metathesis & vowel lengthening <*melti. See p.40, #1.

OLD SLAVONIC

2. Derived verbs (all vowel stems):—

2. A (a) дѣлаѥтъ (=work) дѣлати *a*-stem. This group is the origin of almost all -*am* verbs in West and South Slav.

(b) цѣлѣѥтъ (=get well) цѣлѣти *ě*-stem.

B коупоуѥ (=buy) коуповати Pres. -*u*- stem; Infin. -*ova*- stem.

IV. A хвалитъ (=praise) хвалити -*i*- stem throughout.
видитъ (=see) видѣти Pres. -*i*- stem; Infin. -*ě*- stem.

слъішитъ (=hear) слъішати Pres. -*i*- stem; Infin. originally -*ě*- stem, now -*a*- after *chuintante*.

V. Athematic "*m*" verbs. Cf. Ancient Greek verbs in -μι, also Sanskrit verbs in -*mi*.

ѥсмь	I am	бъіти	
дамь	I shall give	дати	(Pfve.)
ѣмь	I eat	ѣсти	—generally written ѩмь, ѩсти
вѣмь	I know	вѣдѣти	

The Personal Endings of the Tenses.

    Sing.   Plur.   Dual
   1, 2, 3   1, 2, 3   1, 2, 3

Present
  -ѫ,-ши,-тъ   -мъ, -те, -ѫтъ -вѣ, -та, -те
  (-ѧтъ *i*-stems)

Imperative, -и characteristic for sing., -ѣ- typical for plur., except after palatal consonants and in -*i*- stems which have -и- throughout.

—, -и , -и   -ѣмъ,-ѣте, —   -ѣвѣ,-ѣта, —
               -имъ,-ите, —   -ивѣ,-ита, —
—added to the Present stem.

"*Simple*" *Aorist*, e.g. падъ, двигъ, can only be formed from verbs of Class I. A (*a*), some consonant-stem verbs of Class II, and rarely Class III, e.g. обрѣтъ= I found.

  -ъ,-е ,-е   -омъ,-сте, -ѫ -овѣ,-ета,-ете

"*S*" *Aorist*, formed from all other classes of verbs.
-съ(-хъ),[1]—,— -сомъ(-хомъ),-сте, -совѣ;-ста;-сте
                        -сѧ (-шѧ)

Imperfect. Verbs with Infin. in -ѣ- or -а- have -ахъ; the remainder -ѣахъ, changing to -аахъ after velars and palatals.

-ахъ,-ше,-ше;-хомъ,-шете(-сте),-хѫ; -ховѣ,-шета(-ста),-шете(-сте)

[1]No simple rule can be given as to which kind of verbs have either -съ or the later -хъ, -охъ type of "S"Aor. in verbs of Cl. I. Texts vary in their use of these forms.

The Participles.
All five are declined in gender, number, (and case) like indefinite and also definite adjectives. We give here the endings of the Nom. sing. only:—

	Masc. and Neut.	Feminine
Present Active:	несы̑	несѫшти
	знаѩ	знаѭшти

Only *i*-stems have:—
(хвал-) ѧ   (хвал-) ѩшти

Past Active I: несъ   несъши
i-stems:—   хваль   хвальши
Verbs with Infin. in -ѣ- or -а- have -ѣвъ, -авъ,
e.g.:—   горѣвъ   горѣвъши
                 = having burnt
                 дѣлавъ   дѣлавъши
                 = having worked

Past Active II: неслъ, -ло, -ла (-л- endings added to the Infin. stem), = carried, used to form the Perfect tense; Nom. only.

Present Passive: нес-о-мъ (masc.), несомо (neut.), несома (fem.) = being carried.

Past Passive: generally ends in -нъ (masc.), -но (neut.), -на (fem.), (-енъ, etc., after consonants), or -тъ, -то, -та, e.g.:—
несенъ=carried   клатъ=cursed
дѣланъ=worked   витъ =woven
хвалѥнъ = praised
The *Verbal Noun* in -ньѥ, -тьѥ is formed from this participle.

The *Conditional Mood* is formed by the Past Participle Active II in -лъ, compounded with the auxiliary verb:—
бимь, би, би; бимъ (бихомъ), бисте, бѫ (бишѧ);
бивѣ, биста, бисте
or else with the corresponding person of the Aorist of бъіти: бъіхъ, бъі, etc. (See p. 69)

The *Infinitive* always ends in -ти and the *Supine* in -тъ, except for velar stems of Class I: e.g. пешти (Infin.)=to bake : Supine пештъ. The *Supine* is used to express purpose after verbs of motion only and governs the Genitive, e.g. идѫ ръібъ ловитъ = I am going to catch fish.

OLD SLAVONIC

Examples of the Conjugation of the Simple Tenses of Verbs

-e verb.

нѫсѫ = I carry (Class I)

		Present	*Imperative*	*Imperfect*
Sing.	1.	несѫ	—	несѣахъ
	2.	несеши	неси	несѣаше
	3.	несетъ	неси	несѣаше
Plur.	1.	несемъ	несѣмъ	несѣахомъ
	2.	несете	несѣте	несѣашете (-сте)
	3.	несѫтъ	—	несѣахѫ
Dual	1.	несевѣ	несѣвѣ	несѣаховѣ
	2.	несета	несѣта	несѣашета (-ста)
	3.	несете	—	несѣашете (-сте)

		Aorist IIA	*Aorist IIB*	*Aorist I*
Sing.	1.	нѣсъ	несохъ	могъ†
	2.	несе	несе	може
	3.	несе	несе	може
Plur.	1.	нѣсомъ	несохомъ	могомъ
	2.	нѣсте	несосте	можете
	3.	нѣсѧ	несоша	могѫ
Dual	1.	нѣсовѣ	несовѣ	моговѣ
	2.	нѣста	несоста	можета
	3.	нѣсте	несосте	можете

Participles:—
    Present Active:— несы
    Present Passive:— несомъ
    Past Active I:— несъ
    Past Active II:— неслъ
    Past Passive:— несенъ
Infinitive:— нести
Supine:— нестъ

†From мошти = to be able.

-ne verbs (Class II)

двигнѫ = I lift (Pfve.). (Consonant stem двиг-)
ринѫ = I push (Pfve.) (Vowel stem ри-)

		Present	*Imperative*	*Imperfect*
Sing.	1.	двигнѫ	—	двигнѣахъ
	2.	двигнеши	двигни	двигнѣаше
	3.	двигнетъ	двигни	двигнѣаше
Plur.	1.	двигнемъ	двигнѣмъ	двигнѣахомъ
	2.	двигнете	двигнѣте	двигнѣашете
	3.	двигнѫтъ	—	двигнѣахѫ
Dual	1.	двигневѣ	двигнѣвѣ	двигнѣаховѣ
	2.	двигнета	двигнѣта	двигнѣашета
	3.	двигнете	—	двигнѣашете

OLD SLAVONIC

		Aorist I	*Aorist II*	
Sing.	1.	двигъ	двигохъ	ринѫхъ
	2.	движе	движе	ринѫ
	3.	движе	движе	ринѫ
Plur.	1.	двигомъ	двигохомъ	ринѫхомъ
	2.	движете	двигосте	ринѫсте
	3.	двигѫ	двигошѧ	ринѫшѧ
Dual	1.	двиговѣ	двиговѣ	ринѫховѣ
	2.	движета	двигоста	ринѫста
	3.	движете	двигосте	ринѫсте

Participles:—
   Present Active:— —
   Present Passive:— —
   Past Active I:— двигъ   ринѫвъ
   Past Active II:— двиглъ   ринѫлъ
   Past Passive:— движенъ   риновенъ
Infinitive:— двигнѫти   ринѫти
Supine:— двигнѫтъ   ринѫтъ

-je verbs (Class III)

знаѭ = I know

		Present	*Imperative*	*Imperfect*	*Aorist II*
Sing.	1.	знаѭ	—	знаахъ	знахъ
	2.	знаѥши	знай	знааше	зна
	3.	знаѥтъ	знай	знааше	зна
Plur.	1.	знаѥмъ	знаимъ	знаахомъ	знахомъ
	2.	знаѥте	знаите	знаашете	знасте
	3.	знаѭтъ	—	знаахѫ	знашѧ
Dual	1.	знаѥвѣ	знаивѣ	знааховѣ	знаховѣ
	2.	знаѥта	знаита	знаашета	знаста
	3.	знаѥте	знаите	знаашете	знасте

Participles:—
   Present Active:— знаѩ
   Present Passive:— знаѥмъ
   Past Active I:— знавъ
   Past Active II:— зналъ
   Past Passive:— знанъ
Infinitive:— знати
Supine:— знатъ

-je verbs with consonant stem (Class III)

мелѭ = I grind   колѭ = I stab

		Present	*Imperative*	*Imperfect*	*Aorist II*
Sing.	1.	мелѭ	—	мелѥахъ	млѣхъ
	2.	мелѥши	мелӥ	мелѥаше	млѣ

OLD SLAVONIC

		Present	Imperative	Imperfect	Aorist II
Sing.	3.	мелѥтъ	мелӥ	мелѣаше	млѣ
Plur.	1.	мелѥмъ	мелӥмъ	мелѣахомъ	млѣхомъ
	2.	мелѥте	мелӥте	мелѣашете	млѣсте
	3.	мелѭтъ	—	мелѣахѫ	млѣшѧ
Dual	1.	мелѥвѣ	мелӥвѣ	мелѣаховѣ	млѣховѣ
	2.	мелѥта	мелӥта	мелѣашета	млѣста
	3.	мелѥте	—	мелѣашете	млѣсте

Participles:—
    Present Active:— мелѧ̑
    Present Passive:— мелѥмъ
    Past Active I:— клавъ
    Past Active II:— млѣлъ
    Past Passive:— -колѣ̑нъ (-кланъ)
Infinitive:— млѣти клати
Supine:— млѣтъ клатъ

important: вѧжѫ = I bind, tie (Class III)

		Present	Imperative	Imperfect	Aorist
Sing.	1.	вѧжѫ	—	вѧзаахъ	вѧзахъ
	2.	вѧжеши	*вѧжи	вѧзааше	вѧза
	3.	вѧжетъ	вѧжи	вѧзааше	вѧза
Plur.	1.	вѧжемъ	вѧжимъ	вѧзаахомъ	вѧзахомъ
	2.	вѧжете	вѧжите	вѧзаашете	вѧзасте
	3.	вѧжѫтъ	—	вѧзаахѫ	вѧзашѧ
Dual	1.	вѧжевѣ	вѧживѣ	вѧзааховѣ	вѧзаховѣ
	2.	вѧжета	вѧжита	вѧзаашета	вѧзаста
	3.	вѧжете	—	вѧзаашете	вѧзасте

Participles:—
    Present Active:— вѧжѧ
    Present Passive:— вѧжемъ
    Past Active I:— вѧзавъ
    Past Active II:— вѧзалъ
    Past Passive:— вѧзанъ
Infinitive:— вѧзати
Supine:— вѧзатъ
    *Reconstructed form.

коупоуѭ = I buy (Class III)

		Present	Imperative	Imperfect
Sing.	1.	коупоуѭ	—	коуповаахъ
	2.	коупоуѥши	коупоуи	коуповааше
	3.	коупоуѥтъ	коупоуи	коуповааше
Plur.	1.	коупоуѥмъ	коупоуимъ	коуповаахомъ
	2.	коупоуѥте	коупоуите	коуповаашете
	3.	коупоуѭтъ	—	коуповаахѫ
Dual	1.	коупоуѥвѣ	коупоуивѣ	коупова аховѣ

OLD SLAVONIC

Dual 2. коупоуюста коупоуита коуповаашета
     3. коупоуюсте —   коуповаашете

Aorist II

Sing.1. коуповахъ   Plur.1. коуповахомъ   Dual 1. коуповаховѣ
     2. коупова   2. коуповасте   2. коуповаста
     3. коупова   3. коуповаша   3. коуповасте

Participles:—
    Present Active:—   коупоуѩ
    Present Passive:— коупоуѥмъ
    Past Active I:—   коуповавъ
    Past Active II:—   коуповалъ
    Past Passive:—   коуповамъ
Infinitive:— коуповати
Supine:—   коуповатъ

-i verbs (Class IV)

хвалѭ = I praise.

	Present	*Imperative*	*Imperfect*	*Aorist II*
Sing. 1.	хвалѭ	—	хвалꙗахъ(вельахъ)	хвалихъ
2.	хвалиши	хвали	хвалꙗаше	хвали
3.	хвалитъ	хвали	хвалꙗаше	хвали
Plur. 1.	хвалимъ	хвалимъ	хвалꙗахомъ	хвалихомъ
2.	хвалите	хвалите	хвалꙗашете	хвалисте
3.	хвалѧтъ	—	хвалꙗахѫ	хвалиша
Dual 1.	хваливѣ	хваливѣ	хвалꙗаховѣ	хвалиховѣ
2.	хвалита	хвалита	хвалꙗашета	хвалиста
3.	хвалите	—	хвалꙗашете	хвалисте

Participles:—
    Present Active:—   хвалѧ
    Present Passive:— хвалимъ
    Past Active I:—   хвальˆ, хваливъ
    Past Active II:—   хвалилъ
    Past Passive:—   хвалѥнъ
Infinitive:— хвалити
Supine:—   хвалитъ

So also e.g. велѣти = to order. Aor. велѣхъ

Athematic 'm' verbs (Class V)

ѥсмь = I am

	Present	*Imperative*	*Imperfects*	
Sing. 1.	ѥсмь*	бѫдѣмь	(бѣахъ)	бѣхъ
2.	ѥси	бѫди	бѣаше	бѣ
3.	ѥстъ	бѫди	бѣаше	бѣ
Plur. 1.	ѥсмъ	бѫдѣмъ	(бѣахомъ)	бѣхомъ

		Present	*Imperative*	*Imperfects*	
Plur.	2.	ѥсте	бѫдете	бѣашете	бѣсте
	3.	сѫтъ *	бѫдѫ	бѣахѫ	бѣша
Dual	1.	ѥсвѣ	бѫдевѣ	(бѣаховѣ)	бѣховѣ
	2.	ѥста	бѫдета	бѣашета	бѣста
	3	ѥсте	бѫдете	бѣашете	бѣсте
			– та		

		Aorist			*Aorist*
Sing.	1.	бъіхъ	Dual	1.	бъіховѣ
	2.	бъі or бъістъ		2.	бъіста
	3.	бъі or бъістъ		3.	бъісте
Plur.	1.	бъіхомъ			
	2.	бъісте			
	3.	бъіша			

Participles:—
    Present:— съі, (masc. and neut.), сѫшти (fem.)
    Future (Present
    Perfective):— бѫдъі (masc. and neut.), бѫдѫшти (fem.)
    Past I:— бъівъ   "   "   "   бъівши   "
    Past II:— бъілъ
    (Past Pass.):— (за-)бъвенъ=forgotten
Infinitive:— бъіти
Supine:— бъітъ

Conditional:— бъілъ бимь, etc.
Future: бѫдѫ, бѫдеши, etc., regular, like несѫ. Also used as Perfective Present and auxiliary verb in compound tenses (See pp. 71-72.)

*Special negative form: нѣсмь, нѣси, нѣстъ, etc., except 3rd pers. plur. не сѫтъ.

    дамь = I shall give (Perfective)

		Present	*Imperative*	*Aorist*	*Imperfect*
Sing.	1.	дамь	—	дахъ	дадѣахъ, etc.
	2.	даси	даждь	да or дастъ	(regular)
	3.	дастъ	даждь	да or дастъ	
Plur.	1.	дамъ	дадимъ	дахомъ	
	2.	дасте	дадите	дасте	
	3.	дадѧтъ	—	даша	
Dual	1.	давѣ	дадивѣ	даховѣ	
	2.	даста	дадита	даста	
	3.	дасте	—	дасте	

Participles:—
    Present Active:— дадъі (masc. & neut.), дадѫшти (fem.)
    Past Active I:— давъ (masc. & neut.), давъши (fem.)
    Past Active II:— далъ
    Past Passive:— данъ

Infinitive: — дати
Supine: — датъ

ꙗмь = I eat

		Present	Imperative	Imperfect
Sing.	1.	ꙗмь* (ѣмь)	—	ꙗдѣахъ
	2.	ꙗси	ꙗждь	ꙗдѣаше
	3.	ꙗстъ	ꙗждь	ꙗдѣаше
Plur.	1.	ꙗмъ	ꙗдимъ	ꙗдѣахомъ
	2.	ꙗсте	ꙗдите	ꙗдѣашете
	3.	ꙗдатъ	—	ꙗдѣахѫ
Dual	1.	ꙗвѣ	ꙗдивѣ	ꙗдѣаховѣ
	2.	ꙗста	ꙗдита	ꙗдѣашета
	3.	ꙗсте	—	ꙗдѣашете

Aorist (II)

Sing.	1.	ꙗсъ or ꙗхъ
	2.	ꙗстъ (but: нз-ѣ)
	3.	ꙗстъ (but: нз-ѣ)
Plur.	1.	ꙗсомъ or ꙗхомъ
	2.	ꙗсте
	3.	ꙗсѧ or ꙗшѧ
Dual	1.	ꙗсовѣ or ꙗховѣ
	2.	ꙗста
	3.	ꙗсте

Participles: —
   Present Active: — ꙗдꙑ (masc. & neut.), ꙗдѫшти (fem.)
   Past Active I: — ꙗдъ ("   "   "), ꙗдъши (fem.)
   Past Active II: — ꙗлъ
   Present Passive: — ꙗдомъ
   Past Passive: — ꙗденъ
Infinitive: — ꙗсти
Supine: — ꙗстъ

*Similarly вѣдѣти = to know (Fr. savoir, as opposed to знати = connaître), Pres. вѣмь or вѣдѣ, Imperat. вѣждь, Imperf. вѣдѣахъ, Aor. вѣдѣхъ, Pres. Part. Act. вѣдꙑ, Pres. Part. Pass. вѣдомъ or вѣдимъ, Past Part. Act. I вѣдъ, Past Part. Act. II вѣдѣлъ, Past Part. Pass. -вѣдѣнъ, Supine вѣдѣтъ.

Irregular Verbs.
   There are very few really *irregular* verbs in O.S. Their conjugations are as follows: —

хоштѫ = I want
Present

Sing.	1.	хоштѫ	Plur.	1.	хоштемъ	Dual	1.	хоштевѣ
	2.	хоштеши		2.	хоштете		2.	хоштета
	3.	хоштетъ		3.	хотѧтъ		3.	хоштете

Imperat. хоштн, Present Participle Active хотѧ(masc., neut.), хотѧштн (fem.), Imperfect хотѣахъ, Aorist хотѣхъ are all regular. Infin. хотѣтн.

нмѣтн = to have, besides нмѣѩтъ (3rd pers. pl. regular), has нмамь, нмашн, нматъ, нмамъ, нмате, нмѫтъ, нмавѣ, etc., in the Present, with нмы, нмѫштн or нмѣѩ, as the Present Participle, and a regular Imperfect нмѣахъ, Aorist нмѣхъ, Imperative нмѣн, Past Participle, нмѣвъ, etc.

вндѣтн = to see, has an Imperative внждь! on the ahalogy of вѣдѣтн, вѣждь! = to know, Present Participle Passive вндомъ or внднмъ.

Notice also: нматн = to take, Imperfective, Pres. ѥмлѩ (Class III), and
ѩтн = to take, Perfective, Pres. нмѫ (Class I).

					Class
доутн	= to blow	Impfve.,	Pres.	дъмѫ	I
-соутн	= to spread	"	"	-съпѫ	I
лештн	= to lie down	Pfve.,	Pres.	лагѫ	I
сѣстн	= to sit down	"	"	сѧдѫ	I
статн	= to stop, intrans.	"	"	станѫ	II
обрѣстн	= to find	Pfve.	"	обрѧштѫ	III
дѣтн	= to put	Impfve.,	Pres.	деждѫ or дѣѭ	III
пѣтн	= to sing	"	"	поѭ	III
спатн	= to sleep	"	"	сплѩ, спншн	IV
нтн	= to go	"	"	ндѫ	I

Aorist: ндъ and ндохъ
Past Participle Act. I: шьдъ, II шьлъ

| ѩхатн | = to go (conveyed) | Impfve., | Pres. | ѩдѫ | I |

Aorist: ѩдъ and ѩдохъ
Past Participle Act. I: (прѣ)ѩвъ
and: ѩхавъ

| грѧстн | = to come | Impfve., | Pres. | грѧдѫ | I |

This verb has only Present, Present Participle Active, Imperative, and Imperfect (all regular).

Examples of the Compound Tenses.

Perfect   прншьлъ ѥсмь,* etc.   = I have come.
Pluperfect   прншьлъ бѣхъ,* etc.   = I had come.

Imperfective Future имамь, хоштѫ, наѹьнѫ or бѫѹьнѫ } пити, etc. = I shall drink

Future Perfect далъ бѫдѫ,* etc. = I shall have given
Conditional (see above) имѣлъ бимь ,*etc. = I would have
*The Past Participle Active in -лъ varies according to gender and number. The auxiliary verb may also precede it.

Aspects.

There is no sure guide from the form or termination as to whether a given verb is Perfective or Imperfective, but on the whole there are few Perfective verbs not compounded with a prefix. Prefixes make Imperfective verbs perfective; but Perfective verbs remain perfective when compounded with a prefix, the corresponding Imperfective being formed with the same prefix and the Iterative, lengthened or extended verb stem. From this the Present tense is formed for such a compound verb, since the Present form of Perfective verbs is *Future* in meaning in *main* (though not in some subordinate) clauses.

It should be noted that the Imperfect (past) tense is seldom formed from Perfective verbs, but the Aorist *can* be formed from Imperfective verbs. Such an Aorist then gives the action as past, without stressing its continuousness. The Perfect tense (compound Past) is used to translate the Greek Perfect tense mostly and expresses a present state as a result of a past action.

A few verbs use different roots to express the aspects:

Imperfective		*Perfective*
глаголати	=to say, speak	решти
видѣти	=to see	оѹзрѣти
метати	=to throw	врѣшти (Pres. врьгѫ)

In the following important verbs different (vowel gradation) stages of the same root are used for the formation of Iterative forms:—

Imperfective		*Iterative*
ити	=to go (see above)	ходити
нести	=to carry	носити
вести	=to lead (Pres. ведѫ)	водити
вести	=to convey (Pres. везѫ)	возити
влѣшти	=to pull (Pres. влѣкѫ)	влачити
гънати	=to drive (Pres. женѫ)	гонити

OLD SLAVONIC TEXTS

I. CODEX ZOGRAPHENSIS. Luke VI, 20-44.

20. і тъ възведъ очи своі на оученикъі своѩ глаголааше· блажени ништиі доухомь, ѣко ваше естъ цѣсарьствие божие. 21. блажени лаѫщтеі нъінѣ, ѣко въі насъітите сѧ. блажени плачѫщтеі сѧ нъінѣ, ѣко въі въсмѣете сѧ. 22. блажени бѫдете, егда възненавидѧтъ въі уловѣци і егда разлѫчатъ въі і пронесѧтъ імѧ ваше ѣко ѕѣло съі на уловѣчьскааго ради. 23. въздрадоуіте сѧ въ тъ дьнь і възіграіте, се мъзда ваша многа на небесехъ· по сихъ бо творѣахѫ пророкомъ отьци іхъ. 24. шбаче горе вамъ богатъімъ, ѣко въсприѩсте оутѣхѫ вашѫ. 25. горе вамъ насъіштениі нъінѣ, ѣко възлачете сѧ. горе вамъ смѣѭщтімъ сѧ нъінѣ, ѣко въздъіхаете і възплачете сѧ. 26. горе егда добрѣ рекѫтъ о васъ вси уловѣци, по семоу бо творѣахѫ лъжиімъ пророкомъ отьци іхъ. 27. нъ вамъ глаголѭ слъішаштимъ· любите врагъі ваша, добро творите ненавидѧштимъ васъ. 28. благословите клънѫштаѩ въі, молите сѧ за творѧштаѩ вамъ обидѫ. 29. бьѭштюмоу тѧ въ деснѫѭ ланитѫ подаі дроугѫѭ, і отемлѭщтюмоу тебѣ ризѫ і срачицѧ не възбрани. 30. всѣкомоу просѧштюмоу оу тебе даі, і отѧмлѭщтааго твоѣ не істѧзаі. 31. і ѣкоже хоштете да творѧтъ вамъ уловѣци, і въі творите імъ такожде. 32. і аште любите любѧштаѩ въі, каѣ вамъ хвала естъ; ібо і грѣшьници любѧштаѩ любѧтъ. 33. і аште благотворите благоворѧштимъ вамъ, каѣ вамъ хвала естъ; ібо і грѣшьници тожде творѧтъ. 34. і аште въ заімъ даете, отъ нихъже чаете въсприѩти, каѣ вамъ хвала естъ; ібо і грѣшьници грѣшьникомъ въ заімъ даѭтъ, да въспримѫтъ равьно. 35. обаче любите врагъі ваша і благотворите і въ заімъ даіте ничесоже чаѭште· і бѫдетъ мъзда ваша многа, і бѫдете сънове въішьнѣаго, ѣко тъ благъ естъ на невъзблагодѣтънъіѩ і зълъіѩ. 36. бѫдете оубо милосръди, ѣкоже отьць милосръдъ естъ. 37. і не сѫдите, да не сѫдѧтъ вамъ· і не осѫждаіте, да не осѫдѧтъ васъ· отъпоустите, і отъпоустѧтъ въі. 38. даіте, і дастъ сѧ вамъ· мѣрѫ добрѫ натъканѫ і потрѧсънѫ і прѣлиѣѭштѫ сѧ дадѧтъ на лоно ваше· тоѭ бо мѣроѭ, еѭже мѣрите, възмѣрѧтъ вамъ. 39. рече же притъчѫ імъ· еда можетъ слѣпьць слѣпца водити; не оба ли въ ѣмѫ въпадета сѧ; 40. нѣстъ оученикъ надъ оучителемь своімь· съвръшенъ же всѣкъ бѫдетъ ѣкоже і оучитель его. 41. чьто же видиши сѫчьць, іже естъ въ очесе брата твоего, а бръвъна, еже естъ въ очесе твоемь, не очюеши; 42. ли како можеши решти братроу твоемоу· братре, остави да ізъмѫ сѫчьць, іже естъ въ оцѣ твоемь, самъ бръвъна въ оцѣ твоемь не видѧ; лицемѣре, ізъми прѣвѣе бръвъно ізъ очесе твоего, і тъгда прозьриши ізѧти сѫчьць, іжь естъ въ очесе братра твоего. 43. нѣстъ бо древо добро творѧ плода зъла ни древо зъло творѧ плода добра. 44. всѣко оубо древо отъ плода своего познаетъ сѧ· не отъ трьнѣ бо чешѫтъ смокъви ни отъ кѫпинъі грозда обемлѭтъ.

OLD SLAVONIC

II. CODEX ZOGRAPHENSIS. Luke VIII, 20-40.

20. і възвѣстишѧ ємоу глаголѭште, ѣко мати твоѣ і
братрьѣ твоѣ вьнѣ стоѩтъ видѣти тѧ хотѧште. 21. онъ же
отъвѣштавъ рече къ нимъ· мати моѣ і братрьѣ моѣ си і сѫтъ
слъішѧштеі слово божье і творѧште є. 22. бъістъ же въ
єдинъ отъ дьниі і тъ вълѣзе въ корабль і оученици єго, і
рече імъ· прѣідѣмъ на онъ полъ єзера, і прѣѣдж. 23. ѣдѫ-
штемъ же імъ оуспе исоусъ. і съниде боурѣ вѣтръна въ єзеръ,
і исконьчаваахѫ сѧ і вълаахѫ сѧ. 24. пристѫпьше же възбоу-
дишѧ і глаголѭште· наставьниче, наставьниче, погъібнемъ. онъ же
въставъ запрѣти вѣтроу і влъненью морьскоумоу, і оулеже і бъістъ
тишина. 25. і рече къ нимъ· къде єстъ вѣра ваша; оубоѣвъше
же сѧ учюдишѧ сѧ глаголѭште къ себѣ· къто оубо сь єстъ, ѣко
і вѣтромъ велитъ і водѣ і послоушаѭтъ єго; 26. і прѣѣдошѧ
на землѭ ѣенисаретьскѫ, ѣже єстъ об онъ полъ галилеѩ.
27. і ишьдъшемъ імъ на землѭ сърѣте і мѫжь єтеръ отъ града,
іже імѣаше бѣсъ отъ лѣтъ многъ, і въ ризѫ не облачааше сѧ і
въ храмѣ не живѣаше нъ въ гробѣхъ. 28. оузьрѣвъ же ісоуса
припаде къ немоу і гласомь вельемь рече· чьто єстъ мьнѣ і
тебѣ, ісоусе съіне бога въішьнѣєго; молѭ ти сѧ, не мѫчи
мене. 29. прѣштааше бо доухови нечистоумоу· ізиди отъ
чловѣка. отъ многъ бо лѣтъ въсхъіштааше і, і вѧзаахѫ і жи
желѣзнъі і пѫтъі стрѣгѫште і, і растръзааше ѫзъі гонимъ бъі-
вааше бѣсомь сквозѣ поустъінѫ. 30. въпроси же і ісоусъ
глаголѧ· чьто ти імѧ єстъ; онъ же рече· леѣеонъ, ѣко бѣси
мнози вьнидѫ въ нь. 31. і молѣахѫ і, да не повелитъ імъ въ
бездънѫ іти. 32. бѣ же тоу стадо свиниі много пасомо въ горѣ,
і молѣахѫ і, да повелитъ імъ въ тъі вьнити. і повелѣ імъ.
33. і ишьдъше бѣси отъ чловѣка вънидошѧ вь свиниѩ, і оу-
стръми сѧ стадо по брѣгоу въ єзеро і истопе. 34. видѣвъше
же пасѫштеі бъівъшее бѣжашѧ і възвѣстишѧ въ градѣ і вь селѣхъ.
35. ізидѫ же видѣтъ бъівъшааго і придѫ къ ісоусови і обрѣтѫ
сѣдѧшта чловѣка, іѫ негоже бѣси ізидѫ, обльчена и съмъісляшта
при ногоу ісоусовоу, і оубоѣшѧ сѧ. 36. възвѣстишѧ імъ видѣвъше же і, како съпасе сѧ бѣсъновавъі. 37. і молишѧ і вьсь
народъ области ѣерѣесіньскъіѩ отити отъ нихъ, ѣко страхомь
вельемь одръжими бѣахѫ. онъ же вълѣзъ въ корабль възврати сѧ.
38. молѣаше же сѧ ємоу мѫжь, іѫ негоже ізиде бѣсъ, да би съ
нимь бъілъ. ісоусъ же отъпоусти і глаголѧ· 39. възврати сѧ
въ домъ твоі і повѣдаі, єлико ти сътвори богъ. і иде по
вьсемоу градоу проповѣдаѩ, єлико сътвори ємоу богъ.
40. бъістъ же, єгда възврати сѧ исоусъ, приѩтъ і народъ·
бѣахѫ бо вьси чаѭште єго.

III. CODEX ZOGRAPHENSIS. Luke VIII, 5-8.

5. ізиде сѣѩи сѣатъ сѣмене своєго, і єгда сѣаше, ово
паде при пѫти і попърано бъістъ, і пътица небесьскъіѩ
позобашѧ є· 6. а дроугое паде на камене і прозѧбъ оусъше,

за н̃е не имѣаше влагъі · 7. а дроугое паде по срѣдѣ трьньѣ, і въздрасте трьньѣ і подави е. 8. а дроугое паде на земл̃и добрѣ і прозѧбъ сътвори плодъ съторицеѭ. се глагол̃ѧ възгласи · імѣѩи оуши слъішати да слъішитъ.

SECTION 2. BULGARIAN

INTRODUCTION

The particular service of the Bulgarians to Slavonic literature and European literature generally lies in the fact that a form of language closely related to their own was used as the first literary language of the Slavs, namely Old Slavonic or Old Bulgarian, more precisely the language of the Macedonian Slavs of the tenth and eleventh centuries A.D. These Slavs were closely akin to the Slavs of Bulgaria, who absorbed the Uralo-altaïc Turkic-speaking proto-Bulgars from Asia after the latter had invaded Europe under Asparuch in the seventh century (A.D. 680). This language was developed in Bulgaria when, after the disciples of SS. Cyril and Methodius had been driven out of Moravia, their pupil and disciple, St. Clement, took refuge in Macedonia and started spreading Christianity there. The philological and historical importance of the manuscripts preserved from this period and the Bulgarian Golden Age under Tsar Simeon (893-927) in the tenth century can hardly be exaggerated.

The development of the Bulgarian language falls into three periods: ninth to eleventh centuries—Old Bulgarian; twelfth to sixteenth centuries—Middle Bulgarian; sixteenth century onwards—Modern Bulgarian.

A period of subjugation to Byzantium of 168 years ushered in the Middle Bulgarian period, by the end of which most of the characteristically Bulgarian features of the language had established themselves, such as the loss of the cases, the general use of the definite article, etc. These features crept into the written language involuntarily—through the oversights and ignorance of the writers and scribes. The last Bulgarian Patriarch, Evtímij, in the fourteenth century undertook the task of "purifying" the language, including the orthography, and even forbade unlettered men to write books at all. It was this version of Middle Bulgarian, emanating from Tírnovo, which was carried abroad in church books to Russia, Serbia, and Romania at the end of the fourteenth century. Important from the orthographical and phonetic point of view is the treatise on spelling by Konstantín of Kóstenec who earned the name of "the philosopher" at the court of the Serbian king, Stèvan Lazárević. He supported the reforms of Patriarch Evtímij and inaugurated similar ones in Serbia (the

"Resava" School). From his treatise light is thrown on many points of Middle Bulgarian pronunciation, e.g. that of ѣ, etc. After that followed the dark days of decline under Turkish domination.

In the sixteenth century there appeared a new kind of Sbornik (сбо́рникъ) or almanach which provided popular reading matter in those times. They were also called Damaskini after Damaskin Studit, who wrote such works in popular Greek, and these in translation and adaptation (and with dialectical variations) were popular in Bulgaria till the nineteenth century. Attempts to "popularize" the language, i.e. to make the written language more like the spoken language of the people, were constantly countered by the influence and prestige of the church language which was regarded as the noblest and purest. This is noticeable in the writings of Father Paísij, the great eighteenth century patriot writer whose Slav-Bulgarian History appeared in 1762, and the grammarian and scholar Neófit Rílski at the beginning of the nineteenth century and Konstantín Fótinov.

It is interesting to note that Rilski's *Grammar of Bulgarian*, which appeared in 1835, was anticipated by some thirteen years by the Serbian scholar and reformer, Vûk Kàradžić who, encouraged in his studies by the Slovene Kopîtar, in 1822 published his famous *Supplement (Dodatak) to the St. Petersburg Comparative Dictionaries of all Languages*, in which he gave the first description of the Bulgarian language. He based this on the language of Bulgars from Razlóg, S.W. Bulgaria or N.E. Macedonia, whom he met in Vienna; and it was this treatise that finally refuted the theory of the pioneer Czech scholar, Dobrovský, that Bulgarian is not a separate language, but merely a dialect of Serbocroätian.

Later another famous Czechoslovak scholar, Šafarík, after an exhaustive study of both modern and old Bulgarian, convinced himself of the Macedonian origin of Old Slavonic, contrary to the beliefs of Kopîtar and Míklošič who held it to be the language of the old Pannonian Slavs. Šafarík also gave a competent sketch of Bulgarian in his *Slovanský národopis*. And it was a Russian scholar, Grigoróvič, who in 1848 first pointed out to the outside world the existence of the two main dialects, eastern and western, in Bulgarian, the traces of the nasal vowels still evident in certain Macedonian dialects, etc., later competently investigated by the Yugoslavs Jágić and Oblāk, and in more modern times by the Frenchman Mazon, and the Russian Selíščev and the Bulgar Mátov,

etc.
However, as early as 1824, Dr. P. Berón wrote a Bukvar or primer in the modern Eastern dialect, and Dr. Ivan Bogórov in 1844 published his *First Bulgarian Grammar*, in which he advocated the use of the modern colloquial language. (These schools were parallel to the three schools of thought in Greece, the middle (compromise) school of which was led by the great reformer Koraës.) Nearly all the early writers kept to the Western dialect, but in the 'sixties, a great number of brilliant writers appeared in Eastern Bulgaria, such as the famous poets, publicists, and patriots Pétko Slavéjkov, Ljúben Karavélov, and Hrísto Bótev.

In 1869 the scholar Marín Drínov wrote an article in an important periodical published in Braila, in which he finally chose the Eastern dialect as the basis of the literary language, and put forward a fairly definite plan of orthography. Both before and after the liberation of Bulgaria in 1877 the modern Russian language was already beginning to exercise a particularly strong influence on the development of Bulgarian. It was an easy language from which to borrow. The first complete dictionary of Bulgarian, completed and published in 1904, by Gérov and Pánchev, shows strong Russian influence. A Russian scholar, Duvernois, had already attempted a Bulgarian-Russian dictionary in 1886-9. Indeed, as far back as the 1760's, the Vlach (Aromun) scholar Hadží Daniíl had published at Voskopojë (Moschopolis) in Albania a four language vocabulary giving Modern Greek, Aromun, "Bulgarian," and Albanian equivalents. The "Bulgarian" vocabulary in it was recommended by Vûk Kàradžić for its purity of language greater "than in any previous book." It was also quoted (transcribed in Latin characters) by Martin Leake in his *Researches in Greece*. Actually it is clear to anyone who knows the Macedonian dialects that the language there quoted as "Bulgarian" is really a very pure specimen of Macedonian from the Bitola (Bitolj) region, witness the accent indicated throughout among other evidence. (See chapter on Macedonian.)

In the years before the recent (1939-45) war Russian words, no less than borrowings from West European languages, Turkish and such Asiatic languages as Arabic and Persian, have been banned from Bulgarian as much as possible, the tendency being to keep the language as purely Slav—and primarily Bulgarian, as possible. An attempt at introducing a simplified spelling was made by the ill-fated Stambolíjski régime under the guidance of Omarčévski in

1920, but with the return of more reactionary governments a more conservative and less rational (historical) orthography was reintroduced. It may be said, however, that the retention of ѣ had the advantage of offering a conveniently ambiguous letter which the speaker could pronounce how he liked in accordance with his own dialect, the modern language having a fair admixture of Western features with the Eastern.

Some of the leading modern authorities on Bulgarian are Míletič, Cónev, and Mladénov. Both the latter have expressed themselves in favour of orthographical reform, Mladénov in general approving that of 1920, except for the "senseless" generalization of ѫ for ъ and ь medially, an etymologically "shocking" feature not contained in the previous project of the Bulgarian Academy.

It is interesting to note how very few words of proto-Bulgarian origin have survived in the modern language. This is hardly surprising because the original invading Bulgars numbered only about 50 to 60 thousand, and were completely absorbed and "Slavized" by the Slav inhabitants of Bulgaria, then called Moesia and Thrace. For this reason Bulgarian is essentially a Slav language, and the Bulgars—an essentially Slav people, conscious of their common Slavonic heritage.

NOTE ON THE LATEST SPELLING REFORMS (1945)

Since the writing of this section Bulgaria has been liberated, and the Bulgarian orthography has been reformed and greatly simplified. Historic spelling has been abandoned in favour of a more phonetic spelling. Final mute ъ has been abolished, while ъ now does duty for both vocalic (medial) ъ and ѫ, now also wholly abolished. Final mute ь has likewise been dropped. For ѫ, as mentioned, ъ is now regularly substituted, but сѫ is now written са (= they are). For ѣ one now writes е or я, according to whether е or я was pronounced with ѣ as the old spelling. The dialect of N.E. Bulgaria has been adopted as the model for the correct pronunciation of the old ѣ, so that roughly the old rule about the hardness or softness of the subsequent syllable deciding whether one pronounces я or е respectively, holds good. Thus one writes мля́ко (= milk), тря́бва (= one must), but пе́я (= I sing), те́сен (= narrow); бял (= white, masc. sing.) but бе́ли (= white, pl.); мя́сто (= place), however—plural: места́, where former ѣ was unstressed. (See p.82f., "Pronunciation.")

BULGARIAN

As the British student is still bound to have to deal with books and dictionaries in the old spelling, which prevailed between the two world wars, I have left my explanations of it here in square brackets []. Part of the texts are also given in the old spelling as well, for comparative purposes. But the examples in the grammar have been modernized.

There is no doubt that the new spelling makes Bulgarian much easier both for the native and the foreign learner alike. The simplification is enormous. Only the speakers of the Western dialects who pronounce former ѣ always as e have something new to learn. And the eye will have to get used to the new feature of the alternating vowels e and я where formerly ѣ was written: бял, бели (= white); бях (= I was), беше (= he was), cf. Polish—miasto (= town), Loc.: w mieście; wziął (= he took) but masc. pl. wzięli; or German—Buch, Bücher, Hand, Hände.

THE BULGARIAN ALPHABET

Bulgarian.   *Approximate English Equivalent.*

Bulgarian		Approximate English Equivalent
А	а	(more open and forward than) *ah*
Б	б	*b*
В	в	*v*
Г	г	*g* as in "go".
Д	д	*d*
Е	е	*e* in "met".
Ж	ж	*s* in "pleasure", *zh*.
З	з	*z*
И	и	*ee* in "meet".
Й	й	*y* in "boy", *y* in "yes".
К	к	*k*
Л	л	*l* in both "leaf" and "table".
М	м	*m*
Н	н	*n*
О	о	*o* in "hot".
П	п	*p*
Р	р	*r* rolled.
С	с	*s*
Т	т	*t*
У	у	*oo*, or *u* in "rule".
Ф	ф	*f*
Х	х	*ch* in "loch".
Ц	ц	*ts* pronounced together as in "bits".
Ч	ч	*ch* in "church".
Ш	ш	*sh*
Щ	щ	*sht*

BULGARIAN

Bulgarian.		Approximate English Equivalent.
*ъ		[silent finally], medially like *a* in "about", *er* in southern English "bitter", phonetic ə.
*[ь		usually silent, a sign of softening—see below; with masc. definite article = jъ, e.g. кòньтъ (now spelt кòнят) pron. кòнjът (phon. ˈkoņət) (= the horse)].
	ьо	In modern orthography ь occurs only in ьо, pronounced like *yo* in "yonder", phon. jo; used medially and finally.
*[ѣ	ѣ	*e* in "met", or "yah", see below.]
Ю	ю	"you".
Я	я	"yah".
*[ѫ	ѫ	*a* in "about" = medial ъ, phonetic ə.]

*See introductory note on the latest orthographical reform.

Old Slavonic letters not in the modern Bulgarian alphabet are:—

ѕ, і, ѣ, оу (now y), ш, ы, ꙗ (now я), ѥ, ѧ, ѩ, ѫ, and the Greek letters ξ, ψ, θ, υ. Now also: ѫ.

Russian letters not in Bulgarian are:—

э, ё, ы. щ is *pronounced* differently.

Serbian letters not in Bulgarian are:—

ђ, ј, љ, њ, ћ, џ.

[Only ѫ was a peculiarly Bulgarian letter, preserved for etymological reasons, and indicating the place of the old nasal vowel.]

PRONUNCIATION

The *Accent* in Bulgarian is a strong, purely stress accent, and can fall on any syllable in the word, including the last. It agrees in position with the accent in Russian in well over half the total vocabulary, e.g.:—

BULGARIAN

      награ̀да = prize
      нало̀г   = tax
      обра̀тно = back (adv.)

In a small proportion of words the Bulgarian accent agrees in position with that in Serbocroätian, e.g.:—

      гра̀ница = frontier, Russian—грани̇́ца
      на̀бор   = composition (typ.)

In some instances the same unexpected stress position is to be found as in Slovenian, e.g.:—

      месо̀ = meat, Sln. mesô
      морѐ = sea, Sln. morjê.

There are instances where alternative variants of stress are possible, e.g. in the Aorist tense of verbs; this accounts for a few words bearing two accents in this text.

The Vowels

    The Bulgarian *vowels* are: а, е, и, о, у, ъ, [ѫ (= ъ)] and the two "yotated" or *j*-vowels ю and я [and lastly ѣ. This was pronounced either *e* or *ya*, in the literary language according to no absolutely consistent rule, though generally "softness" in the subsequent syllable or ending, i.e. the presence of е, и, or ь, caused a ѣ in the preceding syllable to be pronounced е, e.g. лѣто = ля̀то (this is now the modern spelling) "summer", but про̀лѣть = про̀леть (now written simply про̀лет) "spring"; however, вѣкъ "century" was pronounced век (which is also the modern spelling). ѣ was never pronounced я when unstressed or, under stress, before the *chuintantes* ж, ч, ш, щ, or another vowel.]

    й is the short or glide *i* vowel, phonetically *i̯* or *j*, equivalent to the Russian й and the Serbian *j*, and like the latter may be used initially, as in Йо̀сиф (= Joseph). For *jo* medially and finally ьо is used, e.g. гьон = sole. The combination *je* does not occur in the literary language except in words of foreign origin, such as иерѐй = priest, phon. je'rei̯.

    The only true diphthongs in Bulgarian are those with this *j* glide as the second element, e.g. край (= end), бой (= fight), тъй (= so), etc.

    In Bulgarian the yotated vowels я and ю are pronounced with a full yot initially and after vowels, e.g.:—

      яйцѐ = egg   ваятел = sculptor
      юзда̀ = bridle   воювам = I make war

But when я, ю and also ьо are preceded by consonants,

they are pronounced themselves like a, y and o respectively, but cause the preceding consonant[1] to be pronounced soft or palatalized. The softening is not as great as in Russian. It affects all consonants except the *chuintantes* ш, ж, ч and дж, which are always hard. E.g.:—

    бял   = white (masc.)   гюл   = rose
    тя   = she   гьол   = marsh
    тютюн = tobacco   актьòр = actor

я, like a, is pronounced ъ in verbal and article terminations, and я then = ьъ = phon. jə and palatalizes preceding consonants, e.g.:—

    градà   = the city (Oblique case), pron.
                градъ̀, gra'də
    кòня   = the horse (Oblique case), pron.
                'koɲə
    трѣ̀гнат = they start out, Pfv., pron.
                трѣ̀гнът, 'trəgnət
    тъ̀рсят = they seek, pron. 'tərʂət

The vowels e and и also cause velars *only* to be pronounced soft before them, e.g.:—

    керемѝда = tile   блàги   = sweet, kind (plur.)
    кѝсел   = sour   хигиèна = hygiene

The vowels e and и also cause л to be pronounced as medium l before them, as in Serbocroätian and Czech, e.g.:—

    лèсно = easily   лѝжа = I lick

while before я, ю and ьо л is pronounced soft ļ, practically as in Russian:—

лю̀лка = cradle   лèльо! = auntie!
кòля   = I slaughter, pron. 'koļə   ля̀то   = summer

and before the "hard" vowels a, o, y, ъ, [ѫ], it is pronounced as a hard ł, as in Russian, e.g.:—

    лàком = greedy   лук   = onion
    лош   = bad   лък [лѫкъ] = bow

Unstressed vowels, similarly (but not identically) to Russian, are often modified, viz. a to ъ, o to y (this is a characteristically Bulgarian feature!), but this is censured in the literary language as dialectal, e.g.:—

---

[1] With consonant groups, palatalization affects only the consonant immediately preceding the yotated vowel and not the whole group; e.g. in сгъстя̀ (= I thicken, trans.) the second с is hard, phon. zgə'sţa.

гласу́вам (= I vote), pronounced глъсу́въм
освѣн (= except), pronounced усвѣн

е and и also tend to be "centralized" or less distinctly pronounced, especially in some dialects, and also у, but the modification is not nearly as noticeable as it is in Russian, e.g.:—

ѐсен = autumn
извиня́вам = I excuse
удо́бно = convenient

ъ, ь [and ѫ].

[As has already been indicated, ъ and ь, though silent finally, were used as vowels medially (though never initially until the recent reform), e.g.:—

пръвъ = first
градѣтъ = the city
кра́льтъ pron. кралјът = the king]

These are now written:—

пръв
градѣт, but
кра́лят,

because silent final ъ and ь have been abolished and only ъ is used as a vowel medially. [ь was the sign of "softening" for forming the Oblique case of masc. nouns with the article (see below), e.g. конь (= (a) horse), (now кон), Nom., but ви́ждам ко́ня (= I see the horse), not кона. In nouns ending in a consonant ь was often the sign of feminine gender, e.g. нощь (= night), нощьта̀ (the night), (all fem. nouns formerly ending in ь have the definite article stressed and the ь silent)], now: нощ, нощта̀, see below.

[ѫ, the phonetic equivalent of medial ъ, was never mute and could occur initially and finally as well as medially, e.g.:—

ѫгълъ = an angle
вѫ́тре = inside
аслѫ̀ = actually]

now—

ѣгъл
вѣ́тре
аслѣ̀

[These three letters ъ, ь, ѫ, as well as а and я in unstressed positions, rendered the so-called "neutral vowel", phonetic ə, see also p. 82.]

In the new orthography, owing to the abolition

of ѫ, ъ now occurs initially in a few words, e.g.:—

    ъ̀гъл

ь is still used medially and finally for the *j* consonant before *o* (see above), e.g.:—

    Кòльо a man's name
    Кьолн = Cologne

(As in Serbian, all former ы's have developed into и's, e.g.:—

    син = son)

The Consonants

    The *Consonants* in Bulgarian do not present any particular difficulties. They are of the usual "continental" Slavonic-Romance non-aspirated type, as opposed to the aspirated English type. As in English, as well as in other S. and W. Slav languages, н is pronounced ŋ, i.e. as *ng* in "sing", when followed by velars and, with some speakers, in other positions, e.g.:—

    ся̀нка (= shadow), pron. ся̀ŋка

The difference, as from Russian, in the pronunciation of щ (as *sht*) should also be noted. As in Russian, the *English j* sound, rendered in Serbian џ, is written дж in Bulgarian.

    As in all other Slav languages except Serbocroätian and Ukrainian sometimes, final voiced consonants in the spelling are pronounced unvoiced, e.g.:—

    град (= city), pron. грат
    зъб (= tooth), pron. зъп
    нож (= knife), pron. нош
    аз   (= I), pron. ас
    рев (= roar), pron. реф

In mixed groups of consonants, assimilation is generally regressive, the nature of the second one deciding whether the whole group shall be voiced or unvoiced, e.g.:—

    втор (= second), pron. фтор

    Double consonants in compound words are pronounced as long consonants, e.g.:—

    беззъ̀б = toothless
    оттà̀м   = from there
    стѐнна = mural (fem.)

    Colloquially, final ст[ь] and зд[ь] are sometimes pronounced simply c,[1] e.g.:—

  млàдос for млàдост[ь] (= youth)

 Also medial щ is sometimes pronounced simply as ш, e.g.:—

  мòщно (= powerfully), pron. мòшно.

 тд is reduced to д as in

  петдесèт = fifty

where colloquially the final т is also dropped, as in the other numerals with this ending.

 в is dropped colloquially in the group вс[1]:—

  всѝчки = all (plur.), всèки = every

(For the softening of consonants before я, ю, and ьо see above, under "*The Vowels*".)

THE BULGARIAN DIALECTS

 Bulgarian dialects do not lend themselves readily to classification and subdivision, because on the territory of Bulgaria proper they present a certain homogeneous unity, even though the details of the picture, when examined closely, are very variegated and confusing. In this brief survey we do not take into account the dialects of Greek and Yugoslav Macedonia, which are closely allied to Bulgarian and are briefly described in our separate chapter on Macedonian. These Macedonian dialects have many features which also occur in various Bulgarian dialects, but mostly not in literary Bulgarian, from which they are sharply differentiated, particularly by accent and phonetic system. These features, together with the growing literature in Macedonian, have contributed to the establishment of a separate Macedonian literary language, based on the central and western dialects of Macedonia.

 On the territory of Bulgaria proper many features, such as accent shifts and vowel changes, occur in scattered and disconnected regions all over the country. But in one respect all Bulgarian dialects are uniform: in all of them the accent is free, i.e. it can occur on any syllable in a word, even in Bulgarian Macedonia (the south-western corner of Bulgaria).

 Three other features enable one to see fairly clear divisions in the Bulgarian dialects, as Cònev

---

[1]Not recommended in the literary language, where the pronunciation voiced v, not *f*, is preferred in вс—.

has shown:—
- (1) The various developments of O.S. ѣ (C.S. ě).
- (2) The various developments of C.S. *tj* (and *ktj*) and *dj*.
- (3) The various developments of O.S. ѫ (C.S. ǫ).

(1) ѣ: By this criterion the dialects are subdivided into three main regions: Western, North-Eastern and South-Eastern. West of a line running obliquely across Bulgaria from N.N.E. to S.S.W. and starting from a point a little west of Nikòpol on the Danube, running east of Plèven and Etropòle and forming a big bulge eastward round Čèpino and then running west of Razlòg and Mèlnik and east of Pètrič to the Greek frontier—west of such a line original O.S. ѣ develops into the vowel e. (In the north-west of this region this *e* has a variant ъe.)

The larger eastern half of Bulgaria is divided in two by a line starting a little south of Pàzardžìk and running east, south of Plòvdiv, Čirpàn, Nòvo Sèlo, the villages of Borìsovo and Slìvovo (south of Jàmbol) to the Black Sea south of Burgàs. South of this line ѣ develops in both stressed and unstressed positions into various varieties of 'a (я); (these are the рỳпски гòвори according to Mladènov). North of this line ѣ develops into я only when stressed and followed by a hard consonant or syllable; otherwise it is pronounced *e* (with various shades of clarity). This is the North-Eastern feature adopted as the rule for literary Bulgarian. There are naturally transitional stages, e.g. the pronunciation ä (ě as in French, according to Vûk Kàradžić) round Razlòg, and 'ä round Pavlikiàne.

(2) C.S. *tj* (also *ktj*) and *dj*: These generally develop in Bulgarian into št (щ) and žd (жд) respectively, one of the features peculiar to Bulgarian. But in S.W. Bulgaria, south-west from Sàmokov and into Bulgarian Macedonia up to the frontiers, we have what Cònev regards as the older pronunciations preserved: šč (шч) for št (щ) and phon. ždž (жџ) for žd (жд) (as also in South Macedonia). In the extreme west and north-west of Bulgaria, however, *tj* (and *ktj*) develop into ч, phon. t͡ʃ (hard) and *dj* into џ, phon. d͡ʒ (hard), as in the Kòsovo-Mòrava (Eastern) dialect in Serbia.

(3) ѫ—develops in Bulgarian generally into ъ in the roots of words and into a in terminations (so

BULGARIAN

in literary Bulgarian).[1] But in a large area of Central Bulgaria east, south-east, south and south-west of Sòfia, including the towns of Vràca, Orhanè, Pirdòp, Ihtimàn, Sàmokov (and well beyond it to the south-east), Dùbica, Kjustendîl and Ràdomir, ѫ develops into a. Also, in the central Rhodope Mountains south-west of Plòvdiv, ѫ develops into a sound between o and a, noted oa and õ and ã. This area extends into Bulgarian-speaking areas of Greek Thrace. In a few isolated areas in E. Bulgaria (and in Macedonia) ѫ develops into a variety of e (noted ê or ẽ).

The term šòpski (шòпски) is not a scientific dialectological term, but is used popularly to indicate the speech of the area around and to the west of Sòfia.

Many of the Western dialects are noted for their clearer pronunciation of unstressed vowels. This feature is one of their main contributions to the model pronunciation of literary Bulgarian, as advocated also by Cònev in whose terminology they are called central.[2]

VOWEL GRADATION AND VOWEL LENGTHENING

As in other Slavonic languages, in Bulgarian too both Ablaut or vowel gradation and vowel lengthening play their full part in word formation.

Vowel gradation:—

    да отнесà = that I should carry away:
        прѝнос = contribution;
    зов = a call: прѝзив = an appeal;
    цъфтя̀ = I blossom: цвят = flower;
    дъх = breath: дух = spirit: дѝшам = I
        breathe.

Lengthening:—

    говòря = I speak: отговàрям = I answer;
    нòся = I carry: пренàсям = I transfer, or
        пренѝсам.

SLAVONIC CHARACTERISTICS

1. Metathesis[3]: a regular feature, e.g.:—

    град = city   мля̀ко = milk, formerly млѣко

---

[1] Pronounced ə, see p. 80.
[2] See Б. Цоневъ: История на българский езикъ, Sofia, 1940, vol. i, p. 414. [3] See p. 40, No. 1.

владѣя = I rule   ра̀бота = work, thing
бряг = shore, pl. бреговѐ; брегъ̀т = the shore

2. The 1st Palatalization:—

к, г, х, to ч, ж, ш before е, и, ь, [ѣ from ē], e.g.:—

пека̀ = I bake, печѐх = I was baking (Impf.)
мо̀га = I can, мо̀жех = I was able (Impf.)
страх = fear, стра̀шен = dreadful.

2*a*. As in Serbocroätian, ц and з when originating from к and г respectively, also change to ч and ж, as in the 1st Palatalization, e.g.:—

княз = prince, кня̀же Voc. sing., cf. княгѝ-
      ня = princess, кня̀жество = principality
Отѐц = Father, О̀тче! Voc. sing.

3. The 2nd Palatalization:—

к, г, х, to ц, з, с before е and и, when originating from I.E. diphthongs with *i* as the second element: *ai*, *ei*, *oi*, but not before -и in the plural of fem. nouns and adjectives, e.g.:—

ръка̀ = hand, formerly рѫка, ръцѐ = hands
зало̀г = pledge, зало̀зи Nom. plur.
сирома̀х = a poor man, сирома̀си Nom. plur.
вълк = wolf, вѣлци Nom. plur.

4. The influence of the *j* element, compared with that in Serbocroätian, is rather restricted in Bulgarian, where there are no Comparative adjectives in -*ji* and the *j* in Past Participles Passive of *i*-verbs seems to be lost. This yotation can be observed in the case of:—

к and г which change, as usual, to ч and ж respectively, e.g.:—

плака̀х = I wept (Aor.), пла̀ча = I weep, from
        *плакjѫ
лѣга̀х = I lied (Aor.), лѣжа = I lie, from
        *лъгjѫ

с which changes, as usual, to ш, e.g.:—

писа̀х = I wrote (Aor.), пѝша = I write, from
        *писjѫ

and з, which changes, as usual, to ж, e.g.:—

ма̀за̀х = I smeared (Aor.), ма̀жа = I smear,
        from *мазjѫ

In the case of the other consonants, these remain unchanged for *i*-verbs before the -ен ending of

the Past Partic. Pass., while in the 1st pers. sing.
of the Pres. the *j* element is preserved by the final
vowel being written я (formerly spelt ѫ), e.g.:—

изпра̀тен = dispatched, Pfve. Pres. изпра̀тя, but also
    изпра̀щане = dispatch
изва̀ден = extracted, Pfve. Pres. изва̀дя, but also
    изва̀ждам, Ipfve. Pres., рождѐние = birth (see
    below, Features Characteristic of Bulgarian,
    No. 1), also ра̀ждане = birth, delivery, but
    родѐн = born.
хва̀лен = praised, Impfve. Pres. хва̀ля
напъ̀лнен = filled, Pfve. Pres. напъ̀лня
сто̀рен = made, Pfve. Pres. сто̀ря

    Labials also remain unchanged, e.g.:—

    земя̀ = earth   търпя̀ = I suffer
    тръбѐне = trumpeting   вървя̀ = I go

    Words like оживлѐние (= animation) are Russian
loan words; the corresponding adjective is оживѐн.

    The group ст also remains:—

прекръ̀стя = I make the sign of the cross (Pres.
Pfve.), Past Part. Pass. прекръ̀стен, but we have—
    прекръщѐние = nicknaming. (Cf. below, Features
Characteristic of Bulgarian, No. 1.)

    5. There are many cases of the dropping of consonants from certain groups. Besides the long established S. and E. Slav—

    плел = wove, for *плетлъ, etc.

we have—

    дѝгам (or вдѝгам) = I lift, beside движѐние
        = motion
    влак = train, but о̀блак = cloud
    творя̀ = I create, but сто̀ря = I do (Pfve.
        Pres.)
    загѝна = I perish (Pfve. Pres.), with Impfve.
        Pres. загѝвам or загѝнвам.
    (го̀твя = I prepare, cook, бесѐдвам = I converse, give examples of similar simplifications in Bulgarian by dropping vowels. We even have чер for чѐрен = black, in folk poetry.)

    6. The opposite process of epenthesis, or insertion of consonants, is also to be found in such words as:—
        но̀здри = nostrils
        нѐго = him (full form)
        знаха̀р = fortune-teller

FEATURES CHARACTERISTIC OF BULGARIAN

* marks exclusively Bulgarian features.
† marks features shared with Macedonian.

1.* Common Slav $t + j$, $d + j$ become щ, жд respectively, e.g.:—

        свещ = candle
        рождѐн ден = birthday
        междỳ = between

2.* Common Slav $kt + j$ also becomes щ:—

        нощ = night
        мощ = might (subst.)

cf. more modern—

        кѣща (= house), cf. Macedonian куќа.

But, in contrast to Serbocroätian, foreign loan words preserve the combination $k + j$ or front vowel:—

        кьошѐ = corner, cf. Serbocr. ћо̀шак
        килѝм = carpet, cf. Serbocr. ћѝлим

similarly—

        гюл = rose, cf. Serbocr. ђу̏л

3.* Development of the nasal vowels:—

C.S./O.S. ѫ, formerly preserved orthographically, now written phonetically ъ (= ə):—

        [пѫть, now] път = way
        [рѫка̀, now] ръка̀ = hand

The modern spelling of the Present tense, however, is an exception, e.g.:—

мо̀га = I can, 3rd pers. plur. мо̀гат, cf.
    O.S. могѫ, могѫтъ

†C.S./O.S. ѧ develops into e:—

        пет = five
        ред = order, as in Serbocroätian.

4.* C.S./O.S. ѣ, formerly partly preserved orthographically (see above, Section on Pronunciation, page 83), now я or e (cf. Polish):—

        [свѣтъ, now] свят = world

    but—

        [врѣме, now] врѐме = time
        [мѣсецъ, now] мѐсец = moon, month

5.* C.S./O.S. ъ [formerly consistently preserved orthographically and] pronounced as ə, the neutral vowel, medially (see above, Pronunciation):—

  сън = dream [formerly сънъ]
  мъх = moss [" мъхъ]

6. [ь formerly preserved orthographically and pronounced medially, in the Nom. sing. of soft masc. nouns with the definite article (see above, Pronunciation):—

 e.g. краль = king, pron. крал, phon. kraĺ, *now spelt* крал, but кра̀льтъ = the king (Nom.), pron. кра̀љът, *now spelt* кра̀лят.]

ьо is used mostly in spelling foreign words, in rendering, for instance, the Russian ё and the German ö sounds, the resulting sound in Bulg. being [jo]! (cf. Ukrainian):—

актьо̀р = actor   гьол = bog (< Turkish: göl = lake)
  Кьолнъ = Köln, Cologne

†In strong position C.S./O.S. ь develops into е: ден = day, O.S. дьнь.

7. ъ used as the "fill-vowel", as in Old Slavonic, but even more frequently (cf. the pronunciation of Russian *o* fill-vowel and Slovenian *e* = ə):—

мо̀зък = brain   о̀гън = fire
добѣ̀р = good (masc. sing.)   егои̇̀зъм = selfishness

Occasionally *e* is used as a fill-vowel:—

  [пѣсень, now] пѣ̀сен = song

8.* Common Slav hard and soft vocalic ļ, ļ' and ŗ, ŗ́, and also C.S. lъ, lь and rъ, rь are confused and develop respectively into лъ and ръ in monosyllables, and in polysyllables before two or more consonants, but into ъл and ъp in polysyllables before single consonants. There are many exceptions to this rule, especially for *l* in its various forms—due to analogy, in compound words, etc. (Bulgarian лъ, ъл and ръ, ъp contain the vowel ъ (ə) and are not identical with the true vocalic *l* of Czech and Slovak and with the true vocalic *r* of these two languages and Serbocroätian). E.g.:—

  From ŗ : скръб = affliction, sorrow, but
        скѣ̀рбен = sorrowful
   "   ŗ́ : пръв = first (masc.) but
        пѣ̀рва (fem.)
   "   ŗ́ : пръст = finger

From rъ : кръв = blood, but
кървав = bloody
" rь : кръст = cross and
крѣстя = I christen
" l̥ : тлъст = fat, but
дълг = debt and
длѣжен = owing, due
" l̥' : млък = hush!, but
мълча̀ = I am silent
" l̥' : вълк = wolf, plur. вѣлци.
" l̥' : пѣлен = full (masc.), with fill-vowel, fem. пѣлна.
" lъ : плът = flesh, and so плѣтски = carnal
" lь : сълза̀ = tear

9.† Initial *e* instead of *je*:—

è зеро = lake
е = is
еди́н = one (masc.)

10. Vowel reduction in unaccented syllables, especially the characteristic changing of unaccented o to y (see "Pronunciation" above).

11.* Reduplication of Personal Pronouns for emphasis (as in French and Spanish), e.g.:—

Мѐне ме ма̀ма не да̀ва = mother does not give *me* (to...)

In Macedonian this is the regular practice also when there is *no* emphasis.

12.† The loss of the declensions, see below.

13.* The development of a single definite article, see below.

14.† The loss of the Infinitive in -*ti*, regularly replaced by clauses introduced by да (cf. Serbocroätian where this usage is not quite so widespread).

15.† Formation of Comparative adjectives by prefixing по- to the Positive degree, see below.

16.† Development of new compound tenses in "Renarration" (преизказване—see below), e.g.:—

пи́шел (Imperfect Past Part. Act.) съм = they say I was writing

17.† The preservation in conversation of the Aorist and Imperfect tenses. Cf. Lusatian.

18.* ще + Pres. Pfve. or Impfve. for the Future tense, see below: e.g.:—

ще до̀йдат = they shall come

The following features, thought not exclusively Bulgarian, also characterize the language:—

19. As in Serbocroätian and Slovenian, ы has developed into и, see above "Pronunciation", p. 86: e.g.:—

    ти = thou

20. Palatalized *r* has become hard except before я and ю: e.g.:—

  морè = sea, phon. moˈrɛ, but цàря = the king (Oblique case), phon. ˈtsarə

21. Free accent, as in E. Slav—on *any* syllable.
22. In common with S. and E. Slav languages, the dropping of final dentals of roots before the л of the Past Part. Act.: e.g.:—

    плел = wove, from *плетл

23. In common with S. and E. Slav, original *kv*, *gv* become цв, зв: e.g.:—

    цвят = flower
    звездà = star

24. As in other S. and E. Slav languages, palatal consonants can change a subsequent *o* in a termination to *e*: e.g.:—

  вол = ox, волòве = oxen (plur.)

but—

 брой = number, брòеве = numbers (from брòјеве)

25. Reduction of unstressed verbal ending -ува- to -ва- (cf. Byelorussian), e.g.:—

 вя́рвам = I believe, слéдва = he follows

26.† -т termination for 3rd pers. plur. Pres. (see below "Morphology"), as in Russian and O.S. Bulgarian verbs, however, have only -ат or -ят.

The student will observe that from the phonetic and phonological point of view, Bulgarian is closer to Old Slavonic than other Slav languages.

MORPHOLOGY

The morphology of modern Bulgarian occupies a special place among the Slavonic languages of today. It is a partly simplified version of the general Slavonic system, and reminds one of other modern Balkan languages, such as modern Greek, and West European languages. Points 12-18 in the preceding section on the characteristics of Bulgarian sum up its main features. Mladénov considers that the simplification of the substantival system, the development of the postpositive definite article, as well as the elaboration of the verbal system, are part of a general Bulgarian striving after precision and clarity, which is a tendency inherent to Indo-European languages from earliest times.

THE TREATMENT OF NOUNS IN BULGARIAN

As in other Slav languages, the three genders survive in full, and of the three old Numbers the Dual is lost as in all other Slav languages except Slovenian and Lusatian. But the loss of the declensions with their seven cases is peculiar to Bulgarian and Macedonian only. It is true that traces of certain oblique cases, e.g. the Dative, survive in folk poetry, and that traces of the old five declensions can be observed in the formations of the Plurals and in the Vocatives singular masculine. But for practical purposes, in the modern literary language we have to deal with only two cases in *masculine singular* nouns *with the definite article*—the Nominative and the Oblique case, which latter does duty for the Accusative and all the other cases (except the Vocative) with the aid of various prepositions, as in English and the Romance languages (cf. English, he, him, to him, of him, etc.). The use of the same preposition на for both the Genitive and the Dative cases may be considered to seem contrary to Mladénov's contention, but in practice ambiguity due to this usage seems to be rare. In the feminine and neuter genders and in the plural of all genders with or without the definite article even the distinction between the Nominative and the Oblique case does not exist; while the Vocative (sing. only!) has a separate form in the masc. and fem. genders only. And so we have for masc. sing. nouns *without* article the following constructions, where the other Slavonic languages would use various cases:—

Nom. sing. masc.

    град = city   учѝтел = teacher   път = road

Voc. sing. masc.

    гра̀де   учѝтелю   (пъ̀те)

Acc. sing. masc.

    Вѝждам град, учѝтел, път = I see a city, teacher, road.

Gen. sing. masc.

> Назва̀нието на град, учѝтел, пъ̀т = The name of a city, teacher, road.

Dat. sing. masc.

> Да̀вам на град, учѝтел, (пъ̀т) = I give to a city, teacher, (road).

Instr. sing. masc.

> Говоря̀ с учѝтел = I am speaking with a teacher
> Пѝша с мо̀лив = I am writing with a pencil

Loc. sing. masc.

> Живѐя в град = I live in a city
> Прика̀звам за учѝтел = I am talking about a teacher

And likewise in the plural. Feminine and neuter nouns also make no difference between the Nom. and the Oblique case, e.g.:—

> жена̀ = a woman
> вѝждам жена̀ = I see a woman

[Bulgarian used to preserve the distinction between hard and soft nouns in the Nom. sing. In the masculine the hard ended in ъ, while the soft ended in ь (which was also mute and without any phonetic effect finally). But] in the Oblique case the soft masc. nouns *with the definite article*[1] have я instead of а in the singular. In the Plural there is no regular difference.

Feminine hard nouns end in а, while fem. soft nouns end in я or a consonant [formerly in ь], but this makes no difference in the plurals (see below).

In the neuter, hard nouns end in о and soft in е with the same difference in the plur. as in other Slavonic languages: -а for hard and -я for soft nouns as a rule, but see below!

Plural

The plural of most masc. nouns, except monosyllables, ends in -и:—

> мо̀лив = pencil, plur. мо̀ливи
> учѝтел = teacher " учѝтели
> поро̀й = torrent " поро̀и
> слуга̀ = servant " слугѝ
> съдия̀ = judge " съдиѝ

Masculine nouns ending in a velar undergo the

---

[1] See p. 101, also pp. 84, 85 and 93 (No. 6).

2nd Palatalization:—

    войни́к   = soldier, plur. войни́ци
    съпру́г   = husband   "   съпру́зи
    сирома́х = poor man   "   сирома́си

Nouns· ending in -(н)ин, drop the -ин in the plural and end in -(н)и:—

    англича́нин = Englishman, plur. англича́ни
    ту́рчин   = Turk   "   ту́рци

Exceptions:—

    домаки́н = host, plur. домаки́ни
    господи́н = Mr.   "   господа́

Some nouns with ъ or e in the final syllable, drop these vowels in the plural:

         лове́ц = hunter, plur. ловци́
         ко́съм = a hair   "   ко́сми
    but: ко́рен = root   "   ко́рени
         пи́сък = scream   "   пи́съци

Notice: дя́до = grandfather, plur. деди́[1] = ancestors, but дя́довци = grandfathers; and—

    чи́чо = "uncle", plur. чи́човци

Most *monosyllables* have their plural ending in -ове (variously stressed):—

    хляб = bread, loaf, plur. хля́бове
    вол = ox   "   воло́ве
    град = city   "   градове́;

with soft stems, -еве:—

    брой = number, plur. бро́еве

(See "Features Characteristic of Bulgarian", No. 24.)
Some common exceptions with plural in -и:—

    роб = slave, гост = guest, зъб = tooth,
    трън = thorn, пръст = finger

and, with the 2nd Palatalization:—

    вълк = wolf,   plur. въ́лци
    рак = lobster   "   ра́ци
    грък = a Greek   "   гъ́рци

A few (soft) nouns have their plural in -è:—

    мъж = man, plur. мъже́, also крал = king,
    кон = horse, княз = prince, цар = czar, king.

[1] Literary, poetical.

BULGARIAN

A few nouns (not animate) have a *neuter* plural in -ища (not stressed):—

    край = end, plur. кра̀ища, also път = road, сън = dream.

път meaning "time" after numbers, etc., has plural in -и:

    два (мно̀го) пъ̀ти = twice (many) times.

крак = leg, has a (neuter) plural: крака̀.

After *all* numerals the "Secondary Plural" (the old Dual) is used with masc. nouns:—

    пет гра̀да = five cities

and also after ко̀лко? = how many?, то̀лкова = so many, ня̀колко = a few.

The Plural of all feminine nouns regularly ends in и:—

Hard:— жена̀ = woman, plur. женѝ

Soft:—
    земя̀ = land, plur. земѝ
    кост = bone, plur. ко̀сти
    нощ = night, plur. но̀щи

Some feminine nouns ending in a consonant preceded by ъ or е, drop these vowels in the plural:—

    мѝсъл = thought, plur. мѝсли
    пѐсен = song   " пѐсни

Exceptions are:—

    ръка̀ = hand, plur. ръцѐ
    нога̀[1] = leg   " нозѐ[2]
    (survivals of the old Dual forms.)

(As in E. and W. Slav, the *a*-declension has predominated.)

In the neuter the plural of hard stems in -о ends in -а, e.g.:—

    сѐло̀ = village, plur. села̀, ѐзеро = lake, plur. езера̀

Soft stems in -е have their plural in -я or -ета, e.g.:—

полѐ = field, plur. поля̀ or полѐта
обяснѐние = explanation, plur. обяснѐния (only)

[1] Dialectal for крак, pl. крака̀.
[2] Literary.

Verbal nouns in -не have their plural in -ния:—
искане = wanting, plur. искания
After ц and щ the plural is in -а, e.g.:—
сърцè = heart, plur. сърцà
учѝлище = school, plur. учѝлища

There are many survivals of the old consonantal neuter stems and even an extension of their use in the plural ending, as in полèта above:—

врèме = time, plur. временà
небè = sky, plur. небèса
телè = calf, plur. телèта
рàмо = shoulder, plur. раменà
момѝче = girl, plur. момѝчета

    (-че is one of the regular endings for neuter diminutives, the other being sing. -це, plur. -ца, e.g.:—

    очèнце = little eye, plur. очèнца.)

The plural of детè = child, is децà.

Neuter nouns formed from adjectives have a masc.-fem. plural in -и:—

живòтно = animal, plur. живòтни
насекòмо = insect, plur. насекòми

Окò = eye, and ухò = ear, show survivals of the feminine Dual form for their plural: очѝ, ушѝ.

Vocative

Separate endings exist for the Voc. sing. of masc. and fem. nouns. These are largely the same as those in Serbocr.:—

-е for hard masc. nouns,
-ю for soft masc. nouns, and
-о for feminines, e.g.:—

господѝне! = Sir!
крàлю! = o King!
мàйко! = mother!

The endings -о for hard masc. nouns and -о or -е for soft masc. nouns are also used:—

глупèцо! = fool!
войнѝко! or войнѝче! = soldier!
слàвейо! = o nightingale!

BULGARIAN

    кòньо! or кòню! = (my) horse!
Гòспод (= Lord) has Voc. Гòсподи, and бащà (= father) has Voc. тàтко!

  Soft fem. nouns have the Voc. ending in -ьо or -йо:—

    зèмьо! = o earth!
    Марѝйо! = Mary!

  Those ending in -ца generally have a Voc. ending in -це:—

    сестрѝце! = little sister!

  Nouns and especially names ending in a consonant + ка also have the Voc. in -е:—

    учѝтелке! = teacher! (fem.)
    Стàнке = Stanka!

Дъщерà (=daughter) has a Voc. дъ̀ще!

THE DEFINITE ARTICLE

  This is a postposition or suffix varying according to gender and number, derived from the old demonstrative тъ (= that). (Cf. French "le" from Latin "ille".) Only the masc. sing. differentiates the Nom. from the Oblique case.[1] Colloquially this Oblique case is often used for the Nom. sing. masc.
  According to the modern orthography the forms of the definite article now are:—

Sing. *Masc.*
  Nom. Hard -ът, e.g. градѐт = the city
     Soft -ят, e.g. кòнят[2] = the horse
           бòят   = the fight
  Obl. Hard -а, e.g. градà
     Soft -я, e.g. кòня
           бòя

Sing. *Fem.*
    -та, e.g. женàта = the woman
         земя̀та = the earth
         коsттà[3] = the bone

Sing. *Neut.*
    -то, e.g. сèлото = the village
         полèто = the field

Plur. *Masc.* and *Fem.*
    -те, e.g. градовèте
         конèте

---

[1] Cf. pp. 96, 97, also pp. 84, 93 (No. 6).
[2] So also: ден = day, деня̀(т), plur. днѝте.
[3] All fem. nouns ending in a consonant (formerly а ь), when compounded with the def. article, have the latter stressed.

боевѐте
женѝте
земѝте
кòстите

Plur. *Neut.* only
    -та, e.g. селàта
          полѐтата

Nouns with irregular endings take the article according to their *apparent* gender:—

    бащàта   = the father
    чѝчото   = the uncle
    пѐтищата = the roads

It will be noted that in certain older writers the Oblique case for masc. sing. nouns can be the same for the noun with or without the def. article, e.g.:—

    вѝждам градà = I see the (*or* a) city,

but the modern language prefers to reserve this form for the Oblique case of masc. nouns *with* the article.

When a noun is preceded by one (or more) qualifying adjectives, the definite article is attached to the (first) adjective. In the masc. singular the article then has a form different from those given above, namely:—

Sing. *Masc.* Nom. -ият, e.g. голѐмият хỳбав град стоѝ в долѝна = the big fine city stands in a valley.
           Obl. -ия, e.g. вѝждам голѐмия хỳбав град за кòйто прикàзвате = I see the big fine city about which you are talking.

Sing. *Fem.*   бѐрзата рекà = the fast river
Sing. *Neut.*   мàлкото детѐ = the small child

Plurals: in this case the Neuter is the same in form as the Masc. and Fem. def. article:—

Plur. *Masc.* голѐмите градовѐ = the big cities
Plur. *Fem.* бѐрзите рекѝ   = the fast rivers
Plur. *Neut.* хỳбавите селà   = the beautiful villages

ADJECTIVES

As will be seen from the preceding examples, adjectives in Bulgarian vary in gender and number, and when compounded with the article they distinguish the Nom. from the Oblique case in the masc. sing. only.

The endings for the three genders are:—

	Masc.	Fem.	Neut.	PLUR. *All Genders*.
SING.	consonant or и	-а -я	-о -е	-и
Hard:	бял[1]	бя́ла	бя́ло	бе́ли = white
	ла̀нски	ла̀нска	ла̀нско	ла̀нски = last year's
Soft:	син	си́ня	си́ньо	си́ни = blue

Possessive adjectives (soft)—

ко̀зи   ко̀зя   ко̀зе   ко̀зи   = goat's

with *chuintante*—

о̀вчи   о̀вча   о̀вче   о̀вчи   = sheep's

Many adjectives maintain the same number of syllables in all genders by omitting the last vowel of the masc. sing. in the other genders and in the plural, e.g.:—

добъ̀р, добра̀, добро̀, добрѝ = good
лѐсен, лѐсна, лѐсно, лѐсни = easy
извѐстен, извѐстна, извѐстно, извѐстни = well-known

Other adjectives shorten e after a vowel to й:—

случа̀ен (= casual, fortuitous), fem. случа̀йна, etc.

Some adjectives in -ен, keep the e in all forms: студѐн = cold, fem. студѐна; копрѝнен = silken, fem. копрѝнена.

The Comparison of Adjectives in Bulgarian is very simple. For the Comparative degree the prefix по̀- is added to the Positive degree, and for the Superlative най- is prefixed to the Positive, e.g.:—

       добъ̀р = good
       по̀-добъ̀р = better
       на̀й-добъ̀р = best

These prefixes are sometimes used with other parts of speech, e.g.:—

Това̀ ми най лежѝ на душа̀та = This weighs most heavily on my conscience.

There are no irregular Comparatives in Bulgarian except the adverb по̀вече = more, Comparative of мно̀го = many, much.

---

[1] Like бял go the hard possessive adjectives such as: бра̀тов = brother's, ма̀мин = mother's.

Than	= откòлкото
Rather better	= мàлко по-добрè.
Rather good	= дòста добъ̀р.
Less than	= по-мàлко от (*or* откòлкото).
The more, the better	= кòлкото пòвече, тòлкова по-добрè.
As big as	= (тòлкова) голя̀м кòлкото
As soon as possible	= кòлкото е възмòжно по-скòро

THE NUMERALS

The following is a list of the principal *Cardinal Numerals*. Only 1 and 2 change according to gender. 2 onwards are followed by the noun in the plural, but in the case of the masc. nouns this is the so-called secondary plural, or the old Dual, which is in fact the same in form as the Oblique case of the singular with definite article. The verb is also in the plural after all numerals from 2 onwards. Numerals ending in 1 properly take the noun and the verb in the plural, in contrast to Russian. едѝн is often used as an indefinite article, in all genders.

	Masc.	*Fem.*	*Neut.*
1	едѝн	еднà	еднò
2	два	две	две
3	три		
4	чèтири		
5	пет		
6	шест		
7	сèдем		
8	òсем		
9	дèвет		
10	дèсет		

	Literary.	*Conversational.*
11	единàдесет	единàйсе(т) [1]
12	দванàдесет	дванàйсе(т)
13	тринàдесет	тринàйсе(т)
14	четиринàдесет	четиринàйсе(т)
15	петнàдесет	петнàйсе(т)
16	шестнàдесет	шеснàйсе(т)
17	седемнàдесет	седемнàйсе(т)
18	осемнàдесет	осемнàйсе(т)
19	деветнàдесет	деветнàйсе(т)
20	двàдесет	двàйсе(т)
21	двàдесет и еднò	двàйсе(т) и еднò

[1] The final т can be dropped in colloquial pronunciation in the numerals 11-90.

30	тр́идесет		тр́ийсе(т)
40	чет́иридесет		чет́ирисе(т)
50		петдес̀е(т)	
60	шестдес̀ет		ш̀ейсе(т)
70		седемдес̀е(т)	
80		осемдес̀е(т)	
90		деветдес̀е(т)	
100		сто	
101		сто и едн̀о	
121		сто дв̀адесет и едн̀о	
200		дв̀есте (дв̀еста)	
300		тр̀иста	
400		ч̀етиристотин	
500		п̀етстотин	
600		ш̀естстотин	
700		с̀едемстотин	
800		̀осемстотин	
900		д̀еветстотин	
1,000		хил̀яда	
2,000		две х̀иляди	
5,000		пет х̀иляди	
1,000,000		милио̀н	

The *Ordinal Numerals* are adjectives. In compounds only the last figure is made ordinal:—

	Masc.	Fem.	Neut.	Plur.
1st	пръв *or* п̀ърви	п̀ърва	п̀ърво	п̀ърви
2nd	втор *or* вт̀ори	вт̀ора	вт̀оро	вт̀ори
3rd	тр̀ети	тр̀ета	тр̀ето	тр̀ети
4th	четв̀ърти	etc.		
5th	п̀ети			
6th	ш̀ести			
7th	с̀едми			
8th	̀осми			
9th	дев̀ети			
10th	дес̀ети			
11th	един̀адесети			
20th	дв̀адесети			
100th	ст̀отни			
101st	сто п̀ърви			
200th	двест̀отни			
1,000th	х̀илядни			

As in Serbocroätian, *Collective Numerals* in -ица, signifying male persons, exist; besides these there is another series in -(и)ма or -(и)на which are alternatives with the same meaning. These and the Cardinals can have the def. article added for greater clarity, as in English. When numerals are preceded by и collectiveness is expressed, e.g.:—

и три́те (= all three), fem.
and
и трима́та (= all three), *masc.* only.

2 два́ма, дваминa, дво́ица
3 три́ма, тро́ица
4 чети́рма
5 пети́ма
6 шести́ма
7 седми́на
8 осми́на
9 девети́ма
but
десети́на, стоти́на, however, = *about* 10, 100, etc.

The forms in -ма and -ина are regularly used with nouns signifying male persons instead of the ordinary Cardinals. They are followed by the noun and verb in the *plural*:—

три́ма бъ́лгари са дошли́ = three Bulgarians have come.

Half = полови́на: еди́н мѐтър и полови́на = one and a half metres; but *before* nouns it is used without the final -a:

полови́н мѐтър = half a metre.

Distributive Numerals are expressed by по followed by the Cardinals: по три я́бълки = three apples each.

THE PRONOUNS

The pronouns in Bulgarian vary in gender and number, but only the Personal Pronouns have remnants of the old cases in regular use. They include all the familiar categories, to be found in the list below:—

```
            SING.                    PLUR.
  Masc.    Fem.      Neut.      All Genders
Demonstrative:
  то́я      та́я       това̀       ти́я      = this
  то́зи     та́зи      туй        тѐзи     = this (more colloquial)
  о́ня      она́я      онова̀      они́я     = that
  о́нзи     она́зи     ону́й       онѐзи    = that (more colloquial)
Interrogative:
  кой      коя́       коѐ        кои́      = who?
  какъ̀в    каква̀     какво̀      какви́    = what kind of? (Latin:
                                                   qualis)
  какво̀ (occasionally що)        = what?
(Interrog. Possessive)
  чий      чия́       чиѐ        чии́      = whose?
```

Relative (characterized by the suffix -то):—
  ко̀йто   коя̀то   коѐто   коѝто = who, which
  що or дѐто   = that (colloq.)
  чѝйто   чия̀то   чиѐто   чия̀то = whose

Definitive: всѐки   = every
               всѝчко sing.⎫
               всѝчки plur.⎭ = all
               съ̀щ, съ̀ща, etc. = the same
               са̀м, сама̀, etc. = -self, alone
такъ̀в   така̀ва   тако̀ва   такѝва = such
то̀лкав   то̀лкава   то̀лкаво   то̀лкави = so great, such

Indefinite: нѐщо   = something
              ня̀колко   = some (a few)
              ня̀кой   = someone
              кой да ѐ = whoever, any

Negative: нѝщо   = nothing
            нѝкой   = nobody
            нѝкакъв = no, none

Possessive: мой, мо̀я = my
             твой   = thy
             свой   = (own)
             наш   = our
             ваш   = your
             нѐгов   = his
             нѐин,-йна = her
             тѐхен, тя̀хна, тя̀хно, тѐхни = their

The possessive pronouns often take the article, e.g.:—

    мо̀я(т) ху̀бав брат = my handsome brother,
    мо̀ята ма̀лка къ̀ща = my small house,
    мо̀ето ма̀лко детѐ = my small child.

Personal:
	Full form	Enclitic[1]	Full form	Enclitic[1]
Nom.	аз	= I	ти	= you (famil-
Dat.	на мѐне,	ми	на тѐбе,	ти iar)
Oblique	мѐне,	ме	тѐбе,	те
Nom.	нѝе	= we	вѝе	= you (polite
Dat.	на нас,[2]	ни	на вас,[2]	ви and plural)
Oblique	нас,	ни	вас,	ви

[1] The enclitic forms of the *Oblique* case are used mostly as Accusatives, and also after ѐто; e.g. ѐто ни = here we are!
[2] Note the corresponding, rarely used, archaic Datives: нам, вам.

	Full form	Enclitic[1]		Full form	Enclitic[1]	
Nom.	той	= he	тя		= she
Dat.	на нѐго,[2]	му	на нѐя,[2]	й	
Oblique	нѐго,	го	нѐя,	я	
Nom.	то	= it	те		= they (all
Dat.	на нѐго,[2]	му	на тях,[2]	им	genders)
Oblique	нѐго,	го	тях,	ги	

As in Serbocr., the enclitic forms are always used when there is no special emphasis on the Personal Pronouns in the oblique cases. In the Nom., where only one form exists, the Personal Pronoun can be omitted when unimportant. The Dat. enclitics are frequently used instead of the Possessive adjectives, e.g.:—

книгата ми = мо̀ята книга = my book
ма̀йка му = нѐгова ма̀йка = his mother

When the Dative enclitic Personal Pronoun is used as a possessive adjective the article is omitted with nouns denoting relationship, except син = son, and мъж = husband, in the singular.

The Reflexive сѐбе is declined exactly like (ти), тѐбе:—

Nom. — Dat. на сѐбе, си Obl. сѐбе, се[1]

and its enclitic Dat. is similarly used, e.g.:—

вѝкам сина̀ си = I call my son

Frequently, for the sake of emphasis, both forms of the Personal Pronoun are used in the same clause (as in French and Spanish—see above, "Features Characteristic of Bulgarian," No. 11):—

Нѐго го вѝкат = It is him they are calling
Нѐя я нѧ̀ма = *She*'s not there

As in Russian, си is used simply for emphasis or intensity:—

той си пѝше (Russ. он себѐ пѝшет) = he is
    busy writing

Сѐбе is very often coupled with си, e.g.:—

Всѣ̀ки глѣ̀да сѐбе си = everyone looks after
    himself.

---

[1]The enclitic forms of the *Oblique* case are used mostly as Accusatives, and also after èто; e.g. èто го = here he is!
[2]Note the corresponding, rarely used, archaic Datives: нему (m. and n.), ней (f.), тям (pl.).

Notice also: приЯ́тно ми е = (it is pleasant for me), I am glad to...
              спи ми се = I feel sleepy
but, with a noun, страх ме е = I am afraid

ADVERBS

As in other Slavonic languages, only adverbs formed from adjectives have any regular ending. It is generally -о, the same as the neut. sing. adj., though it can be -е, and from adjectives in -ски we have adverbs also in -ски:—

        хỳбаво = beautifully
        добрѐ = well
        приЯ́телски = amicably

The comparison of adverbs is identical with the comparison of adjectives—by means of the prefixes: по- for the Comparative and най- for the Superlative: по̀-добрѐ = better, на̀й-добрѐ = best.

Other adverbs, derived from nouns, numerals, verbs, prepositions, etc., have a great variety of endings:—

Place:—

тук, тỳка	= here	вѐтре	= inside
там	= there	в кѐщи	= at home
до̀лу	= down below	напрѐд	= forward

Time:—

сега̀	= now	най-по̀сле }	= at last, finally
тога̀ва	= then	най-сѐтне }	
днес	= to-day	вѝнаги	= always
ỳтре	= to-morrow	веднàга	= at once
вчѐра	= yesterday	веднàж, -ѣж	= once
ско̀ро	= soon	но̀щем	= by night
нѝкога	= never		

Manner:—

такà	= thus, so	за̀едно	= together
бѐрзо	= quickly	напра̀зно	= in vain
ба̀вно	= slowly	наро̀чно	= on purpose
тичешко̀м	= running		

Degree:—

мно̀го	= much, very	съвсѐм	= quite
по̀вече	= more (N.B. irregular Comparative)	почтѝ	= almost
		са̀мо	= only
най-мно̀го }	= most	понѐ	= at least
най-вѐче }		дово̀лно }	= enough
ма̀лко	= (a) little	доста̀тъчно }	

Interrogative:—

когà?	= when?	как?	= how?
къдè? }	= where?,	кòлко?	= how much?
где? }	whither?	защò?	= why?
накъдè?	= whither?	далѝ?	(interrogative particle)
откъдè?	= whence?	налѝ?	(interrogative particle expecting the answer "yes")

Not = не; no = не; yes = да.

CONJUNCTIONS

The coördinating and subordinating conjunctions of Bulgarian have no special forms or difficulties.

Coördinating:—

и	= and		ѝли	= or
а	= and, but		обàче	= however
но	= but		та	= and then
амà, алà	= but, however			

Subordinating:—

àко	= if	щом	= as soon as
когàто	= when	за да	= in order that
катò	= as, when	понèже	= because, since
докатò	= while	макàр че	= though
след катò	= after	катò че	= as if
защòто	= because	предѝ да	= before

It is important to note that, in contrast to Serbocroätian, Bulgarian uses да + the Pres. (Pfve. or Impfve.) to replace the Infinitive of other languages, but че (= that) to introduce an indirect statement:—

той ѝска да... = he wants to...
той кàзва че... = he says that...

Каквò is used as a variant for че when there are many successive "that's".

PREPOSITIONS

Owing to the loss of the declensions, in Bulgarian prepositions have a wider use than in other Slavonic languages. One may therefore divide them roughly into three categories:—

1. uses where other languages use plain cases;
2. uses similar to those in other languages;
3. uses, as well as forms of the prepositions themselves, peculiar to Bulgarian (see above, "The Treatment of Nouns.")

BULGARIAN

The Oblique case is always used.

	Cf. Serbocroatian:	Cf. Russian:
1.		
Орà с плуг = I plough with a plough	Орем плугом	
Говòря на брàта = I am speaking to my brother	Говорим брату	
Вървя̀ из у̀лицата = I am going down the street	Идем улицом	по улице
На трèти май = on the 3rd of May	Трећег маја	
По слу̀чай (ро̀жден ден) = on the occasion of (a birthday)	Приликом	при случае
Учѝтел по фрèнски езѝк = a teacher of French	Учитељ француског језика	
По пòщата = by post	Поштом	
2.	Cf. Serbocr.:	Cf. Russ.:
Живèя в Плòвдив (Proper names remain in Nom.) = I live in Plovdiv	Живим у Пловдиву	
Влѝзам в стàята = I enter the room	Улазим у собу	
Към нèя = towards her	К њој	
Между̀ у̀лицата и къ̀щата ѝмаше градѝна = between the street and the house there was a garden	Међу улицом и кућом беше башта	
На мàсата = on the table	На столу	
Пред свидèтели = before witnesses	Пред сведоцима	
3.	Cf. Serbocr.:	Cf. Russ.:
От врèме на врèме = from time to time	С времена на време	от времени до времени
Предѝ всѝчко = above all	Пре свега	прежде всего
През планинàта = over the mountain	Преко планине	через гору

	Cf. Serbocr.:	*Cf. Russ.:*
През есентà = in autumn	У јесен	осенью
През прозòреца = through the window	Кроз прозор	
При клàденеца = by the well	Код бунара	
Спорèд закòна = according to the law	По закону	
Срещỳ тỳрците = against the Turks	Против Турака	
У бèлгарите = among the Bulgarians	Код Бугара	
Кнѝга върхỳ бèлгар-ското стопàнство = a book on Bulgarian economics	Књига о бугарској привреди	
За каквò прикàзвате? = about what are you talking?	О чему причате?	
Глèдам из прозòреца = I am looking out of the window	Гледам са прозора	из окна
Пътỳвам из Югослà-вия = I travel about Yugoslavia	Путујем по Југосла-вији	
Излѝзам към два часà = I go out about two o'clock	Излазим око два сата	
По любòв = Out of love	Из љубави	
Под мòя отговòрност = on my responsibility	На моју одговорност	
Отвèд Дỳнава = beyond the Danube	Преко Дунава	за Дунаем

Also: зарадѝ = because of, подѝр = after, behind, въз = on (to).

After *Verbal Nouns*[1] the object is very often translated by a further noun in the Oblique case not connected by any preposition:—

[1] See pp. 100, 115.

```
    чѐтене кни̇ги   = reading books
    лѐене оцѐт     = pouring vinegar
    пи̇ене чай     = drinking tea
```

Partitive and other Genitives are also thus rendered:—

```
    ча̀ша вода̀          = a glass of water
    нача̀лник отделѐние = head of department
but, еди̇н от тях       = one of them
```

в and с are usually pronounced във and със, especially въф before в, вс, ф, хв, and със before з, ж, с, ч, ш, щ, вс, and also in cases where confusion can arise or where the preposition is emphasized:—

в Ва̀рна (= in Varna), pron. въф...
с(ъс) чѐсън = with garlic
в(ъф) и̇мето на крали̇цата = in the name of the queen
та̀зи ду̀ма се пи̇ше с(ъс) е, а не с(ъс) я = this word is written with an е and not with я
пиши̇ ми за сви̇чко, що ста̀ва с(ъс) и чрез нѐго = write to me about everything that happens with and because of him

The spelling във is recommended before words beginning with в and ф, and the spelling със is recommended before words beginning with с, з, ш and ж.

With monosyllables and in cases of emphasis these prepositions may also be spelt thus.

Про-, раз-, об-, and пре- are used in Bulgarian only as prefixes.

THE CONJUGATION OF VERBS

Voices and Tenses

While the declensional system in Bulgarian has become greatly simplified in the course of its development, the conjugational system has been considerably elaborated and enriched, so that in this respect too Bulgarian occupies a special place among the modern Slavonic languages. In practice, in the ordinary language of conversation, the newspapers, etc., the usage of verbs does not differ very markedly from that in Serbocroätian, but a number of variants and possibilities exist for rendering subtler shades of meaning which in Serbocroätian would be rendered more analytically by means of adverbs and other more explicit means. In Bulgarian a system of tenses has been developed for relating about facts not witnessed by the speaker without using an introductory verb, similar to the English system of reported speech, but more widely used, e.g. in conversation, narration, etc. This system is called преизка̀зване (Renarration or the Indirect Mood). The sign for this shade of meaning, often also expressing incredulity, uncertainty, etc., is the use of one of a series of special compound tenses with the auxiliary verb e or ca always omitted when the 3rd person singular or plural is used. There can be two Past Participles Active for many verbs in Bulg., one formed from the Aorist and one from the Imperfect tense—another characteristic feature of this language. The one formed from the Imperfect is used *only* in Renarration.

The Dual number as a regular grammatical category has been lost in the verbs, as in the nouns. And the Passive voice is rendered, as in other Slavonic languages, by the usual three alternatives: the reflexive verb,[1] the verb "to be" + the Past Participle Passive, or the 3rd pers. plur. of the verb used impersonally, making what is the subject in English, the object of the verb, e.g.:—

    Къ̀щата се вѝжда отту̀к   = the house is seen from here
    Той е хва̀лен *or* Хва̀лят го = he is praised.

The negative is separated from its verb by ce and all enclitic Personal Pronouns.

The only simple tenses are the Present, the Imperfect, and the Aorist Indicative, as in Serbocroätian. And the use of the Perfective Present (the Aspects are in vigorous use in Bulgarian, too!) is usually restricted to subordinate clauses introduced by да (= that), а̀ко (= if), кога̀то (= when), etc., also as in Serbocr. conversational style, and to the "Historic Present" which expresses a habitual action not connected with any point of time; e.g. сѐдне и запу̀шва = he would sit down and start smoking. Of the other *Moods*, only the Imperative has independent forms—for the 2nd pers. sing. and plur. only! The Supine has been entirely lost, and also the Infinitive in -*ti*; the latter is regularly replaced by a subordinate clause after да, but in certain cases (see below) the so-called "truncated Infinitive", generally just the root of the verb, can be used alternatively, notably in prohibitions. Of the *Gerunds*, only the Present Active exists, while of the *Participles*, the Pres. Act. and the Past Act. in -л (No. II in O.S.) and the Past Passive survive.

---

[1]This is formed by using the separable enclitic Accusative Reflexive pronoun ce with an Active verb.

BULGARIAN

The remnants of the Pres. Partic. Pass. are regarded as adjectives. *Verbal Nouns* in -не or -ние or in -тие are formed from the Past Participle Passive, those in -ние (as opposed to -не) having the more abstract meaning. The plural of both the latter forms ends in -ния. Cf. pp. 100, 112.

Classification of Verbs according to their Present endings

The loss of the Infinitive and the "hardening" of the vowel e (the fact that it no longer implies -*je*, though regularly causing the 1st Palatalization, as in мо̀га, мо̀жеш = I, you can) has greatly simplified the classification of verbs in Bulgarian according to their Presents.

The first three classes of O.S. and Serbocr. fall here into one single class characterized by the vowel e; verbs with и dominant form the second class, while the third and last class is made up of verbs characterized by Present endings featuring *a* in all persons—a new formation arrived at by the contraction of ae to a, as in other S. and W. Slav languages. The former athematic -м verbs can now be regarded as irregular verbs in Bulg. Their characteristic м in the 1st pers. sing. has been generalized as a regular feature of verbs of the abovementioned 3rd modern Bulg. class in -ам.

The only possible subdivision of the above classes would be according to the Aorist endings, for which certain alternatives exist (see below) following no fixed rule and which consequently have to be learnt for every verb, the more so as this is an important tense in Bulg., as opposed to Serbocr.

According to the Present endings we therefore have the following classes of verbs:—

1. чета̀ = I read, Aor. чѐтох
   тъка̀ = I weave, " тъка̀х
   пора̀сна (Pfve.) = I grow, " пора̀снах
   зна̀я = I know, " зна̀ях
   чу̀я = I hear, " чух
   пѝша = I write, " пѝсах
   владѐя = I rule, " владя̀х

2. мѝсля = I think, " мѝслих
   търпя̀ = I suffer, " търпя̀х
                           (formerly spelt: търпѣхъ)
   стоя̀ = I stand, " стоя̀х
   доя̀ = I milk, " доя̀х
   държа̀ = I hold, " държа̀х

3. глѐдам = I look, Aor. глѐдах
   вàлям = I roll, " валя̀х
   поглѐждам = I glance, " поглѐждах

Tense Endings
Present

    1.
Sing. 1 четà = I read   знàя = I know
     2 четѐш   знàеш
     3 четѐ   знàе

Plur. 1 четѐм (or четѐме)   знàем (or знàеме)
     2 четѐте   знàете
     3 четàт   знàят

(а pron. ъ, from ѫ, formerly spelt ѫ; я pron. jъ, from jѫ, formerly spelt ѭ.)

    2.
Sing. 1 мѝсля = I think   държà = I hold (1st sing., see note after четà above)
     2 мѝслиш   држѝш
     3 мѝсли   държѝ

Plur. 1 мѝслим (or мѝслиме)   държѝм (or държѝме)
     2 мѝслите   държѝте
     3 мѝслят   държàт (-ат from -ѧтъ, 3rd plur., irregular development, due to analogy.)

(държà follows the orthographical rule of not writing я after *chuintantes*.)

    3.
Sing. 1 глѐдам = I look   стрѐлям = I shoot
     2 глѐдаш   стрѐляш
     3 глѐда   стрѐля

Plur. 1 глѐдаме   стрѐляме
     2 глѐдате   стрѐляте
     3 глѐдат   стрѐлят

    These are new contracted endings, as in Serbocr., etc., and most newly formed verbs go into this category, e.g. планѝрам (= I plan). -ме for the 1st pers. plur. is obligatory in this class to avoid confusion with the 1st pers. sing. -м.

Aorist
    In this tense the personal endings are the same for all categories of verbs, while the connecting vowel varies. Those that end in -ох in the 1st pers.

sing. have -e in the 2nd and 3rd pers. sing. The two latter persons are always identical. All verbs whose stem ends in a vowel add the endings direct to the stem without a connecting vowel. It will be observed that in contrast to modern Serbocroätian and O.S., analogy has made the consonant x prevail also in the 2nd and 3rd pers. plur. The stress in this tense is very often the opposite to that in the Present. This tense can be formed from verbs of either aspect, but is more usual in the Perfective.

чèтох[1] = I read	чèте	чèте	чèтохме	чèтохте	чèтоха
рàснах (Pfve.) = I grew	рàсна	рàсна	рàснахме	рàснахте	рàснаха
чух (Pfve.) = I heard	чу	чу	чỳхме	чỳхте	чỳха
мѝслих[1] = I thought	мѝсли	мѝсли	мѝслихме	мѝслихте	мѝслиха
тъ̀рпях[1] = I suffered	тъ̀рпя	тъ̀рпя	тъ̀рпяхме	тъ̀рпяхте	тъ̀рпяха
глèдах[1] = I looked	глèда	глèда	глèдахме	глèдахте	глèдаха
валях = I rolled	валя	валя	валяхме	валяхте	валяха

The Imperfect

The endings of this tense are the same as those of the Aorist except in the 2nd and 3rd pers. sing.; but in the 1st and 2nd classes this tense is characterized by the joining vowel e or, under stress, я for the 1st pers. sing. and all the plural [formerly ѣ, written e after vowels and *chuintantes*]; and in the 3rd category, where the joining vowel is a or я and this distinguishing feature is lacking to mark it off from the Aorist, the stress, which for all three categories is *the same* as in the Present, helps to distinguish the Imperfect from the Aorist. This tense can also sometimes be formed from Perfective verbs.

четях = I was reading	четèше	четèше	четяхме	четяхте	четяха
пѝшех = I was writing	пѝшеше	пѝшеше	пѝшехме	пѝшехте	пѝшеха
знàех = I used to know	знàеше	знàеше	знàехме	знàехте	знàеха
мѝслех = I used to think	мѝслеше	мѝслеше	мѝслехме	мѝслехте	мѝслеха

[1]The corresponding *Perfective* Aorists are: прочèтох, etc., помѝслих, претъ̀рпях, поглèднах.

държѐх държѐше държѐше държѐхме държѐхте държѐха
  = I used to hold (or -а̀х, -а̀хме, -а̀хте, -а̀ха
  stressed after a *chuintante* or with -я̀-
  after a vowel)
глѐдах глѐдаше глѐдаше глѐдахме глѐдахте глѐдаха
  = I was looking
ва̀лях ва̀ляше ва̀ляше ва̀ляхме ва̀ляхте ва̀ляха
  = I was rolling
сѐднех сѐднеше сѐднеше сѐднехме сѐднехте сѐднеха
  = I used to sit down (сѐдна Pfve.), more vivid
  than ся̀дах, ся̀даше, etc., from ся̀дам (Frequentative) [formerly сѣ̀дамъ].

The Imperative Mood
   This has an independent form for the 2nd pers. sing. and plur. only.

   In categories 1 and 2—
those verbs whose stems end in consonants add:
sing. -ѝ (stressed),[1] plur. -ѐте.[1]
those verbs whose stems end in a vowel add:
sing. -й, plur. -йте.

   Verbs in category 3 have sing. -ай (unstressed), plur. -айте, or sing. -яй
plur. -яйте
according to the original vowel of the Present ending.
   The 1st pers. plur. and the 3rd pers. sing. and plur. are formed with да or нѐка (да) + Present Pfve. or Impfve.
   Prohibitions are mostly expressed by недѐй, plur. недѐйте + truncated Infinitive (see below).
   If expressed by не + Imperative, the Impfve. aspect is used. But after недѐй the Present preceded by да *can* also be used (see below).
   Examples:—
Sing.
2 четѝ = read![1] бро̀й = count! глѐдай = look! стрѐляй = shoot!
3 нѐка четѐ нѐка бро̀й нѐка глѐда нѐка стрѐля

Plur.
1 нѐка да   нѐка да   нѐка да   нѐка да
  четѐм   бро̀им   глѐдаме   стрѐляме
2 четѐте[1]   бро̀йте   глѐдайте   стрѐляйте
3 нѐка четя̀т   нѐка броя̀т   нѐка глѐдат   нѐка стрѐлят

[1] Velar stems undergo the *1st* Palatalization before these endings, e.g.:—
   пека̀ = I bake, Imper. печѝ, печѐте.

Prohibitions: недѐй(те) глѐда,
не глѐдай(те),
недѐй да глѐдаш

in 3rd persons and 1st pers. pl. with нѐка: нѐка да не глѐда.

For the 1st and 3rd pers. sing. and plur. one can use стѝга or дòста + Compound Past (see below). This construction with 2nd persons expresses a wish, e.g.:—

    дòста сме я̀ли! = let us stop eating, let us not eat!
    стѝга си глѐдал! = stop looking, don't look (any more)!

The Infinitive

The old Infinitive in *-ti*, as well as the old Supine, have been lost in modern Bulgarian. These are regularly replaced by clauses introduced by да + Present, even in sentences where the Infinitive replaces a noun, e.g.:—

    да крадѐш, е грехота̀ = it is wrong to steal,
    or stealing is wrong

After a few expressions, such as недѐй, (see above, the Imperative), не мòга (= I cannot), не смѐя (= I dare not), the "truncated Infinitive" can be used. In form this is the pure root of the verb, identical in form with the 2nd and 3rd pers. sing. Aorist, e.g.:—

    глѐда = to look

In verbs whose stems end in a dental, this too is cut off, e.g.:—

    че = (to) read
    я = (to) eat
    да = (to) give

—all ending in a vowel, as well as—

    пя = sing
    ка̀зва = say
    хва̀ли = praise, etc.

Present Gerund Active (Verbal Adverb)

    Categories 1 and 2 end in -ейки
    Category 3—in -айки or -яйки, e.g.:—

    четѐйки = reading
    мѝслейки = thinking
    глѐдайки = looking
    ва̀ляйки = rolling

These are formed from Impfve. verbs and can be paraphrased by a clause with a verb in the Indicative introduced by катò (= as, when).

As in other Slavonic languages, gerunds in Bulgarian can only qualify a main verb and therefore refer only to the subject of the sentence.

(There is no Past Gerund in Bulgarian.)

Participles (Verbal Adjectives)
These vary in gender and number, and also in case for the masc. sing. with article, and can have the article suffixed.

Present Active, formed only from Impfve. vbs.:—

Categories 1 and 2 end in -ещ, or, if finally stressed, -èщ, *or* -ящ.
Category 3 ends in -ащ/-ящ.

Examples:—

пламтèщ = flaming, fem. пламтèща, neut. -що, plur. -щи.
пламтèщият òгън = the flaming fire (Nom.)
гàрвани прелùтащи из мрàка = ravens flying about in the dark

Past Active.—In contrast to Serbocroätian and other Slavonic languages, Bulgarian has, for verbs with different stems in Present and Aorist, *two* Past Participles Active in -л (masc.), -ла (fem.), -ло (neut.), -ли (plur.):—

(1) one formed by adding these endings to the 1st pers. sing. Imperfect less the final -x—the Imperfect Past Participle Active, used only in Renarration;
(2) the other formed by adding the same endings to the 2nd/3rd pers. sing. Aorist—the Aorist Past Participle Active.

E.g.:—

пùша = I write (Impfve.)
Imperfect: пùшех (1) Imperfect Past Part. Act.: пùшел
Aorist: писàх (2) Aorist Past Part. Act.: писàл
напùша = I write (Pfve.)
Aorist: напùсах (2) Aorist Past Part. Act.: напùсал
трèгна = I set out (Pfve.)
Imperfect: трèгнех (1) Imperfect Past Part. Act.: трèгнел

Aorist: тръ́гнах   (2) Aorist Past Part. Act.:
                  тръ́гнал

Verbs with Aorist in -ох add -ъл, e.g.:—

донѐсох = I brought, Past Part. Act.: донѐсъл

but dental stems lose their final т or д before the л, e.g.:—

     плѐтох = I wove, Past Part. Act.: плел
     бо̀дох = I pricked, Past Part. Act.: бол

These participles are mostly used in compound tenses (see below), but they can also be used by themselves in Renarration to give a description of events not witnessed by the speaker:—

Живѐел едѝн цар...   = There once lived a king...
Той вдѝгнал тоя́гата и ка̀зал = They say (or: Once) he lifted his stick and said...

These Past Participles Active are actually the Compound Past (Perfect) tense with the auxiliary verb (quite regularly) omitted in the 3rd persons. (See "The Compound Past or Perfect" tense below.)

Past Participle Passive. This is obtained by adding—

-н, -на, -но, -ни   to verbs whose 2nd/3rd pers. sing. Aorist ends in -а or -я;

-ен, -ена, -ено, -ени to verbs whose 2nd/3rd pers. sing. Aorist ends in -е or -и;

sometimes also (under stress) -я́н, -я́на, -я́но, -ѐни;

-т, -та, -то, -ти   to verbs which add the Aorist endings direct to vocalic verb stem, or whose 1st pers. sing. Present ends in -на.

Past Participles Passive in -ен should be distinguished from adjectives in -ен:—

     побѐден, fem. побѐдна = victorious, conquering
     победѐн, fem. победѐна = conquered

These participles can be formed from transitive verbs of either aspect according to the meaning required, though perfective Past Participles Passive are more common. Examples:—

```
писа̀н    = written        хра̀нен   = fed
търпя̀н   = endured        чут      = heard
мъ̀чен    = tormented      трѐснат  = struck
```

Compound Tenses

Future. This is formed with the invariable (unstressed) particle ще + Present Pfve. or Impfve.:—

```
            ще чета̀ = I shall read
            ще четѐш
              etc.
```

The negative is often formed with ня̀ма да + Present:—

```
            ня̀ма да четѐш = you will not read
```

Far more rare and dialectal is the Future formed by using the Truncated Infinitive with the variable auxiliary—

```
   ща   = will        щем (щеме)
   щеш    etc.        щете
   ще                 щат
```

This form is archaic and is to be found in special expressions and "popular" (наро̀дна) speech.

Future of Renarration

The Compound Past of ща (щял съм) is here followed by да + Present with omission of the 3rd person auxiliaries, e.g.:—

```
   Той щял да замѝне = I have heard that he was
            starting out (was going to...)
```

This tense also serves as the Renarration form of the Past Conditional (Past Future)—see below.

Future Perfect

The Future of "to be" is compounded with the Aorist Past Participle Active of either aspect, viz.:—

either— ще съм (про)чѐл
or—   ще бъ̀да (про)чѐл = I shall have read
                                 (through)

```
   Negative form:—
            ня̀ма да съм (бъ̀да)(про)чѐл.
```

There is also a *Past Future Perfect*:—

щях да съм пра̀вил = I was going to have done

The *corresponding form of Renarration* serves to render a *Future Perfect* as well as a *Past Future Per-*

fect of direct speech:—

щял съм да съм пра̀вил = They say I would have done;
or: They say I was going to have done

The Compound Past or Perfect

This tense is formed with the Present of "to be" + the Aorist* (or, for Renarration only, the Imperfect) Past Participle Active. In the most correct language it is used:—

    (a) as an indefinite Past tense, generally equivalent to the English Perfect, e.g.: "I have done," or "I have been doing";
    (b) in Renarration (преизка̀зване), when the omission of the auxiliary verb in the 3rd persons sing. and plur. (е, са) is obligatory.

(In Renarration the speaker or writer describes events not witnessed by himself, but learnt of indirectly. This is, of course, quite different from "Reported Speech".)

    Чел си = (1) You have been reading, or
            (2) They say (or: I have heard) that you read

In Renarration this form corresponds *only* to an Aorist of direct statement.

No introductory verb is necessary to render the second alternative meaning.

In the 3rd person:—

    (1) Той е боледу̀вал годѝни = he has been ill for years

But—

    (2) Боледу̀вал годѝни = they say he was ill for years

(corresponding to an original Imperfect *or* Aorist, because the stem of both is identical).

Четя̀л си (with Imperfect Past Participle Active), however, can only mean: I hear (or: they say) you are *or* were reading.

    *N.B. of *either* aspect, with corresponding change of meaning, i.e.:—

чел си   > <   прочѐл си
= (1) you have been reading   = (1) you have read through
= (2) they say you read   = (2) they say you have read through,

    Nos. (2) corresponding to direct—чѐте > < прочѐте.

This form, therefore, corresponds either to an original Present or to an Imperfect. (Cf. under Past Participle Active.)

Compound Past (Perfect) in Renarration
The Renarration form of Nos. 1 above adds a бил, making the report more remote, e.g.:—

    бил си чел   = they say you have read
    бил боледу̀вал годѝни = they say he has been
                                   ill for years

These forms are also used to renarrate an original Pluperfect—see below.

The Pluperfects
The same principle applies here. When the Aorist Past Participle Active of either aspect is compounded with the Imperfect or Aorist Indicative of "to be", they represent direct continuous or completed Pluperfects respectively, e.g.:—

    бе(ше) чел   = he had been reading
    бе(ше) прочѐл = he had read through

Pluperfect of Renarration
But when these participles are compounded with the Compound Past of "to be" with the usual omission of the auxiliary verb in the 3rd persons, they imply reported information which the speaker does not necessarily believe, i.e. Renarration (also used in historical accounts). E.g.:—

    Той бил пѐел из у̀лиците = They say he was
        singing in the streets.

This form, e.g. бил съм пѐел = they say I have sung, etc., also corresponds to an original direct Compound Past (Perfect), e.g.: пѐел съм (see above).

The Conditional
This Mood is formed by compounding the Aorist Past Participle Active of either aspect with бих, би, би, бихме, бихте, биха.

    бих чел   = I would read (I would be reading)
    бих прочѐл = I would read (through)

Very rare is the form obtained by adding -вам, -ваш, -ва, -ваме, -вате, -ват to the root of the verb:—

    я̀двам = I would eat, also = I may eat

The Past Conditional or Past Future is formed either with the Imperfect of ща (щях, etc.) + да + Pres. Pfve. or Impfve., or more rarely with the invariable auxiliary ще + the Imperfect. E.g.:—

щях да четà or ще четях = I would have been reading, or: I was going to read
щях да прочетà = I would have read, or: I was going to read through

Negative form:—

нямаше да четà = I would not have read, or: I was not going to read

These tenses can express "Unreal Conditions in the Past".

There also exists a *Past Conditional of Renarration* made up of the Compound Past (or Pluperfect) of ща + да + Present:—

щял съм да четà = they say that I would have read or been reading

This tense is also used to render in Renarration a Future of direct speech (see above).

The use of the Pluperfect with its бил makes the Renarration even more remote.

той щял бил да замѝне = they say he would have started off, or: meant to start off

Irregular Verbs
   Originally Athematic Verbs

съм = I am (Frequentative бѝвам — regular)

		Present	Imperfect	
Sing.	1	съм	бях (*formerly* бѣхъ) or бъ̀дех (*formerly* бѫдѣхъ)	
	2	си	бе or бѐше "	бѣ(ше) (regular, used only after àко and да in conditional clauses)
	3	е	бе or бѐше "	бѣ(ше)
Plur.	1	сме	бяхме "	бѣхме
	2	сте	бяхте "	бѣхте
	3	са (*formerly* сѫ)	бяха "	бѣха

BULGARIAN

Aorist

Sing. 1 бях (*formerly* бѣхъ) or бидо́х (used only with Past Participle Passive to render the Aorist Passive)
    2 бе or беше   "   бѣ(ше)   бидѐ
    3 бе or беше   "   бѣ(ше)   бидѐ
Plur. 1 бя́хме   "   бѣхме   бидо́хме
    2 бя́хте   "   бѣхте   бидо́хте
    3 бя́ха   "   бѣха   бидо́ха

Future   *Conditional*

Sing. 1 ще бѣ́да (*formerly* бѫда) or ще съм   бих   бил(ѐ)
    2 ще бѣ́деш   etc.,   ще си   би   "
    3 ще бѣ́де   etc.   би   "
Plur. 1 ще бѣ́дем   бѝхме били́
    2 ще бѣ́дете   бѝхте   "
    3 ще бѣ́дат   бѝха   "

Present Gerund: бидѐйки
Present Participle: (бѣ́дещ)[1]
Past Participle: бил, била́, било́, били́
Imperative: 2nd pers. sing. бѫ́ди! (*formerly* бѫди!)
           2nd pers. plur. бѫ́дѐте! (*formerly* бѫдете!)

ям = I eat   дам = I give (Pfve.)

Present Imperfect Aorist Present Imperfect Aorist

Sing. 1 ям   ядя́х   я́дох   дам   дадя́х   да́дох
    2 ядѐш ядѐше я́де   дадѐш дадѐше да́де
    3 ядѐ   ядѐше я́де   дадѐ   дадѐше да́де

Plur. 1 ядѐм   ядя́хме я́дохме дадѐм(е) дадя́хме да́дохме
    2 ядѐте ядя́хте я́дохте дадѐте   дадя́хте да́дохте
    3 ядя́т   ядя́ха   я́доха   дадя́т   дадя́ха   да́доха

Present Gerund: я́дейки   (да̀вайки)
Present Participle: я́дещ   (да̀ващ)
Imp. Past Participle:
  ядя́л, -а, -о, ядѐли   дадя́л, -а, -о, дадѐли
Aor. Past Participle:
  ял, я́ла, я́ло, я́ли   дал, да̀ла, да̀ло, да̀ли
Past Part. Pass.: я́ден   да̀ден
Imperative: яж! я́жте!   дай! да̀йте!

[1]This form is really an adjective, meaning "future"; cf. същ = real, true.

The old verb вѣмъ (= I know) survives only in the adverb невям (= maybe).

Other Irregular Verbs

ща = I will (aux. verb in the literary language), cf. йскам (reg.) = I want

	Present	Imperfect			Aorist	
Sing. 1	ща	щях	(*formerly*	щѣхъ	щях	(*formerly*	щѣхъ
2	щеш	щѐше		щѣше	щя		щѣ
3	ще	щѐше		щѣше	щя		щѣ
Plur. 1	щем	щяхме		щѣхме	щяхме		щѣхме
2	щѐте	щяхте		щѣхте	щяхте		щѣхте
3	щат	щяха		щѣха)	щяха		щѣха)

Past Participle: щял, щяла, щяло, щѐли
(*formerly* щѣл, щѣла, щѣло, щѣли)

мо̀га, мо̀жеш, = I can, has Impf. мо̀жех, Aor. можа̀х, Aor. Past Part. Act. (можа̀л or) могѐл, могла̀, могло̀, моглѝ.

спя, спиш = I sleep, Impf. спях, спѐше, Impf. Past Part. спял, -а, -о, спѐли, Aor. спах, Aor. Past Part. спал.

Verbs of Going and Conveying

I go on foot = вървя̀ (reg. Class 2)
I go regularly (Freq.) = хо̀дя (reg. Class 2)
I go away (Impfve.) = отѝвам (Class 3)
    (Pfve.) = отѝда (Class 1) with Past Part. отѝшъл, fem. отѝшла (otherwise both regular).
I go out (Impfve.) = излѝзам
    (Pfve.) = излѣ̀за, излѣ̀зеш, Aor. излѣ̀зох, Aor. Past Part. излѣ̀зъл, -зла, -лезли, Imperative излѣ̀з! излѣ̀зте!
I come (Impfve.) = доха̀ждам
    (Pfve.) = до̀йда, -еш, Aor. дойдо̀х, Imperative ела̀! ела̀те! Past Part. дошѐл or дошѐл, дошла̀, дошло̀, дошлѝ.
I lead (Impfve. and Freq.) = во̀дя 2nd pers. sing. во̀диш, (Pfve.) = заведа̀, заведѐш, Past Part. Act. завѐл.
I convey (Impfve. and Freq.) = во̀зя, 2nd pers. sing. во̀зиш; or ка̀рам or отка̀рвам
    (Pfve.) = *only* отка̀рам, отка̀раш, Past Part. Act. отка̀рал
I carry (Impfve. and Freq.) = но̀ся, 2nd pers. sing. но̀сиш, (Pfve.) = занеса̀, занесѐш, Past Part. Act. занѐсъл, занѐсла.

The regular verb ѝмам (= I have) has a special

negative form: нямам, used also for forming the negative Future tense, see above. няма also means "there is not", French "il n'y a pas".

The Aspects of the verb
These are as important in Bulgarian as in any other Slavonic language and are formed in the same various ways:—

1. Pfve. from (simple) Impfve. by adding a prefix—

пѝша   = I write   мо̀ля   = I request   пѝя   = I drink
напѝша   помо̀ля   изпѝя

2. Impfve. from simple or compound Pfve. by vowel lengthening or by inserting a syllable—

отгово̀ря = I answer   ку̀пя   = I buy
отгова̀рям   купу̀вам

дам   = I give   убѝя   = I kill
да̀вам   убѝвам

3. Impfve. from Pfve. by changing the Present ending—

пу̀сна = I let   вдѝгна = I lift
пу̀скам   вдѝгам

ста̀на = I become, I get up   уда̀ря   = I strike
ста̀вам   у̀дрям (with contraction)

лѐгна = I lie down   запо̀чна = I begin
ля̀гам (with lengthening,   запо̀чвам
   < лѣг-)

4. Different forms of the same root or two entirely different roots sometimes occur for the two aspects—

Pfve.   *Impfve.*
взѐма   = I take   взѝмам
умра̀   = I die   умѝрам
помо̀гна = I help   пома̀гам
донеса̀   = I bring   дона̀сям
до̀йда   = I come   доха̀ждам
доведа̀   = I bring (a person)   довѐждам
оба̀дя   = I report   оба̀ждам
платя̀   = I pay   пла̀щам
простя̀   = I forgive   проща̀вам
прокълна̀ = I curse   проклѐвам or проклѝнам

Most Frequentative verbs belong to Class 3.

BULGARIAN

WORD ORDER WITH ENCLITICS

The only enclitics in Bulgarian are:—

1. The auxiliary verbs of the Compound Past (Perfect) tense:

      съм, си, е, сме, сте, са:

2. The short forms of the Accusative (= Oblique) and Dative Personal Pronouns and of the Reflexive Pronoun:—

Pers. Pron.		Sing.			Plur.			Reflex.
	1st pers.	2nd pers.	3rd pers. masc. and neut.	3rd fem.	1st pers.	2nd pers.	3rd pers.	
Acc.	ме	те	го	я	ни	ви	ги	се
Dat.	ми	ти	му	ѝ	ни	ви	им	си

3. Some particles: бе, ле, ма (emphatic, with Vocative), ли (interrogative).

None of these enclitics can start a sentence. They regularly come after the first emphatic word *or word group* in the sentence.

1. Ку́пѝл съм къ̀щата   = I have bought the house

   Вче́ра съм бил в къ̀щи   = Yesterday I was at home

   Цял ден е у́чѝл   = He was studying the whole day

2. Тъ̀рсят те   = They are looking for you

   Кажѝ ми!   = Tell me!

   Кажѝ ѝ!   = Tell her!

   Тая скръб на селянката го смая = lit. That sorrow of the peasant woman astonished him

After the negative не, however, these enclitics take the stress.

Не го̀ да̀вай!   = Do not give it!
Не тѐ тъ̀рсят   = They are not looking for you
Не ѝ ка̀звай!   = Do not tell her!
Не съм хо̀дѝл отда̀вна на Вѝтоша = I haven't gone up the Vitosha (mountain) for a long time

Contrary to the usage in Serbocroätian, these enclitics can occur directly after и (= and), но (= but), etc., e.g.:—

Обѝчай родѝната си и ѝ служѝ вя̀рно	= Love your country and serve it faithfully
Дѝрен е и у тях, но го не намѐрили	= He was sought (i.e. they looked for him) in their house, too, but they did not find him.

When an auxiliary verb of the Compound Past tense occurs with an enclitic Personal or Reflexive Pronoun, the auxiliary verb takes precedence unless it is the 3rd pers. sing. auxiliary verb e, e.g.:—

Кỳпѝл съм си но̀ви дрѐхи	= I have bought myself some new clothes
Мно̀го пѣ̀ти съм го наблюда̀вал	= I have often observed it
Той го е поглѐднал, та го е поразѝл	= He looked at him and struck him down
Той добрѐ разбра̀ какво̀ се е слỳчѝло	= He understood well what had happened
Той се е борѝл с мѐчка	= He fought a bear

If a Dative and an Accusative Personal Pronoun occur in the same clause, then the Dative Pers. Pronoun comes first. This is true even when the Acc. Pers. Pronoun is the Acc. Reflexive ce (as in Serbocroätian, and contrary to the usage in Slovenian, Czech and Slovak). E.g.:—

Стрỳва ми се	= It seems to me
Кой ти го да̀де?	= Who gave it to you?
Кỳпѝх си го отда̀вна	= I bought it for myself long ago
Не съм му я дал	= I have not given him it (fem.)

'He' can be separated from its main verb only by the enclitic Personal and Reflexive Pronouns, as in Macedonian and in contrast to Serbocroätian:—

Не го̀ вѝждам но го чỳвам	= I do not see it but I hear it
Това̀ не се ка̀зва	= That is not said
Въ нѐго не се чỳвствува прекѣ̀сване	= In it one does not feel a break

But with the Compound Past tense, не cannot be separated from the auxiliary verb by enclitic pronouns unless the auxiliary is in the 3rd pers. sing. —e, e.g.:—

Не съм го виждал	= I have not seen him
Не сѐ е обадил	= He has not called

The interrogative particle ли takes precedence over other enclitics, but it cannot come between the negative не and its auxiliary verb. It follows the word asking the question, not necessarily the verb. E.g.:—

Не си ли го виждал?	= Have you not seen him?
Не ѐ ли излизал тъдява?	= Has he not come out here?
Ти ли си идвал?	= Did *you* come?
Ти вчера ли си идвал?	= Was it yesterday you came?
Не ви ли се струва, че...?	= Does it not seem to you that...?

The Dative enclitic Pers. Pronouns used as possessives occur after or before the noun they qualify, if it is without an adjective, e.g.:—

Взех шапката си *or* Взѐх си шапката	= I took my hat.

But if the noun is also qualified by an adjective, the possessive enclitic comes between the adjective and the noun, e.g.:—

Взех голямата си шапка	= I took my big hat

The Vocative particles follow their noun:—

Иване бе! = I say, John!
Марийке ле! Марийке ма! = I say, Mary!

The auxiliary verb of the Future tense, ще, is a *pro*clitic. It may start a sentence and can only be separated from its verb by the enclitic Pers. and Reflexive Pronouns and rarely by ли.

Ще му кажа това	= I shall tell him that
(Ще ли дойдеш?) Better: Ще дойдеш ли?	= Will you come?

The auxiliary verb of the Conditional Mood, бих, би, etc., is neither proclitic nor enclitic. It, too, can only be separated from its main verb by the enclitic Pers. and Reflexive Pronouns and ли.

Бих се обадил	= I would call
Не би го видял никога	= He would never see him
Бихте ли ми услужили?	= Would you do me a favour?

TEXTS

For purposes of comparison, passages are given in both the old and the new spelling.

I. *(Old Orthography)*
Евангелие отъ Лука,
    VIII, 5-8.

5. Сѣячътъ излѣзе да сѣе семето си; и когато сѣеше, едно падна край пѫтя; и затъпка се, и небеснитѣ птици го изкълваха.

6. А друго падна на канарата; и щомъ поникна, изсъхна, защото нѣмаше влага.

7. Друго пъкъ падна всрѣдъ трънитѣ; и заедно съ него порастоха трънитѣ, та го заглушиха.

8. А друго падна на добрата земя и, като порастна, даде стократенъ плодъ. Като каза това, извика: Който има уши да слуша, нека слуша.

(New Orthography)
Евангелие от Лука,
    VIII, 5-8.

5. Сеячът излезе да сее семето си; и когато сееше, едно падна край пътя; и затъпка се, и небесните птици го изкълваха.

6. А друго падна на канарата; и щом поникна, изсъхна, защото нямаше влага.

7. Друго пък падна всред тръните; и заедно с него порастоха тръните, та го заглушиха.

8. А друго падна на добрата земя и, като порасна, даде стократен плод. Като каза това, извика: Който има уши да слуша, нека слуша.

II. *(New Orthography)*
И. Вазов

            Габровският манастир.

    Сред глухите недра на Стара планина, сред чаровните балкански самотии, в една от най-разкошните гънки на северния склон на тая планина, е кацнал не далеко от изворите на кристалната Янтра Соколският манастир.

    Кацнал със своите чардаци и с блестящето на слънцето кубе, между зелени гористи висоти, над един дълбок дол, пълен с вечен шум на реката, той приветливо и радостно се изпречва пред погледа на поклонника, който иде по върлия път от към Габрово да го посети.

    Четири дена бях мил гост на тая балканска светиня.

    От което място на манастиря да погледнах,—от звона ли, от чардаците ли, из стаята си ли—аз виждах отвред чудесен изглед. На север, на запад се спущаха и вълнуваха зелени планински върхове с пасища, ниви и гори по тях. На изток и юг—високи урви, които от манастиря се качваха към небето, за да стигнат гръбняка на Стара планина. Столетни букови гори шумят там.

И аз още от сутринта, разбуден от шума на водите и на славеите в ближния букак, изкачах из манастиря и се залутвах по висотите, през гори и пасища, запъстрели с хиляди разноцветни цветя, за да се любувам още по от високо на безкрайната картина.

И не се нагледвах, и не се насищах на тези красоти.

Господи, колко хубаво!...

III. *(New Orthography)*
Любен Каравелов

   Хубава си, моя горо...

Хубава си, моя горо, меришиш на младост,
Но вселяваш в сърцата ни само скръб и
  жалост.

Който веднъж те погледне, той вечно жалее,
Че не може под твоите сенки да изтлее.

А комуто стане нужда веч да те остави,
Той не може, дорде е жив, да те забрави...

IV. *(New Orthography)*
Пею Яворов
     ЗАТОЧЕНИЦИ.

  От заник-слънце озарени,
  Алеят морски ширини;
  В игра стихийна уморени,
  Почиват яростни вълни...
  И корабът се носи леко
  С попътни тихи ветрове—
  И чезнете в мъгли далеко
   Вий родни брегове.

  И вече нам за път обратен
  Едва ли ще удари час:
  Вода и суша—необятен,
  Затворен е светът за нас!
  А Вардар, Дунав и Марица,
  Балканът, Странджа и Пирин
  Остават сенки върволица
   На спомена един.

  Но корабът, уви, не спира:
  Все по-далеч и по-далеч
  Лети, отнася ни... Простира
  Нощта крилото си... И веч

> Едва се мяркат очертани
> На тъмно модър небосклон
> Замислените великани
> На чутния Атон.

(New Orthography)   *(Old Orthography)*
                              Пѣю Яворовъ.

И ний през сълзи накипели	И ний прѣзъ сълзи накипѣли
Обръщаме за сетен път	Обръщаме за сетен пѫть
Назад към скъпи нам пределия	Назадъ къмъ скѫпи намъ прѣдѣли
Угаснал взор,—за сетен път	Угасналъ взоръ,—за сетенъ пѫть
Простираме ръце в окови	Простираме рѫцѣ въ окови
Към нашия изгубен рай...	Къмъ нашия изгубенъ рай...
Горчива скръб сърца ни трови,	Горчива скръбъ сърца ни трови,
Прощавай, роден край!	Прощавай, роденъ край!

V. *(New Orthography)*
Елин Пелин

From « ЗАНЕМЕЛИТЕ КАМБАНИ »

Но игумена искаше още веднъж да провери. Може би е забравил нещо. И той отново влезе в черквицата. Малка, ниска стара черквица, градена кой знае в кои години, запомнила старите царе, преживяла робството и благословила новото царство. Вътре вече бе влязъл вечерният мрак и се молеше пред запалените кандилца, чиито малки пламъчета се губеха пред благите усмивки на светиите. Те бяха умилително тържествени пред деня на големия празник.

Дядо игумен спря очудено на прага, защото видя пред светата икона тъмния силует на жена с дете в ръка. Старецът се ядоса. —На днешната вечерня не се влизаше в черква преди да ударят тържествено камбаните. Така беше обичаят.

Той пристъпи тихо към влязлата и я изгледа. Тя беше дрипава, мръсна, забрадена с нечиста кърпа така, че само очите ѝ се показваха. Тя беше стъпила на плочите с боси, изцапани крака, които бяха отпечатали стъпките си по пода и това ядоса повече чистия старец. Жената не го усети. Тя се молеше високо, с плач, и поднасяше пред стъпките на Светата Майка своето болно дете, бледо, изсъхнало, като ланско цвете. То бе склопило очичките си, дишаше тежко и болезнено стенеше.

—Запази ми го и го спаси, майко Богородичке, едничко ми е, шепнеше жената и се навеждаше ниско, като дърво под силата на вятъра. Сълзите ѝ капеха по студените плочи, както капеше восъкът от горещите свещи.

Жената извади от пазухата си игличка с синьо топченце на края и я заборе на новото коприненo перде.
—Приеми това от мен, Света Майко.   Нямам нищо друго!
—Защо си влязла тука?   —каза сърдито старецът.
—Камбаните още не са били. Не знаеш ли обичая?
—Не знам, отче, —каза объркано жената.
—Излез сега. После, после ела!
Жената покорно се обърна, стисна детенцето си в прегръдките и тръгна. Отец Иоаким я проследи с поглед. И когато тя мина през светлината на вратата, още един път забеляза, колко е дрипава и нечиста.
Игуменът видя, че по плочата, на която стоеше жената, бяха останали кални петна. Той видя върху завесата простата игличка със синята топчица на края. Тая топчица личеше като дървеница върху хубавата завеска и я грозеше. Отец Иоаким я извади и захвърли в ъгъла. След това се прекръсти пред иконата, оправи хубаво завеската и излезе.
Без тая случка, всичко друго беше в ред. Но неговото добро сърце забрави това, като видя, че дворът бе изпълнен с богомолци, които държеха свещи и чакаха да ударят камбаните, за да влязат в черквата. Братята също бяха готови. Те бяха слезли долу и разговаряха с народа за предстоящия празник.

VI. *(New Orthography)*
Н. Й. Вапцаров

ВЯРА

Ето—аз дишам,
работя,
живея
и стихове пиша
(тъй както умея).
С живота под вежди
се гледаме строго
и боря се с него
доколкото мога.

С живота сме в разпра,
но ти не разбирай,
че мразя живота.
Напротив, напротив!—
Дори да умирам,
живота със грубите
лапи чилични
аз пак ще обичам!
Аз пак ще обичам!

Да кажем, сега ми окачат
въжето
и питат:
« Как, искаш ли час да
    живееш? »
Веднага ще кресна:
« Свалете!
Свалете!
По-скоро свалете
въжето, злодеи! »

За него—живота—
направил бих всичко.—
Летял бих
със пробна машина в
    небето,
бих влезнал във взривна
ракета, самичък,
бих търсил в простора

далечна
планета.

Но все пак ще чувствам
приятния гъдел
да гледам как
горе
небето синее.
Все пак ще чувствам
приятния гъдел,
че още живея,
че още ще бъда.

Но ето, да кажем,
вий вземате, колко?—
пшеничено зърно
от моята вера,
бих ревнал тогава,
бих ревнал от болка
като ранена
в сърцето пантера.

Какво ще остане
от мене тогава?—
Миг след грабежа
ще бъда разнищен.

И още по-ясно
и още по-право—
миг след грабежа
ще бъда аз нищо.

Може би искате
да я сразите
моята вяра
във дните честити,—
моята вяра,
че утре ще бъде
животът по-хубав,
животът по-мъдър?

А как ще щурмувате,
 моля?
С куршуми?
Не! Неуместно!
Ресто! —Не струва! —

Тя е бронирана
здраво в гърдите
и бронебойни патрони
за нея
няма открити!
Няма открити!

SECTION 3. MACEDONIAN

INTRODUCTION

By an irony of history the people whose ancestors gave to the Slavs their first literary language, were the last to have their modern language recognized as a separate Slavonic language, distinct from the neighbouring Serbian and Bulgarian. In medieval times the Macedonian people formed part of the Bulgarian and Serbian kingdoms and of the Byzantine Empire, until they were finally swallowed up by the Osmanli Turks in the fifteenth century. The majority of them remained under Turkey till the beginning of the twentieth century, when she was finally expelled from the Balkans in 1912. Then the Macedonian people were split up between the three neighbouring countries of Serbia, Bulgaria, and Greece—a state of affairs which still partially persists to-day, as there are still about a quarter of a million Macedonians in both Greece and Bulgaria. The Macedonians, though thus divided and small in numbers and though exploited economically and politically, nevertheless managed to preserve their distinctive dialects and culture, largely in their villages and smaller towns. The bigger centres were in earlier centuries for the most part turkicized, at least superficially.

Their own poets and scholars, such as the brothers D. and K. Miladinov in the nineteenth century, and B. Koneski, V. Iljoski, and K. Toševx in our day, as well as scholars from Russia and Western Europe, such as A. M. Seliščev, A. Mazon, and A. Vaillant, have collected many beautiful folk-songs and delightful folk-stories, treasures of folk-lore preserved by the people. The melodies of their songs, in beauty and subtlety, compare favourably with any in the Balkans, which are one of Europe's richest regions in this respect. Thus the Macedonians, though oppressed and poor, preserved their national identity and their cultural and artistic individuality.

Macedonian was recognized as a literary language quite recently, during the struggle for liberation by the Yugoslav peoples during the last (1939-45) war. On 29th September, 1943, at the second session of AVNOJ (Anti-fascist Council for the National Liberation of Yugoslavia) at Jajce, the Macedonian people was recognized as a separate nationality with its own language. And on 2nd August, 1944, at a meeting in the monastery of St. Prohor Pčinski, the Macedonian people formally joined the new federal Yugoslavia, as

an independent people with their own official and
literary language. Since then much publishing of
books, periodicals, and newspapers in Macedonian has
taken place, and great progress has been made in developing a complete official and literary language.
But in certain smaller points the language is still
in a state of active development and stabilization,
especially as regards the spoken language of educated
speakers. The last orthographical reforms took place
in 1970 with the publication of the new Правопис.

One of the earliest records of Macedonian is to
be found in the *Lexicon tetraglosson* of Hadži Daniil,
first published in 1764 at Voskopojë (Moschopolis)
in Albania.[1] Hadži Daniil was a Vlach (Aromun)
scholar whose object in this work was to teach Greek
to, and hellenize the non-Greek inhabitants of the
southern Balkans. His *Lexicon in four languages* contains passages in Greek translated into Albanian,
Vlach, and what he calls "Bulgarian". But as Mazon
and Vaillant point out,[2] the language recorded is actually a fairly exact picture of the language *spoken*
in the region of Bitolj (Monastir—in Macedonian
Bitola) in the middle of the eighteenth century.

It was not till some fifty years later that native Macedonians tried to use their own language in
literary works. The first to do so were two monks,
Joakim Krčovski and Kiril Pejčinovič. Krčovski, born
in the region of Kičevo, worked also as a teacher and
moved about from place to place. He published four
religious works, printed in Buda between 1814 and
1819, and died in 1820. Pejčinovič was born in 1771,
in the village of Tearce in the Tetovo district of
Western Macedonia and spent most of his life in monasteries. He was a pupil of Krčovski for a time.
His two works, also of a religious character, appeared at Buda in 1816 and at Salonika in 1840. He
died in 1845. Both these writers tried to write in a
simple popular language, comprehensible to the people, and modelled themselves on the Bulgarian
writer , Sofronij Vračanski, and the Serbian reformer, Vuk Karadžić. Krčovski's language is rather more
artificial and is a mixture of various dialects—
doubtless due to his many changes of habitat. Pejčinovič attained a more lively and popular style and
based his language mainly on the dialect of the
Tetovo district. His writings are more emotional and
personal, though also on religious themes (e.g. his

[1] See also our chapter on Bulgarian.
[2] See Mazon and Vaillant, *L'Evangéliaire de Kulakia*,
p. 8.

"Ogledalo" = Mirror), and are exclusively inspired by a zeal to spread and heighten Christian morality. Neither he nor Krčovski sound any note of protest on behalf of their people, or show any sign of an awakened national consciousness.

The second half of the nineteenth century saw the fight of the Southern Slavs of Orthodox faith against the domination of Greek influence, centred in Constantinople, over all their church and cultural affairs. The famous national champion, Dimitar Miladinov, was born in Struga on Lake Ohrid in 1810, and was brought up in Greek schools. In 1840 he was a teacher in his native town, teaching in Greek. The Russian scholar, Grigoróvič, visited him at his school in 1845 and asked why he did not teach in his native tongue, and encouraged him to do so. "Are you not our brothers?" he said. From then on, D. Miladinov turned more and more toward his native Slav language and the Cyrillic alphabet, and became a resolute opponent of Panhellenism. He gradually became absorbed in the struggle and developed a fanatical *Bulgarian* national consciousness. (The Macedonians did not regard themselves as a separate nation yet.)

He had a number of famous pupils, among them his younger brother, Konstantin Miladinov (born in Struga, 1830), Rajko Žinzifov (b. in Veles, 1839), Grigor Prličev, Partenij Zografski, and Kuzman Šapkarev. He directed them to Russia for their education; and his brother Konstantin, Žinzifov and Zografski were able to attend Russian universities where they studied Slavonic philology in the late fifties.

K. Miladinov, Žinzifov, and Prličev laid the foundations of modern Macedonian poetry, into which they introduced entirely novel and inspired elements.

K. Miladinov, a born poet, contracted consumption in Moscow under the rigours of student life in those days. His poems often express his aversion to the northern climate and his longing for his native South. He based his style and language on Macedonian folk poetry which he knew well, and succeeded in writing genuine poetry. In Moscow he and Žinzifov fraternized with prominent Bulgarian leaders of the day, such as Ljuben Karavelov, the poet, and Marin Drinov. Their whole group was under the influence of the democratic wing of the Russian Slavophils, led by Aksákov. In 1861, K. Miladinov went to Zagreb. There the Croat bishop and patriot, Josip Štrosmajer, helped him to publish his big collection (Zbornik) of six hundred Macedonian folk epics and lyrics. It was the first publication of its kind, and Štrosmajer had persuaded him to transcribe it from the Greek alphabet into the Cyrillic.[1] That year his brother Dimitar was arrested by the Turks, who were influenced by the slander of the Greek church authorities and imprisoned him in Constantinople. Konstantin promptly went there to intercede for his brother and was himself imprisoned. The two brothers died in captivity early the following year.

Rajko Žinzifov remained in Russia all the rest of his life, working as a secondary school teacher. He was a Slavonic scholar and translated the "Слово о полку Игореве", the poems of Шевченко, and even the Czech Ossianic forgery, the Královédvorský rukopis. He was also an active publicist for the Macedonian cause. He was the first to protest against the economic oppression of Macedonia. He also wrote the first short story in Macedonian ("Прошетба"), describing the sufferings of the Macedonian peasants at the hands of the Greek priests. He was an ardent Slavophil and loved the folklore of his native land. In Russia he felt himself isolated, and his poetry expresses his longing for his native land and his doubts as to the reality of his achievements. The Ukrainian poet, Шевченко, exercised the most powerful influence on him. Žinzifov wrote in a mixed language, strongly influenced by Bulgarian. His accentuation and prosody also show the influence of Russian and Ukrainian.

Grigor Prličev showed that he was undoubtedly a gifted poet when he wrote in Greek; but when he tried to write in Slavonic, he wrote in a painfully mixed language, apparently unaware that his own native Macedonian would best serve him as a medium of expression. He translated the *Iliad*, and at the end of his life he lamented that he could never completely master Bulgarian.

Kuzman Šapkarev and Marko Cepenkov both collected folk songs, stories, proverbs, and riddles. Šapkarev published a big collection in 1891. Cepenkov, who was a tailor in Prilep, published his many contributions in collections published by the Ministry of Education in Sofia.

But these preparations did not lead to an immediate growth of Macedonian literature on a big scale owing to the expansion at that time of Pan-Serb and Pan-Bulgar political influences, for both Bulgars and

---

[1] The Greek alphabet was at that time freely used for Macedonian. For instance, in 1852, Kirjak Dražilovec of Voden (Edessa) printed in Salonika in the Greek alphabet a translation of the Gospels into Macedonian, made by the monk Pavel Božigropski who was born in the village of Konikovo, near Voden.

Serbs laid claim to Macedonian folk poetry as their
own. And Greek church influence held education
firmly in its own hands. Šapkarev's school textbooks
in Macedonian were forbidden.

One of the most interesting and important figures of the Macedonian national revival was the
writer, publicist and teacher, Krste P. Misirkov
(1874-1926). He was born in Postol (Aegean Macedonia) and first went to the Greek primary school
there; but he finished his rather troubled schooling
mainly in Belgrade, and in 1895 completed his course
at the teachers' training college there. He then
decided to go for further study first to the Ecclesiastical Seminary in Poltava (Ukraine) and then to
the University of St. Petersburg, where he graduated
in the faculty of history and philology in 1902. He
was acutely aware of the political dilemma of his
people under Turkish rule, being as they were the
target of propaganda from Serbia and Bulgaria alike,
as well as from the great powers interested in the
Balkans. His main work, "За македонските работи"
(On Macedonian affairs) was suppressed after being
printed in Sofia in 1903, and very few copies survived destruction. His periodical, "Вардар", suffered a similar fate after the first issue was
printed in Odessa in 1905 but was never published.
His main advocacy was for the independence of the
Macedonian people who he thought at first should remain loyal to the Turkish Sultan. In respect of the
Macedonian language he advocated basing the literary
language on the dialects of Veles, Prilep, Bitola and
Ohrid, remarkably enough the very dialects on which
the modern literary language was founded after 1944,
the dialects of central and western Macedonia. Due
to the suppression of his publications, his views
expressed in these works were only known to an extremely small circle until after the second world
war. In 1913 he advocated his ideas in the Macedonian émigrés' paper published in St. Petersburg in
Russian, called "Македонский голос". At the time of
the Russian revolution he was a teacher in Kishinëv
(Moldavia) which was annexed by Romania. Misirkov
then went again to Bulgaria where he worked mostly as
a teacher, in difficult material circumstances. He
died in poverty and obscurity in Sofia, Bulgaria, in
1926. But even though he was not in a position to
evolve and finalize the orthography and grammatical
norms of Macedonian as we know them today, he is now
honoured in Macedonia as one of the chief founders of
modern literary Macedonian.

Only after the first world war was there an opportunity for the nation to consolidate culturally and gather strength. Curiously enough, drama led the way. B. Iljoski, A. Panov, and R. Krleski wrote plays about local life and customs ("бит"), which accorded with the interest of Serbian theatres in this subject at that time and were allowed to be performed. The first play in Macedonian had actually been written considerably earlier—in 1900, by Vojdan Černodrimski.

Soon afterwards three of Macedonia's best-known modern poets started their activity: Kosta Racin, Kole Nedelkovski, and Venko Markovski. They all three took the national folk-poetry as their starting point and basis.

Racin (b. 1909) was the son of a poor potter in Veles, and at first followed his father's trade. He was largely self-educated. His poetry expresses the bitterness of his nation's struggle for freedom against oppression and poverty and a presentiment of her coming liberation. He took an active part in illegal political work for his nation, and was hounded by the police. His only volume of poems (Бели мугри) was published in Zagreb in 1938. In 1942, when he was arrested by the police in Skopje, his landlady burnt his unpublished poetry. Earlier the Serbian police had burnt the manuscript of his novel *Opium*. He joined the Partisans during the second world war and died on service in the summer of 1943.

Nedelkovski was born in the village of Vojnica in the district of Veles in 1912. He grew up in great poverty and had to leave school early and became a house painter in Skopje. In 1933, he went to live a lonely life in Sofia. There he met Venko Markovski, whose poetry greatly moved him. He started publishing in 1939, and later produced two small volumes of very successful and moving lyrics. He was an active political worker in his nation's cause. In 1941, he committed suicide to avoid arrest by the police in Sofia, when he found he could not escape.

Markovski was born in 1915. His first lyrics were in the folk style and of extreme beauty. Later he published poetry in a more individual style and on political and war themes, not dissimilar to that of the Soviet modernists. He also was an active political worker, and went to Sofia at the end of 1937. During the second world war he fought in the ranks of the Partisans. He has described the long struggle of the Macedonian people for liberation. His many volumes of poetry, both because of their aesthetic value and also their progressive ideas, have greatly contributed to the formation of the modern Macedonian literary language.

These three poets helped finally to establish[1] the central dialect as the basis of the modern literary language. Thus the speech of some of Macedonia's biggest towns, Prilep, Bitola, Veles, and Kičevo, round which lives the most compact mass of Macedonian population, became the model for the whole nation. The dialects of western Macedonia stand closest to this central one. (See § on "Dialects" and "Features Characteristic of Macedonian" for further details.) The Cyrillic alphabet, on phonetic principles, had now long been in use, and in 1945 the main rules of the orthography were laid down in the official "Правопис", slightly revised in 1948.[2] Since then, publishing in Macedonian of papers, text-books, translations, and original literature has gone on apace in the new federal Yugoslavia. The Macedonians in Yugoslavia at last have their own National Republic. Their language has been recognized, their literature is growing.

THE MACEDONIAN ALPHABET

Macedonian		*Approximate English Equivalent*
А	а	(more open and forward than) *ah*
Б	б	*b*
В	в	*v*
Г	г	*g* in "go"
Д	д	*d* (dental)
Ѓ	ѓ	voiced midpalatal plosive, cf. *d* in "dew"
Е	е	*e* in "met"
Ж	ж	*zh*, *s* in "pleasure"
З	з	*z*
Ѕ	ѕ	*dz* pronounced together, as in "adze"
И	и	*ee*, *i* in "machine"
Ј	ј	*y* in both "boy" and "yes"
К	к	*k*
Л	л	*l* [3]
Љ	љ	medium *l* in "let"
М	м	*m*
Н	н	*n*
Њ	њ	soft *n*, *ni* in "onion"

[1] Other notable modern poets are: Blaže Koneski, G. Ivanovski, and S. Janevski. [2] See also p. 138, lines 9-10.
[3] Л, л is pronounced hard [ł] before the back vowels а, о, у, and medium before е and и, and ј.

Macedonian		Approximate English Equivalent
О	о	*o* in "for"
П	п	*p*
Р	р[1]	*r* rolled
С	с	*s* in "see"
Т	т	*t* (dental)
Ќ	ќ	unvoiced midpalatal plosive, cf. *t* in "tune"
У	у	*oo* in "boot", *u* in "rule"
Ф	ф	*f*
Х	х	*ch* in "loch"
Ц	ц	*ts* pronounced together, as in "bits"
Ч	ч	*ch* in "church"
Џ	џ	*j* in "jam"
Ш	ш	*sh*

The Macedonian alphabet is the same as the Serbian Cyrillic, except that it replaces ђ and ћ by the typically Macedonian palatal plosives ѓ and ќ respectively, and adds the letter ѕ to represent the typically Macedonian sound *dz*. The form ѕ goes back to a letter of similar shape and representing the same sound in Old Slavonic. Otherwise, the same differences between the Macedonian and the Old Slavonic (and also the Russian) alphabets exist, as between Serbian Cyrillic and Old Slavonic (and Russian) Cyrillic.

PRONUNCIATION

The spelling of literary Macedonian is phonetic —one letter represents one sound only, as in Serbocroätian. The only exceptions to this rule are due to the assimilation of consonants in groups and to the unvoicing of final voiced consonants, apart from the two variants of *l* mentioned on page 143, footnote No. 3.

The Accent
The accent in Macedonian is a purely stress ac-

---

[1] Р, р can be vocalic, as in дрво (= wood), крвав (= bloody). When it is vocalic initially, an apostrophë is used before it: 'рж (= rye), 'р̀а (= rust).

The apostrophë is also used to indicate the "neutral vowel", ə (= *a* in Eng. "about"), which occurs in foreign and dialectal words, e.g.:—

        к'смет = fate
        В'чко (a name)

cent, as in Bulgarian and East Slav. ("Musical accent" or intonations do not exist here.) In literary Macedonian the stress is placed on the third syllable from the end in words of three or more syllables and on the first syllable of dissyllables,[1] e.g.:—

> плàнина = mountain
> дỳкан = shop

When a monosyllabic suffix is added, e.g. the definite article, to words of three or more syllables the accent shifts forward by one syllable, keeping to the third from the end. E.g.:—

> планѝната = the mountain

On dissyllabic words with a suffix it is kept on the third from the end, e.g.:—

> дỳканот = the shop
> кỳќата = the house

Monosyllabic nouns never have the article stressed, in contrast to Bulgarian, e.g.:—

> град = city   грàдот = the city,
>   cf. Bulg. град, градèт
> леб = bread,   лèбот = the bread
> ноќ = night,   нòќта = the night

Irregular accents occur with monosyllabic prepositions, conjunctions, pronouns, the negative не, and with adjectives before nouns and the article when attached to an adjective, owing to a tendency of shorter words to form dactylic groups (´ ˘ ˘) on the model of the trisyllabic and longer words. See the accented text at the end of this section in which there occur:—

> кàj него   = to him
> дò неа   = to her
> пò глава   = on the head
> дà прави   = to do
> àко не гò сториш тòа = if you do not do this
> болнатà нога   = the sick foot

See also on the Enclitics and Proclitics under "Word Order with Enclitics".

Foreign words also have an irregular accent, mostly in accordance with that in the language of origin, e.g.:—

[1] The words однàj = hardly, тамàм = just, all accented on the final syllable, are exceptions.

>   клишѐ   = clichet
>   помàда   = pomade
>   бирò   = office
>   мемора̀ндум   = memorandum
>   досиѐ   = dossier
>   литератỳра   = literature

The Present Gerund of all verbs is always stressed on the penultimate syllable. (see p. 205.)

The Vowels

In literary Macedonian the vowels should always be clearly pronounced, whether stressed or unstressed, as in Serbocroätian and West Slav. This is one of the main characteristics of literary Macedonian, distinguishing it from the Bulgarian of many speakers (also from Russian) and from certain Macedonian dialects. In contrast to Serbocroätian, Slovenian, Czech and Slovak, there are no long vowels in literary Macedonian.

The Macedonian o is pronounced like a short o in Serbocroätian.

The neutral vowel, indicated by an apostrophë, occurs only in foreign words and in Macedonian dialects.

Vocalic p is as frequent as in Serbocroätian.

C.S. vocalic ļ has become -ол-.

For consecutive vowels see under "The use of j" below.

A "movable a" occurs in words ending in -изам (= -ism), e.g.:—

>   романтизам   = romanticism, but—
>   романтизмот = the romanticism (of...)

E and a are used as the "fill-vowels" in consonant groups, e.g.:—

>   ветер = wind, cf. O.S. вѣтръ
>   храбар = brave, cf. O.S. храбръ

But the C.S. semivowels ъ and ь become o and e in Macedonian, when developed, e.g.:—

тежок (masc.) = heavy, fem. тешка, O.S. тѧжькъ
редок (masc.) = rare, fem. ретка, O.S. рѣдъкъ
ден   = day, O.S. дьнь

Borrowed words preserve the fill-vowel used in the language borrowed from, e.g.:—

метар   = metre   ⎫
Александар = Alexander   ⎬ from Serbocroätian
Днепар   = Dnieper   ⎭

MACEDONIAN

The Consonants

	Bi-labial	Labio-dental	Dental	Dento-alveolar	Al-veolar	Palatal	Velar
Plosive	п б		т д			ќ ѓ	к г
Affricate				ц ѕ	ч џ		
Fricative		ф в		с з	ш ж	ј	х
Nasal	м		н			њ	(ŋ)
Lateral			л (ɫ)		љ		
Rolled					р		
Semivowel						ј	

The consonants of Macedonian are the same as those of Serbocroätian and Bulgarian, except in the following respects:—

1. Macedonian possesses the sound *dz*, written ѕ, in contrast to Serbocr. and most words in Bulg. E.g.:—

   ѕвезда = star
   ѕид = wall
   ѕвонец = bell
   ѕвер = beast
   јанѕа = ague, chill; "jitters"

and in some foreign words:—

   сенѕер = (kind of) apricot

2. Macedonian ќ, ѓ are midpalatal plosives (or affricates with some speakers) and usually correspond to Serbocr. ћ, ђ, e.g.:—

			Sbcr.	cf. also Bulg.
куќа	=	house	кỳћа	кѣ́ща
цвеќе	=	flowers	цвѐће	цветя̀
ќе	=	will, shall	ће	ще
дуќан	=	shop	дỳћан	дукя̀н
меѓа	=	boundary	мѐђа	межда̀
туѓ	=	strange	тỳђ	чужд
ѓавол	=	devil	ђа̏вол	дя̀вол
шеќер	=	sugar	шѐћер	(за̀хар)
калуѓер	=	monk	ка̀луђер	калу̀гер

But cf. also:—

| ангел | = | angel | а̑нђео | а̀нгел | |
| луѓе | = | people | љу̑ди | (хо̀ра), лю̀де |

Ќ is never written before и.
 Serbian names with ђ and ћ are regularly tran-

scribed in Macedonian with ŕ and ḱ respectively.
E.g.:—

Ђурић = Ѓуриќ

3. љ, њ were described by Kepeski as "half-soft" palatal consonants. For practical purposes the pronunciation of њ may be regarded as the same as in Serbocr. But Macedonian љ is much less palatal than љ in Serbocr. and much nearer medium 1, as in Czech and л in Serbocr., e.g.:—

љубов = love
Кољо   man's name

In many words in Macedonian either hard л or лј occur where Serbocr. has љ, e.g.:—

недела	= Sunday	cf. Sbcr.	нȅдеља
постела	= bed		пȍстеља
учител	= teacher		у̑читељ
лут	= angry, hot (in taste)		љу̑т
луѓе	= people		љу̑ди
	etc.		

On the other hand:—

волја	= will	cf. Sbcr.	вȍља
зелје	= greens		зе̑ље
илјада	= thousand		хи̏љада
	etc.		

л is pronounced medium before *j* as in волја (= will) above.

Before е and и it is also a medium *l* as in Bulg. before е and и and as in Sbcr. before all vowels.

Before а, о, у it is a hard *ł* as in Bulg. and Russian.

4. The affricates ч and џ in Macedonian, though hard, are not as hard as in Serbocroätian. Being compounds of ш and ж (i.e. т̑ш and д̑ж) and not having to be distinguished from ћ and ђ, they are pronounced with the tip of the tongue further forward than in Serbocr.

5. A characteristic feature of Macedonian is the frequent dropping of х or the replacing of х by в or ј, e.g.:—

леб	= bread	зедов	= I took (Aor.)	сторив	= I did
страв	= terror	зедовме	= we took	сторивме	= we did
тивко	= quietly	зедоа	= they took	сторија	= they did
итно	= urgently	виор	= whirlwind	уво	= ear
убав	= beautiful	мува	= a fly	глув	= deaf

Хв becomes ф, as in Serbocr. dialects and colloquially in Serbocr., e.g.:—

  ѓакам = I seize, begin
  фрлам = I throw, cf. Bulg. хвѣрлям

  6. *The use of j.*—When two vowels occur consecutively in a word, j is used to avoid hiatus only between и and a, and when three vowels would otherwise occur consecutively. E.g.:—

    пијам = I drink
    сторија = they did
    Македонија = Macedonia
    знаеја = they knew

  In foreign words, too, there is now, according to the latest orthography, a j between и and a, e.g.:—

    материјáл = material
    варијáнта = variant

 -aa- is frequent in Macedonian, e.g.:—

    траам = I last
    бараат = they seek
    оваа = this (fem.)
    бегаа = they were running

  Other examples of consecutive vowels:—

знае	= knows
заим, dial. for заем	= loan
пеам	= I sing
грее	= warms
пее	= sings
трофеи	= trophies
ножеи, dial. for ножеви	= knives
неугоден	= unsuitable
ние	= we
пиеше	= he was drinking
судии	= judges
виор	= whirlwind
нашиот	= our (masc.)
стоам	= I stand
тоа	= this (neut.)
зборои, dial. for зборови	= words
поубав	= more beautiful
пишуат	= they write ⎫ in pre-1948
пишуе	= writes ⎭ spelling;
	now: пишувам, пишува

  These consecutive vowels are pronounced with their full value and are not reduced, except sometimes in the dialectal and poetic masc. plur. forms such as:—

зборои, ножеи

where и is reduced to ј (i̯).
Ј is lost before the endings -ски, -ство,
e.g.:—

 историја = history убиство = murder
 историски = historical

Unvoicing and Assimilation of Consonants
 As in Bulgarian, Slovenian, Russian, Byelorussian and West Slav, final voiced consonants are pronounced unvoiced. E.g.:—

  леб pron. леп = bread
  снег " снек = snow
  мраз " мрас = frost
  Охрид " Охрит (a town)

 Assimilation of consonants in Macedonian is regressive,[1] the final consonant deciding by its nature whether a group of consonants shall be all voiced or unvoiced. (Consonants with no unvoiced counterparts, such as ј, л, м, н, р, and also в[1] do not have this effect on consonantal groups.) The phonetic orthography of Macedonian shows most of these changes, cf. Serbocroätian:—

Voiced > unvoiced:—

леб = bread   but: лепче = roll of bread
sид = wall   " sитче = small wall
тежок = heavy (masc.) " тешка = heavy (fem.)
редок = rare (masc.) " ретка (fem.)
пре*т*седател = chairman; бе*с*платно = free, gratis;
 о*п*фатен = included

Unvoiced > voiced:—

сват = wedding guest but: свадба = wedding (both
                pronounced *sf-*)
гостин = guest   " гозба = feast
шетам = I walk   " шедба = walking

 Assimilation of consonants occurs in Macedonian also in word juncture, but is not shown in the spelling, e.g.:—

пет гроша = five piastres (coins) is pronounced пед гроша
шест години = six years   "   " шез години
млад човек = young man   "   " млат човек

 [1]Only with в, especially after с, is the assimilation *progressive*; hence, e.g.:—

свеќа = candle, is pronounced [sfeca], сфеќа
сват = wedding guest, " " [sfat], сфат

н before к or г becomes ŋ (like -*ng* in "sing"), as in other South and West Slav languages and English, e.g.:—

    Венко (a man's name), pron. 'vεŋkɔ

Orthographical, though not phonetic, exceptions to the above laws of assimilation in consonant groups occur in the four following cases:—

    1. With the consonant в, which is preserved in spelling, although in pronunciation it becomes ф before an unvoiced consonant. E.g.:—

    овца (= sheep), is so spelt, though pronounced: офца
    тревка (= grass, dim.) is so spelt, though pronounced: трефка

    2. Before the endings -ски, -ствен, -ство, -д- does not change to -т-, e.g.:—

град = city,   adj. градски   pron. гратски, i.e. грацки
суд = law court,   "   судски   "   суцки;
                          судство   "   суцтво = (department of) justice
сосед = neighbour,   "   соседство   "   сосецтво = neighbourhood
родствен = related   "   роцтвен

    3. Before the feminine article -та, e.g.:—

челад = family, children;
    челадта = the children, pron. челатта
'рж = rye;
    'ржта = the rye,   "   'ршта

    4. Before ч,—с and з are pronounced ш, though they are *both* spelt с. Thus before ч, the prefixes из-, без-, раз- become ис-, бес-, рас- in spelling and иш-, беш-, раш- in pronunciation. E.g.:—

счеличам = I harden (into steel), pron. шчеличам
расчешлам = I comb apart,   "   рашчешлам, from разчешлам

    Similarly:—

    исчешлам = I comb out,   pron. ишчешлам
    бесчестам = I dishonour,   "   бешчестам

    Likewise з before џ and ж is pronounced ж but is preserved as з in spelling; e.g.:—

разџавка (се) = starts yapping, pron. ражџавка (се)
разжвакам¹   = I chew up,   "   ражжвакам

Double Consonants

Double consonants are generally avoided in Macedonian, as in:—

      одамна = long ago < оддамна < оддавна

Similarly з, after changing to с, is dropped in:—

      исечам = I cut out < иссечам   < изсечам
      расипам = I spoil   < рассипам < разсипам
      бесмртен = immortal < бессмртен < безсмртен

and:

      раширам = I widen   < рашширам < разширам

Feminine nouns in -ст, when the definite article -та is added, lose one -т-, e.g.:—

      радост = joy,   but радоста = the joy
      маст   = grease,   "   маста
      свест = consciousness,   "   свеста
             conscience

but e.g. пролет = spring, пролетта, pronounced with double т.

Prefixes, the original meaning of which is emphasized, are not reduced. E.g.:—

      одделам   = I divide off
      оттука   = from here
      наддавам   = I give extra, add
      раззеленам = I make green
      бессилен   = powerless
      најјасен   = clearest

н is never written or pronounced as a double consonant in Macedonian.

Further Consonantal Changes

Notice the peculiarly Macedonian change of с, з, ч, ш, ж and ј all to в before the diminutive ending -че. This change is reflected in the spelling. E.g.:—

мовче   = little bridge   <   мост-че
гувче   = gosling   from гуска = goose
мавче   = kitten   "   мачка = cat
појавче = little belt   "   појас
гровче = little bunch   "   грозд = bunch of
                                                    grapes

---

[1]More usually: разџвакам.

```
тровче   = little crumb         from трошка
крлевче  = little tick            "  крлеж
шамивче  = little kerchief        "  шамија (See p. 161,
                                               No. 5)
```

Notice the change of в to м before н in:—

```
одамна = long ago              < оддавна
рамно  = on a level with       < равно
```

MACEDONIAN DIALECTS

These are divided according to their accent and certain other linguistic features into:—

1. The Western dialects. These are further subdivided into:—

(a) the central group of the Veles, Prilep, Kičevo, and Bitola (Bitolj) regions, with the accent fixed on the third syllable from the end of a word. If a word is lengthened by the addition of a suffix, the accent still remains on the third syllable from the end by shifting forward a syllable, e.g.:—

воде́ница = water-mill, водени́цата = the watermill

The Western dialects (central group) are also characterized by the following main features:—
I. Three forms of the article, e.g.:—

```
              волот = the ox
              волов = the ox here
              волон = the ox there
```

II. The clear pronunciation of all vowels, whether accented or not.
III. The vowel a representing C.S. ϱ (O.S. ѫ). E.g.:—

```
              рака = hand, O.S. рѫка
              пат  = road, O.S. пѫть
```

This group of dialects is the basis of modern literary Macedonian.

(b) the dialect of the Debar-Galičnik region, with features:—
I. o for literary a (from ѫ), e.g.:—

```
              пот (for пат) = road
```

II. мие = we, instead of ние

2. The South-western dialect of the Kostur (in Greek: Castoria)—Lerin (Greek: Florina) region, spoken mainly in Northern Greece, and characterized by having the accent on the penultimate syllable, e.g.:—

бабичка = grandmother
бабичица = granny

Closely related are the dialects of Tikveš and Mariovo, which accent the penultimate or propenultimate, but never the final syllable of words. They also drop vowels, as in дѐт'то = the child, дѐц'та = the children, с'те = all (pl.).

3. [1]The South-eastern dialect, spoken in the region of Gevgelija, Strumica, and Lake Dojran, characterized by a stress which gravitates towards the penultimate syllable, and by the shortening of words, e.g. учѝт'ле = teachers, and by the ending -ум in the 1st pers. sg. Present, e.g. нòсум = I carry.

4. [1]The dialect of the Kukuš and Voden (in Greek: Kilkis and Edessa) region in Northern Greece, with a mobile (shifting) accent which has a tendency to fall on either of the last two syllables of a word, and with modified (reduced) vowels, e.g.:—

јабу̀лка = apple
синòви = sons
дубѝт'к = cattle, income
ура̀ч = ploughman
чувѐк = person, man

5. The Eastern dialect of the Štip and Pirin (Bulgaria) region, with a mobile accent which tends towards one of the final three syllables of a word, e.g.:—

ѝстина = truth
рабòта = work, thing
дојдѐ = he came

The closely related dialect of Maleševo and Gòrna Džumаја̀ (Bulgaria) is characterized by the masc. definite article ending -o and by a mobile accent: гласò = the voice, гла̀совето = the voices; Станкѐ Voc. (girl's name).

6. The Northern dialect of the Kumanovo-Kratovo region, with features showing a transition to the Serbian dialects of the Morava valley, e.g.:—

дън for lit. ден (O.S. дьнь) = day
сън "   " сон (" сънъ) = dream
Видеа с'м га Стојан = I have seen Stoyan
Ја ву кажа = I told her
Поздрави гу мајку = Greet mother

[1]These two dialects could be counted as one, according to K. Tošev,—see Македонски јазик, I, 9-10, p. 199.

MACEDONIAN

In scattered areas of S. Macedonia we have traces surviving of the old nasal pronunciation of former nasal vowels. The most solid area is in the region of Kostur (Castoria). There are also six villages north-east of Salonica and four villages near Seres (Sĕr) with this pronunciation. Here we have the pronunciations ън/ъм in many words for former ѫ, but not consistently, e.g. бънди! = be!, and the pronunciations ен/ем, also after *chuintantes* and j, for former ѧ: гренди! = come!, женден = thirsty, ензик = tongue.

VOWEL GRADATION AND VOWEL LENGTHENING

These two features exist also in Macedonian. Examples:—

Vowel Gradation

донеси!	= bring (Pfve.); носеше = she was carrying
смрт	= death; да умрат = that they (should) die (Pfve.); умреа = they died; уморен = tired
разбрав	= I understood; да разбере = that he should understand; избор = a choice
изведени	= derived (Nom. pl.); наводи = quotes
реков	= I said, реченица = sentence (with 1st Palatalization); прирок = predicate
смрзнува	= freezes; мраз = frost
дујам	= I blow; здив = breath, gasp
пее	= sings; пој! = sing!

Vowel Lengthening

роден	= born; раѓање = birth
разбрав	= I understood; разбирам = I understand
одам	= I go away, walk (< ход-); доваѓа = comes (< дохадја)
се разлеат	= they overflow, *or* are poured out; наливаше = he was pouring (in)
говор	= speech; разговарав со М. = I was talking to M.

SLAVONIC CHARACTERISTICS

1. The Metathesis of liquids. In Macedonian this takes place, as in other South Slav languages, with the vowel o becoming a after the preceding *l* or *r* in all cases and with no further developments. E.g.:—

град	= town	млеко	= milk
глава	= head	работа	= work, thing
брег	= coast, hill		

2. The 1st Palatalization of velars, in which к, г change to ч, ж respectively, is a regular feature of Macedonian. E.g.:—

јунак = hero	—	јуначе!	(Voc. sg.)[1]
реков = I said (1st p. sg. Aorist)	—	рече =	he said (3rd p. sg. Aor.)
сок = juice	—	сочен =	juicy
Бог = God	—	Боже!	(Voc. sg.)
могов = I was able (dialectal)	—	може	(3rd p. sg. Pres.) = he can
	also:	можам	(1st p. sg. Pres.) = I can
		можат	(3rd p. pl. Pres.) = they can
тага = sorrow	—	тажен =	sad

In the case of x, it has mostly been replaced by в, pronounced ф, in modern Macedonian, so that we have the change в > ш, e.g.:—

страв (< страх) = fright — страшен = frightful
but (literary): дух = spirit — душевен = spiritual, sincere

2*a*. ц and з also change to ч and ж respectively, like к and г, e.g.:—

месец = month — месечно (neut. adj. and adv.) = monthly
кнез = prince, duke — кнежевина = dukedom

3. The 2nd Palatalization of velars is also a regular feature of Macedonian. Here к, г change to ц, з respectively, e.g.:—

волк = wolf	—	plur.	волци	
рака = hand	—	"	раце =	hands (Old Dual)
кружок = circle	—	"	кружоци =	circles
ученик = pupil	—	"	ученици =	pupils
бубрег = kidney	—	"	бубрези	
нога = leg, foot	—	"	нозе =	(old Dual)
митинг = meeting	—	"	митинзи	

In the case of x, which is replaced by в, we have the correspondence в:с here:—

Влав = a Vlach, Aromun — plur. Власи, but—
успех = success — " успеси, and
орев = walnut, plur. ореви; кожув = sheepskin coat, plur. кожуви; etc. Cf. p. 168.

[1] Notice the further change to ш in e.g. јунаштво < јуначьство = heroism. Cf. филолог = philologist, adj. филолошки <*филоложьск- = philological, by analogy, as in Sbcr.

MACEDONIAN

4. *Yotation*, or the influence of *j* on preceding consonants has a very limited field in Macedonian, as in Bulgarian. In Macedonian it is confined to the velars and dentals, and to the sibilants in certain instances. Examples can be found in the formation of nouns and verbs. With other consonants the yot (*j*) is preserved, being written immediately after the consonant concerned. As in Bulgarian, there is no yotation either in the Past Participle Passive or in the Comparative of adjectives, q.v.

The velars к, г, х change to ч, ж, ш respectively before *j*, as in other Slavonic languages. E.g.:—

плакав	= I wept	—	плаче	= he weeps
стругало	= a plane	—	струже	= he planes
лага	= a lie	—	лаже	= he lies
душа	= soul (from духја);		дишам	= I breathe

The dentals т, д before *j* undergo a change peculiar to Macedonian, and become ќ, ѓ respectively. E.g.:—

Cf. пратиме = we follow, send, and испраќаме
 = we see off
се вратил = he has returned, and се враќаш
 = you are returning;
меѓа (< medja) = boundary
се раѓа = is born, cf. род = race

With the sibilants с, з the older changes to ш, ж respectively can be seen in:—

пишувам = I write (with new ending),
 cf. писмо = letter
кажувам = I say, tell (with new ending),
 cf. доказ = proof

But сј, зј occur where a ь formerly came between the с or з and the ј, e.g.:—

лисја = leaves
лозје = vineyard

н + ј becomes њ, e.g.:—

камен = stone камења = stones

and in all Verbal Nouns from Imperfective verbs, e.g.:—

ослободување = liberation

л + ј are preserved as лј and do not fuse into љ, in contrast to Serbocroätian. E.g.:—

волја = will, зелје = greens

N.B. љ is an independent phoneme in Macedonian, as

in:—

      љубов = love
 беља = misfortune >< бела = white (fem. sg.)
  Кољо (a name) >< коло = wheel, series

 After p, ј disappears in Macedonian, except when derived from -ьј-, e.g.:—

   море = sea, cf. O.S. мор҄ѥ
but—
  приморје = littoral, coast, from -рьје
  борје = pines (collective plural)

 The labials п, б, в, м are preserved before ј, which itself also remains unchanged and is not preceded by any kind of /l/, e.g.:—

     копје = lance
     сабја = sabre
     дрвје = trees
     земја = earth

 Both ст and ск become шт before ј, e.g.:—

напуштам = I leave (root: пуст-)
огниште = fireplace, hearth (< огнискје)
трештен = cracked, mad; cf. треска =
     to knock; to talk nonsense

 ж is preserved before ј, as in:—

     оружје = arms

5. The dropping of consonants.

 The dropping of x or its replacement by в or ј, as mentioned in point 5 under the heading "Pronunciation—The Consonants", p. 148, is the most frequent and characteristic phenomenon in this sphere in Macedonian.

 в is omitted in certain instances:—

тоа   = this (neut.), cf. Bulg. товà
зема (Ipfv.) = takes, Pfv.земе
Малески   (a surname)
се(то)   = all (neut.)

 Further, т is dropped in the groups стј, стл, стн, штн, e.g.:—

лисје = leaves
послан = spread out; polite; well brought up
жалосн-а, -о, -и and in masc. by analogy
   жалосен = sad, pitiful
Similarly:

  радосн-а, -о, -и and радосен = joyous
  свесн-а, -о, -и " свесен = conscious, etc.

But some more literary adjectives restore the -т- in the masc. sing., e.g.:—

    месн-а, -о, -и = local, but masc. местен
    усн-а, -о, -и = oral,   "   "   устен

Similarly:

    немошн-а, -о, -и = sick, masc. sing. by analogy немошен
    помошн-а, -о, -и = auxiliary, masc. sing. by analogy помошен

    Also помошник = assistant
    but:
    училишн-а, -о, -и = school (adj.), masc. sing. училиштен
    чудовишн-а, -о, -и = monstrous, masc. sing. чудовиштен

д is dropped in the groups здj, здн, ждн; e.g.:—

    грозjе = grapes
    празн-а, -о, -и and празен = empty
    нужн-а, -о, -и   " нужен = needed, necessary

    But notice the literary words:—

    бездна = abyss
    sвезден, sвездн-а, -о, -и = starry

The combination -jе- is foreign to Macedonian, as it is to Bulgarian. Therefore, in contrast to Serbocroätian, Russian and other Slavonic languages, there is no j before e in words like:—

е   = is   ткае   = weaves
еден = one   кое   = which (neut.), cf. Sbcr. коjе
езеро = lake
               претприjатие = undertaking, company

    6. Epenthetic н always appears in the Personal Pronoun of the 3rd person, when used in its full, non-enclitic form in the two oblique cases, e.g.:—

    Acc. sing. masc.:   него = him
    Dat. plur. all genders: ним = to them

Also in:—

        внимавам = I pay attention
        внимание = attention

Notice the prothetic в in вистина = truth, and its derivatives.

FEATURES CHARACTERISTIC OF MACEDONIAN

Exclusively Macedonian features are the following: —

1. C.S. ǫ (O.S. ѫ) represented by *a* in most words: —

        рака = hand, O.S. рѫка
        пат = road, O.S. пѫть

According to the latest orthography (1970), in the following words and in words derived from them, original ǫ (ѫ) is represented in modern literary Macedonian by у: —

кука	= house	судбина	= fate
кус	= short	сушт	= real, genuine
пупка	= bud, pimple	сопруг(а)	= spouse, (wife)
суд	= law court	труба	= trumpet
гуска	= goose	гужва	= a crowd
круг	= circle	густ	= thick
мудар	= wise	желудник	= stomach
орудие	= tool	скуден	= scanty, sparse
оружје	= arms	нуди	= to offer
отсутен	= absent	су-	= as a verbal prefix, e.g. суреди = to put in order
присутен	= present		

2. C.S. *tj*, *dj* represented by ќ, ѓ respectively, e.g.: —

        свеќа = candle
        меѓа = boundary

A few words have -шт-, -жд-; e.g.: —

        горешт = hot
        свештеник = priest
        пештера = cave
        нужда = need, etc.

Similarly C.S. *ktj* becomes ќ, e.g.: —

        ноќ = night

3. C.S. *ě* (O.S. ѣ) represented everywhere by plain e (phon. ε) without differences of length (as in Slovenian and Serbocroätian) and without palatalization of the preceding consonant. E.g.: —

        место = place
        век = century, age
        дело = a work

4. C.S. *ch* (O.S. х) replaced by в in ordinary, not specifically literary Macedonian words,

MACEDONIAN

(cf. p. 148, No. 5), e.g.:—

мов	= moss (cf. Russ. мох, Sbcr. мах)
грав	= pea
мува	= a fly
видов (Aor.)	= I saw
можев (Imperfect)	= I was able

But (lit.) успех = success, дух = spirit. Final в is pronounced ф [f].

5. The change of с, з, ч, ж, ш and ј to в (pron. f) before -че and, rarely, before -ци, -ца, -це (see p. 152-153); e.g.:—

      гувче = gosling (< гуска)
      мавче = kitten (< мачка)
      глушец = mouse, plur. глувци
      мавца = fat (< маст)
      мевце = a bit of meat (< месо)

6. Fixed accent on the third syllable from the end. (See p. 144-145.)

7. Three forms of the definite article (see Morphology below), e.g.:—

вол (= ox), волот (= the ox), волов (= the ox here), волон (= the ox there)
рака (= hand), раката (= the hand), ракава (= the hand here), ракана (= the hand there); etc.

8. The regular use of double Personal and Interrogative Pronouns, and of corresponding enclitic pronouns when the object is definite. E.g.:—

    Него *го* носам = I am carrying him
    Фатете *ја* мачката = Catch the cat!

Cf. the Bulgarian use of double Personal Pronouns for emphasis.

9. The generalization of the ending -ам for the 1st pers. sing. Pres. of verbs of all classes, e.g.:—

    идам = I come, 2nd pers. sing.: идеш
    носам = I carry, " " " : носиш
    викам = I call, " " " : викаш

10. The use of a Past Tense formed with the verb 'I have' + Past Participle *Passive* similar to the usage in Modern Greek, e.g.:—

    имам работено = I have worked

11. The use of ќе + Pres. Pfve. or Impfve. to express the Future tense (cf. Bulg. ще), e.g.:—

ќе викам = I shall call (Impfve.)
ќе паднам = I shall fall (Pfve.)

12. The use of ќе with the Imperfect and Compound Past (Indefinite Past) tenses to express unfulfilled conditions in the past (cf. Bulgarian), e.g.:—

јас ќе викав, да дојдеше татко.
= I would have shouted, if father had come

тој ќе дојдел тогаш, ако го пуштеле.
= He would have come then, I hear, if they had let him.

13. Past Participle Active plural in -ле for all genders.

FEATURES CHARACTERISTIC OF MACEDONIAN AND BULGARIAN

In common with Bulgarian, Macedonian has the following features:—

14. C.S. initial *je* (O.S. ѥ) becomes e, e.g.:—

езеро = lake
е = is
еден = one

15. The loss of the declensions (see Morphology below).

16. The formation of Comparative adjectives by prefixing по-, e.g.:—

поубав = more beautiful

17. The preservation in conversation (see Morphology below) of the Aorist and Imperfect tenses. (Cf. also Lusatian.)

18. The loss of the Infinitive, replaced by finite verbs in the Present preceded by да.

19. The ending -ат for 3rd pers. plur. Pres. of all verbs, e.g.:—

викаат = they call
носат = they carry
идат = they come

20. The development of new compound tenses: for examples see No. 12 above,—ќе викав, ќе дојдел, etc.

MACEDONIAN

FEATURES CHARACTERISTIC OF MACEDONIAN AND SERBOCROATIAN

In common with Serbocroätian, Macedonian has the following features: —

21. The clear pronunciation of all vowels, whether stressed or unstressed, as also in West Slav.

22. The loss of x, as is frequent in East Serbocroätian dialects, e.g.: —

        леб for хлеб = bread

23. The development of ч into ц before vocalic p (p̥), e.g.: —

        црн = black
        црв = worm
  Notice цврст = firm, cf. Sbcr. чврст

24. The preservation of vocalic p, as in Serbocroätian, Czech, and Slovak.

25. In common with Serbocroätian, (Slovenian), Polish and Lusatian, Macedonian has the ending -ње (phon. ɲɛ) for (Imperfective) Verbal Nouns, e.g.: —

        пишување = writing
        седење   = sitting

FEATURES CHARACTERISTIC OF ALL SOUTH SLAV LANGUAGES

In common with all South Slav languages, Macedonian has the following features: —

26. C.S. ę (O.S. ѧ) develops into e, e.g.: —

        месо = meat
        пет = five

27. C.S. *y* (O.S. ъı) becomes и, e.g.: —

        син = son
        ти = thou

28. Soft *r*'s are hardened,[1] e.g.: —

        море = sea

29. Dentals are dropped before -л in the Past Participle Active, as also in East Slav, e.g.: —

        плел = woven
        повел = lead

---

[1] For Bulgarian see p. 95, No. 20.

30. C.S. *kv* becomes цв, e.g.:—

цвет = flower

OTHER FEATURES

31. On the other hand, C.S. *gv* becomes sв- as in:—

sвезда = star

Other words with original *zv* in C.S. have been changed to *dzv* (sв) by analogy. This *dzv* is also found in Polish, cf.:—

sвонец = bell, Pol. dzwonek
sвечи = rings, Pol. dźwięk = sound

but-

sвер = wild animal, Pol. zwierzę

also-

sвиждук = a whistle, Pol. gwizdnąć = to whistle

32. As in South and East Slav, palatal and formerly palatal consonants are followed by front vowels, e.g.:—

возови = trains, but ножеви = knives

33. C.S. vocalic l develops into -ол- as in Slovenian, East Slav and Lusatian, e.g.:—

волк = wolf
долг = long

34. C.S. semivowels ъ, ь develop into о, е respectively, cf. Russian and Bulgarian, e.g.:—

сон (O.S. сънъ) = dream
пес (O.S. пьсъ) = dog

35. The fill-vowel is a or e, e.g.:—

ветар or ветер = wind
оган (also: огин) = fire
добар (masc. sg.) = good

(see "Pronunciation: The Vowels".)

36. The metathesis of liquids occurs without further development, as in other South and West Slav languages. (See "Slavonic Characteristics", No. 1.)

MORPHOLOGY

THE TREATMENT OF NOUNS

In Macedonian the full declension of nouns has been lost, as in Bulgarian.

Most nouns have a singular and a plural form. Masculine and feminine nouns that represent persons that can be addressed, also distinguish the Vocative from the Nominative in the singular. Masculine names and masculine nouns denoting relationship, if they end in a consonant, *can* also distinguish an Oblique singular from a Nominative singular. (Nouns with the definite article, see below, only distinguish number but not case, in contrast to Bulgarian.) The other cases which are used in other Slavonic languages, are replaced analytically by prepositions, viz.:—

The Genitive	is expressed by	од	= from, of,
		на	= of
The Dative	" "	на	= to, кај = by, near, кон = to(wards),
		до	= to, при = to near
The Instrumental	" "	со	= with
The Locative	" "	в(о)	= in, на = on, при = near

(See also under "Prepositions").

In the *masculine nouns* we have therefore the following types of declensions:—

1. Proper names ending in a consonant have three cases:—

    Nom. sing. Гроздан
    Obl. sing. Гроздана or Гроздан
    Voc. sing. Гроздане or (еј) Гроздан

2*a*. Proper names ending in -о, however, do not have a separate Vocative sing.:—

    Nom./Voc. Марко
    Obl. Марка

2*b*. Proper names in -е also have no Vocative sing. The Obl. is formed with the addition of the syllable -та, e.g.:—

    Nom./Voc. Диме
    Obl. Димета

3. Proper names in -а do not decline at all, e.g.:—

    Nom./Voc./Obl. Илија, Методија

4. Nouns denoting a male relation or member of a family and ending in a consonant such as: брат (= brother), зет (= brother-in-law, or son-in-law),

маж (= husband), син[1] (= son), distinguish a Nom., a Voc., and an Obl. in the singular when they have no article, like proper names under No. 1, and in addition they have a plural form. The Oblique form is often followed directly by a Dative enclitic pronoun (see "Pronouns" below) to indicate the "possessor" and define the noun more closely. The nouns човек (= man, person), Бог (= God) (Voc. sg. Боже!, with 1st Palatalization), Господ (= Lord) (Voc. Господи! as well as Господе!) are declined in the same way, except that the plural of човек is irregular: луѓе (= people). E.g.:—

```
Sing.: Nom.        зет
       Obl.        зета (ми, ти, ви, му, etc.) or
                   зет (ми, etc.)
       Voc.        зете! or зету!
Plur.: (all cases) зетови
```

Other masculine nouns ending in a consonant, when personified, can also be declined like this, e.g.:—

леба ми така е = By my bread, it is so!
лежи лебе, да те јадам = lie bread, let me eat you!

Likewise:—

јунак = hero, Voc. sg. јуначе!

5. Nouns denoting a relation and ending in -о, -е or -а, such as: татко (= daddy), вујко (= uncle), дедо (= grandad), чиче or чичо (= uncle (familiar)), тате (= dad), have no separate Voc. sing., and distinguish only Nom. and Obl. in the singular. Those ending in -е form Obl. sing. in -ета. Notice the special plural forms. E.g.:—

```
                          (a)        (b)
Sing.: Nom./Voc.  татко      тате       чиче
       Obl.       татка      татета     чичета
Plur.:            татковци              чичевци
```

6. Nouns ending in -а have no separate Obl. sing., e.g.:—

```
Sing.: Nom./Obl.  војвода = commander, duke
       Voc.       војводо or војвода
Plur.:            војводи
```

7. Nouns ending in a consonant and denoting an occupation, such as: овчар (= shepherd), орач (= ploughman), воловар (= oxherd), поп (= priest),

---

[1] Voc. sing.: сине, сину, or синко!

MACEDONIAN

only distinguish a Voc. sing. and have no separate Obl. sing. The same rule applies to masculine names of animals. The plural of most of these nouns usually ends in -ови, e.g.:—

Sing.: Nom./Obl. поп   коњ = horse
       Voc.   попе!   коњу!
Plur.:   попови   коњи

Notice:—

Sing.: Nom./Obl. сват = bridegroom's companion   вол = ox
      Voc.   свате! or свату!   волу! or воле!
Plur.:   сватови   волови

Sing.: Nom./Obl. пес = dog   волк = wolf
      Voc.   песу!   волче! (with 1st Palatalization)[1]
Plur.:   пци   волци (with 2nd Palatalization)

The *plural* of most monosyllabic masculine nouns ends in -ови after hard consonants and sometimes in -еви after formerly soft consonants. (The forms retaining -в- are from the Eastern Macedonian dialects and have been adopted as standard in literary Macedonian). E.g.:—

Plur.
леб = bread   лебови = loaves
град = city   градови
број = number   броеви
грош = small coin, groat   грошеви
цар = king   цареви

ден is treated as a hard stem in modern Macedonian: plur. денови, but also дни.

A few monosyllabic masculine nouns and *all* other masculine nouns have or may have a plural in -и. E.g.:—

       прст = finger   пост = fast   крст = cross
Plur.: прсти   пости or постови   (крсти or) крстови

Some nouns ending in -ец and -ел drop the vowel e in forming their plural, e.g.:—

     старец = old man,   Pl. старци
     скакулец = grasshopper,   " скакулци
     петел = cock,   " петли
     орел = eagle,   " орли

[1] Cf. Бог = God, Voc. sg. Боже!; Влав from Влах = Aromun, Voc. sg. Влаше!

Notice also:—

    ветер or ветар = wind, pl. ветрови
    оган = fire, " огнови *or* огневи

Nouns ending in -ин and denoting an inhabitant of a country, town, etc., drop this syllable in the plural,[1] e.g.:—

    граѓанин = citizen, Pl. граѓани
    Бугарин = Bulgarian, " Бугари
Notice Турчин = Turk, " Турци

Similarly *some* nouns in -нец also denoting an inhabitant, drop the final -ец but not the н in the plural, e.g.:—

    селанец = peasant, pl. селани
    скопјанец = inhabitant of Skopje, pl. скопјани
But: Македонец = Macedonian, pl. Македонци
    Германец = German, pl. Германци

Some nouns in -ар lose the -а- in the plural, e.g.:—

    метар = metre   центар = centre
  Plur.: метри   центри

Nouns ending in velars г, к undergo the 2nd Palatalization in forming their plural, e.g.:—

    белег = sign   Plur.: белези
    бубрег = kidney   " бубрези
    волк = wolf   " волци

Nouns ending in -в from -х either have a plural with the 2nd Palatalization of the original х to с, or they have a plural in -(во)ви, cf. p. 156, No. 3. e.g.:

  Влав = a Wallachian or Aromun, Plur.: Власи
  страв = terror   " стравови

Like страв:—

    прав = dust   грав = pea, haricot bean

A few monosyllabic nouns have a (neuter) plural in -ишта, e.g.:—

пат = road, plur. патишта
сон = sleep, dream, plur. соништа or сништа
крај = end, region, plur. краеви or краишта
град = city, plur. градови or градишта
ѕид = wall, plur. ѕидови, ѕидје or ѕидишта

---

[1] Exception: домаќин = host, pl. домаќини.

After the numeral два = two, and after неколку = some, a plural in -a can be used for masculine non-personal nouns, cf. Bulgarian. This is a remnant of the old Dual form. With other numerals either this or the ordinary plural may be used. E.g.:—

два коња = two horses   два метра = two metres
обата вола = both the oxen   неколку дена = a few days

Masculine personal nouns are more often used in the plural after *Collective* Numerals:—

    двајца синови = two sons

The ordinary plural is used if the noun *precedes*, e.g.:—

    Си прегна коњи четири = He harnessed four
          (poet.)   horses.

Feminine nouns

Feminine nouns ending in -a only distinguish Nom. and Voc. sing., and have no Obl. form. Feminine nouns ending in a consonant only have one form in the sing. In the plural all feminine nouns end in -и.

We thus have two types:—

1. Hard:—
    Sing.: Nom./Obl. жена = woman, wife
          Voc.   жено
    Plur.:   жени

  Soft:—
    Sing.: Nom./Obl. Марија = Mary
          Voc.   Маријо

    Sing.: Nom./Obl. боја = colour, идèја = idea
    Plur.:   бои   идèи

So also-
    песна = song, plur.: песни
    мисла = thought, "   мисли

2.   Sing.: ноќ = night   радост[1] = joy
    Plur.: ноќи   радости

рака = hand, has an irregular plural: раце (from the old Dual)
нога = foot, " " " " нозе (from the old Dual)

Neuter nouns

These distinguish only singular and plural.

---

[1] Fem. nouns in -ст are often colloquially pronounced without the final -т.

1. Those ending in -о have plural in -а.
2. Most of those ending in -е, except those in -иште, -је, -це, -ие and Verbal Nouns, have plural in -иња, including diminutives in -е.

1. Sing.: сел<u>о</u> = village езер<u>о</u> = lake писм<u>о</u> = letter
   Plur.: сел<u>а</u>   езер<u>а</u>   писм<u>а</u>

2. море = sea; поле = field; име = name; прасе = pigling; куче = dog

   Sing.: мор<u>е</u>   пол<u>е</u>   им<u>е</u>   прас<u>е</u>   куч<u>е</u>[1]
   Plur.: мор<u>ињ</u>а пол<u>ињ</u>а[2] им<u>ињ</u>а прас<u>ињ</u>а куч<u>ињ</u>а

But, e.g.—

   Sing.: чудовиште = monster   решение = decision
   Plur.: чудовишта   решенија

   Sing.: лозје = vineyard   орање = ploughing
   Plur.: лозја   орања

         Sing.: лиц<u>е</u>[3] = face, person
         Plur.: лиц<u>а</u>

дете   = child,   has an irregular pl.: деца, or af-
                                          fectionately:
                                          дечиња
око   = eye,   "   "   "   очи
уво   = ear,   "   "   "   уши
животно = animal,   "   "   "   животни
чудо   = marvel,   "   "   "   чудеса (also
                                          чуда)
небо   = sky,   "   "   "   небеса (also
                                          неба)
рамо   = shoulder, "   "   "   рамена, ра-
                                          мења or ра-
                                          миња

Nouns of all three genders can form *collective* plurals in -је, which (except for feminine nouns) have a further plural in -ја. E.g.:—

Masc. лист   камен   сноп   друм
       = leaf   = stone   = sheaf   = highway
coll. лисје   камење   снопје   друмје
plur. лисја   камења   снопја

[1] кутре = puppy.
[2] poet. поља.
[3] Diminutives in -енце, e.g. детенце = little child, have no plural form.

срце = heart, plur. срца, and јајце = egg, plur. јајца, have affectionate plural diminutives: срциња, јајциња.

Fem.			Coll./Pl.
планина	=	mountain	планиње
ливада	=	meadow	ливаѓе
трева	=	grass	тревје
година	=	year	годиње

Neut.			Coll.	Plur.
крило	=	wing	крилје	крилја
дрво	=	tree	дрвје	дрвја
перо	=	feather, pen	перје	перја
гумно	=	threshing floor	(гумење)	гумења

These collective plurals take the *neuter* (sing. and plur.) articles, e.g. лисјето, лисјата, but adjectives and verbs in agreement are in the *plural* in Macedonian. (See below for these parts of speech.)

Nouns borrowed from other languages take their gender according to their ending in Macedonian, irrespective of their gender in the language of origin, e.g.:—

ниво	neut.	= level (Fr. le niveau)
кино	neut.	= cinema
радио	neut.	= wireless
метод	masc.	⎫
or		⎬ = method
метода	fem.	⎭
адреса	fem.	= address

THE ARTICLES

The definite article in Macedonian has three alternative forms, each with a different meaning—a peculiarly Macedonian feature. They have the form of suffixes and are derived from Demonstrative Pronouns.

In contrast to Bulgarian, nouns of masculine gender with the article suffixed, do *not* distinguish a Nom. from any other case.

The ordinary form of the article is:—

Sing.: Masc. -от   Fem. -та   Neut. -то

Plur.: Masc./Fem. -те   Neut. -та

E.g.:—

Sing.			Plur.
волот	=	the ox	воловите
мечката	=	the bear	мечките
селото	=	the village	селата

Masc. nouns in -изам, lose the -a- when the definite article is used, but foreign nouns in -ар keep the -a-. E.g.:—

романтизам = romanticism, with article: романтизмот
центар   = centre   "   "   центарот

Notice that feminine nouns in -ст lose one т when the definite article -та is used. E.g.:—

радост = joy   радоста = the joy

All other feminine nouns retain the -та in full, and the unvoicing of voiced consonants before this article is not indicated in the spelling. E.g.:—

пролет = spring, with art. : пролетта
смрт   = death,   "   " : смртта
заповед = order,   "   " : заповедта
                              (pron. заповет-та)

The form of the article with -в- instead of -т- indicates someone or something near the persons speaking:—

Sing.: Masc. -ов Fem. -ва Neut. -во

Plur.: Masc./Fem. -ве Neut. -ва

E.g.:—

волов ќе треба да го нараниме = We shall have to feed
                                the (this) ox here
воловиве   = the oxen here

On the other hand, the form of the article with -н- refers to someone or something at a distance from, but visible to, the persons speaking:—

Sing.: Masc. -он Fem. -на Neut. -но

Plur.: Masc./Fem. -не Neut. -на

E.g.:—

Човекон врви по мостон = The man there is going over
                         the (that) bridge (there)
Планинине   = the mountains yonder

Notice that masculine nouns in -a, take the feminine article, e.g.:—

судијата = the judge

All (neuter) plurals in -a also take -та:—

морињата = the seas
патиштата = the roads

Some nouns can have either masculine or feminine gender as indicated by the article, e.g.:—

```
песокот or песоктa = the sand
лојот     "  лојта   = the tallow
потот     "  потта   = the sweat
жарот     "  жарта   = the red-hot coal
животот   "  животта = the life
```

The definite article can be attached to an adjective qualifying a noun instead of to the noun itself (see p. 175 for "Adjectives"), e.g.:—

```
белиот¹ вол    = the white ox
арната книга   = the good book
белото пиле    = the white chicken
```

Also—

```
белиов¹ вол    = the white ox here
белион¹ вол    = the white ox there, etc.
```

In the plural the article is -те, -ве, or -не for all genders when it is attached to the adjective, e.g.:—

```
белите петли    = the white cocks
белите кокошки  = the white hens
белите пилиња   = the white chickens
```

and—

```
беливе пилиња   = the white chickens here
```

When two or more adjectives qualify and precede a noun, only the *first* has the article suffixed, when there is no special emphasis expressed:—

```
брзата планинска река = the fast-flowing
                        mountain river
```

With inversion of order the noun takes the article:—

Гората густа и висока беше преминâта = The thick, tall forest was passed.

Notice the irregular behaviour of the articles with луѓе (= people). When луѓе is not qualified by an adjective, it takes the neut. sing. article, e.g.:—

луѓето = the people

But with an adjective, we have—

првите луѓе = the first people

with the regular plural -те. Likewise with: -во/-ве and -но/-не. (Compare the note on collective plurals, p. 170 (bottom) and p. 171 (top).)

---

[1]See p. 175 concerning the -и- of the masc. sing. adjective with the article.

The article is used with certain geographical names, e.g.:—

Охридско(то) езеро = Lake Ohrid; Алпите = the Alps

But it is *not* used in adverbial expressions, e.g.:—

на пазар = to market; на пролет = in spring
со глава = with one's head

ADJECTIVES

Adjectives in Macedonian vary according to gender in the sing. In the plur. one form serves for all genders. They do not decline.

The masculine form ends in a consonant except for adjectives ending in -ски, which denote belonging to something or somebody. But in address (i.e. as a Vocative) the masc. form ends in -и: драги татко = dear father!
E.g.:—

	SING.		PLUR.	
Masc.	*Fem.*	*Neut.*		
кус	куса	кусо	куси	= short
црвен	црвена	црвено	црвени	= red
бел	бела	бело	бели	= white
сплескан	сплескана	сплескано	сплескани	= flat
златен[1]	златна	златно	златни	= of gold, golden
длабок	длабока	длабоко	длабоки	= deep
селски	селска	селско	селски	= (of the) village
козји	козја	козјо	козји	= goat's

Notice that adjectives formed from nouns in -ст lose the -т, e.g.:—

радост = joy   радосен, радосна, радосно, радосни = joyful
чест   = honour чесен, чесна, etc. = honourable, honest
пост   = fast   посен, посна, etc. = (of a) fast (day, food)
But from место = place, we have местен, месна, etc. = local

Negative adjectives with the prefix не-, including those formed from participles, are always written in one word, e.g.:—

[1] With movable -*e*-.

MACEDONIAN

```
неубав    = not beautiful
нетрпелив = impatient
невиден   = not seen (before)
нечуен    = unheard of
```

Possessive adjectives end in -ов, -ова, etc., when formed from masculine nouns, and in -ин, -ина, etc., when formed from feminine nouns, e.g.:—

```
Петров  Петрова  Петрово  Петрови = Peter's
Верин   Верина   Верино   Верини  = Vera's
мајчин¹ мајчина  мајчино  мајчини = mother's
```

The article can be used attached to the adjective, instead of to the noun qualified, as already mentioned under "The Article". Notice that the masc. sing. form of the adjective with the article then ends in -и, e.g.:—

белиот, црвениов, златнион петел	= the white, this red, that golden cock
белата кокошка	= the white hen
црново пиле	= the black chicken here
белите, црните петли	= the white, the black cocks
црниве прасиња	= the black piglings here

Notice: новиот судија = the new judge, although one says: судијата = the judge (cf. p. 172).

The Comparison of Adjectives

This is very simple in Macedonian, as in Bulgarian. The Comparative degree for *all* adjectives that can logically be compared, is formed by prefixing по- to the Positive degree, and the Superlative by prefixing нај- also to the Positive degree. Both forms vary in gender and number like ordinary adjectives. E.g.:—

	Comparative	*Superlative*
голем = big	поголем, -а, -о, -и	најголем, -а, -о, -и
висок = high	повисок	највисок
арен = good	поарен, поарна, etc.	најарен
силен = strong	посилен, посилна, etc.	најсилен
бел = white	побел	најбел
низок = low, small in stature	понизок, пониска, etc.	најнизок

¹From мајка (= mother), with 1st Palatalization.

		Comparative	*Superlative*
лош	= bad	полош	најлош
убав	= beautiful	поубав	најубав

In Macedonian certain nouns, pronouns, adverbs, prepositions and verbs may also be compared, e.g.:—

Тој е арен мајстор	= He is a good (master) craftsman
Стојан е помајстор	= Stoyan is more of a craftsman
Милан е најмајстор од сите	= Milan is the best craftsman of all
Тој ми е посвој	= He is nearer to my heart
Дојди поваму	= Come more this way, nearer here
Дојди по кај нас, по до него	= Come more towards us, more up to him
Никола работи	= Nicholas works
Вера по не работи од него	= Vera does not work as much as he does
Пецо нај не работи	= Pete does the least work of all
Very	= многу, мошне
Than	= од (before a noun), отколку, одошто
Rather better	= нешто поарен
Much better	= многу поарен
Rather good	= прилично арен, доста арен
Less than	= помалу отколку
The bigger...*the* better...	= што поголем...(то) поарен...
As (good) as	= исто така (арен) колку
As soon as possible	= што поскоро; што порано
As fast as possible	= што побргу (побргу колку можеш)
The (very) best of all	= најарен од сите
Too	= многу, прекалено; прекумерно (= excessively)
The same as	= исти како
In the same way as	= исто така како

Notice: прȩ́стар = 1. too old; 2. very old, but: прѝстар = rather old.

THE NUMERALS

The *Cardinal* numerals do not decline in Macedonian, and only "one" and "two" vary according to gender. "Two" onwards count as plurals and are followed by nouns in the plural. Masculine nouns after the numeral "two", as already mentioned, can have a special plural in -a (the old Dual ending),[1] cf. Bulgarian. Adjectives qualifying nouns with numerals are also in the plural, except with "one". Numerals ending in "one" take the noun in the singular, e.g. сто и една година = a hundred and one years. Едни, plural of "one", means "some". All simple numerals can take the article -те, (though some only rarely): e.g. дванаесетте апостоли = the Twelve Apostles. Compound numerals prefer the demonstrative тие = those, e.g. тие сто и педесет динари = the 150 dinars (already mentioned). Notice: шесте (with one т) = the six. Cf. радоста (= the joy).

	Masc.	Fem.	Neut.
1	еден	една	едно
2	два[2]		две[2]
3	три		
4	четири		
5	пет		
6	шест		
7	седум		
8	осум		
9	девет		
10	десет		
11	единаесет	(pronounced -најсе[3])	
12	дванаесет	"	"
13	тринаесет	"	"
14	четиринаесет	"	"
15	петнаесет	"	"
16	шеснаесет	"	"
17	седумнаесет	"	"
18	осумнаесет	"	"
19	деветнаесет	"	"
20	дваесет	("	двајсе)
26	дваесет и шест		
30	триесет		
40	четириесет		
50	педесет		
60	шеесет		
70	седумдесет		
80	осумдесет		
90	деведесет		

[1] The plural in -a may also be used after the other numerals. See p. 169.

[2] обата (masc.), обете (fem. and neut.) = both, always have the article.

[3] Pronounced with the article: единајсетте, etc., (with double т!)

100	сто
150	сто и педесет[1]
200	двесте
300	триста
400	четиристотини
500	петстотини
600	шестотини
700	седумстотини
800	осумстотини
900	деветстотини
1,000	илјада
1,000,000	милион

The *Ordinal* numerals are adjectives and vary in gender and number. 1-4 have alternative forms for the masculine. The ordinary form ends in a consonant, the form ending in -и is used with the article. E.g.:—

Кој е прв по успех во класот? = Who is first (in success) in class?
Првиот ученик е Стојан. = The first pupil is Stoyan.

or:—

Стојан е прв во класот. = Stoyan is first in class.

Notice below the double -тт- in the endings of most numerals, whose cardinal form ends in -т.

		Fem.	Neut.	PLUR. All Genders
1st	прв -и	-а	-о	-и
2nd	втор -и	-а	-о	-и
3rd	трет -и			etc.
4th	четврт -и			
5th	петти			
6th	шести			
7th	седми			
8th	осми			
9th	деветти			
10th	десетти			
11th	единаесетти,[2] etc.			
19th	деветнаесетти[2]			
20th	дваесетти,[2] etc.			
50th	педесетти, etc.			
90th	деведесетти			
100th	стоти *or* стотен			

[1] Pronounced: стојпедесет.
[2] In the ending -аесетти ае is contracted to аj in pronunciation and the stress falls on the а: pronounce единáјсетти, etc.

200th   двестотен
500th   петстотен
1,000th   илјаден
1,000,000th милио̀нен or мѝлионски (pron. мѝлјонски)

Collective numerals ending in -ина are used in Macedonian to indicate the approximate[1] number of things in a group, e.g.:—

Имам десетина овци, стотина динари.
= I have about ten sheep, about a hundred dinars

Collective numerals or "Numeral Nouns" ending in -ца or -мина are used only of groups including male persons,[2] and can have the article attached.

2   двајца = a pair, обајцата = both (always with article)
3   тројца
4   четворица
5   петина   or петмина
6   шестина or шесмина
7   седмина or седуммина
8   осмина   or осуммина
9   деветмина
10   десетмина
20   двајсемина
50   педесемина
100 стомина
1,000 илјадамина

With article, e.g. тројцата = the three; also седумтемина = the seven.

Numeral Adverbs

Once = еднаш

The other numeral adverbs are formed with the suffix -пати, e.g.:—

двапати = twice
трипати = thrice
стопати = a hundred times, etc.

---

[1] Approximate numbers can also be expressed by using *some* two consecutive numbers pronounced together as a group, e.g. два - три = two or three. In the teens, tens and hundreds the second part of the numeral is not repeated: два - тринаесет = 12 or 13, три - четириесет = 30 or 40, три - четири стотини = three or four hundred. пет - шест is pronounced печес (phon. 'peʧes). 1-2, 4-5, 6-7, 8-9 and the corresponding teens, tens and hundreds are not usually expressed in this way.

[2] I.e. groups exclusively of, or containing, men.

Notice also: двојно = doubly
             тројно = trebly
                      etc.

             вудве = two by two, in twos
             вутри = in threes
             надве = (divided) into two
             натри = ("   ) into three

Fractions
             половина = half
             третина = a third
             четвртина = a quarter

Distributive Numerals are expressed by по + Cardinal or Collective Numeral, e.g.:— по три = three each; по десетина сливи = ten plums each.

THE PRONOUNS

The Pronouns in Macedonian constitute a group of words many of which have a distinctive form when compared with the corresponding words in other Slavonic languages, e.g. some of the Personal Pronouns, the Relative Pronoun, the Demonstrative Pronouns, and the word for "all", below. In Macedonian, the word for "who" (interrog.) and its compounds decline in the Acc. and Dat. sing. masc.,[1] as do also the Personal Pronouns (which latter in Bulgarian are the only pronouns that ordinarily decline). The other pronouns only vary in gender and number. After prepositions the *Accusative* form is used.

The following is a list of the main pronouns in Macedonian:—

Demonstrative:—

Masc.	SING. *Fem.*	*Neut.*	PLUR. *All Genders*	
овој	оваа	ова	овие	= this here (near me or us)

This pronoun can have a special form for the Acc. sing. masc.: овега.

| тој | таа | тоа | тие | = that (near you) |
| оној | онаа | она | оние | = that (yonder) |

---

[1] Only when used independently, i.e. not with a noun following.

Interrogative: —

	SING.			PLUR.	
Masc.	*Fem.*		*Neut.*	*All Genders*	
кој[1]	која		кое	кои	= who? which?
Dat.: кому му *or* на кого(му)					= to whom?
Acc.: кого го					= whom?
			што (Nom. and Acc.)		= what?

A Dat. form exists in the expression: чуму ти е тоа? = what do you need it for?

каков	каква	какво	какви	= what kind of?
колкав	колкава	колкаво	колкави	= how great? of what size? of how many?
чиј	чија	чие	чии	= whose? (interrogative only, rare)

Relative: —

кој (што)	која (што)	кое (што)	кои (што)	= who, which
Dat.: кому (што) *or* на кого				
Acc.: кого (што)				
		што[2]		= that
чиј што	чија што	чие што	чии што	= whose (rare)

Definitive: —

секој	секоја	секое		= every, everyone
Dat.: секому *or* на секого				
Acc.: секого				
сиот	сета	сето, сѐ[3]	сите	= all
сиов	сева	сево	сиве	= all this
сион	сена	сено	сине	= all that
цел	цела	цело	цели	= (the) whole
исти	иста	исто	исти	= the same

[1] кој and its compounds decline only when they are used independently and when they do not qualify nouns.

[2] This is the commonest relative pronoun and for the Accusative and Dative cases it is amplified by the enclitic pronouns Acc. s. m., n. го, f. ja; Dat. s. m., n. му, f. ѝ; Acc. pl. ги, Dat. pl. им (see p. 184); e.g. Дојде човекот што го видовме вчера = The man whom we saw yesterday has come.

[3] сѐ is written with an accent to distinguish it from се, the Reflexive Pronoun, and also from the 3rd pers. plur. Pres. of the verb "to be". It it used by itself and means "everything" or "all": сѐ знае = he knows everything.

	SING.		PLUR.	
Masc.	*Fem.*	*Neut.*	*All Genders*	
друг	друга	друго	други	= other
сам	сама	само	сами	= -self
ваков	ваква	вакво	вакви	= of this kind, like this here
таков	таква	такво	такви	= of this kind
онаков	онаква	онакво	онакви	= of that kind
инаков	инаква	инакво	инакви	= different
секаков	секаква	секакво	секакви	= of all kinds
олкав	олкава	олкаво	олкави	= so great, as big as this
толкав	толкава	толкаво	толкави	= so great
онолкав	онолкава	онолкаво	онолкави	= as big as that

Indefinite:—

некој	некоја	некое	некои	= some, someone

Dat.: некому *or* на некого
Acc.: некого

кој било која било, etc.			= any (you like)
кој да е			= anybody
кој годе			= any you like
		нешто	= something
		што било	= anything
некаков	некаква	некакво некакви	= some kind of

Negative:—

никој	никоја	никое	никои	= no, no-one

Dat.: никому *or* на никого
Acc.: никого

		ништо		= nothing
никаков	никаква	никакво	никакви	= no, none

Possessive:—

мој	моја	мое	мои[1]	= my, mine
твој	твоја	твое	твои[1]	= your(s) (familiar)

[1]These plural forms are often pronounced мој, твој, but are spelt with -и to distinguish them from the masc. sing., cf. the colloquial and dialectal pronunciation -oj of the plur. ending -ои for lit. -ови of masc. nouns.

	SING.		PLUR.	
Masc.	*Fem.*	*Neut.*	*All Genders*	
свој	своја	свое	свои[1]	= own (referring to the subject)
наш	наша	наше	наши	= our(s)
ваш	ваша	ваше	ваши	= your(s) (pl. and polite)
негов	негова	негово	негови	= his
нејзин	нејзина	нејзино	нејзини	= her(s)
нивни	нивна	нивно	нивни	= their(s)

These are frequently used with the article:
мојот, твојот, нашиот, вашиот, неговиот, нивниот брат, коњ, etc. (= my, your, our, your, his, their brother, horse, etc.) (Notice the added и underlined.) Fem. мојата, neut. моето, pl. моите; etc. (regular).

Personal: —

The Personal Pronouns in Macedonian are characterized by three alternative forms in the Dat. and Acc. cases.

1. The *double* form is frequently used with verbs, especially but not only for emphasis, and is a distinctive feature of Macedonian. Its use is spreading at the expense of the other forms.

2. The short "enclitic" form can also be used with verbs when there is no emphasis, and is then a *proclitic preceding* the verb. But with the Imperative and Present Gerund it follows after and is enclitic. It is also used to repeat a definite object which itself occurs in the sentence. These two usages are also distinctively Macedonian. It is also used after the demonstrative adverbs: еве = here is (are), ете = here is, ене = there is.

3. The *full* form is used mainly after the negative не, after the conjunctions а = but, и = and, after prepositions, in answers to questions, and in curses. It consists of the first, longer half of the double form.

The third person Personal Pronoun in the Nom. (sing. and plur.) is тој, таа, тоа, тие, which are also Demonstrative pronouns meaning "that". Cf. Bulgarian forms beginning with т for the 3rd pers. pro-

---

[1] This plural form is often pronounced свој, but is spelt with -и to distinguish it from the masc. sing., cf. the colloquial and dialectal pronunciation -oj of the plur. ending -ои for lit. -ови of masc. nouns.

noun, differentiated, however, from the Demonstratives. Alternative forms, used only in poetry, are: он, она, оно, они.

Nom. јас = I ние = we ти = you (fam.) вие = you (pl. and polite[1])
Dat. мене ми, ми нам ни, ни тебе ти, ти вам ви, ви
Acc. мене ме, ме нас нè, нè[2] тебе те, те вас ве, ве

Nom. тој (он) = he таа (она) = she тоа (оно) = it тие (они) = they
Dat. нему му, му нејзе ѝ, ѝ[3] нему му, му ним им, им
Acc. него го, го неа ја, ја него го, го нив ги, ги

Reflexive:—

Dat. себе (себеси) си, си = -self
Acc. себе (себеси) се

Examples of the use of the Personal Pronouns:—

1. The double form:—

Мене ми рече = He told (me)
Мене ме виде = He saw me
Тебе ти реков = I told you
Вас ве најдов = I found you
Нему му е арно = He is fine, all right, in a good position
Го видов денеска на ручек него = It was him I saw at lunch today

2. The short form (*proclitic*):—

(a) with verbs:—

Ми рече Никола оти ќе дојде = Nicholas told me that he would come

---

[1]The polite use of вие in Macedonian is copied from other languages and is not used in the speech of ordinary people; hence one meets some variations of agreement. According to Конески, with вие verbs, including the participle in the compound tenses, go in the plural but an adjectival compliment goes in the singular if one person is addressed. E.g. Вие сте станале нервозен = (We hear that) you became ill at ease. See Б. Конески: *Граматика на македонскиот литературен јазик*, (1967), p. 332, §213.

[2]The Acc. plur. нè (= us) is written with an accent to distinguish it from не (= not).

[3]Dat. sing. ѝ (= to her) is written with an accent to distinguish it from и (= and).

Ме најде брат ми[1] = My brother found me
Удри ме пȍ глава! = Hit me on the head!

(b) repeating a definite object:—

Фатете *ја* мачката! = Catch the cat!
Го видов Гроздана = I saw Grozdan
Трудбениците *ја* манифестираа својата готовност...
= The workers demonstrated their readiness...
Младината...со чест ќе *ги* исполни тие задачи...
= The young people will carry out those tasks with distinction
Барајќи го волкот, ја нашол лисицата
= Looking for the wolf, he found the fox
Кого го виде? = Whom did he see?

(c)

Еве ме, идам = Here I am, I'm coming
Еве ви = Here you are! (giving something)
Ене му = There! He's got it!
Еве ти ја = Here it (f.) is (for you)![2]

3. The full form (alone):—

(a) after a negative:—

Не тебе, а нив ги видов = I did not see you, but them...
Не вам, а на Стојана му реков = I did not tell you, but Stoyan

---

[1] Here we also have an example of the Dative short form, used enclitically, to indicate the "possessor", instead of the Possessive Pronoun-adjective—a common usage in Serbocroätian and Bulgarian too, but in Macedonian used only with nouns indicating relations and close associates, e.g.:—

мајка му = his mother
сестра ми = my sister
со другара ти = with your friend, comrade
мајстор си = his master (referring to the subject)

Notice the omission of the article with nouns indicating relationship and close ties.

[2] The Dative of interest, expressed by a short pronoun, is commonly used in Macedonian. Notice: си одам = I am going away. See p. 184.

(b) after prepositions (the Accusative form):—

Со мене дојде	= He came with me
Во нас е клучот	= The solution lies in us
Од тебе и од него глава не можам да кренам	
	= Because of you and him I can't budge, move an inch (lit. lift my head)

(c) as an answer to a question:—

(Кого го најде?) Него.   = (Whom did he find?) Him.

(d) in curses and imprecations:—

Тешко тебе   = Woe to you!

ADVERBS

Adverbs formed from adjectives end in -o and are identical in form with the neut. sing. of the adjective, e.g.:—

арно	= good (neut. adj.) and = well (adv.)
убаво езеро	= a beautiful lake
тој пее убаво	= he sings beautifully
криво	= wrong (ȧdj. крив)
лесно	= easily (adj. лесен)
мачно	= with difficulty (adj. мачен = difficult)
кусо	= short, lacking

Other adverbs have the most various forms and are sometimes the petrified remains of nouns with old case endings, prepositional expressions, verb roots with adverbial endings, etc. E.g.:—

зиме	= in winter	дома	= at home, home(ward)
лете	= in summer		
горе	= above	ноќе	= by night
долу	= below	дење	= by day
збогум	= good-bye	пеш	= on foot
всоне	= in one's sleep	прекусила	= with great efforts, with difficulty
квечерум	= towards evening		
вкуќи	= at home	сосила	= by force; with difficulty

Peculiarly Macedonian adverbial endings are:—

1. -ица, -ница, e.g.:—

бодинаница	= at a gallop
вјаваница	= on horseback
турканица	= pushing(ly)
трчаница	= (in a) running (manner)

2. -ум, for adverbs formed from verbs, e.g.:—

    викум = shouting
    ќутејќум = silently

3. -ана, e.g.:—

    препинана = stumbling
    рипана = jumping
    со куцана = limping
    на трчана = running

Notice the compound, hyphenated adverbs, such as:—

  лека-полека = quietly, gently
  згора-згора = superficially
  пошто-зашто = for a trifle, for a song; somehow
  надве-натри = somehow
  криво(-)лево = all the same, whatever it is

The Comparison of Adverbs

The Comparison of Adverbs is made in the same way as the comparison of adjectives. For the Comparative degree по- is prefixed to the Positive adverb, and for the Superlative degree нај- is prefixed also to the Positive adverb. E.g.:—

тивко = quietly   потивко = more quietly   најтивко = most quietly
арно = well   поарно = better   најарно = best

The only irregular comparison of an adverb in Macedonian is:—

многу = much   повеќе = more   најмногу = most

We give below some of the commonest adverbs, mostly those not formed from adjectives, and classified according to their meaning.

Place:—

    овде(ка), тука = here, hither
    ваму = on this side
    таму = there, thither
    онаму }
    онде(ка) } = over there
    одовде = hence, from here
    оттаму = thence
    секаде = everywhere
    другаде }
    на друго место } = elsewhere
    некаде = somewhere
    никаде = nowhere
    внатре = inside
    надвор = outside, out

Place:—

однадвор	= from outside
дома	= home(ward)
вкуќи	= at home
горе	= above, upstairs
долу	= below, downstairs
наместа	= here and there
надолу	= down
близу *or* блиску	= near
одблизу	= from near
далеку	= far
оддалеку	= from afar
назад	= back
напред	= forward
дома, в земја	= at home (not abroad)
в туѓина	= abroad
напреку	= opposite
преку	= across
отстрана	= aside
понатака	= further
(на)лево	= to the left
(на)десно	= to the right
среде	= in the middle
прекутрупа	= straight, cross country

Time:—

сега	= now
тогаш	= then
денеска	= to-day
утре	= to-morrow
вчера	= yesterday
некни	= the day before yesterday
веќе	= already
уште	= still
не...веќе	= no longer
уште не	= not yet
часум	= in a moment
веднаш } начас }	= immediately, at once
секога(ш)	= always
секојдневно	= daily
токму, баш	= just
на утро	= in the morning
изутрина	= during the morning
сабајле	= in the morning, tomorrow morning
утринава	= this morning
квечер(ум) } приквечер }	= towards evening
вечерва	= this evening

Time:—

сношти, синоќа	= last night, last evening
досега	= up to now
отсега	= from now, henceforward
навреме	= in time
пак / одново	= again
никогаш	= never
никојпат	= at no time
понекојпат / понекогаш	= sometimes
некогаш	= once (upon a time)
постојано	= all the time
секојпат	= every time
отпосле	= later, subsequently
доцна	= late
рано	= early
често	= often
ретко	= seldom
потоа, после	= afterwards
одамна	= long ago
првин, првен	= first
најсетне	= lastly
окончателно	= finally
најпосле	= at last, finally
само, дури	= only
летоска	= last summer
преѓе(ска)	= just recently
во иднината	= in future
скоро, неодамна	= recently
годинава	= this year
лани	= last year
оломлани	= the year before last
истовремено	= at the same time, simultaneously
набргу / (на)скоро	= soon
во исто време	= meanwhile
зиме	= in winter
лете	= in summer
дење	= by day
ноќе	= by night
са ноќ	= all night
потака	= further (in time)
понатаму	= still, further
ден-денес(ка)	= to this day
довека	= for ever
напладне	= at midday
наручек	= at dinnertime
призори	= at dawn

Manner:—

вака	= so, thus, in this way
така	= so, in that way
инаку	= otherwise
(на)опаку	= the wrong way round
полека } бавно }	= slowly
бргу	= quickly
наеднаш	= suddenly
веднага	= immediately
намерно } нарочно }	= on purpose
залудо } напусто }	= in vain
необично	= exceptionally, unusually
обично	= usually
случајно	= by chance
некако	= somehow
никако	= in no way
вистински	= really
навистина	= certainly
неочекувано	= unexpectedly
патем	= en route
молкома	= silently
назорум	= stealthily
грабаданица	= galloping
исто така	= likewise
прекумерно	= excessively
вклучително	= including
наедно	= together
редум	= in turn
ничкум	= prone
простум	= upright

Degree:—

многу } мошне }	= very
малку } трошка }	= a little
толку } олку }	= so much
неколку	= some
малку	= little
одвàј	= hardly
доста	= enough
најмногу	= mostly
наполно, исцело	= fully
сосем(а)	= quite
навистина	= indeed, really, definitely

MACEDONIAN

Degree:—

бар(ем)	= at least
може би	= perhaps
особено нарочно	= especially
едночудо	= a great deal
тукутака	= for no reason, just so
тронsа трошѝчка	= just a little
доволно достаточно	= sufficiently
само туку саде, сал (colloq.)	= only
скоро готово	= nearly, almost
еднакво	= equally
горе(-)долу околу	= roughly
воопшто	= in general
тама̀м баш токму	= just
дури	= even
речиси	= almost
донекаде	= up to a point
воглавно	= chiefly
тукурѐчи	= so to speak, maybe
делум	= partly
непремено	= certainly

Interrogative:—

кога?	= when?
каде?	= where? whither?
откаде?	= whence?
зошто? зашто?	= why?
како?	= how?
колку?	= how much?
...ли...?	enclitic interrogative particle
дали...?	interrogative particle introducing a question (rarer)
зар...?	interrogative particle expressing incredulity
нели...?	interrogative particle expecting the answer "yes"; = surely, don't (you)...?, e.g. Нели знаете сѐ? = Don't you know everything?

Not = не; no = не, (јок); yes = да
         догледање = au revoir
         збогум   = good-bye

CONJUNCTIONS

Many Macedonian conjunctions have forms slightly different from those of Bulgarian and Serbocroätian, but the tenses used after them are the same in the main. The following conjunctions are important:—

Coördinating:—

и	= and
па	= and then, and (in enumeration), well
та	= and (so)
пак	= yet, but (usually enclitic)
потоа	= then, after that
затоа	= therefore
ни	= nor
ни(ту)...ни(ту)	= neither...nor...
(или...) или	= (either...) or...
а	= and, but (contrasting)
ама	= however, but
сепак	= still, nevertheless
туку	= only, but (after a negative)
но	= but
ами	= but (in remonstrance)
ту...ту / де...де	= now...now
то ест / имено	= namely, i.e.
например	= for example, e.g.
освен тоа	= apart from that, besides
впрочем	= anyhow, by the way, actually
исто(и)	= likewise, also
само(што)	= only (that)
не само	= not only
камо ли	= let alone
меѓутоа	= on the other hand, however
притоа	= at the same time, in addition
белки	= maybe
бездруго	= certainly
секако / нема збор / се разбира	= of course

Note: ем...ем = both...and, ја...ја = either...or, are both dialectal.

Subordinating:—

кај, каде што	= where	
кога (што)[1]	= when	
штом, а, едно	= as soon as, (also штомтуку and тукушто)	
тамàм	= hardly, as soon as	
до каде (кај)	= while	
дури (да)	= until, while	
додека	= till, while	
откако, откога	= since	
одошто	= as, because	
пошто	= after	
пред но што, пред да	= before	
да, за да	= (in order) that	
да, та	= so that (of consequence), usually preceded by:— така = so, толку = so much	
така што	= so that	
дека, оти, како	= that (after verbs of saying, thinking, etc.); (also што and да)	
да	= that, to (after verbs of commanding, requesting, etc.)	
(за) дека, (оти), чунки(м) (dial.)	= because, as	
бидејќи	= since	
зашто, пошто	= because, since	
како (што)	= as (after така = so, in main clause)	
колку што	= as much as	
божем, како да	= as if	
иако, (ако)[2], макар да, макар што	= although	
макар и да	= even if	
без да	= without (doing)	
дали(...дали)	= whether (in indirect questions) ..., (or...)	
ако[2] (ли), ...ли (enclitic)	= if; лели = once, if, when	

[1] Notice кога да + Imperfect of Pfve. verb = whenever, e.g. Кога да дојдеше = whenever he came.

[2] When stressed, ако means 'although' - a rare use.

да = if (in unfulfilled conditions), e.g.:—
Јас би ти кажал, да знаам = I would tell you if I knew

да + Pres. Imperfective or Perfective is regularly used in Macedonian to replace the lost Infinitive, which in Bulgarian and other Balkan languages has also largely been lost, e.g.:—

сакам да читам = I want to read

PREPOSITIONS

The prepositions in Macedonian are always followed by nouns in the Nom. case (of such nouns as have a rudimentary declension). No special form (Oblique case) is used after prepositions for masculine nouns with the definite article, in contrast to the usage in Bulgarian.
Thus we have:—

на Рацин	= of Racin
со Рацин	= with Racin
со син ми	= with my son
кај јагленар<u>от</u>	= to (at) the charcoal burner's

Pronouns after prepositions are put in the Acc. full (non-enclitic) form, e.g.:—

во нас = in us

Most of the prepositions in Macedonian are easily recognizable to those knowing other Slavonic languages. In the list below we give the majority of the most important prepositions, italicizing those which are peculiar in form or meaning.

Prepositions corresponding to cases in Slavonic languages with full declensions

To replace:—

Genitive
- *од* = of (used more frequently in this meaning than in Bulgarian); from
- *на* = of; *also for Dative*: to, for

Dative
- до = to: писмо до... (= a letter to...)
- (*на*) *кај*[1] = to (like Serbocroätian код + Gen. = to [someone])
- *кон* = towards
- при = (to) near

---

[1]Alternative forms to кај are: накај, докај, каде.

Instrumental: co (always with -o) = with (also of an instrument), e.g.:—

                со нож   = with a knife
                со таа форма = with this form

Locative ⎰ на   = at, in, on (on to), e.g.:—
                      на масата = on (to) the table, or
                      врз масата
             врз   = on
             при   = near, by (also: кај)
             в (во) = in, into

The form в is used with nouns without the definite article:—

                в град = in (a) town
                в река = in (a) river

(But see 2 and 4 below.)

The form во is used:—

1. with nouns with the definite article, or other defining word (adjective, adverb, numeral or demonstrative pronoun), e.g.:—

            во градот   = in the city
            во реката   = in the river
            во литературниот = in the literary
               јазик   language

2. before nouns beginning with в and ф even *without* the definite article, e.g.:—

                во Велес = in Veles
                во вода = in water
                во фурна = in an oven

3. before pronouns:—

                  во мене   = in me
                  во кого? = in whom?
                  во нив   = in them

4. with nouns without the definite article, when emphasized or contrasted, e.g.:—

      Јас во река сум се капел, а во море не.
= I have bathed in a river, but not in (any, Eng. "the") sea

5. to avoid agglomerations of consonants, e.g.:—

                во Скопје = in Skopje (Skoplje)

In folk poetry, в is found also with nouns *with* the definite article, e.g.:—

в полето = in the field, lit. во полето

Notice (with the days of the week):—

              во среда = On Wednesdays, every Wednesday
              во средата = on (last) Wednesday
              в среда = on (next) Wednesday
but: вторник = on (next) Tuesday (omitting в)

Other prepositions

до	= by, next to, against, as far as, till, e.g.:—
	до станицата = as far as the station
	до ѕидот = by the wall
	близу до = near
без	= without
освен	= except
од	= *off, out of*
против	= against
спроти(в)	= opposite, on the eve of
преку	= through, by means of, over (also of numbers)
за	= for; about, concerning; by; after; in
низ	= through, down
над	= over, above
под	= under
пред	= in front of; before (of time),... ago
зад	= behind
меѓу, помеѓу	= between, among
по	= after; over; in respect of
покрај	= near, with, along; past; besides
спрема	= according to
во врска со	= in relation to
поради	= because of
заради	= because of, for the sake of
околу	= near, about, around
надвор	= outside
внатре	= inside
во време на	= during
место, наместо	= instead of
далеку	= far from
близу	= near
одзади	= beyond
крај	= near by, next to
вопреки	= in spite of

Notice also:

врз	= on, after
докај	= about, towards (of time)
накај	= to, towards; about
накрај искрај (rarer)	= at the edge of
наспроти	= against, despite; as regards; on the eve of
насред (посред)	= in the middle of
одавде	= this side of
онанде отаде	= beyond
откај	= from, since, about
потем (rare)	= after, in (of time)
през (rare)	= during
сосе	= together with
според	= according to, compared with
спрема	= to, towards, according to, compared with, on the eve of
сред(е)	= in the middle of
у (rare) = кај	= at, etc.

кај also means: at, approximately

Double prepositions also occur, e.g.:—

од пред	= from before
од под	= from under
од одавде	= from this side of
до кај	= to (a person)
до под	= to under

на or од (= of) is omitted in certain cases, as in:—

чаша вода = a glass of water
разни видови вршења на глаголското дејствие
(lit. = different kinds *of* performance of the action of the verb)

The following verbal prefixes are not used as prepositions in Macedonian:—

о(б)-, пре-, про-, раз-, воз-

THE CONJUGATION OF VERBS

Macedonian verbs are most like verbs in Bulgarian in their classes, number of tenses and use. The use of tenses consisting of an auxiliary verb and a Past Participle Active in -л for "Renarration" (Mac. прекажаност, repeating other people's reports, etc.) is also to be found in Macedonian, though there are fewer such tenses in the literary language. Маcedonian also lacks Future Perfect tenses and a Present Participle Active (corresponding to the variable forms in -ещ, -ащ in Bulgarian).

Four uniquely Macedonian features in the verbs are:—

1. the generalization of the ending -ам for the 1st person singular Present of *all* classes of verbs, both of the -е- and the -и- type;

2. the use of the verb имам (= I have) with the Past Participle Passive in the neuter (or сум = I am, for intransitive verbs, with Past Partic. Pass. in the gender of the subject) to express a Perfect (Active) tense on the model of Modern Greek and the Romance languages. Thus:—

> имам работено = I have worked
> јас сум дојден[1] = I have come

3. the ending of the Past Participle Active in the plural for all genders, which is -ле, e.g.:—

> тие биле = they have been (I heard)

4. Many verbs, which are intransitive in other Slavonic languages, are used transitively in Macedonian, and transitive verbs can be used intransitively. E.g.:—

Тој шета	= he goes for a walk
Го шета детето	= (She) takes the child for a walk
Приближи го прстот до уста	= bring your finger near your mouth
Приближавме до село	= we approached a village
Тој ги седна	= he sat them down
Тој ги умре	= he killed them
Го загинав саатот	= I have lost my watch
Ме смееш	= you make me laugh

In other respects Macedonian and Bulgarian largely agree. Macedonian has no Dual number and no Infinitive at all (not even a "truncated" one!).

The Present tense has -ме in the 1st pers. plur. and -ат in 3rd pers. plur.

The Imperative has no 1st pers. plur.

The Aorist and Imperfect tenses survive in Macedonian and also the Compound Past and the Pluperfect.

The Future is formed by an *invariable* ќе + Pres. Pfve. or Impfve. Its negative form is mostly

---

[1] Note this Passive form which is Active in meaning. This is typical of Macedonian and there are many such participles from intransitive verbs, e.g. even умрен = dead.

нема да + Pres. The auxiliary ќe is also used to express habit and to make one form of Conditional (apart from that with би).

Macedonian has only one Gerund—Present, and two Participles—Past Part. Active in -л, Past Part. Passive with -н or -т.

The classification of verbs is also similar to that for Bulgarian despite the generalization of -ам in the 1st pers. sing. Pres. There is no separate class of "athematic" verbs. The Aorists, in Macedonian too, point to the subdivisions.

The Present, the Aorist and the Imperfect are the only simple tenses in Macedonian.

The Passive Voice is rendered in Macedonian in three ways:—

1. By using the verb "to be" followed by the Past Part. Passive, e.g.:—

Тој е тепан многу често = He is beaten very often
Тој беше истеран од училиште = He was expelled from school

2. By using a reflexive verb,[1] e.g.:—

тој се вика = he is called (lit. calls himself)
тоа не се знае = that is not known

3. By using an "impersonal" 3rd pers. plur., e.g.:—

го викаат = he is called (lit. they call him)
го отепале = he was killed (lit. they killed him)

The Present

The personal endings of the Present for all types of verb (of both aspects) stems:—

Sing.	1	-(а)м	Plur. 1	-ме
	2	-ш	2	-те
	3	-	3	-(а)т

In the 1st pers. sing. the joining vowel between the ending -м and the stem of the verb is always -а-.

In the 3rd pers. plur. the ending -ат can be preceded by a consonantal stem, e.g.:—

[1]The reflexive verb in Macedonian is formed with the separable enclitic *or proclitic* Acc. Reflexive pronoun ce used with an Active verb.

N.B.—As in Bulgarian, the negative не is separated from its verb by ce and other enclitic pronouns, as in the example above. (See "Word Order with Enclitics".)

идат = they go,

or a vowel stem, e.g.:—

стоат = they stand

The *Classification of verbs in Macedonian* is based on the joining vowel in the remaining four persons.

I. The modern -*e*- group includes all verbs of Classes I and II of Old Slavonic and all verbs of Class III except most *a*- (vowel) stems. (-e- is always pronounced ε, not jε!), e.g.:—

Old Class I:

Sing. 1	идам = I come	можам = I can	земам = I take[1] (Pfve.)	изберам = I choose[1] (Pfve.)
2	идеш	можеш	земеш	izбереш
3	иде	може	земе	избере
Plur. 1	идеме	можеме	земеме	избереме
2	идете	можете	земете	изберете
3	идат	можат	земат	изберат

Old Class II:

Sing. 1	викнам = I call[1] (Pfve.)	паднам = I fall[1] (Pfve.)
2	викнеш	паднеш
3	викне	падне
Plur. 1	викнеме	паднеме
2	викнете	паднете
3	викнат	паднат

Old Class III:

Sing. 1	добијам* = I get[1] (Pfve.)	покажам = I show[1] (Pfve.)
2	добиеш	покажеш
3	добие	покаже
Plur. 1	добиеме	покажеме
2	добиете	покажете
3	добијат	покажат

*So also пеам (= I sing), преживеам (= I live through, Pfve.), дочујам (= I hear, Pfve.).

[1] The Pfve. Present is not used in main clauses, and does not have a future meaning as in East and West Slav. It is used, as in other South Slav languages, in subordinate clauses after да, кога (= when), or other introducing conjunction.

II. This class consists of all verbs with -и- joining vowel.

Old Class IV:

		стоам = I stand	видам = I see[1] (Pfve.)
Sing. 1	носам* = I carry	стоам	видам
2	носиш	стоиш	видиш
3	носи	стои	види
Plur. 1	носиме	стоиме	видиме
2	носите	стоите	видите
3	носат	стоат	видат

*So also: сторам, сториш, etc. = I do[1] (Pfve.)

III. This class consists of verbs with -а- joining vowel and, as in Bulgarian and other South and West Slav languages, is a new class produced by coalescence of -а- stems with -е- endings. To this class now belong all verbs in -увам, -уваш, etc., -уваат which until the orthographical reform of 1948 were conjugated -уам, -уеш, -уат (i.e. modern Class I), e.g. купувам, below.

викам = I shout, call (Impfve.); пливам = I swim (Impfve.); добивам = I get (Impfve.); купувам = I buy (Impfve.)

Sing.	1	викам	пливам	добивам	купувам
	2	викаш	пливаш	добиваш	купуваш
	3	вика	плива	добива	купува
Plur.	1	викаме	пливаме	добиваме	купуваме
	2	викате	пливате	добивате	купувате
	3	викаат	пливаат	добиваат	купуваат

So also: напаѓам (= I attack, Impfve.), земам (= I take, Impfve.*), бегам (= I run, Impfve.), избегам (= I run out[1], Pfve.).

Like купувам:—

кажувам = I tell, пишувам = I write, зборувам = I talk

Notice the double -аа- in the 3rd pers. plur.

*The student will observe that the ending -ам in the 1st pers. sing. is no guide as to the class of the verb. This depends on the endings in the 2nd and 3rd pers. sing. and 1st and 2nd pers. plur.

The Aorist

This tense is formed from Pfve. verbs and indicates a completed action in the Past witnessed by the

---

[1]See footnote on p. 200.

speaker, more precisely "a moment of an action, whether it be its beginning or full performance".

In literary Macedonian the original х in the endings has become unvoiced в (i.e. ф, = f) and has been generalized for the 1st and 2nd pers. plur., as in Bulgarian. In the 2nd and 3rd pers. sing. the form ends in a vowel, and in the 3rd p. plur. the х before -а becomes ј only after и and у or after two consecutive vowels. After other vowels х is dropped before the final -а.

The formation of the Aorist corresponds to the Infinitive in other Slavonic languages, as originally the Aorist was formed from the Infinitive. The Infinitive being lost in Macedonian, the Aorist is now the only other guide left for subdividing the three modern main classes of verbs.

Modern Class I.

    Old Class I:—

PRESENT			AORIST		
2nd sg.	Sg.: 1	2 and 3	Pl.: 1	2	3
дојдеш	= you come (Pfve.)				
	дојдов	дојде	дојдовме	дојдовте	дојдоа
донесеш	= you bring (Pfve.)				
	донесов	донесе	донесовме	донесовте	донесоа
земеш	= you take (Pfve.)				
	зедов	зеде	зедовме	зедовте	зедоа
избереш	= you choose (Pfve.)				
	избрав	избра	избравме	избравте	избраа

    Old Class II:—

паднеш	= you fall (Pfve.)				
	паднав	падна	паднавме	паднавте	паднаа

    Old Class III:—

дочуеш	= you hear (Pfve.)				
	дочув	дочу	дочувме	дочувте	дочуја
преживееш	= you live through (Pfve.)				
	преживев	преживе	преживевме	преживевте	преживеа
покажеш	= you show (Pfve.)				
	покажав	покажа	покажавме	покажавте	покажаа

Modern Class II.

    Old Class IV:—

сториш	= you do (Pfve.)				
	сторив	стори	сторивме	сторивте	сторија
претрпиш	= you suffer (Pfve.)				
	претрпев	претрпе	претрпевме	претрпевте	претрпеа

PRESENT			AORIST		
2nd sg.	Sg.: 1	2 and 3	Pl.: 1	2	3

видиш = you see (Pfve.) [irregular]
    видов   виде   видовме   видовте   видоа
постоиш = you stand for a moment (Pfve.)
    постоав постоа постоавме постоавте постоаја

Modern Class III.

избегаш = you run out (Pfve.)
    избегав избега избегавме избегавте избегаа

The Imperfect

    The Imperfect normally indicates a continued action in the past witnessed by the speaker and is therefore usually formed from Imperfective verbs only.
    Its personal endings are the same as those of the Aorist except in the 2nd and 3rd pers. sing., which end in -ше. But in this tense these endings are added to the Present stem. Verbs of modern Classes I *and* II have -e- as the joining vowel, and verbs of modern Class III have -a- as the joining vowel. In the 3rd pers. plur. -j- is used before the final -a when two vowels precede.

Class I.

Sing. 1 идев = I was going
     2 идеше
     3 идеше
Plur. 1 идевме
     2 идевте
     3 идеа

    можев = I was able
    можеше
    можеше   врнеше = it was raining.
    можевме   (Pres. врне)
    можевте
    можеа

Sing. 1 пеев = I was singing
     2 пееше
     3 пееше
Plur. 1 пеевме
     2 пеевте
     3 пееја

Class II.

Sing. 1 носев = I was carrying   стоев = I was standing
     2 носеше   стоеше
     3 носеше   стоеше
Plur. 1 носевме   стоевме
     2 носевте   стоевте
     3 носеа   стоеја

Class III.

Sing. 1	бегав = I was running	викав = I was shouting	купував[1] = I was buying
2	бегаше	викаше	купуваше
3	бегаше	викаше	купуваше
Plur. 1	бегавме	викавме	купувавме
2	бегавте	викавте	купувавте
3	бегаа	викаа	купуваа

An Imperfect in form only, is formed from Pfve. verbs in conditional constructions. Thus:—

дојдам = I come (Pfve.)
да дојдеше = if he had come (if he would have come)
паднам = I fall (Pfve.)
ќе паднеше = he would have fallen

The Imperative

Separate Imperative forms exist in Macedonian only for the 2nd pers. sing. and the 2nd pers. plur. They are formed from the Present stem.

Verbs of modern Classes I and II with 2nd pers. sing. Pres. in -еш and -иш respectively, have the endings:—

2nd pers. sing. -и
2nd pers. plur. -ете   if they are consonant stems

and—

2nd pers. sing. -ј
2nd pers. plur. -јте   if they are vowel stems

E.g.:—

Sing. иди[2] = носи! = BUT: стој! = stand! пиј![3] =
   go!   carry!   stop!   drink!
Plur. идете! носете! стојте!   пијте!

All verbs of modern Class III are treated as vowel stems; verbs with Pres. in -увам, etc., use either -у- or -ува- as the stem; hence we have:—

Sing. бегај!   викај!   купуј! or купувај! = buy!
  = run!   = shout!
Plur. бегајте! викајте! купујте! or купувајте!

---

[1]So also: кажував = I was saying.

[2]Velar stem verbs of *old* Class I keep the stem with 1st Palatalization in the Imperative:

речам = I say, Imper. речи! речете!;
поможам = I help, "   поможи! поможете!

[3]The j is *not* pronounced after и.

For the 1st and 3rd pers. sing. and plur. periphrases with да or нека + Pres. (Pfve. or Impfve.) are used, e.g.:—

    да викам   = let me shout!
    да викаме   = let us shout!
    нека вика   = let him shout!
    нека викаат = let them shout!
    да пееме   = let us sing!

Prohibitions are expressed by не + Imperfective Imperative or by немој(те) да + Pres. (Impfve. or Pfve.), e.g.:—

не смејте се *or* немојте да се смеете = do not laugh!
немој(те) да мислите (дека...)   = do not think (that...)

Notice the idiomatic use of the Imperative in narration:—

    Ние кинисавме по патот: *оди, оди*; одвàј стасавме в село.
= We started along the road; we walked and walked; with great difficulty (lit. hardly) we reached a village.

    Тамо имаше многу свет пред вратата: едни *влези*, други *излези*.
= There, there were many people at (in front of) the door: some were going in, others were going out.

The particles ама before the Imperative and де after it are used to express urgency:—

Ама брзај кога ти велам = Hurry up when I tell you!
Побрзај де!   = Well, hurry up then!

The Present Gerund (Active)
    In Macedonian this is the only Gerund (verbal adverb), as in Bulgarian. It is invariable and refers to the subject of a sentence. It describes an action contemporary to that of the main verb (in any tense) and is formed only from Impfve. verbs. The stress falls always on the penultimate syllable.
    For Verbs of Classes I and II the Gerund ends in -ејќи, and for verbs of Class III it ends in -ајќи. It can be regarded as being formed from the 1st pers. sing. Imperfect tense by dropping the final -в and adding -јќи. E.g.:—

Imperf. идев = I was пеев = I was   носев = I was
                 going   singing   carrying
Gerund идејќи = going пеејќи = singing носејќи =
                                                   carrying

Imperf.	бегав = I was running	купував = I was buying	кажував = I was saying
Gerund	бегајќи = running	купувајќи = buying	кажувајќи = saying

The Participles

Macedonian has only two kinds of participles: the Past Participle Active in -л and the Past Participle Passive in -н or -т.

1. The *Past Participle Active* ends in: —

Sing. masc. -л fem. -ла neut. -ло
Plur. all genders -ле

For Imperfective verbs it is formed from the Imperfect tense (as in Bulgarian) by substituting the above endings for the final -в of the 1st pers. sing. E.g.: —

Imperf.   *Past P.A.*

можев = I was able   можел = been able
пеев = I was singing   пеел = been singing
носев = I was carrying   носел = carried, been carrying
викав = I was shouting   викал = shouted, been shouting
купував = I was buying   купувал = been buying
кажував = I was saying   кажувал = been saying

For Perfective verbs it is formed from the Aorist tense (also as in Bulgarian) by substituting the same endings for the final -в of the 1st pers. sing. E.g.: —

Aorist   *Past P.A.*

донесов = I brought   донесол[1] = brought
паднав = I fell   паднал = fallen
дочув = I heard   дочул = heard
покажав = I showed   покажал = shown
сторив = I did   сторил = done
избегав = I ran out   избегал = run out
напишав = I wrote   напишал = written

As Imperfective verbs do not have an Aorist tense in literary Macedonian (in contrast to Bulgarian and Serbocroätian), Macedonian as opposed to Bulgarian has no Past Part. Act. formed from Aorists of Impfve. verbs (e.g. *писал does not exist in Macedonian). Thus the two Past Participles Active cor-

---

[1] Verbs with Past Part. Act. masc. sing. in -ол drop the -о- in the other genders and plur., e.g. fem. донесла, neut. донесло, plur. донесле.

respond to the aspects.

On the other hand to form a *direct* and also the *Reported* Past Conditional or Future in Renarration (see the Compound Tenses below under these headings) Imperfective Past Participles Active have to be formed from Perfective verbs, e.g.:—

               паднел = fallen

The Past Part. Active is very important in Macedonian as it is used to form the compound tenses (see below) which express a reported event not witnessed by the speaker but recounted to him by some one else and related by the speaker to a third person (i.e. in Renarration).

2. The *Past Participle Passive* with a passive *meaning* is formed from transitive verbs and ends in:—

Sing.
    masc. -т   fem. -та   neut. -то   Plur. all genders -ти
or
Sing.
    masc. -н   fem. -на   neut. -но   Plur. all genders -ни

The same endings can be used to form a Past Participle which is Passive in form but *Active in meaning* and which is used with имам (= I have) and сум (= I am) to form a peculiarly Macedonian Past tense (already mentioned under "The Conjugation of Verbs"; see also "The Past Definite" under "Compound Tenses" below).

The endings with -т- are used for verbs with stems ending in -н or -њ. These endings with joining vowel -*e*-, where necessary, are added to the Aorist stem. E.g.:—

Passive
in meaning: заколнат   = slaughtered
                ранет   = wounded
                скаменет   = fossilized
                соединети   = united (pl.), cf. Sbcr. сједињени
                изменет   = changed
                бањат   = bathed
Active
in meaning: тргнат   = started off, set off
                минат   = passed, past
                загинат   = died
                овената трева = faded grass
                настанат   = become, happened

The endings with -н- are used for all other verbs of modern Classes I, II, and III. Verbs of

Class I and II (except for those with Aorist in -ав) have the vowel -е- preceding these endings, while verbs of Class III and those of Class I with Aorist in -ав have -а- before them. E.g.:—

Passive in meaning:
  Class I:
  донесен = brought (Pfve.)
  избран = chosen (Pfve.)
  убиен = killed (Pfve.)

  Class II:
  носен = carried (Ipfve.)
  сторен = done (Pfve.)
  крпен = patched (Ipfve.)

  Class III:
  тепан = beaten (Ipfve.)
  купуван = bought (Ipfve.)
  изорана и посеана нива = a field ploughed and sown
  венчана жена = a married woman

Active in meaning:
  Class I:
  дојден = come (irreg.—see below, "Verbs of going and conveying") (Pfve.)
  умрен = dead (Pfve.)

  Class II:
  спан = slept (Ipfve.)

  Class III:
  беган = run (Ipfve.)

There is no yotation before the endings -ен, -ена, etc., as also in Bulgarian. Only velar stems undergo the 1st Palatalization, e.g.:—

  испеков = I baked, Past Part. Pass. испечен

Verbal Nouns are formed from Past Participles Passive by changing the final -н to -ње for Impfve. verbs and to -ние for Pfve. verbs. The latter group are mainly literary words expressing more abstract notions and processes. E.g.:—

  носен = carried, носење = carrying
  одење = going, walking
  кажување = saying
  купување = buying
  тепање = beating
  бегање = running
  орање = ploughing

but—

издание	=	publishing
образование	=	forming, education
решение	=	decision
соопштение	=	announcement
уверение	=	assurance

COMPOUND TENSES

The Future

The Future of verbs of *both* aspects is formed with the *invariable* auxiliary ќе (cf. Bulg. ще) and the Present (Impfve. or Pfve.). Thus:—

Ние ќе викаме = We shall shout (be shouting), Impfve.

Ние ќе го викнеме = We shall call him (Pfve.)

This form is also often used to express habits, e.g.:—

Ќе свири и ќе пее поручек = He plays and sings after dinner

The Future can also be expressed by the invariable има да + Pres. (Impfve. or Pfve.), e.g.:—

Има да носиш = you will carry (Impfve.)

The negative form of this is the regular way of expressing a negative Future in Macedonian, e.g.:—

Нема да носиш = you will not carry

The Reported Future in Renarration

The auxiliary ќе is used with the Compound Past (see below) to express a Future in Renarration, i.e. a future action about which we have heard from others that it is going to take place. The auxiliary verb е or се is always omitted with the 3rd persons sing. and plur. E.g.:—

Ќе си викал = they say you will be shouting

Ќе сум паднел¹ = they say I shall fall

Утре ќе оделе другарите в село = To-morrow the chaps will go to (the) village, I hear.

Другиден ќе дојдел Спиро на пазар = Spiro will come to market the day after tomorrow, they say.

---

¹Special Impfve. Past Partic. Active formed from Pfve. verb,—see p. 207. The use of the *Imperfective* P.P.A. is more usual in this tense.

The forms are the same as for the *Reported Past Conditional*, q.v. (pp. 215, 216).

The Compound Past

The Compound Past tense (by natives called the Indefinite Past tense—минато неопределено време) is formed in the 1st and 2nd pers. sing. and plur. with the Present of the verb "to be" always preceding a Past Part. Active of either aspect. In the 3rd pers. sing. and plur. there is no auxiliary verb, and this tense consists of the Past Part. Active in the appropriate gender and number by itself. Thus:—

Impfve.:

сум бегал (-ла, ло) = I have been running
си бегал   = you have been running
бегал   = he has been running
сме бегале   = we have been running
сте бегале   = you have been running
бегале   = they have been running

So also: сум купувал (-ла, -ло) = I have been buying; сум носел = I have been carrying.

Pfve.

сум сторил (-ла, -ло) = I have done
си сторил   etc.
сторил
сме сториле
сте сториле
сториле

The meaning of the tense in the 2nd and 3rd persons.—1. This tense expresses a past action without reference to any particular time in the past, or a fact freshly observed, e.g.:—

      Гледам, гората се свршила
      = I see, the forest has finished

Карпата се надвисила над патот, ти се чини ќе падне
      = The rock hangs over the road;
      it seems to you it will fall

2. (Reported Past (sometimes Present) in Renarration): This tense is used to express an action about which the speaker has heard from someone else, but which he has not witnessed himself. E.g.:—

Тој работел цел ден = he worked all day (they say)
                       (Ipfve.)
Ти си паднал од дрво = I have heard you fell off a
                      tree, or You are supposed to
                      have fallen off a tree (Pfve.)

Вие сте направиле куќа, а нам не сте ни кажале
= You have built a house (we hear), and have not told *us*

In the 1st person this tense has the meaning of:—

1. a past action not connected with any particular point in time, e.g.:—

Јас сум го правел тоа, и пак ќе го правам
= I have been doing this and shall do it again

2. a statement in Renarration as if quoting another person's false statement, e.g.:—

Ами! Сум зел, како не?
= What! I have taken it, of course?
(It isn't true what you say!)

3. a statement about an action by the speaker, done unconsciously and only subsequently noticed, e.g.:—

Леле, сум го загубил кесето!
= Oh dear, I have lost my purse!
(I have only just noticed it)

Ноќеска на сон сум станал, сум излегол надвор, и пак сум се вратил, и ништо не сум сетил што сум правел.
= Last night I got up in my sleep, I went outside, and came back again, and I did not feel anything of what I was doing.

Further uses of the compound Past:—

1. Referring to the Future:—

Бегај оттука, дури не сум те отепал!
= Run away from here, while I haven't killed you!

Си пропаднал, ако не дојдеш!
= You are lost (will perish), if you do not come.

2. To express a command:—

Да не си мрднал од местото, оти тешко ти тебе!
= Don't budge from the spot, or you will get it!

3. In proverbs and sayings:—

Ни лук си јал, ни лук мирисал
= I don't like to take the risk (lit. (If) you have not eaten onion, you have not smelt of it)

4. In wishes:—

Ристос ти помогол! = May Christ help you!

The Past Definite or Perfect

In direct contrast in meaning to the Compound Past is the peculiarly Macedonian Perfect tense constructed with the Past Participle "Passive", already mentioned. Such forms state facts definitely known by the speaker as performed.

Intransitive verbs use the Past Part. "Passive" in the appropriate gender preceded by the verb "to be" in the Present. E.g.:—

Јас сум дојден *or*   = I have come (here I am)
  Дојден сум
Тој е сега заспан   = He is now asleep (has fallen asleep)

This construction is widely used.

Constructions with имам: Transitive and intransitive verbs are used with the Past Part. Passive in the neuter preceded by the auxiliary verb имам (= I have). имам can be used in all its forms and tenses with the corresponding changes of meaning. This also is a common Macedonian construction and virtually creates a whole parallel series of tenses in which the completeness of an action is stressed. E.g.:—

   Ние имаме пратено едно писмо дури до Белград
   = We have sent a letter as far as Belgrade

     Тој нема видено такви луѓе
     = He has not seen such people

(As a Pluperfect:)

     Немав чуено такви работи
     = I had not heard (of) such things

    Јас имам слегувано многупати овде
    = I have often been (lit. come) down here

The Pluperfect

The Pluperfect tense is formed with the Imperfect of "to be" + the Past Participle Active of either aspect, though the Perfective is more frequently used. It expresses an action in the past preceding another action also in the past. Thus we have:—

Impfve.: бев викал (-ла, -ло) = I had been shouting
       беше викал   = you had been shouting
       беше викал   etc.
       бевме викале
       бевте викале
       беа викале

Pfve.:   бев викнал, etc.   = I had called out, shouted, etc.

Тие беа дошле, кога го пишував писмото
= They had (already) come (Pfve.),
  when I was writing the letter

Бевме си легнале, кога некој затропа на порта
= We had (already) gone to bed,
  when someone knocked on (the) door

A rarer form of this tense with the same meaning is:—

беше сум викал	беше сме викале
беше си викал	беше сте викале
(беше викал)	беше викале

The Conditional Mood

The ordinary Conditional referring to Present, Future, or Past in main clauses is constructed with the invariable auxiliary verb би + Past Participle Active in -л, -ла, etc.[1] With such forms the Nom. Personal Pronoun is required to indicate the person, if the subject is not otherwise expressed or understood.

A less frequently used form has the Present of "to be" in the 1st and 2nd persons after the би, thus indicating the person meant (cf. Slovak), e.g.:—

Јас би дошол, дошла	= I would come,	or	(јас) би сум дошол, -ла
ти би дошол, дошла	= you would come,	"	(ти) би си дошол, -ла
тој би дошол	= he would come,	"	(тој) би дошол
таа би дошла	= she would come,	"	(таа) би дошла
ние би дошле	= we would come,	"	(ние) би сме дошле
вие би дошле	= you would come,	"	(вие) би сте дошле
тие би дошле	= they would come,	"	(тие) би дошле

Examples:—

Јас би го зел, да имам пари
= I would take it if I had (the) money

Ти би дошол вчера, да знаеше дека имавме работа
= You would have come yesterday, if
  you had known that we had work

Тале би го направил тоа, ако се *сетел*[2]
= Tale would have done (or: do)
  this, if he had remembered

---

[1] Perfective Past Participles Active are most usual for perfective verbs in this mood, and imperfective P.P.A.—for imperfective verbs.

[2] Special Impfve. Past Partic. Active formed from Pfve. verb, mentioned under the "Past Participle Active".

Јас би сум се скарал со него, да знаев за тоа
= I would have quarrelled with
him, had I known about this

Тој би се отепал во барање, да не му *кажев*[1]
= He would have killed himself with
searching if I had not told him

The Conditional is also used to express a doubt, e.g.:—

Јас би рекол, дека ти тоа не го правиш од срце
= I would say that you are not doing
this sincerely (lit. from the heart)

To express the *Past Conditional* ("would have"), more commonly ќе is used with the Imperfect of Impfve. verbs in the main clause, followed by the Imperfect after a suitable conditional conjunction in the "if" clause. For Pfve. verbs a special "hybrid Imperfect" is constructed for both clauses, by adding the Imperfect endings to Aorist stems. (See under "The Imperfect".)[2]

Examples:—

Јас ќе земев (Pfve.) пари, да дојдеше (Pfve.) татко ми
= I would have taken (the) money, if my father had come

Тој ќе викаше (Impfve.) по мене, ако се забавев (Pfve.)
= He would have called for me, if I had been late

Јас ќе паднев (Pfve.), ако не ме придржеше (Pfve.) ти
= I would have fallen, if you had not held me

Ќе ја видев таа работа, ако имав време
= I would have seen this thing, if I had had time

This form of the Past Conditional is also used to express intention in the past and also habit in the past, e.g.:—

Ќе одев   = I was going to walk, go.
Ќе влезев = I was going to go in.[2]

Ќе седнеше, ќе ја земеше тамбурата и ќе свиреше убави песни, а ние тогаш ќе го слушавме
= He would sit down, take his tambura (kind of mandoline) and play lovely songs, and we would then

---

[1] Special Conditional Imperfect formed from Pfve. verb, mentioned under "The Imperfect".

[2] Negative form: немаше да одам (влезам) = I would not have walked (gone in), *or* = I was not going to walk (go in).

listen to him

Поручек ќе ја земев книгата и ќе читав
= After lunch I would take the book and read

There is a further indirect or *Reported Past Conditional* in Macedonian in Renarration to express conditions heard about by the speaker from others. This is formed by ќе followed by the Compound Past tense. To form this Reported Past Conditional from Pfve. verbs a special "hybrid Past Part. Active" is formed by adding the Impfve. endings -ел, -ела, etc., to the Aorist stems of Pfve. verbs of Classes I and II. Pfve. verbs of Class III have no special endings. The aux. verbs e or ce are omitted in the 3rd persons, as in other Renarration tenses. E.g.:—

    Impfve.:—

        ќе сум викал, -а = I would have been shouting, they say etc.
        ќе си викал
        ќе викал
        ќе сме викале
        ќе сте викале
        ќе викале

    Pfve.:—

        ќе сум паднел, -а = I would have fallen, they say
        ќе си паднел
        ќе паднел
        ќе сме паднеле
        ќе сте паднеле
        ќе паднеле

These forms are also used for the *Reported Future*, q.v. above.

Examples:—

Тој ќе дојдел тогаш, ако го пуштеле
= He would have come then (they say), if they had let him

Тие ќе купеле жито, ами немале пари
= They would have bought (some) wheat (I hear), but they had no money

Петре ќе стасал на време, да не беше му се поболел коњот
= Peter would have arrived in time (I am told), if his horse had not gone sick

This form can also be used to express past habits not witnessed by the speaker, e.g.:—

Спиро ќе земел леб и ќе одел на нива
= (They say) Spiro would take some bread and go into (the) fields

As this form is also used to express the Reported Future, the last example could also mean: They say Spiro will take (some) bread and go into the fields (but I don't believe it, or: I don't think so).

Irregular and Noteworthy Verbs

Of the old "athematic" verbs, modern Macedonian has preserved only: сум (= I am).

јадам, јадеш (= I eat) and дадам (or дам), дадеш (= I give, Pfve.) are now regular verbs of Class I with dental stem in the Present. The Imperative of дадам is дај!, Aor. дадов. Past Part. Act. дал (Pfve.), дадел (Ipfve.), Past Part. Pass. даден; Impfve. давам, regular. јадам has Past Part. Act. јадел (Impfve.), Past Part. Pass. јаден.

сум = I am

		Present	*Imperfect*	*Future*[1]	*Imperative*
Sing.	1	сум	бев (or бидев, etc., reg.)	ќе бидам	—
	2	си	беше	ќе бидеш	биди
	3	е[2]	беше	ќе биде	нека биде
Plur.	1	сме	бевме	ќе бидеме	—
	2	сте	бевте	ќе бидете	бидете
	3	се	беа	ќе бидат	нека бидат

Present Gerund: бидејќи
Past Participle: Sing. masc. бил, fem. била, neut. било; Plur. (all gend.) биле
Past Participle (Impfve.): Sing. masc. бидел, fem. бидела, neut. бидело; Plur. (all gend.) биделе

The form би, originally an Aorist of this verb, is now only used as an *auxiliary* for forming the Conditional mood: јас би бил, etc. = I would be, etc.

The negative form of сум, etc. is не сум, не си, etc., written separately in Macedonian.

"I know" is знам or знаам (Impfve.), Pres. знаеш etc., 3rd p. plur. знаат
Imperfect: знаев, Past Part. Act. знаел
"I find out" is: дознам or дознаам (Pfve.)

---

[1] A Future composed of ќе + Present is also occasionally to be found in modern texts.
[2] Pronounced је when emphasized and after an accented word ending in a consonant.

Notice also:—

		2nd pers. sing.	
можам	= I can	можеш	3rd p. pl. можат, Cl. I. Imperfect можев, P.P.A. можел
сакам	= I wish, I love	сакаш	regular Class III.

The negative form of сакам—нејќам, нејќеш, is sometimes used in dialects and idioms with -и- endings: сакате, нејќите (= nolens, volens). P.P.A. нејќел

чујам	= I hear (Pfve.)	чуеш	irreg. Cl. I, Aor. чув, чу, P.P.A. чул
успеам	= I manage, succeed (Pfve.)	успееш	irreg. Cl. I, Aor. успеав
спијам	= I sleep	спиеш	reg. Class I
видам	= I see (Pfve.)	видиш	irreg. Cl. II, Aor. видов, P.P.A. видел
гледам	= I see (Impfve.)	гледаш	reg. Cl. III
пулам	= I look at	пулиш	reg. Cl. II
барам	= I look for	бараш	reg. Cl. III
паѓам	= I fall	паѓаш	reg. Cl. III
земам	= I take (Impfve.)	земаш	reg. Cl. III

but—

земам	= I take (Pfve.)	земеш	irreg. Cl. I, Aor. зедов, зеде, etc., P.P.A. зел, P.P.P. земен, -а
имам	= I have	имаш	reg. Cl. III

Negative form: немам (= I have not), Imperfect: немав, немаше, etc.; нема = there is no(t)

разбирам	= I understand	разбираш	reg. Cl. III, has Pfve. разберам, разбереш, Cl. I, Aor. разбрав, P.P.A. разбрал
кревам	= I lift up (Impfve.)	креваш	reg. Cl. III

		2nd pers. sing.	
кренам	= I lift up (Pfve.)	кренеш	reg. Cl. I
стасам	= I arrive (Pfve.)	стасаш	reg. Cl. III
на(в)оѓам or најдувам	= I find (Impfve.)	-аш	reg. Cl. III
најдам	= I find (Pfve.)	најдеш	irreg. Cl. I, Aor. најдов, P.P.A. нашол (Ipfve. најдел)
кинисам	= I start out (Pfve.)	кинисаш	reg. Cl. III
кинисувам	= I start out (Impfve.)	кинисуваш	reg. Cl. III
бендисам	= I please, satisfy	бендисаш	reg. Cl. III
клавам	= I put down (Impfve.)	клаваш	reg. Cl. III
кладам	= I put down (Pfve.) Imper. клај	кладеш	reg. Cl. I, Aor. кладов, P.P.A. кладол
велам	= I say (Ipfve.)¹	велиш	
речам	= I say (Pfve.)	речеш	Aor. реков, рече, etc., P.P.A. рекол
кажам	= I say, show (Pfve.)	кажеш	Aor. кажав

Verbs of Going and Conveying

To come =

    Impfve. and Freq.:
Pres. идам   Imperfect идев   P.P.A. ишол
    идеш²   идеше   (Pfve.)
                                                            идел
To go (off) =   (Ipfve.)

    Pfve.:
Pres. појдам   Aorist   појдов   P.P.A. пошол
    појдеш   појде   (Pfve.)
                                                            појдел
                                                            (Ipfve.)

---

¹You *speak* = зборуваш or говориш, both reg.
²The form идвам, -аш, etc., is now considered bad style and is no longer used in good writing.

To come =

    Impfve. and Freq.:
Pres. доаѓам   Imperfect доаѓав   P.P.A. доаѓал
      доаѓаш

    Pfve.:
Pres. дојдам   Aorist   дојдов   P.P.A. дошол m.
      дојдеш   (Pfve.)
                                                                       дошла f.
                                                                       дојдел
                                                                       (Ipfve.)
        Imper. дојди! дојдете! or ела! елате!

To go (away), to walk =

    Impfve. and Freq.:
Pres. одам   Imperfect одев   P.P.A. одел
      одиш   одеше
    (одам is often used for 'to go')

To go away (only) =

    Pfve.:
Pres. отидам   Aorist   отидов   P.P.A. отишол m.
      отидеш   (Pfve.)
                                                                    отишла f.
                                                                    отидел
                                                                    (Ipfve.)

To go out =

    Impfve.:
Pres. излегувам Imperfect излегував P.P.A. излегувал
      излегуваш

    Pfve.:
Pres. излезам   Aorist   излегов   P.P.A. излегол
      излезеш   излезе,   (Pfve.)
                                                          etc.   излезел
                3rd p. pl. излегоа   (Ipfve.)
So also: влегувам (Impfve.) = to go in, (Pfve.) влезам

To lead =

    Impfve. and Freq.:
Pres. водам   Imperfect водев   P.P.A. водел
      водиш   водеше

    Pfve.:
Pres. поведам   Aorist   поведов   P.P.A. повел
      поведеш   поведе   (Pfve.)
                                                                    поведел
                                                                    (Ipfve.)

To bring (a person) =

    Impfve.:
Pres. доведувам Imperfect доведував P.P.A. доведувал

    Pfve.:
Pres. доведам   Aorist   доведов   P.P.A. довел
     доведеш   доведе   (Pfve.)
                                                                         доведел
                                                                          (Ipfve.)

To carry, to convey =

    Impfve. and Freq.:
Pres. носам   Imperfect носев   P.P.A. носел
     носиш

    Pfve.:
Pres. понесам   Aorist   понесов   P.P.A. понел
     понесеш   (Pfve.)
                                                                      понесел
                                                                          (Ipfve.)

To bring (or convey in a vehicle to a place) =

    Impfve.:
Pres. донесувам Imperfect донесував P.P.A. донесувал

    Pfve.:
Pres. донесам   Aorist   донесов   P.P.A. донесол[1]
     донесеш   донесе   (Pfve.)
                      Imperat. донеси!   донесел
                                                                      (Ipfve.)

For "to convey" we also have:

 Impfve. and Freq.: Pres. возам, возиш, reg. Cl. II,
  Pfve.: Pres. повезам, повезеш, Aor. повезов,
  P.P.A. повезол (Pfve.), повезел (Ipfve.)

and for "to bring (in a vehicle)" we also have:

    Impfve.: Pres. довезувам, Cl. III,
    Pfve.: Pres. довезам, Cl. I, (like повезам)

The Aspects

    The formation of aspects in Macedonian is similar to that in other Slavonic languages.

    1. Pfve. from simple Impfve. verbs by means of prepositional prefixes, e.g.:—

Impfve.		Pfve.
прашам	= I ask	запрашам
пишувам	= I write	напишувам
молам, -иш	= I request	замолам, -иш

    [1] In poetry also: донел.

2. Impfve. from Pfve. verbs by lengthening the root, e.g.:—

Pfve.		Impfve.
дадам, or дам	= I give	давам
купам, -иш	= I buy	купувам
донесам, -еш	= I bring	донесувам
помогнам, -еш	= I help	помагам

3. Impfve. from Pfve. verbs by changing the ending of the Present, e.g.:—

Pfve.		Impfve.
викнам, -еш	= I shout	викам
земам, -еш	= I take	земам, земаш
фатам, -иш	= I seize, start	фаќам, -аш

4. Different forms of the same root or occasionally different roots are used to express a difference of aspect, e.g.:—

Impfve.		Pfve.
разбирам	= I understand	разберам, -еш
излегувам	= I go out	излезам, -еш
доаѓам	= I come	дојдам, -еш

The Pfve. Pres. is only used in subordinate clauses.

A special feature of Macedonian in connection with the aspects is the formation of the Aorist tense from Pfve. verbs only, and a corresponding Pfve. Past Participle Active, and an Imperfect tense from Impfve. verbs only with a corresponding Impfve. Past Participle Active, e.g.:—

Impfve.	доаѓам	= I come	Pfve.	дојдам
Imperfect	доаѓав, доаѓаше etc.	= I used to come, or was coming	Aor.	дојдов, дојде, etc. = I came
P.P.A.	доаѓал		P.P.A.	дошол
Impfve.	разбирам	= I understand	Pfve.	разберам
Imperfect	разбирав, разбираше		Aorist	разбрав
P.P.A.	разбирал		P.P.A.	разбрал

The Aorist is not formed from Impfve. verbs in Macedonian, nor the Imperfect from Pfve. verbs, in contrast to Bulgarian.

WORD ORDER WITH ENCLITICS

A peculiar feature of Macedonian is that its short, unemphatic forms of the Personal Pronouns are more often treated as proclitics preceding the verb than as enclitics following it.[1] As already mentioned in "The Pronouns", they are often repeated by an emphatic pronoun in the same case earlier or later in the sentence.

Се разбира	= It is understood; of course. Cf. Bulg. разбѝра се, Sbcr. разу̀ме се
Ми ја дава мене книгата	= He gives me the book
Земи ја	= Take it (fem.)!
Удри ме	= Hit me!
Дај му го	= Give it to him!

The proclitic negative не precedes other proclitics, cf. Bulg. E.g.:—

Не се прави тоа никогаш	= That is never done

The auxiliary verb ќе, used for forming the Future tense and a form of Conditional, etc., is always proclitic; it precedes pronominal proclitics, e.g.:—

Ќе дојде	= He will come
Ќе му речам нему	= I will tell him

The interrogative particle ли is always enclitic (only) and precedes other enclitics, e.g.:—

Работи ли Петар?	= Is Peter working?
Ви дава ли леб?	= Does he give you bread?

The verb сум when used as an auxiliary verb is always enclitic or proclitic, e.g.:—

Сте биле } Вие сте биле }	= (They say, or we hear) you have been

The negative не is *usually* proclitic; it *sometimes takes the stress*, e.g.:—

Не ра̀збирам	= I do not understand

but—

нè сакам	= I do not want

When не occurs with an auxiliary verb, the interrogative particle ли, and two proclitic pronouns, the order is: negative, aux. verb, ли, Dat. pronoun, Acc. pronoun. E.g.:—

Не сум ли му се јавил?	= Did I not let him know?
Не сум ли му го дал?	= Have I not given it to him?

---

[1] See pp. 183-186.

Monosyllabic conjunctions and prepositions are usually proclitic; but they may also attract the accent—the prepositions[1], before Personal Pronouns and before nouns without the article in adverbial expressions, e.g.:—

У̀дри ме си̍лно по̀ глава	= Strike me hard on (the) head
Еден ден дошла ка̀ј него мечката	= One day the bear came to him
Јагленарот немал што да̀ прави	= The charcoal burner had no choice (lit. had not what to do)

(See Text No. II—accented.)

TEXTS

(Printed as in the source used)

I. Од Лука, VIII.
   5. излезе сејач да сее семе; и кога сееше, едно падна покрај патот и беше изгазено, и птиците небески го исколваа;
   6. а друго падна на камен, па штом никна се исуши, оти немаше влага;
   7. едно пак падна меѓу трње; и израснаа трњето, па го задушија;
   8. а друго падна на добра земја, и кога изникна, донесе стократен плод. Зборувајќи го ова, извика: кој има уши да слуша, нека чуе.

II. Folk tale (народна прикаска) accented by K. Кепески

ЈАГЛЕНАРОТ И МЕЧКАТА

Си би́л еден ја́гленар и жи́веел в пла́нина. Еден де́н до́шла ка́ј него една ме́чка што си ја набо́дила но́гата на гло́гов тр́н. Но́гата на ме́чката и́ би́ла гнојо́сана од тр́нот. Кога до́шла кај јагле́нарот, по́чнала да ја кре́ва болната́ нога како да са́ка да му ка́же: ја бо́ли но́гата и го мо́ли да и́ по́могне. Јагле́нарот ра́збрал што сака ме́чката, се при́ближил до́ неа и и́ го и́звадил тр́нот. На ме́чката и́ поми́нала но́гата. О́ттога се спријате́лиле јагле́нарот и ме́чката и живе́еле за́едно.

---

[1] со and во only take the accent when written together with a noun and forming an adverb: со̀сила = by force, во̀двор = outside.

Една но́ќ, како што спи́еле ме́чката и јагле́нарот за́едно, јагле́нарот ќе и́ ре́че на ме́чката: „Их, мори ме́цо, ко́лку ти смрди зди́вот". Ме́чката ни́што не му одгово́рила, ту́ку му ре́кла: „Зе́ми ја се́га секи́рана и у́дри ме си́лно по́ глава. Ако не го́ стори́ш то́а, ќе те и́зедам". Јагле́нарот не́мал што да́ прави и го сто́рил о́на што му ре́кла ме́чката. На гла́вата на ме́чката и́ на́правил го́лема ре́занка. После, ме́чката си о́тишла и не се вра́тила за до́лго вре́ме кај јагле́нарот.

Поми́нале мно́гу го́дини. Еден де́н се сре́ле па́к ме́чката и јагле́нарот. То́гај ме́чката го натера́ла јагле́нарот да ви́ди по гла́вата дали се по́знава не́каква тра́га од секи́рата. Јагле́нарот по́гледал и ре́кол дека ни́што не се по́знава. А ме́чката ќе му ре́че то́гај: „Е́те, ви́диш, секи́рата тра́га не о́стави; ами што ми ре́че дека ми смрди зди́вот, у́ште го ду́мам". То́гај ско́кна и го и́зеде јагле́нарот.

III. Folk poem (народна песна)

„Рачај, порачај, бела Бојано: сега сум овде, утре ќе одам, утре ќе одам туѓа туѓина. Рачај, порачај, што да ти пратам, ал' пари сакаш, ал' книга сакаш?"
„Ни пари сакам, ни книга сакам, и јас си сакам овде што нема, овде што нема таму што има, таму што има до три биљбиља, до три биљбиља рано што пеат: првиот пее за вечерање, вториот пее за легнување, третиот пее за станување!
„Ај вечерајте, две луди млади, две луди млади, две неженети!"
„Ај легнете си, две луди млади, две луди млади, две неженети!"
„Ај станете си, две луди млади, две луди млади, две неженети!"
Ах, да би знала тој што ми пее, рано што пее за вечерање, јас ќе го ранев со топен шеќер. Ах, да би знала тој што ми пее, рано што пее за легнување, јас ќе го ранев со суво грозје. Ах, да би знала тој што ми пее, рано што пее за станување, јас ќе го ранев отров и катран!"

MACEDONIAN

IV. Константин Миладинов (*modernized spelling*)

ТАГА ЗА ЈУГ

Орелски крилја как' да си метнех,
и в наши страни да си прелетнех!
На наши места ја да си идам,
да видам Струга, Кукуш да видам;
да видам дали сонце и тамо
мрачно угрева, како и вамо.

Ако как' овде сонце ме стрети,
ако пак мрачно сонцето свети;
на пат далечни ја ќе се стегнам,
и в други страни ќе си побегнам,
каде сонцето светло угрева,
каде небото ѕвезди посеваат.

Овде е мрачно, и мрак м' обвива,
и темна магла земја покрива;
мразои и снегои, и пепелници,
силни ветришта, и вијулици;
околу магли и мразои земни,
а в гради студои, и мисли темни.

Не, ја не можам овде да седам:
не, ја не можам мразои да гледам:
дајте ми крилја ја да си метнам,
и в наши страни да си прелетнам,
на наши места ја да си идам,
да видам Охрид, Струга да видам.

Тамо зората греи душата;
тамо дарбите—природна сила
со сета раскош ги растурила:
бистро езеро гледаш белеи
и си од ветер сино темнеи;
поле погледниш или планина,
сегде божева е хубавина.

Тамо по срце в кавал да свирам,
сонце да зајдва, ја да умирам.

V. Венко Марковски

АЛТАНА

Кој не ја видел Алтана?
Кому не памет свртела,
Алтана — алтан на грло,
Алтана — жива приказна!

Една е мома Алтана,
на лице — пупка трендафил,
на снага — стројна калина,
на мерак — огин разгорен!

Седи ли — гори земјата,
гледа ли — рани отвара,
мине ли — луња планинска,
пее ли — мртви скорива!

Кога се Алтана родила,
три пати зора зорила,
три пати светот се менил,
три пати рајот с' отворил.

Пролет ѝ била постела,
горска ја срна доила,
ангели песни пеале,
над неа солнце греало!

Кој не ја видел Алтана?
Кому не срце однела? —
Женети венец фрлаат,
ергени горат за неа!

VI. Коста Рацин

ТУТУНОБЕРАЧИТЕ

На кантар студен со туч го мерат
и можат ли да го измерат
нашиов тутун — нашава мака,
нашава солена пот!

Од темни зори на утрини летни
до никоја доба на вечери зимни
тој гладно пие тагата наша
и потта и крвта и снагата ни.
Жолт — жолти прави лицата бледни
и жолта гостинка у градите носи.

По утрини росни, по мугрите пресни
наведени ничкум по полињата родни
зачмаени ние го береме.
Лист по лист кини,
лист по лист нижи,
лист по лист превртуј, притискај,
лист по лист милно, таговно реди
и на долга низа од капки пот
и надеж со клетва и зелена јад,
со корав поглед на очите матни
по кревките лисја жолтозлатни
прикаска горка на живот клет
нанижи безгласна а така јасна.

Та не знаеш ли?
Денот ли дојде тој да се мери —
мерка му нема, а в градите длаби
без да се запре, без дно да најде
не тага а клетва, и в очите матни

и не сакајќи сама се дига
фуријата.

Кантарот носи лисјето златно
а в гради луто далгите беснат
на жолтата мака — на жолтиот тутун
на жолтата пот на раците ни!

VII. Коле Неделковски

ВРАЌАЊЕ

О страдна земјо јунашка,
одбради образ набразден,
одви и срце поврати
од лути рани вековни.

Еве ти чеда, погледни,
радоста твоја, мајчице,
со очи полни правдини,
гордост за свет и светлина.

Зошто, ох, така немееш,
уште ли не си верует,
или ти сила истина,
мајчински да нè погледнеш?

Разбрав, о грозна грешнице,
мајка на црни сираци,
земја на коски прснати
од борци — млади јунаци.

А за нас, мајко, не прашам —
гладни и голи скитници —
колку си горка тлеала,
колку си отров голтнала.

Ај нека тија останат —
темни и стари времиња,
а сега гради разгрни,
својте си чеда прибери.

И викни, мајко, извикај,
радост и песни истури
за твојте гладни сираци,
за твојте клети скитници.

VIII. Гого Ивановски

ВО СЕЛСКАТА СОБА

Миризма топла од пченичен леб
на сачот што се пече,
те гали во гради, те опива сет,
во тиха, заспана вечер.

Во ламбата мижи, потрепнува плам,
на софра грав се пари,
а селанец корав започнува пак,
приказни стари, стари.

Расправа како во нивјето клас
при ветрец тих се љушка,
а топол ко оран неговиот глас,
чиниш божем те гушка.

И петлите дури не запеат пак,
тој збор по збор ќе ниже —
приказна јасна ко дневниот зрак,
жива ко мајчини грижи.

IX. Славко Јаневски

СВАТОВСКА

Во село ми, во село ми
ситно оро виловито,
надвишило класје класој,
срп се сплеткал в тешко жито.

Натежнале зрели црешни,
искршиле сочни гранки,
и прокапал мед од саќе
на момини топли дланки.

Грозје зрее, сокој лее,
сонце-свадбар дели злато,
закитува бели дреи
на жетвари, селски сватој.

Во село ми, во село ми
свадбената песна снови,
нараснале над јасики
двокатници наши нови.

Се сокриле бели ѕидој
под тутунски низи тешки,
од погачи, од погачи
вршниците раснат жешки.

Гиздав младич по лозјата
наточува рујно вино,
бело моме дарој ткае
в лененово поле сино.

Блеат трла, амбар стежнал,
свадба слави село збрано,
под сватовско крилно знаме
мине оро разиграно.

X. Блаже Конески

ОХРИД

1.
Ој разбуди се, росо девојче,
ти да погледаш долу полено,
како е поле раззеленето,
и по полето бели сватови —
коњи виловни што разиграле,
песна сватовска што запеале.

— Ој та не ми е поле широко,
поле широко раззеленето.
Ој туку ми е сино езеро,
сино езеро разлелеано.

Ој та не ми се бели сватови,
ој туку ми се бели бранови.

Ој та не ми е песна сватовска,
ој туку ми е песна жалосна.

Шуми езеро, играј езеро,
летај, галепче белокрилесто,
Летај долетај мене на рака,
да те затоплам на бели гради!

2.
Три дена веќе езерото,
три ноќи пее бурна песна,
како во чуден занес сето,
како во игра страсна и бесна
бучи и јачи,
клика и плачи!

О таква сила! Да можеш така
во занес бескрај сет да тонеш!
Да можеш таков глас да имаш,
над бурни водје да заѕвони,
од сури ридје да се рони!

XI. Блаже Конески

ЗА МАКЕДОНСКАТА ЛИТЕРАТУРА

Кога треба кратко да се определи состојбата на македонската литература, првата мисла ми е да побарам формулација за едно чувство што не е само мое субјективно, ами претставува вистински плод на нашиот литературен процес. Тоа е чувството на интимен допир со јазичната материја, чувството на податливост на јазикот, би рекол дури—на онаа галовност на говорот што нè обзема во својата полнота. Не е тоа, се разбира, некое посебно откритие—секој творец го доживеал тоа во некаков вид, па макар доживувањето и да не го

подбудило да размислува за појавата. Но тоа чувство
е особено изразито во почетокот на создавањето на
една литература, и тогаш тоа има подлабоко значење—
знак е за нејзиното зреење.

Зошто кај нас, како и другаде, спонтано се почна
од народната поезија? Кажувањето облагородено од
силата на уметничкиот чин е онаа атмосфера што творецот треба да ја чувствува околу себе за да може и
самиот да создава. Слухот на нашиот поет беше природно привлечен од звукот на единствениот извор на
уметничкиот збор во нашиот јазик. Малку подалеку од
него уште траеше тишината. Но на тоа блажено место
можеше да се задржиме само многу кратко време. Требаше да ја разбудиме тишината, со полна вера во нови-
те созвучја што таа ни ги ветува. Тоа што ние го
направивме за изминативе десетина години, нас самите
нѐ богати со животно чувство на полифоничноста на
нашиот уметнички јазик, нашиот слух е веќе обземен од
неа. Не можеше, се разбира, за тоа време да се
постигне којзнае колку, но самото тоа чувство е дра-
гоцено, оно не се губи ами се продолжува, се предава
како по законот на споените садови. Би го спoредил
по тоа чувство македонскиот поет со човек што, учејќи
да плива, одеднаш првпат сетува дека морето го држи
на површината, го сетува милувањето на брановите.
Јазикот нѐ прима, ни ги открива значи своите својст-
ва, не е мимолетен звук, ами богата сушност што нѐ
опфаќа и нѐ исполнува со своето бучење.

Можеби ќе речат дека сум премногу опфатен од
таа една мисла, кога велам дека сите различни
настојувања на литерарното поле кај нас за последниве
неколку години вредат пред сѐ толку колку што беа во
служба на узревањето на тоа чувство. Под непосредно
влијание на литерарните борби во другите југословен-
ски центри но, се разбира, и во согласност со законо-
мерноста на нашиот книжевен процес, се поведоа темпе-
раментни спорови, се истакнаа ознаките на „реализмот"
и „модернизмот". Многу`нешто во тие спорови не спаѓа
во литературата. А тоа што спаѓа во неа, па и кога
ќе се обележи со ознаки кои и другаде се употребу-
ваат, не е сосем истото—зашто ѝ е потчинето и, во
својата сушност, мора да ѝ биде потчинето на основ-
ната задача што неминовно ја налага овој момент од
нашиот литературен развиток: постигање на споменатото
чувство на полнота и податливост на јазичната материја, на она, би рекол, роење на уметнички облагоро-
дени звуци кои го привлекуваат слухот на творецот и
му овозможуваат да се откине од јазичниот прав на
делничноста. Поинаку, значи, ја поставува таа работа
кај нас фактот што требаше да се постигне првпат тоа
чувство во еден нов литературен јазик.

XII. С. Шарски

ШАР ПЛАНИНА

Ако тргнеме од нашиот главен град Скопје кон запад со малечкото влакче, што ги соединува градовите на северна и западна Македонија—Тетово, Гостивар, Кичево, Струга и Охрид—скоро ќе навлеземе по Дервенскиот Провлак. Овој провлак ја дели Жеденската Планина од Сува Гора. Провлакот е тесен и многу пречи на погледот. Но кога ќе го минеме селото Групчин, ние ќе видиме дел од голема и висока планина. А штом ќе излеземе од Дервенскиот Провлак, пред нашите очи наеднаш се открива една чудесна и неописно убава слика. Пред нас се испречува целата Шар Планина. Нашите очи гледаат и не можат да ѝ се начудат на височината и на убавината на таа наша македонска планина, за која толку многу се пее во нашите народни песни.

Гледаш, но срцето ти тупка од радост и гордост и не знаеш на што повеќе да го задржиш својот зачуден поглед: дали на рамното како морско огледало и плодородно Тетовско Поле, што изгледа како цветна градина, дали на острите врвови Љуботен, Кобилица, Турчин, Војводица и други, што гордо се издигаат дури до облаците; или пак на прочуените шарски гори. Сите тие убавини на природата ја исполнуваат твојата душа со чиста и возвишена радост и ти не можеш да не се осетиш горд оти си се родил како син на убавата и славна македонска земја....

XIII. Јован Бошковски

From the story „РАСТРЕЛ"

Надвор есенското зајдисонце ги златеше крошните од високите буки. Низ плитарите на котарот се цедеше слаба светлина, што полека се промрежуваше, толку полека, што на Иља му се чинеше дека никогаш нема да се стемни а да дојде стариот бач, кого тој со душа го чекаше да му каже што станува во планината.

Кога чкрапна вратничето, беше веќе мрак. Иљо олеснето се издиши и за миг заборави на своите тегобни мисли, постана од сламеното легало. Сламата шушна. Во темницата одвај се насираше малата приведена фигура од старчето, но гласот јасно му го чу: тој ги тераше овците в котар.

— Ти си, стрико Танасе?

— Јас сум...Еве, сега ќе го запалам виделничено.

Чкртна чкорче. Мало жолтникаво пламенче ја процепи темнината и затрепка светлина по благото лице на старецот покриено со снежно-бела брада. Сенката му заигра по ѕидот, голема и трепкава и кога старецот појде да го земе виделничето, сенката му порасна, се извиши дури до исчадените греди. После се доближи до него со запалено виделниче в рака, мил и поднасмеан како секогаш:

— Е, се крепиш ли?...

— Арен сум сега. Туку ми здодеа на едно место. И знаеш—јас не сум за седење. Уште ли се штураат наваму? Нема ли да скршат глава?... — нетрпеливо одговори Иљо и се загледа во стариот планинец, чекајќи од него да чуе нешто.

А тој спокојно се готвеше да си врши работа.

— Потрај малу, додека ги измолзам овцине... — одговори старецот и се сврте кон котарот, од каде што допираше блеење и овците нетрпеливо подаваа глави преку плетот.

Стрико Танас отиде покроце, а со него зашета и виделото. Иљо остана пак по темница, сам, со своите мисли. Шуркањето на млекото, гласот на старецот што си збореше нешто со овците, нивното блеење, го нишкаше пријатно в сон и го враќаше со мисли далеку, во деновите на неговото детинство. Потклекнат, стариот бач ги молзеше овците покроце, без брзање, како во таа работа да се криеше некаква чудна милина. Кога сврши и пак пријде, Иљо се поткрена до половина во легалото, се протегна, а во жилите му заструи крвта. Зачека.

— Е?...

— На, напи се. Ти, безбели си гладен? — место одговор му принесе стрико Танас каленица со пресно млеко, што уште се пенеше, шумеше и слатко мирисаше на некосена трева. Иљо го испи наеднаш, со големи голтки. Со нескриена радост сети како по снагата му се разлеа свежа струја. Полека му се враќаше старата сила.

SECTION 4. SERBOCROATIAN

INTRODUCTION

The remarkable beauty of the Serbocroätian language finds its parallel in the remarkable character of the people of Yugoslavia who speak it. By their fearless decision to resist in the spring of 1941, with no other result in prospect but that of untold suffering and certain disaster, they wrote a heroic page in the history of human courage.

Serbocroätian could be defined roughly as the language of the Slav inhabitants of the western half of the broad part of the Balkan peninsula, i.e. the greater part of modern Yugoslavia, whose inhabitants immigrated there about the sixth century A.D. Despite differences of dialect, regional names, religion, and varying historical fortunes, it should be emphatically stated that the language of Serbia, Croätia, the Voivodina (to the north of the Sava and the Danube), Bosnia, Herzegovina, Dalmatia, and Montenegro, is mutually intelligible without previous study or preparation, and for this reason alone the union of these peoples in 1918 was not a fortuitous or illogical event. Together with Slovenian, Macedonian and Bulgarian, as well as Old Slavonic, Serbocroätian forms the South Slav group of languages. Owing to the greater divergences of Bulgarian and Macedonian, some philologists class them as East S. Slav, as opposed to Serbocroätian and Slovenian, which they call together West S. Slav.

The beauty of the sound of Serbocroätian will be found in its system of five simple, clear vowels, which do not vary according to the position of the stress in the word, and in its clear consonants (only a few of which are palatalized). These give a forceful and virile impression, while the mobile "musical" accent, occurring mostly early in the word, and the varying vowel lengths give the language a unique lilt and pattern of changing pitch which charms the ear. At one of the historic Slavonic conferences, Serbocroätian was voted the most pleasant-sounding Slav tongue. Professor Jopson has also described it as "the most beautiful, yet manly, of the Slav tongues".

The purest tradition of the Serbocroätian language was preserved through historical times in the famous folk ballads and folk stories which were handed down orally but not systematically recorded till Vûk Kàradžić undertook this task at the beginning of the nineteenth century. But the literary language of the previous periods was not modelled on this tradition, being first written in a Serbianized form of Church Slavonic. During the dark days of Turkish subjugation, Dalmatia, though from 1409 largely ruled by Venice, kept the torch burning together with the reformer and counter-reformation writers of Croätia and Bosnia. One of the most outstanding writers of this period is Ìvan Gùndulíć, 1589-1638, a native of the free city of Dubrovnik—better known in English as the Ragusan Republic. Later, in the eighteenth century, the persecution under Maria Theresa caused the Serbs under her rule to look to Russia for salvation. The influence of the Russian teachers sent out to help them brought about the strong admixture of Russian Church Slavonic to the literary language of the time, and produced the terrible hybrid "slavjanoserbski" language of the eighteenth century.

The first writer effectively to combat these corrupt tendencies in the literary language was Dosìtej Obrádovíć, 1742-1811, a scholar and a widely travelled man who visited England and was a great admirer of Addison and Steele. But he was in an unfortunate position, because in combating the Russian influence on the language he seemed to be combating the one political power that was prepared to support his people during their persecution under Austria and Turkey. Despite his convictions and efforts, Obradovíć did not wholly succeed in freeing his own writings from the largely ecclesiastical literary traditions of his time. He prepared the way; and one can note in passing, he was the first writer to use the letter ћ for the sound ć [t͡ɕ].

The greatest work of linguistic and literary reform was done by Vûk Stefánovíć Kàradžíć, 1787-1864, who was taught and inspired by the "romantic" nationalist ideas of Jèrnej Kopìtar, the Slovene scholar and writer who worked as a censor for the Austrian government. He believed that the only genuine living language was the language of the common people, the speech of "the ploughman and the digger", and this language he regarded as the only rightful model for the literary medium of the Yugoslavs. Furthermore, he advocated that one should "write as one speaks", and to this end reformed the spelling on a purely phonetic basis, and even simplified the Serbian alphabet, abolishing certain letters and adopting finally six new ones: ђ, ј, љ, њ, ћ, џ, thereby crystallizing the efforts at orthographical reform of such people as Sòlaríć and Mŕkalj. His first *Grammar of the Serbian Language, written according to the speech of the common people*, appeared in 1814, and the first edition of his Serbian dictionary appeared in 1818, giving some 26,000 words with copious explanations, especially of expressions in folklore. Both these works were subsequently greatly expanded. He visited Russia and Germany, and lived much of his time in Vienna, and all the while was tirelessly collecting and editing the folk ballads and folk stories and proverbs of his people, encouraged and aided by Kopîtar and travelling round the Yugoslav districts when his means would allow. By his reforms he made many literary enemies, but in his later years his reputation became international, although he had no academic training; and he received subsidies from the Russian and Serbian governments to carry on his work. The final edition of his folk ballads, nine volumes, did not start appearing till 1891, after his death.

In Croátia a similar work of linguistic and literary reform was carried out by Ljůdevit Gâj, 1809-1872, who was inspired and encouraged by the two great Czechoslovak Slavophils, the poet Jân Kollár and the scholar P. J. Šafarík. His aim was to create a uniform "Illyrian" language for all western Yugoslavs, to awaken their national consciousness and help the spread of education and the cultural defence of his people, dominated at the time by alien powers. In 1836, in his *Illyrian National Newspaper* and his *Illyrian Morning Star* (Dànica Ìlirska) he finally chose the *je-* version of the *što* dialect as the most fitting medium for the literary language, the same dialect as that chosen by Vûk Kàradžić and one of the most widely spoken in the Yugoslav lands. His orthographical reforms were based on Czech models, supplemented by the suggestions of Bàbukić; using the Latin alphabet with diacritical signs, he introduced a phonetic spelling exactly corresponding to that introduced by Vûk for Cyrillic. Thus he helped the Croäts to give up their local dialect as a literary medium and enter a far wider field. His movement had such a great success that in 1843 the Austro-Hungarian authorities put a ban on the name "Illyrian" and suppressed his paper and the movement it stood for. Gâj, who was not a political revolutionary but always tried to live as a law-abiding citizen, was forced to live in obscurity and poverty till his death in 1872. But his great work had already been accomplished—the literary and cultural fusion of the peoples of Yugoslavia.

The final seal to this work was set by the so-called Vienna Literary Agreement (Bečki književni dȍgovor) in 1850, when all the leading Yugoslav scholars of the time, including both Vûk and Gâj, met in Vienna and agreed on the final adoption of a common literary language on the following basis: the adoption of a single dialect in its unadulterated form rather than a composite language embodying the features of several dialects; this dialect was to be the *je*-version of the *što* dialect, already mentioned above, the most widely spoken dialect except in Serbia. In it the letter *h* was to be preserved, although mute in some dialects, and the vocalic *r* sound was to be written as just *r*. Further details in the work of the *rapprochement* and unification of the Serbocroätian language were subsequently completed, most notably by the Serbian scholar, Đúro Dàničić, a pupil of Vûk, and by Tóma Màretić, a distinguished professor of Zagreb University and author of a standard work on the language.

Since 1918, we have witnessed a period in which the fusion of the main dialects can be regarded, for all practical purposes, as complete: the language can be written either in the Latin alphabet or in Cyrillic, in either the *je*- or *e*-variety of the *što* dialect, which are mutually intelligible straight away; and, although the two alphabets *seem* to create a chasm of difference, these scripts can be simply and directly transcribed from one to the other. Purist tendencies have been strong, aiming at the elimination of foreign loan-words, especially those of eastern origin. But the foreigner, and especially the Slavist, cannot help observing with some surprise the fewness of the borrowings from the kindred Slavonic languages in comparison with the numerous western loan-words for the commonest things of everyday life. Some of the most meritorious work in the ordering and garnering of the language in this period has been done by the eminent Serbian scholar, Professor A. Bélić.

In recent years movements have started in favour of recognizing regional varieties of Serbocroätian as separate languages, notably Croätian, Bosnian, Montenegran, as distinct from Serbian. At this stage we can only register the facts that all these varieties of language are mutually intelligible and that only two distinct literary variants and traditions are recognizable, the eastern one of Serbia centring on Belgrade and using the *ekavština* variant of the *što* dialect, and the western one of Croätia, centring on Zagreb, which uses the *ijekavština* variant of the same *što* dialect.

THE SERBOCROATIAN ALPHABETS—CYRILLIC AND LATIN

Cyrillic. Latin Script.   Approx. English equivalent.

Cyrillic	Latin	Approx. English equivalent
A a	A a	(more open and forward than) *ah*
Б б	B b	*b*
В в	V v	*v*
Г г	G g	*g* in "go".
Д д	D d	*d* (dental)
Ђ ђ	Đ đ or Dj dj[1]	*d* in "due" approaching *j*.
E e	E e	*e* in "met"; long *e* = *ê* in Fr.*êtê*.
Ж ж	Ž ž	*s* in "pleasure", *zh*.
З з	Z z	*z*
И и	I i	*ee* in "meet".
J j	J j	*y* in "yes" and "boy".
К к	K k	*k* (unaspirated)
Л л	L l	*l* in "let" (never as in "all").
Љ љ	Lj lj	*ly-*, *li* in "million".
М м	M m	*m*
Н н	N n	*n* (alveolar)
Њ њ	Nj nj	*ny-*, *n* in "new".
O o	O o	*o* in "for".
П п	P p	*p* (unaspirated)
Р р	R r	*r* rolled.
С с	S s	*s* in "see".
Т т	T t	*t* (dental)
Ћ ћ	Ć ć	*t* in "tune" approaching *ch* in "church".
У у	U u	*u* in "rule".
Ф ф	F f	*f*
Х х	H h	*h* or *ch* in "loch".
Ц ц	C c	*ts* in "bits", i.e. pronounced together.
Ч ч	Č č	*ch* in "church" with the tongue farther back.
Џ џ	Dž dž	*j* in "jam" with the tongue farther back.
Ш ш	Š š	*sh*

Latin Order:—A, B, C, Č, Ć, D, Dž, Đ, E, F, G, H, I, J, K, L, Lj, M, N, Nj, O, P, R, S, Š, T, U, V, Z, Ž.

It will be seen that the Serbian Cyrillic alphabet is an adaptation of the Old Slavonic with the following new letters (see above): Ђ, J, Љ, Њ, Ћ, Џ.

[1] In the Latin alphabet, *dj* for *đ* has now become old-fashioned. The letters ļ for *lj*, ń for *nj*, and ǵ for *dž* have not been generally adopted, although used in certain learned works.

The following O.S. letters are not used in Serbian Cyrillic:—

ѕ, і, ћ (for palatal g), оу (in this form), ѡ, щ, з, ы, ь, ѣ, ю, ꙗ, ѥ, ѧ, ѫ, ѩ, ѭ, ξ, ψ, θ, υ.

Russian letters not used in Serbian are:—

ё, й, щ, ъ, ы, ь, э, ю, я.

In both alphabets Р = R can be vocalic, i.e. can form a syllable by itself, as in:—

врт = vȓt "a garden".

In rare cases this can occur before another vowel, when a diærisis should be printed:—

гр̏оце = little throat   ỳмр̏о је = he died.

PRONUNCIATION

The Serbian alphabet is one of the most "phonetic" and consistent in Europe, since Vûk Kàradžić made it follow the principles of "one letter per sound" and "write as you speak." For foreigners, however, not knowing the position and the kind of accent required in every word, it is difficult to speak and read correctly. Long vowels also differ slightly in quality from short vowels, notably *e* and *o*, which are more closed when long (see below paragraphs on accents).

All *consonants* are pronounced "hard" except:—

ђ, ј, љ, њ, and ћ.

љ and њ are more palatal than soft л and н in Russian and unlike their Russian counterparts, can have a certain amount of friction when stressed.

ћ and ђ are respectively nearest to Polish *ć* and *dź* (voiced); phon. tɕ, dʑ.

ж and ш are also generally pronounced somewhat palatalized, i.e. with the tip of the tongue against the lower teeth, and with a certain amount of lip-rounding.

For hard ч and џ the lips are even more rounded and the tip of the tongue is raised to the alveolar ridge.

н is regularly pronounced ŋ (= *ng* in "sing") before velars, as in English: e.g. ба̑нка =(financial) bank.

All former double consonants except *jj* are reduced to single ones, and this is reflected in the spelling, e.g.: о̏дани = devoted < оддани, but нȃјјачи = the strongest.

The same occurs in pronunciation (only) when one word ends and the next begins with the same consonant, e.g.:—

на пр̑во(м) мȅсту = in the first place

where the first м is not pronounced.

I. Assimilation of consonants in respect of voicing (this does *not* occur in combinations with the sonants р, л, љ, м, н, њ, в and ј) is regularly reflected in the spelling of words, e.g.:—

    Ср̏бин = a Serb, but ср̑пски = Serbian
    на́тпис (<надпис) = inscription
    тȅшко (Nom., Acc. Sing. Neut.) = difficult,
      but masc. те́жак
    дру̏кчијӣ = different (<другчији)
    нѝска (Nom. Sing. fem.) = low, but masc. нѝзак
and то̀бџија = gunner, cf. топ = a gun, cannon
    свȁгдањӣ = daily (<свак-)
    збо̏гом = goodbye! (<с бо̏гом)
    зȁдужбина = endowment (<зȁ ду̑шу)
    свѐдоџба = certificate cf. сведо̀чити = to witness

In word juncture, although it occurs in pronunciation, it is not shown in spelling, e.g.:—

    ко̀д куће, pron. ко̀т‿куће, phon. ˌkot kut͡ɕe = at home
    бе̑з пушке, phon. ˌbes‿puʃke = without a rifle
    с бра̏том, phon. z bratom = with (his) brother
    с ђа̑ком, " z‿d͡ʑakom = with a pupil
    о̀тац га је.., phon. ˌotad͡z‿ga‿je = his father -d him

Only д is retained in spelling before с, ш in the latest orthography, e.g.:—

    пре́дседник = president
    грȁдски = city (adj.)
    одше́тати = to go walking off
    сро̀дство = kinship

II. Assimilation of consonants with regard to place of articulation occurs and is shown in the spelling of words

1. When с and з change to ш and ж before the palatal and formerly palatal affricates and fricatives ћ, ђ, ш, ж, ч, џ, e.g.:—

    лѝшће = leaves, from лӣст = leaf
    гро̑жђе = grapes, from гро̑зд = a bunch of grapes
    па̏шче = little dog, from па̏с = dog

ишárати = to colour (<исш- > ишш- with reduction
           of double consonant)
ражárити = to make to glow (<разж- > ражж- with
           reduction of double consonant)

2. When н changes to м before the labials б and п,
e.g.:—

    о̀брамбен = defensive
    прѐхрамбен = nutritional
    цр̀мпураст = swarthy

This feature does not occur in many compound words,
e.g.:—

    jеда̀нпӯт = once
    ва̀нбра̄чнӣ = illegitimate

III. Final voiced consonants are normally pronounced
voiced, as in Ukrainian, e.g.:—

    бре̂г   phon. bre:g   = hill
    гра̂д   phon. gra:d   = city
    га̀леб   phon. 'galeb   = seagull
    му̂ж   phon. mu:ʒ   = husband
    же̂ђ   phon. ʒe:ʨ   = thirst
    ве̂з   phon. ve:z   = embroidery

All the *vowels* have roughly the same quality, whether
under the accent or not, and can all form diphthongs
with *j*, e.g.:—

    га̂j = wood   бо̂j = fight
    хеj! = hey!   ку̀пуj = buy!
    би̂j! = beat!

    The "soft vowels" of Russian are rendered by the
corresponding "hard vowel" preceded by *j* (or љ or њ),
e.g.:—

бjесно̀ћа = fury   љу̂т = angry   jа̂ = I
љѐто = summer   ња̀кати = to bray   jу̀г = south

THE ACCENTS

    (The following general rules apply to vocalic *r*
as well as to all the five vowels.)
    The accent (and stress) in Serbocroatian can fall
on any syllable of a word except the last. Moreover,
it can vary in position in the course of declension or
conjugation, e.g.:

брȇг	= hill	плѐтēм	= I weave
брȇгу	Loc. sing.	плетémo	= we weave
брȅгови	Nom. plur.	dȃм	= I give (Pfve.)
брегòвима	Dat. Instr. Loc. plur.	dȃмо	= we give (Pfve.)

The stressed syllable or any *subsequent* one can be either long or short; while the stressed syllable can also vary by having an intonation either rising or falling in pitch. There are thus obtained four main varieties of accent, called "musical" because of the rise or fall in pitch:—

       long rising, marked ´
       long falling, marked ˆ
       short rising, marked `, also called
         spȍrī = slow
       short falling, marked ˵, "   "
         bȓzī = fast

The difference between ´ and ˆ is much more clearly audible, than between ` and ˵, and consists in a definite rise or fall on the actual vowel so accented. The ˆ really indicates a considerable fall in pitch preceded by a slight rise, but this rise is observable usually only when the word is in an emphatic position in the sentence. (Sentence intonation naturally modifies the intonation of individual words.) Vondrák has pointed out that ˵ sounds stronger and more abrupt than `, which latter, as also the ´, cause the next syllable quite naturally to be higher in pitch and more smoothly connected.

The two rising accents are intonations newly formed in Serbocroătian, and indicate a shift back by one syllable from the original Slavonic accent, the *position* of which is often preserved in Russian, Ukrainian, Byelorussian, Bulgarian, and Slovenian. This accent shift can be observed in about 75 per cent of Serbocroătian words. The two falling accents can occur *only* on the *first* syllable of words (and can also represent a shifted accent.[1]) Therefore any word accented on any syllable but the first must have one of the two *rising* accents. Monosyllables can bear only one of the *falling* accents. There also occur unaccented words, proclitic and enclitic (conjunctions, prepositions, the negative particle не, the short Personal Pronouns and the auxiliary verbs). However the accent sometimes shifts on to a proclitic when it is followed by a word with one of the *falling* accents.

---

[1] See pp. 329-330 for examples.

Only a demonstration by a native or a gramophone record or tape can give the learner a clear idea of what these intonations sound like in isolated words and in the flow of connected speech. They represent in part a most interesting survival of an ancient feature of Indo-European.

THE DIALECTS OF SERBOCROATIAN

Serbocroätian is divided into three main dialects, rather arbitrarily named after the different word for "what" in each of them, namely *što*, *kaj*, and *ča*, which may be taken to represent the differences of vocabulary between them. But quite considerable differences of accent and accidence also exist. The *kaj* dialect spoken in N.W. Croätia is a transition to Slovenian. The *ča* dialect is confined to N. Dalmatia and certain Adriatic islands, and is slightly more difficult to follow for those knowing standard Serbocroätian (because of its more archaic accent, corresponding in position more nearly to that in Slovenian and Russian, and also because of greater differences in declensions, etc.). The reader will immediately observe that the *što* dialect is by far the most widespread of the three, for it is spoken over the rest of the Serbocroätian-speaking area of Yugoslavia E. and S.E. of these areas.[1]

The *ča* and *što* dialects are subdivided into three subvarieties according to whether the old ѣ is rendered *e*, *je* (or *ije* when long), or *i*: e.g. *vèra*, *vjèra*, or *vĩra* (= faith). The *e* variety of the *što* dialect is used as the literary language of Serbia[1] and most of the Voivodina, while the *je* variety predominates in the rest of the *što* area, including Croätia, Bosnia, and Montenegro, and is also the language of the greater part of the older Serbian literature, including the writings and collections of Vûk Kàradžić. These three sub-varieties especially are mutually intelligible without any real difficulty, just as in English the various pronunciations of *a* and the other vowels present no insuperable obstacle to understanding. It should be noted that the *kaj* dialect has only *e* for former ѣ (ě), like Slovenian.

---

[1]This includes the Kosovo-Resava dialect of E. and S. Serbia, and the more southern dialect called *torlački*, which forms a transition to Macedonian and Bulgarian.

Correspondence of the accents between the e *and* je
sub-dialects.

Whereas both ȅ and ȅ̄ are rendered by *je* bearing the same accent in each instance, e.g.:—

   вȅра (= faith), vjȅra
   сȅдим (= I sit), sjȅdim

the two long accented ȇ and ế are rendered *ȉje* and *ijȅ* respectively, stressing the first or second syllable according to the fall or rise of tone, e.g.:—

   сȇно (= hay), sȉjeno
        but
   рếка (= river), rijȅka

An unaccented ē is rendered *ijē*, e.g.:—

   кȍлēвка (= cradle), kȍlijēvka

But after a consonant + r, *short je* is replaced by *e*, e.g. вријȅме (= time), Gen. sing. врȅмена. There are a number of other instances of the lack of the correspondence outlined above.

In Cyrillic *l* + *j* and *n* + *j* are rendered, of course, by љ and њ, e.g.:—

   љȅто = summer, њȅдра = bosom

t + *j* and *d* + *j* are also sometimes (according to the western dialect) rendered by ћ and ђ, e.g.:—

S. гдjȅ or W. гђȅ = where (*S.* is the literary form.)

Before о, j, and љ, и is used in the *je* dialect instead of je, e.g.:—

   хтȉо je   = he wanted
   смȉjати се = to laugh
   бȉљег   = mark

It should be noted that all three sub-varieties of the *što* dialect can be written in either the Cyrillic or the Latin alphabet in various parts of Yugoslavia, and that the dialects do not generally correspond to the boundaries of the republics or to religious boundaries. The *alphabet* used, on the other hand, is usually an indication of religion, the Cyrillic being preferred by the Orthodox as a matter of tradition.

VOWEL GRADATION AND VOWEL LENGTHENING

The familiar features of vowel gradation or Ablaut and vowel lengthening are both fully alive in

Serbocroatian, e.g.:—

1. Ablaut:—

смр̏т = death у̀мре̄ти = to die умо̀рити = to kill,
да̏х = breath ду̏х = spirit   exhaust
ви̏ти = to wind ве̏нац = wreath
зва̏ти = to call зо̀ве̄м = I call по̏зив = invitation

2. Lengthening:—

одгово̀рити = to answer(Pfve.) одгова́рати = to answer (Impfve.)
у̀мре̄м = I die (Pfve.) у̀мирати = to die (Impfve.)

SLAVONIC CHARACTERISTICS

1. The Metathesis of liquids of O.S. is also a feature of modern S. Slav languages, as well as of W. Slav, in which no "Polnoglasie" exists. Thus:—

вла́да = government бре̑г = hill
мла̑д = young мле́ко = milk
гра̑д = city ра̀бота = labour

2. The 1st Palatalization: к, г, х changing to ч, ж, ш before и, е, e.g.:—

пѐкӯ = they bake Бо̑г = God стра̏х = terror
пѐче = he bakes Бо̏же = Voc. sing. стра̀шити = to terrify

2a. ц and з when originating from к and г respectively, also change to ч and ж, as in the 1st Palatalization, e.g.:—

кне̑з = prince зе̏ц = hare
кне̑же Voc. sing. зе̏че Voc. sing.
кне̑жев Possessive adj. зе̏чица = female hare

The Poss. adj. from the name Ми̏лица is Ми̏личин just as ма̑јка (= mother) has the Poss. adj. ма̑јчин.

3. The 2nd Palatalization: к, г, х changing to ц, з, с before и, when originating from I.E. diphthongs *oi*, *ai*, e.g.:—

ру́ка = hand књи̏га = book
ру́ци Dat., Loc. sing. књи̏зи Dat., Loc. sing.
ву̑к = wolf сиро̀мах = a poor man
ву̑ци Nom. plur. сирома́си Nom. plur.

4. The influence of the *j* element, called in Serbocroatian *jotovanje*.[1] In this language the Comparative adjectives in -ји among other forms afford good examples, e.g.:—

[1] In English: yotation.

к, г, х + ј change to ч, ж, ш:—

  jȃк = strong   дра̏г = dear   ти̏х = quiet
  jȁчи Comp.   дра̀жи Comp.   тѝши Comp.

т, д, + ј change to ћ, ђ[1]:—

    љу̑т = angry   ви̏дети = to see
    љу̏ћи Comp.   ви̏ђен = seen

с, з + ј change to ш, ж:—

  пи́сати = to write   бр̑з = quick
  пи̑ше   = he writes   бр̀жи Comp.

    ве́зати = to bind
    ве̑же   = he binds

л, н + ј change to љ, њ:—

  во̀лети = to like   бра́нити = to defend
  во̀љен = liked   бра́њен = defended

N.B.:— р remains unpalatalized:—

    обо̀рити = to overthrow
    обо̀рен = overthrown

п, б, в, м + ј add љ:—

  љу́бити = to kiss   ста̀вити = to put
  љу́бљен Past Part. Pass.   ста̀вљен Past Part. Pass.
  ма́мити = to entice   то̀пити = to melt
  ма́мљен Past Part. Pass.   то̀пљен Past Part. Pass.

ц + ј changes to ч:—

  ба́цити = to throw   ба̑чен Past Part. Pass.

ст, зд + ј change to шћ, жђ[1]:—

  ли̑ст   = leaf   све̏тлост   = light
  ли̑шће collective plur.   све̏тлошћу Instr. sing.

    гро̑зд = a bunch of grapes
    гро̑жђе = (coll.) grapes

But in older words ст + ј becomes шт:—

  кр̀стити = to baptize   кр̀штен Past Part. Pass.

ск, зг + ј change to шт, жд[1]:—

 и̏скати = to demand   мо̏зак = brain, Gen.sing.мо̏зга
 и̏штем = I demand   мо̏ждани̑ = of the brain, adj.

 хт + ј becomes шћ[1]:—

---

[1] The form of these changes is peculiar to Serbocroätian.

др̀хтати = to tremble   др̀ште̄м = I tremble

сл, сн, зл, зн + *j* change to шљ, шњ, жљ, жњ:—

 ми̏сао = thought, Inst. sing. ми̏шљу
 но̀сити = to wear, cf. но̀шња = costume
 па̀зити = to pay attention, cf. па̀жљив = attentive
 во̀зити = to convey, cf. во̀жња = travelling (in a vehicle)

5. The disappearance of consonants received new prominence in Serbocroatian through the introduction of phonetic spelling. Thus, besides:—

 са̏н = sleep (<root *sup*)
 пото̀нути = to sink (<root *top*)
 плѐла = she was weaving (<*pletla*)

we have

 ср́це = heart, cf. Russ. се́рдце
 ма́сна = greasy (fem.), <ма̄ст = grease
 о̀тац = father, Gen. sing. о́ца
 су́дац = judge: Gen. s. су́ца and су́чев = judge's (adj.) <судчев
 хр̏ва̄т = Croät: хр̀ва̄штина = Croätian language
 го̀дишњӣ = yearly: го̀дӣште a year's produce, issue
 о̀дсуство = absence, leave, < одсутство
 го̀зба = feast, <гостба
 пра̑знӣк = holiday cf. Russ. пра́здник
 на̀прстак = thimble, Gen. sing. на̀прска
 мла̀дӣћкӣ = youthful, <мла̀дӣћ + ски
 ју̀на̄чкӣ = heroic, <ју̀на̄к + ьски
 ју̀на̄штво = heroism, <ју̀на̄к + ьство > јуначтво with dissimilation of ч and т to -шт-

6. Epenthetic *n* is rare, except in the declension of the third person Personal Pronoun (as in other Slavonic languages):—

 о̑н = he
 њѐга = him (emphatic), Acc., also Gen.

FEATURES CHARACTERISTIC OF SERBOCROATIAN

(Those marked * are exclusively Serbocroatian characteristics.)

1.* Common Slav *tj*, *dj* become ћ, ђ respectively, e.g.:—

    све́ћа = candle
    мѐђа = boundary, ро̀ђен = born

2. *t* and *d* dropped before final *o* (formerly final *l*) and before *l*, as in E. and other S. Slav languages, e.g.:—

    па̏о = (he) fell   па̏ла = (she) fell
    пле̏о = (he) weaved пле̏ла = (she) weaved

3. Metathesis of liquids—see above, "Slavonic Characteristics," No. 1.

4. C.S. *kv*, *gv* change to цв, зв respectively (a feature of S. and E. Slav as opposed to W. Slav), e.g.:—

    цве̑т = flower
    зве́зда = star
      cf. Polish—*kwiat, gwiazda*.

5. Labial consonants + *j* add љ, as in Slovenian and E. Slav, e.g.:—

    зѐмља = earth
      cf. Polish—*ziemia*.

6. The C.S. nasal vowels ѧ and ѫ develop into e and y respectively (ѧ as in other S. Slav languages, ѫ as in E. Slav), e.g.:—

пу̑т = way, O.S. пѫть жѐну = woman, Acc.s. O.S. женѫ
ре̏д = order, O.S. рѧдъ ви̑де = they see O.S. видѧтъ

7. C.S. ы develops into и, as in other S. Slav languages, e.g.:—

    ми̑сао = thought си̑н = son
    би̏ти = to be   ти̑ = you (familiar)

8.* Both ъ and ь of C.S. develop into a in strong position:—

па̏с = dog, O.S. пьсь да̑н = day, O.S. дьнь
са̏н = sleep, O.S. сънъ ва̑н = beyond, O.S. вънъ
                                             = out

9.* Three alternative developments of ѣ—see above section on "The Dialects of Serbocroatian".

10.* C.S. vocalic *l̥*, *l̥'*, as well as C.S. lъ, lь, *all* develop into y: e.g.:—

    l̥ ду̑г = debt
    l̥' ву̑к = wolf

    lъ пу̏т f. = human flesh, skin
    lь су̏за = tear

 C.S. vocalic r̥, r̥', as well as C.S. rъ, rь, all develop into Serbocr. vocalic p (r): e.g.:—

    r̥ тр̑г = market
    r̥' пр̏ст = finger
    rъ кр̑в = blood
    rь кр̏ст = cross

 Vocalic r is also to be found in Macedonian, Slovenian, Czech and Slovak.

 11. Final voiced consonants are normally pronounced voiced, as in Ukrainian, e.g.:—

    бре̑г, phon. bre:g = hill
    гра̑д, phon. gra:d = city

See p. 240.

 12. Regressive assimilation of consonants (the Serbocroatian phonetic spelling brings this much more into prominence in writing than the orthography of other Sl. languages, in the *pronunciation* of which this feature is prominent):—

    *povezti is spelt пове̏сти = to convey
    *svatba is spelt сва̏дба = wedding
    *obširan is spelt о̏пширан = exhaustive
   cf. Ср̏бија = Serbia ср̏пскӣ = Serbian

 13.* The Infinitive endings *-gti*, *-kti* become -ћи:—

    мо̏ћи = to be able
    ре̏ћи = to say

 Likewise C.S. ktь, gtь become ћ: но̑ћ = night, мо̑ћ = power

 14. Contraction of vowels with sometimes the first one predominating:—

    мојега > мо̑га = my (Gen. sing. masc.)
    неимам > не̑мам = I have not
    нехоћу > не̑ћу = I will not

 But more frequently the second vowel predominates:—

    зајец > зе̑ц = hare
    појас > па̑с = girdle
    овамо > а̑мо = hither

15.* *a*—the "fill-vowel" in agglomerations of consonants:—

    о̀гањ = fire,   O.S. огнь
    до̏бар = good (masc. s.), O.S. добръ

16. As in other Sl. languages, palatalized consonants generally require to be followed by front vowels, e.g.:—

    гра̀дови = cities

      but

    ци́љеви = aims

Serbocroätian in common with O.S., E. Slav, Slovenian and Slovak, has changed original ѣ after the *chuintantes* ж, ш, ч, into a:—

    бѐжати = to flee

Cf. Czech *běžeti* = to run, but Slovak *bežat'* = to run.

17.* *h* (phon. x) prefixed—this is a characteristic of *spoken* Sbcr.

    хр̀ђав for р̀ђав = bad, ха̀лав for а̀лав = greedy.

18.* въ develops into syllabic у, also as a prefix:—

    у̏ = in
    у̀зе̄ти = to take
    у̀не̄ти = to carry in

The original preposition у is generally rendered код (= by, at the house of, etc.) + Gen.

19. Original palatalized *r* becomes hard, as in Macedonian, Slovak and Byelorussian:—

    ца̀ра = of the king, originally царја
    мо̏ре = sea, O.S. морje

20. Final же becomes pe and then p (cf. Slovenian -*r* for Relative Pronouns, etc.):—

    O.S. ѥже : jѐр = because

21.* Final (in words and syllables) *l* (ł—"dark *l*") becomes o:—

    ку́пио = bought, fem. ку́пила
    вео̀ма = very
    бѐо = white, Nom. sing. masc., fem. бе́ла
    Бео̀град = Belgrade

22.* *h* lost in pronunciation and sometimes in spelling, sometimes replaced by в or j,—an E. Yugoslav characteristic:—

 (х)ла̑д = shade   (х)ла́дан = cold
 му̏ва = fly   (х)ле̏б = bread
 сна̀ја = daughter-   (х)о̀ћу = I will, shall,
     in-law   want

23. Initial ц where other Sl. languages have ч before original vocalic ̦r, as also in Macedonian:—

  цр̑н = black
     Russian: чёрный
     Slovenian: čŕn, Slovak čierny

  цр̑в = worm
     Czech: červ
     Russian: червяк

  цр̀вен = red
     Polish: czerwony
     Bulgarian: червѐн

MORPHOLOGY

Peculiarities of Serbocroatian Morphology (Summary):

(*Denotes features shared with Slovenian.):—

1. Instr. sing. fem. *i*-declension in -и, as an alternative ending to -jy:—

 ко̀сти = with a bone

*2. Gen. sing. and Nom. Acc. plur. fem. *a*-declension in -е, Dat. Loc. sing. in -и:—

 же̏не̄ = of a woman, etc., but жѐне = women
 жѐни = to a woman, etc.

(Cf. also the West Slav languages.)

3. Instr. sing. fem. *a*-declension in -ōм:—

 жѐно̄м

also in Instr. sing. fem. of adjectives, even after soft consonants:—

 вру́ћо̄м (во̀до̄м) = with hot (water)

4. Voc. sing. fem. hard *and* soft *a*-stems both in -о:—

 жѐно = woman!
 зѐмљо = o land!

(In masc. nouns Voc. sing. has -e for hard stems and -y for soft stems:—

    цȁре = emperor!
    кȍњу = horse!)

 *5. The Acc. plur. of masc. *o*-stems in -e, always distinguished from their Nom. plur. in -и:—

    Nom. pl. прȍзори = windows, Acc. pl. прȍзоре
    " " кȍњи = horses   " " кȍње

 6. Gen. plur. in -ā for practically all nouns except fem. *i*-stems:—

    нȃрōдā = of nations
    сȇлā = of villages
    жȇнā = of women

 7. Dat., Instr., and Loc. plur. of declensions of all genders always in -ма, -има for all masc. and neut. *o*-stems (and fem. *i*-stems) and all adjectives, -ама for *a*-stem nouns:—

    прȍзорима = windows
    сȅлима = villages
    ствȃрима = things
    лȇпима = beautiful
    жȅнама = women

 *8. Extended plur. in -ови for masc. hard stems, and in -еви for masc. soft stems:—

    сȕнови = sons
    вȍлови = oxen
    крȁљеви = kings

 9. Collective plural ending -āд (*i*-stem singular declension) used for neuter nouns in -e, denoting human and animal young:—

    ȕнучāд = grandchildren
    пȕлāд = chickens

 10. Survival of the declension of the Indefinite Adjectives (See pp. 269-270 and 272.)

 *11. Generalization of the forms with *n* prefixed for the emphatic (non-enclitic) 3rd person Personal Pronoun (not necessarily with a preposition):—

    њȅга Gen. sing. = of him
    њȕх Gen. plur. = of them

 12. Metathesis of consonants in the word for "all" and cognates:—

Sing. са̏в, сва̏, све̏, Plur. сви̏ = all;
сва̀кӣ = every

*13. Gen. sing. masc. and neut. of Definite Adjectives and pronouns in -*a*, viz. -ora (Slovenian -*ega*):—

дра̑го̄га = dear

14. The possibility of dropping (under certain conditions) the final vowel of adjectives and adjectival pronouns in the Gen., Dat.-Loc. and Instr. sing. masc. and neut. (Definite form for all adjectives), and in the Dat., Instr. and Loc. plur. of all genders (Definite *and* Indefinite forms for adjs.) (See pp. 264-268, 272-273), e.g.:—

Gen. s. m., n.				дра̑го̄г(а) = dear
"	"	"	"	мо̀јег(а), мо̑г(а) = my
Dat., Loc. s. m., n.				дра̑гом(е) or (-у) = dear
"	"	"	"	"	мо̀јем(у) or мо̑м(е) or (-у) = my
Instr. s. m., n.				ти́ме or ти̑м = that
Dat., Instr., Loc. pl.				ти̑ма or ти̑м = that
"	"	"	"	дра̑гим(а) = dear
"	"	"	"	мо̀јим(а) = my

*15. 1st pers. sing. Pres. Ind. for all verbs but two in -м (cf. also Slovak and Macedonian):—

пи̑ше̄м = I write

*16. Loss of final *t* in 3rd p. sing. Pres. (in common with all S. and W. Slav languages, as well as partly in Ukrainian for *e*-verbs):—

су̑дӣ = he judges

*17. 1st pers. plur. Pres., Aor. and Imperf., as well as Imperative in -мо (cf. Ukrainian):—

благосло̀вимо = we bless

*18. 3rd pers. plur. Pres. also without final *t*, as in W. Slav and Slovenian:—

су̑де̄ = they judge
ѝдӯ = they go

19. Future tense compounded with (хо̀)ћу, (хо̀)ћеш, (хо̀)ће; (cf. Bulg. ще, Mac. ќе):—

пи́саћу = I shall write

20. Survival of Aorist and Imperfect tenses, as in Bulgarian, Macedonian and Lusatian.

*21. Loss of declinable Pres. and *Past Active[1] and *Pres. Passive[2] participles.

22. Frequent replacement of Possessive Adjectives by Dat. of corresponding enclitic Pers. Pronoun (so also in Bulgarian and Macedonian):—

    о̀тац му = his father
    ру́ка ми = my hand

THE DECLENSIONS IN SERBOCROATIAN

Nouns

  As in Russian, owing to the disappearance of the *ŭ-* and *ū*-stems, four main types of noun declensions remain:—

    i-stems—all feminine.
    consonant stems—neuter, except for two. (This group, however, in Serbocroätian has taken over the *endings* of the *o*-stems).
    a-stems—mostly feminine.
    o-stems—masc. and neuter.

  The three genders are preserved and all the seven cases of O.S. including the Vocative, which has a form distinct from the Nominative for masc. and fem. nouns in the singular. In the plural, however, the Dat., Instr., and Loc. are identical for each declension. The Dual number, preserved as a grammatical category only in Slovenian and Lusatian of all the modern Slavonic languages, survives in Sbcr. only in isolated examples:—

    о̀чи = eyes
    у̑ши = ears, etc.

  1. *i*-stems, feminine.

  (The masc. *i*-stems have been lost except for the isolated example of пу́тем = along the road, by means of, special Instr. sing. of пу̑т = road, otherwise declined as an *o*-stem.)

    ства̑р = thing

	Sing.	*Plur.*
Nom.	ства̑р	ства̑ри
Gen.	ства̑ри	ства́ри̑

[1] Surviving in Russian, Byelorussian, Czech and Slovak.
[2] Surviving only in Russian.

Dat.	ствȃри	ствȃрима
Acc.	ствȃр	ствȃри
Instr.[1]	ствȃри or -jу	ствȃрима
Loc.	ствȃри	ствȃрима
Voc.	ствȃри	

It will be noted that the Dat., Instr., and Loc. plur. have taken over the old Dat. and Instr. Dual ending, generalizing it for the plural of all nouns.

The form of the Instr. sing. in -jy is preferred when the noun is used by itself, without any qualifying word to indicate the case.

Notice:—

    мȋсао (f.) = thought, Gen. s. мȋсли, but
    смȋсао (m.) = sense, Gen. s. смȋсла (Declension No. 4a)

Notice the alternative Genitive plurals of:

    кȍкōш = hen, Gen. pl. коко̀шиjӯ
    кȍст = bone, Gen. pl. кȍстиjӯ
    ȗш (or вȃш) = louse, Gen. pl. у̀шиjӯ

2. Consonant stems in n and t, neuter, as in Russian. (o-stem endings!)

    пле̏ме = tribe

	Sing.	Plur.
Nom., Voc.	пле̏ме	племѐна
Gen.	племѐна	племе̑нā
Dat.	племѐну	племѐнима
Acc.	пле̏ме	племѐна
Instr.	племѐном	племѐнима
Loc.	племѐну	племѐнима

[1]Fem. nouns in -ост have the alternative Instr. sing. form ending in -шћу owing to the coalescence of the j with the -ст, viz. свȅтлошћу = with light, кȍшћу = with a bone.

Similarly, with yotation:—

    глȃд = hunger, Instr. s. глȃђу
    кр̑в = blood, " " кр̑вљу
    сȏ = salt, Gen. s. сȍли, Instr. s. сȍљу
    зȅлēн = herbs, Instr. s. зȅлēњу
    љу̑бав = love, " " љу̑бављу

and with j dropped after palatals:—

    нȏћ = night, Instr. s. нȏћу
    жȇђ = thirst, " " жȇђу
    о̀битељ = family, " " о̀битељу

Likewise:—

ду̏гме (= button), Gen. sing. ду̏гмета; де́те (= child), Gen. s. дѐтета, Plur. (irreg.) дѐца f. sing. *a*-stem.

не̏бо (= sky) (now an *o*-stem) has an *s*-stem plur.: небѐса. Also чу̏до = a wonder, pl. чудѐса; те̑ло = body, pl. телѐса or те̑ла.

Most nouns in -e denoting young animals have a feminine collective plural in -а̄д:—

те̏ле = calf, Gen. sing. тѐлета, Plur. N.V.A. тела̑д,G.D.I.L. тела̑ди, D.I.L. also тела́дма, but also N.V.A. plur. тѐлићи or тѐоци.

ве̏че̄ = evening, is an irregular *r* consonant stem, usually neut. in the sing., declined like пле̏ме—Gen. s. вѐчера. But sometimes in the sing. and *always* in the plur. it is feminine and declined like ства̑р; Gen. s. and Nom. pl. вѐчери. Only in the greeting can one say: до̀ба̀р вече̄(р) (masc.) as well as до̏бро ве̏че̄ (neut.) = good evening!

др̏во = tree, Gen. s. др̀вета, has plur. Nom. дрвѐта, Gen. дрве́та̄, or collective дрве̑ће which is a neut. sing. *o*-stem; while др̀ва = wood (as material). ја́је = egg, Gen. s. ја̀јета, etc. in sing., but plur. N.V.A. ја́ја, Gen. ја́ја̄, D.I.L. ја́јима.

N.B.—Nom., Voc., and Acc. for all neuter nouns are identical in each number.

The only two surviving fem. consonant stems (*r*-stems) can be regarded as irregular, and are declined as follows:—

ма̏ти = mother[1]   кћи̑ = daughter

	Sing.	Plur.		Sing.	Plur.
Nom.	ма̏ти	ма̏тере (as an		кћи̑	кће̏ри
Gen.	ма̏тере	ма̏тера̄ *a*-stem)		кће̏ри	кће̏рӣ
Dat.	ма̏тери	ма̏терама		кће̏ри	кће̏рима
Acc.	ма̏тер	ма̏тере		кће̑р	кће̏ри
Instr.	ма̏теро̄м	ма̏терама		кће̏ри, кће̏рју	кће̏рима
Loc.	ма̏тери	ма̏терама		кће̏ри	кће̏рима
Voc.	ма̏ти			кће̏ри	

3. *a*-stems, mostly feminine, a few masc. It will be noticed that in Serbocr. as opposed to E. and W. Slav, the endings of the old -*ja* declension (soft *a*-stems) have predominated and become generalized, except in the Instr. and Voc. sing.

---

[1]More commonly: ма̑јка (*a*-stem).

жèна = woman

Nom.	жèна	жèне
Gen.	жèнē	жéнā
Dat.	жèни	жèнама
Acc.	жèну	жèне
Instr.	жèнōм	жèнама
Loc.	жèни	жèнама
Voc.	жèно	жèне

Polysyllabic nouns in -ица have Voc. sing. in -це:—

 гȍспођице = Miss! Мȉлице! (girl's name), but disyllabic nouns and also disparaging appellations have -цо: птȉцо! = bird! пȉјаницо! = drunkard! кȕкавицо! = coward!

Of proper names other than those in -ица only those of two syllables with ´ accent have Voc. sing. in -o:—

 Јêло! but Ра̀дōјка! (girls' names) Ѝлија! (man's name)

Masc. nouns in -a have either -o or -a, except слу́га:—

 вла̀дика! or вла̀дико! = bishop!
 but only слу̂го! = servant!

Nouns in -a denoting relations have Voc. sing. in -a more usually, and for certain nouns—exclusively:—

 ма̀ма! or -o = mummy! but тȅтка! (only) = aunt!

Nouns with stems ending in groups of consonants other than ст, шт, зд, жд, шћ, жђ have a Gen. plur. either in -ā, in which case the elements of the group are usually separated by a second long ā, e.g.:—

 дȅвојка (= girl), Gen. plur. дȅвојāкā

or else they can have a Gen. plur. in -ӣ on the analogy of the i-stems, e.g.:—

 брȅсква = peach, Gen. pl. брȅскви or брȅсāкā
 бо̀рбӣ = of struggles (or бо̂рбā)
 мо̀лбӣ = of petitions (or мо̂лбā)

ру́ка = hand, но̀га = leg, have irregular Gen. plur. (from old Dual forms): ру̀кӯ, но̀гӯ. Similarly: слу́га = servant, G. pl. слу́гӯ or слу́гā.

All *common* nouns with a-stems ending in a velar not preceded by another consonant, change this velar according to the 2nd Palatalization before the final -и of the Dat., Loc. sing., e.g.:—

SERBOCROATIAN

књѝга (= book), Dat. and Loc. sing. књѝзи
ма̑јка (= mother), " " " " ма̑јци
ре́ка (= river), " " " " ре́ци

But к and г are retained before и after ч, ћ, т, ц, с, з and in all proper and affectionate names: hence, тѐтки = to an aunt, се́ки = to little sister, Дра́ги (name); та̏чки (= dot), во̏ћки (= fruit tree), ко̏цки (= dice); да̏ски (= plank), ма̏зги (= mule).

N.B.—Masc. nouns in -*a* are feminine in gender in the plural.

4*a*. *o*-stems, masculine. Here the hard *o*-stem endings predominate, except in the Acc. plur. Nouns ending in the palatalized or formerly palatalized consonants ж, ђ, ј, љ, њ, ћ, ч, ц, ш, and џ retain the soft (*jo*) endings in the Voc. and Instr. sing.

Proper nouns and names ending in -o and -e in the Nom. *and Voc.*, such as Ма̑рко, Мѝлоје, а̏уто, ра̏дио, also follow these models. But in western regions *affectionate* names and nouns, such as Е́ро, Ӥво, по̏бро (= pal) are declined like *a*-stems.

	HARD STEMS		SOFT STEMS	
	про̏зор = window		ко̏њ = horse	
	Sing.	*Plur.*	*Sing.*	*Plur.*
Nom.	про̏зор	про̏зорИ	ко̏њ	ко̏њИ
Gen.	про̏зорa	про̏зо̄рā	ко̏њa	ко̏њā
Dat.	про̏зорУ	про̏зорИМА	ко̏њУ	ко̏њИМА
Acc.	про̏зор	про̏зорe	ко̏њa	ко̏њe
Instr.	про̏зорОМ	про̏зорИМА	ко̏њеМ[1]	ко̏њИМА
Loc.	про̏зорУ	про̏зорИМА	ко̏њУ	ко̏њИМА
Voc.	про̏зорe		ко̏њУ	

Many monosyllables and some other nouns insert the syllable -ов (-ев after soft consonants) before the endings of all the cases of the plural:—

сӣнОВИ = sons, Gen. pl. синȏвā, Dat. Inst. Loc. синȏвима
но̏жеВИ = knives

Velar stems not inserting this syllable change their final consonant according to the 2nd Palatalization before и, e.g.:—

во̏јнӣк = soldier, Nom. pl. во̏јни́ци, Voc. pl. во̏јници!, Dat. pl. војни́цима.

[1] Some nouns with e in the root syllable and stem ending in a palatal consonant nevertheless have Instr. sing. in -ом by a kind of vowel dissimilation, e.g. хмѐљом (=with hops), па́дежом (= by a grammatical case).

цвр̀чак = a cricket; N. pl. цвр̀чци
о̀рах = walnut, N. pl. о̀раси
ко̀вчег = coffer, N. pl. ко̀вчези

In the Voc. sing. their final consonant changes according to the *1st* Palatalization or they have the ending -у:—

во̀јниче! but цвр̀чку!

(See also "Slavonic Characteristics," No. 2*a*.)

Nouns ending in -ин, denoting people belonging to a nation, place or profession, drop the syllable -ин in the formation of the plural (in *all* cases):—

Ср̀бин = Serb Nom. pl. Ср̀би
Ту̀рчин = Turk Nom. pl. Ту̀рци
Бео̀грађанин = Belgrader Nom. pl. Бео̀грађани
чо̀банин = shepherd Nom. pl. чо̀бани

Peculiar to Sbcr. are the masculine nouns ending in -*o*, in which the lost final *l* reappears in the oblique cases:—

во̂ (= ox), Gen. sing. во̀ла.

The characteristic *a* movable vowel appears in many masc. nouns in the Nom. sing. and Gen. plur. only:—

по̀сао = business, Gen. s. по̀сла, Nom. pl. по̀слови or по̀сли, Gen. pl. по̀сло̄ва̄, по̀са̄ла̄ or поса́ла̄
ла́нац = chain, Nom. plur. ла́нци, Gen. plur. ла̄на̄ца̄
мо̀менат or мо̀мент = moment, Gen. plur. момѐна̄та̄
слу̏шалац = listener, G.s. слу̏шаоца, N.pl. слу̏шаоци, G. pl. слу̏шала̄ца̄

When the movable vowel a is dropped in declension before ц or ч, a final т or д in the stem disappears before them:—

о̀тац = father, Gen. s. о̀ца, Voc. s. о̀че, Nom. pl. о̀чеви or о̀цеви
жѐлудац = stomach, Gen. s. жѐлуца
зада́так = task, Gen. s. зада́тка
Pl. Nom. зада́ци, Gen. за̀да̄та̄ка̄, Dat. Instr. Loc. зада́цима

But notice with *long* ā retained in declension, e.g. ју̏на̄к = hero, Gen. s. јуна́ка.

чо̀век = man, Gen. чо̀ве̄ка, Voc. чо̀вече, has a special plural:—

    Nom. Voc. љу́ди, Gen. љу́дӣ, Acc. љу́де,
      Dat. Instr. Loc. љу́дима

1. Other masc. nouns with a Gen. pl. in -ӣ are:

    хва̑т = fathom, G. pl. хва̑тӣ or хва́то̄ва̄
    мра̑в = ant, G. pl. мра́вӣ or -а̄
    цр̑в   = worm, G. pl. цр̑вӣ or -а̄
    ме̏се̄ц = month, G. pl. месе́цӣ or -а̄
    са̑т   = hour, G. pl. са́тӣ or са́то̄ва̄
    па̑р   = pair, G. pl. па́рӣ

2. Notice the alternative forms of Gen. pl. in -ӣ and in -ијӯ (from the old Dual) for го̑ст = guest, G. pl. го̏стӣ or го̏стијӯ; но̀кат = nail, G. pl. нока́та̄ or но̀ктијӯ; пр̑ст = finger, G. pl. пр̏стӣ or пр̏стијӯ or пр̏ста̄.

бра̏т = brother, and госпо̀дин = gentleman, Mr., have special fem. sing. collective plurals:—

    Nom. бра̏ћа   Gen. бра̏ће, etc.
     "   госпо̏да "   госпо̏де, etc., Voc. го̏сподо!

цве̑т = flower, has a neuter (sing.) collective plural:—

    Nom. цве̑ће, Gen. цве̑ћа, etc.

да̑н = day, is regular in Serbocroätian: Gen. s. да̑на, Nom. pl. да̑ни, Gen. pl. да́на̄.

4b. *o*-stems, neuter. Here the soft stems differ from the hard stems only in the Nom.=Acc.=Voc. sing. and Instr. sing.

	HARD STEMS		SOFT STEMS	
	се̏ло = village		по̏ље = field	
	Sing.	*Plur.*	*Sing.*	*Plur.*
Nom. *Voc.*	се̏ло	се̏ла	по̏ље	по̏ља
Gen.	се̏ла	се̏ла̄	по̏ља	по̏ља̄
Dat.	се̏лу	се̏лима	по̏љу	по̏љима
Acc.	се̏ло	се̏ла	по̏ље	по̏ља
Instr.	се̏лом	се̏лима	по̏љем	по̏љима
Loc.	се̏лу	се̏лима	по̏љу	по̏љима

A few relics of the old Dual survive, e.g.:—

    The *plurale tantum*:—пр̏си or пр̏са = breast
                        Gen. пр̏сӣ   пр̏са̄
                       or пр̏сијӯ
      Dat. Inst. Loc. пр̏сима   пр̏сима

о̏ко (= eye) neuter sing.   Likewise: у̏хо (у̏во)
                                     = ear, neut. sing.
о̏чи *fem.* plur. Nom.,Acc.,Voc.   у̏ши
очиjӯ or о̏чӣ plur. Gen.   ушиjӯ or у̏шӣ
о̏чима plur. Dat., Inst., Loc.   у̏шима
but plur.: о̏ка = holes (of a   The form у̏шеса
  net)   is contemptuous.

плѐћи (= shoulders)—has Gen. plur. плѐћā or плѐћӣ.

The movable vowel a can also occur in the neut. Gen. plurals:—

    jу̏тро = morning, acre   Gen. pl. jу̏тāрā
    вѐсло = oar   Gen. pl. вѐсāлā

Velar stems undergo the 2nd Palatalization before the ending -има of the D., I., L. pl., e.g. клу̏пко = ball (of wool), клу̏пцима; па̏зухо = armpit, па̏зусима.

Note the indeclinable neuter nouns: до̏ба = period of time; по̏дне = midday.

The Numerals

Cardinal: 1 is declined and treated as a Definite adjective, agreeing with the noun it defines in gender, number (*sic*) and case. 2, 3, and 4 govern what looks like the Gen. sing. (originally the Dual) and the qualifying adjective is in the Gen. sing. of the *indefinite* declension.[1] 5 onwards govern the Gen. plur., and usually take the verb in the (neuter) singular, e.g. in the Past tense. Only 1-4, 100, 1,000, and 1,000,000 decline. After prepositions, declension is generally avoided. Compounds of 1-4, e.g. 21, 22, etc., govern the case of the final figure.

		Masc.	*Neut.*	*Fem.*
1	Nom.	jѐдан	jѐдно	jѐдна
	Gen.	jѐдног(а)		jѐдне
	Dat.Loc.	jѐдном(е)		jѐдноj, etc.

(See "The Adjectives" below.)

2	Nom.Acc.	два̂	два̂	двѐ
	Gen.	*два́jӯ		двѐjӯ
	Dat.Inst.Loc.	два́ма or два̀ма		двѐма or двѐма

*After prepositions this numeral is usually left undeclined.
  о̏ба, о̏бе = both, is declined like два̂, but Dat., Inst., Loc. is обе́ма for *all* genders.

[1]The corresponding verb is in the plur., but the Past Partic. Act. ends in -a for masc. and neut. nouns and -e for fem.

SERBOCROATIAN

Nom. Acc. *All Genders.*   Gen. *All Genders.*   Dat. Inst. Loc. *All Genders.*

3	трȋ	*трȋјȳ̄	трȉма
4	чѐтири	*четирȋјȳ̄	чѐтирма
5	пȇт		
6	шȇст		
7	сȅдам		
8	ȍсам		
9	дȅвēт		
10	дȅсēт		
11	једàнаест		
12	двáнаест		
13	трѝнаест		
14	четр̀наест		
15	пȅтнаест		
16	шȅснаест		
17	седàмнаест		
18	осàмнаест		
19	девȅтнаест		
20	двáдесēт		
21	двáдесēт (и) јȅдан		
30	трѝдесēт		
40	четрдѐсēт		
50	педѐсēт		
60	шездѐсēт		
70	седамдѐсēт		
80	осамдѐсēт		
90	деведѐсēт		
100	стȏ or стȍтина		
101	стȏ (и) јȅдан		
200	двȅста or двȇ стȍтине		
300	трѝста or трȋ стȍтине		
400	чѐтиристȏ or чѐтири стȍтине		
500	пȇтстȏ or пȇт стȍтинā		
600	шȇстстȏ or шȇст стȍтинā		
700	сȅдамстȏ or сȅдам стȍтинā		
800	ȍсамстȏ or ȍсам стȍтинā		
900	дȅветстȏ or дȅвēт стȍтинā		
1,000	хи̏љада or тѝсућа		
2,000	двȇ хи̏љаде		
5,000	пȇт хи̏љāдā		
1,000,000	милѝјȳ̄н, Gen. Sing. милијȳ́на or милѝо̄н, Gen. Sing. милио̄на		

*After prepositions these numerals are generally left undeclined:

са трȋ прѝјатеља = with three friends

The *Ordinal* Numerals—

1st	пр̂ви	= first
2nd	дру̀ги	= second
3rd	трѐћи	= third
4th	че̂твр̂ти	= fourth
5th	пе̂ти	
6th	ше̂сти	
7th	се̂дми	
8th	о̂сми	
9th	дѐве̄ти	
10th	дѐсе̄ти, etc., obtained by adding -и to the Cardinals.	
100th	сто̂ти	= 100th
1,000th	хи̏љадити or ти̏суђи or ти̏суђни	
1,000,000th	милѝјунти or милѝонти	

are declined like Definite Adjectives (see below, "The Adjectives"). Only трѐћи is a soft stem. The rest follow the hard stem declension. In compound Ordinals only the last figure is made ordinal, e.g.:—

сто̂ пр̂ви = 101st

There are also three sets of *Collective Numerals*:

1. Plur. Collective (adjectival) Numerals, varying in gender, used with nouns used in the plur. only or implying pairs (verb in plur.):—

дво̀је ча̀рапе	= 2 pairs of stockings
тро̀је но̀вине	= 3 newspapers
чѐтвора or чѐтвера ко̏ла	= 4 cars
дво̀ји во̏лови	= 2 pairs of oxen

2. Neuter sing. Collectives used for living things of mixed gender (sometimes absolutely).[1] These can also be used with nouns which have fem. sing. collective plurals instead of normal ones. (The verb can be either masc. plur. or neut. sing.):—

Би́ло је у вр̂ту дво̀је дѐце, тро̀је пѝла̄ди и чѐтворо о̀дра̄слӣх = There were in the garden two children, three chickens, and four adults.

3. Substantival fem. Collectives indicating a number of men (only, and not always specifying at that point who they are), with the ending -ица. The

---

[1]These are (occasionally) declined: Nom.Acc.Voc. дво̀је, Gen. дво̀га or дво̀јега, Dat.Inst.Loc. дво́ма, Dat.Loc. also дво́ме or дво̀јему; Nom.Acc.Voc. чѐтворо, Gen. четво́рга, Dat.Inst.Loc. четво́рма, Dat.Loc. also четворо́ме; or with четвер- throughout.

verb is in the plural, though the participle may be in the fem. sing.:—

Тро̀јица су до̏шли or до̏шла = Three men have come.

The noun or pronoun after this kind of numeral, if expressed, goes in the Gen. pl. when the numeral is in the Nom., Voc., or Acc.: на̑с дво̀јица = we two. Otherwise it agrees in case with the numeral: ње̏ма дво̀јици = to them two.

Distributive Numerals are expressed by the preposition по + Acc.: e.g.:—

Ви̑ у̀змите сва̏ки̑ по три̑ гла̏ве ку̀пуса = Each of you take three cabbages (lit. heads of cabbage) each

The Pronominal Declension

Besides the Personal Pronouns

ја̑ = I   о̑н = he
ти̑ = thou   ми̑ = we, etc.

this category includes the Demonstratives

о̀ва̄ј = this   та̑ј = that

the Interrogatives

ко̀ = who   што̀, шта̏ = what

the Indefinite Pronouns such as

не̏ко   = someone
ко̀ји ... го̏д[1]= whoever, whichever
ма ко̀ји̑   = any
ко̀ји̑ би́ло   = any you like
и̏ко   = anyone (used after без = without, не̏го = than, ни̏ти = not even)

the Negative pronouns such as

ни̏ко = no one   ни̏шта = nothing

the Possessive Pronoun-Adjectives such as

мо̑ј = my, mine   на̏ш = our(s)

the Relatives such as

ко̀ји = which   што̀ = that

---

[1] The two words can be separated by enclitics, if these occur.

and the Definitives, e.g.

са̏в = all   са̂м = -self   и̏сти̑ = the same

From the tables below it will be seen that except for the Personal Pronouns of the 1st and 2nd person, all these Pronouns follow roughly the same lines in declension, with the familiar variation of hard and soft endings, e.g. Gen. sing. masc. -ora hard, -era soft, Loc. s. masc., neut. -ом(е) hard, -ем(е) soft. Note that the endings are often short in contrast to those of the definite adjectives (see below p. 273).

Hard: та̂j = that

SING.	*Masc.*	*Neut.*	*Fem.*
Nom.	та̂j	то̂	та̂
Gen.	то̏г(а)		те̂
Dat.	то̏м(е) or (-у)		то̂j
Acc.	*	то̂	ту̂
Instr.	ти̂м, ти́ме		то̂м
Loc.	то̏м(е) or (-у)		то̂j

PLUR.

Nom.	ти̂	та̂	те̂
Gen.		ти̂х	
Dat.		ти̏ма,	ти̂м
Acc.	те̂	та̂	те̂
Instr.		ти̏ма,	ти̂м
Loc.		ти̏ма,	ти̂м

Soft: о̂н = he, о̀на = she, о̀но = it

SING.

Nom.	о̂н	о̀но	о̀на
Gen.	ње̏га,[1] га		ње̂, је
Dat.	ње̏му,[1] му		њо̂j, joj
Acc.	ње̏га,[1] га, њ[2]		њу̂, је, jy[3]
Instr.	њи̂м,[4] ње́ме		њо̂м,[4] ње́ме
Loc.	ње̏му[1]		њо̂j

*Acc. sing. masc. = Nom. sing. masc. for inanimates,
              = Gen. sing. masc. for animates.

[1] These forms can also have the short falling tone: ње̏га, ње̏му.

[2] Used only after prepositions: на њ = on to him.

[3] Acc. sing. fem. jy is used when je as auxiliary verb occurs in the same sentence, or after a word ending in -je.

[4] The short form is used after prepositions.

SERBOCROATIAN

	PLUR.	*Masc.*	*Neut.*	*Fem.*
Nom.		о̀ни	о̀на	о̀не
Gen.		ње̑х, их		
Dat.		ње̑м(а), им		
Acc.		ње̑х, их		
Instr.		ње̑м(а)		
Loc.		ње̑м(а)		

According to the hard model are declined:—

the Demonstratives, о̀ва̄ј = this
о̀на̄ј, о̀на̄, о̀но̄ = that

the Interrogatives: ко̀ = who? (see below)
ка̀кав*, -ква = what kind of?

the Indefinite Pronouns:

не̏ко = someone, Gen. не̏кога
не̏кӣ = some
не̏какав* = some kind of

the Definitives:

је̏дан = one, је̏днога
са̑м = -self, са́мога
и̏стӣ = the same, и̏сто̄га
та̀кав,* -ква = such
ова̀кав,* -ква = like this
она̀кав,* -ква = like that
то̀лӣкӣ = so great

the Possessives:

ње̏гов* = his
ње̑зин* or ње̑н* = her(s)
ње̑хов* or ње̑н* = their(s)

*These pronouns can also be declined like indefinite adjectives (see below, p. 272), especially in the western literary tradition centred on Zagreb. To them should be added са̑м, fem. са́ма, neut. са́мо, in the sense of 'alone', and the forms то̀лик = so great, ово̀лик, оно̀лик. See the declension of ње̏гов below.

According to the soft model are declined:—

the Interrogative: шта̏ or што̏ (Nom. and Acc.) with the stem ч- in the other cases (see below)

the Possessives: мо̑ј (= my), Gen. s. masc. neut. мо̀јега generally contracted to мо̑га, Dat. Loc. s. m. and n. мо̑ме (see below)
тво̑ј = thine, your   на̏ш = our (see below)
сво̑ј = my, your or   ва̏ш = your
his own

the Possessive Relative and Interrogative:
чѝjӣ = whose, Gen. s. m., n. чѝjега

the Relative and Interrogative:
кȍjӣ = who, which, кȍjега (see below)

and the Definitive: cȁв = all, which was originally soft in the Nom. sing. masc., Gen. s. m. n. свèга, Gen. pl. свӣ̏х or свӣ̏jӯ (see below).

As in the declension of тȃj above, the Accusative sing. masc. for all the declensions below except штȍ is the same as the Nom. sing. masc. for inanimate nouns and the same as the Gen. sing. masc. for animate nouns. Note the important differences of vowel length in the endings.

мȏj = my, mine

SING.	*Masc.*	*Neut.*	*Fem.*
Nom.	мȏj	мȍjе	мо̀jа
Gen.	мо̀jег(а), мȏг(а)		мо̀jē
Dat.	мо̀jем(у), мȏм(у,-е)		мо̀jōj
Acc.	= Nom. or Gen.	мȍjе	мо̀jу
Instr.	мо̀jим		мо̀jōм
Loc.	мо̀jем(у), мȏм(у,-е)		мо̀jōj

PLUR.

Nom.	мо̀jи	мо̀jа	мо̀jе
Gen.		мо̀jӣх	
Dat.		мо̀jима, мо̀jӣм	
Acc.	мо̀jе	мо̀jа	мо̀jе
Instr.		мо̀jима, мо̀jӣм	
Loc.		мо̀jима, мо̀jӣм	

Like мȏj: твȏj = your(s) (fam.), свȏj = own (referring to subject of sentence).

нȁш = our(s)

SING.	*Masc.*	*Neut.*	*Fem.*
Nom.	нȁш	нȁше	нȁша
Gen.	нȁшег(а)		нȁшē
Dat.	нȁшем(у)		нȁшōj
Acc.	= Nom. or Gen.	нȁше	нȁшу
Instr.	нȁшим		нȁшōм
Loc.	нȁшем(у)		нȁшōj

	Masc.	Neut.	Fem.
PLUR.			
Nom.	нȁши	нȁша	нȁше
Gen.		нȁшйх	
Dat.		нȁшима, нȁшйм	
Acc.	нȁше	нȁша	нȁше
Instr.		нȁшима, нȁшйм	
Loc.		нȁшима, нȁшйм	

Like нȁш: вȁш = your(s), (polite sing. and familiar and polite plur.). The fuller forms with the final vowel of the Gen., Dat., Instr., and Loc. sing. and the Dat., Instr., and Loc. plur. of all pronouns such as тȃj, мȏj, нȁш and кȍjӣ are used when the pronoun occurs by itself or follows the noun it qualifies: Рȅкао сам твоjима = I told your people.
Пȍштуj оца свȍга = Honour your father!
Говȍрио сам о тȍме = I have spoken about that.

сȁв = all

	Masc.	Neut.	Fem.
SING.			
Nom.	сȁв	свȅ	свȁ
Gen.	свȅга		свȇ
Dat.	свȅму		свȏj
Acc.	= Nom. or Gen.	свȅ	свȕ
Instr.	свȋм(е)		свȏм
Loc.	свȅм, свȅму		свȏj
PLUR.			
Nom.	свȕ	свȁ	свȅ
Gen.		свȋх, свȕjȳ	
Dat.		свȋм, свȕма	
Acc.	свȅ	свȁ	свȅ
Instr.		свȋм, свȕма	
Loc.		свȋм, свȕма	

кȍjӣ = which (relative and interrogative)

	Masc.	Neut.	Fem.
SING.			
Nom.	кȍjӣ	кȍjē	кȍjā
Gen.	кȍjēга, кȍга		кȍjē
Dat.	кȍjēму, кȍму		кȍjōj
Acc.	=Nom. or Gen.	кȍjē	кȍjȳ
Instr.	кȍjӣм, кȋм		кȍjōм
Loc.	кȍjēму, кȍме		кȍjōj

PLUR.	*Masc.*	*Neut.*	*Fem.*
Nom.	кòjӣ	кòjā	кòjē
Gen.		кòjӣх	
Dat.		кòjӣм(а)	
Acc.	кòjē	кòjā	кòjē
Instr.		кòjӣм(а)	
Loc.		кòjӣм(а)	

Like кòjӣ: чѝjӣ = whose (relative and interrogative)

кò, ткò = who?   штò, штȃ = what?
(animate)   (inanimate)

Nom.	кò, ткò	штò, штȃ
Gen.	кòга (кòг)	чèга (чèг), штȃ
Dat.	кòме, кòму, кòм	чèму
Acc.	кòга (кòг)	штò, штȃ
Instr.	кӣм, кӥме	чӣм, чӥме
Loc.	кòме, кòм	чèму, чèм

According to these models are declined all compounds of these pronouns: e.g. нѝко = no one, нèшто = something. Prepositions come between the prefix and the pronoun; e.g. ни зà што = for nothing, to no purpose, no good.

It is important to distinguish кòга? = (of) whom?, from кòга? = (of) which...?, кòму? = to whom?, from кòму? = to which...?, о кòме? = about whom?, from о кòме? = about which...?.

њèгов = his

SING.	*Masc.*	*Neut.*	*Fem.*
Nom.	њèгов	њèгово	њèгова
Gen.	њèгова[1]		њèгове
Dat.	њèгову[1]		њèговоj
Acc.	=Nom. or Gen.	њèгово	њèгову
Instr.	њèговим		њèговом
Loc.	њèгову[1]		њèговоj

PLUR.

Nom.	њèгови	њèгова	њèгове
Gen.		њèгових	
Dat.		њèговим(а)	
Acc.	њèгове	њèгова	њèгове
Instr.		њèговим(а)	
Loc.		њèговим(а)	

[1]But see "The Adjectives," p. 270, fourth paragraph.

SERBOCROATIAN

Like његов *can* be declined њезин, њен = her(s), њихов, њин = their(s), са̑м, fem. са́ма, neut. са́мо = alone, the group of pronouns in -ав such as та̀кав = such, and in -ик (western form), such as то̀лик = so big.

Personal Pronouns

The Personal Pronouns of the 1st and 2nd person have special declensions of their own:—

jȃ = I   ми̑ = we   ти̑ = you (fam.)   ви̑ = you(pl. and polite)

Nom.	jȃ		ми̑
Gen.	мѐне,[1]	ме	на̑с, нас
Dat.	мѐни,[1]	ми	на̏ма, нам
Acc.	мѐне,[1]	ме	на̑с, нас
Instr.	мно̑м,[2]	мно́ме	на̏ма
Loc.	мѐни[1]		на̏ма

Nom.	ти̑		ви̑
Gen.	тѐбе,[1]	те	ва̑с, вас
Dat.	тѐби,[1]	ти	ва̏ма, вам
Acc.	тѐбе,[1]	те	ва̑с, вас
Instr.	то̀бо̄м		ва̏ма
Loc.	тѐби[1]		ва̏ма

сѐбе (Acc.—no Nom.!) is declined like (ти̑) тѐбе, and means "-self", for all persons sing. and plur. when referring to the subject of the sentence. In literary Serbocroätian there is no Dat. enclitic form *си, only Acc. се.

The shorter, enclitic forms of the Pers. Pronouns for all three persons are retained in full use in Serbocroätian, in contrast to Russian. They are used where there is no emphasis on the pronoun in the sentence. (See section on "Word Order with Enclitics"). The Accusatives ме, те, се can be used after prepositions which then take the accent, e.g. на́ ме = on to me, за́ се = for oneself, by itself.

The Adjectives

In Serbocroätian the category of the Indefinite Adjectives has survived (cf. pp. 47-48 and 56-57 in the chapter on Old Slavonic) beside that of the compound Definite Adjectives. The latter, especially in the

---

[1] In the disyllabic forms the accent (tone) can also be ˶
[2] The form мно̄м is used after prepositions: са̏ мно̄м = with me.

masc. and neut. singular, are more similar in their declension to the "long form" adjectives in other Slavonic languages, such as Russian, Czech, and Polish: cf. Sbcr. Nom. s. m. бе̑ли = the white..., Gen. бе̑лōга, Russ. бе́лый, бе́лого, Cz. bílý, bílého, Pol. biały, białego.

The Indefinite Adjectives are characterized by *o*- and *a*-stem substantival endings with *short* vowels in the Nom. (except in the masc. sing.) and Acc. of both numbers and all three genders, e.g. sing. f. Nom. бе́ла = a white..., Acc. бе́лу, neut. Nom., Acc. бе́ло, plur. m. Nom. бе̑ли, Acc. бе́ле, f. N. A. бе́ле, n. N. A. бе́ла, and by distinctively substantival endings in the masc. and neut. s. Gen. бе́ла, and Dat. and Loc. бе́лу.

The masculine Nom. sing. Indefinite Adj. ends in a consonant or -o (from a final -*l*): e.g. вру̑ћ = hot, ја̑к = strong, мла̑д = young, бе̏о = white, за̏о = bad, wicked (fem. зла̀), дѐбео = fat (fem. дѐбела). Movable -*a*- can appear before a final consonant or -*o*: e.g. до̀бар = good, fem. до̀бра, хла́дан = cold, fem. хла́дна, то̀пао = warm, fem. то̀пла.

All Possessive adjectives such as Пѐтро̄в = Peter's, при̏јатељев = (my, etc.) friend's, ма̑јчин = mother's, originally followed the Indefinite declension and, particularly in the modern western tradition, still often do so. But colloquially, both in eastern and western Yugoslavia, the Indefinite endings are often replaced by the Definite endings, just as they are replaced in the third person Possessive Pronouns, so one hears, and also sees in writing, Пѐтровōг Gen. s. masc., like његовōг, etc.

There is no separate Vocative sing. form distinct from the Nominative for Indefinite Adjectives.

Many adjectives also distinguish the Indefinite form from the Definite by a difference of accent (tone)—rising (except in the Nom. s. masc.) in the Indefinite, and falling in the corresponding Definite, e.g. Nom. s. fem. Indef. мла́да, Def. мла̑да̄ = young; and also in trisyllabic words, by the *position* of the accent (tone)—on the *second* syllable for the Indefinite form (except in the Nom. s. masc.) and on the *first* syllable for the Definite form, e.g. Nom. s. fem. Indef. црвѐна, Def. цр̏вена̄ = red (see the declensions below).

When both forms have the same tone, as in ло̏ш (Nom. s. masc. Indef.) = bad, Def. ло̏ши, the other forms, for the Nom. and Acc. s. fem. and neut. and the Nom. and Acc. plur. for all genders, are distinguished only by the length of the vowel ending, the Indefinite forms having *short* vowels and the Definite forms all having *long* vowels.

The Definite Adjectives are characterized by a long vowel in their endings in *all* cases, on the *first* syllable in the characteristic disyllabic endings of the Gen. and Dat., Loc. sing. masc. and neut.: e.g. Nom. s. до̏брӣ m., до̏бра̄ f., до̏бро̄ n. = the good..., Gen. s. m., n. до̏бро̄га, Dat., Loc. s. m., n. до̏бро̄м (-e or -y). These endings, as in other Slavonic languages, show clearly the compound nature of this declension: до̏бро̄га from добра + јего, до̏бро̄му from добру + јему, etc. Hence its similarity to the pronominal declension.

Soft stems are distinguished from hard stems by having -e- for -o- in the Nom., Acc. sing. neut. and the Def. Gen., Dat. and Loc. sing. masc. and neut., e.g. Nom., Acc. s. n. Indef. вру̂ће = hot, cf. Def. вру̂ће̄, and in the *Definite* Gen. s. m. and n. вру̂ће̄га, and Dat., Loc. s. m. and n. вру̂ће̄м (-e or -y). Note that -o- is retained for soft stems in the fem. sing. endings -о̄j (Dat., Loc. s. Indef.), e.g. вру̂ћо̄j, and -о̄м (Instr. s. Def.), e.g. вру̂ћо̄м.

In the Gen., Dat., Instr. and Loc. sing. fem. and for all genders in the plural of these cases, the *endings*, though not necessarily the accents (tones), of both types of declension are identical.

Adjectives used as predicates are invariably put in the Nominative of the Indefinite form, if such exists: e.g. о̂н је до̏бар = he is good, о̂на је до̏бра = she is good, but та̂j (e.g. и̏звешта̄ј) је да̀нашњӣ = that (report) is today's.

Only Definite adjectives are used:—

(a) after demonstrative and possessive pronouns, e.g.:

мо̂ј ста̏рӣ прѝјатељ = my old friend,
та̂ј ла̀кӣ зада́так = that easy task,

(b) in names: e.g. Но̏вӣ Са̂д = (Novi Sad), Ѝван Гро̏знӣ = Ivan the Dread.

(c) with Vocatives: e.g. дра̂гӣ о̏че! = dear father!

Adjectives in -ни, -ски, -шки, -чки, and -ји and all adjectives of time and place, including those in -њи and -шњи, and also ма̂лӣ = small, and по̀ко̄јнӣ = the late, have no indefinite forms, e.g.:—

на́роднӣ   = national, folk   ју̀на̄чкӣ = heroic
гра̀дскӣ   = city   ву̂чјӣ   = wolf's
сиро̀машкӣ = poor, pauper's   ле̂вӣ   = left

де̏снӣ = right   да̀на̄шњӣ = today's
до̑њӣ = lower

All Comparative and Superlative adjectives are declined like the Definite *soft* declension because of the final soft consonant of the stem. (See below "The Comparison of Adjectives").

The forms of the Gen., Dat., Loc.sing. masc. and neut. Def. and of the Dat., Instr. and Loc. plur. of all genders, with a final vowel (-a, -e or -y), given in the declensions below, are used:—

(a) when the adjective is used by itself, e.g.: Па̏метно̄ме и кома̀рац му̏зика = For the sensible man even a mosquito is music.

(b) when the adjective is put after the noun, e.g.: То̂ о̀н ве̏лӣ о̀цу ро̀ђено̄ме! = He tells that to his own father!

(c) for the first of a string of adjectives qualifying a single noun, e.g.: Је̏днога ле̑по̄г сун- ча̏но̄г да̑на... = One fine sunny day...

црвен = red

INDEFINITE

	Masc.	*Neut.*	*Fem.*
SING.			
Nom.	цр̏вен	црве̏но*	црве̏на
Gen.	црве̏на		црве̏не̄
Dat.	црве̏ну		црве̏но̄ј
Acc.	= Nom. or Gen.	црве̏но*	црве̏ну
Instr.	црве̏ним		црве̏но̄м
Loc.	црве̏ну		црве̏но̄ј
PLUR.			
Nom.	црве̏ни	црве̏на	црве̏не
Gen.		црве̏них	
Dat.		црве̏ним(а)	
Acc.	црве̏не	црве̏на	црве̏не
Instr.		црве̏ним(а)	
Loc.		црве̏ним(а)	

*In these cases soft stem adjectives substitute -e- for -o- (with the same quantity) in the endings. See paragraph on soft stems above, p. 271.

DEFINITE

	Masc.	Neut.	Fem.
SING.			
Nom.	цр̏ве̄нӣ	цр̏ве̄но̄*	цр̏ве̄на̄
Gen.		цр̏ве̄но̄г(а)*	цр̏ве̄не̄
Dat.		цр̏ве̄но̄м(е) or (-у)*	цр̏ве̄но̄ј
Acc.	= Nom. or Gen.	цр̏ве̄но̄*	цр̏ве̄нӯ
Instr.		цр̏ве̄нӣм	цр̏ве̄но̄м
Loc.		цр̏ве̄но̄м(е)*	цр̏ве̄но̄ј
PLUR.			
Nom.	цр̏ве̄нӣ	цр̏ве̄на̄	цр̏ве̄не̄
Gen.		цр̏ве̄нӣх	
Dat.		цр̏ве̄нӣм(а)	
Acc.	цр̏ве̄не̄	цр̏ве̄на̄	цр̏ве̄не̄
Instr.		цр̏ве̄нӣм(а)	
Loc.		цр̏ве̄нӣм(а)	

THE COMPARISON OF ADJECTIVES

Comparative Adjectives are formed with three alternative sets of endings, viz.:—

(a) -шӣ, -ша̄, -ше̄
(b) -јӣ, -ја̄, -је̄
(c) -ијӣ, -ија̄, -ије̄

Only three adjectives form their comparatives with the first set of endings (a), namely:

ла̏к = easy, Comp. ла̏кшӣ
ле̑п = beautiful, Comp. ле̏пшӣ
ме̏к = soft, Comp. ме̏кшӣ

The second set of shorter endings (b) with -јӣ is used for many monosyllabic adjectives and causes yotation of the final consonant of the stem, offering a rich field for the illustration of yotation in Serbocroätian. (Cf. "Slavonic Characteristics," No. 4.)

ја̑к	= strong,	Comp. ја̏чӣ
го̀рак	= bitter,	" го̏рчӣ (from stem горк-)
дра̑г	= dear,	" дра̏жӣ
ду̑г	= long,	" ду̑жӣ, or ду̑љӣ (Irreg.)
стро̏г	= strict,	" стро̏жӣ or стро̀жијӣ
ти̑х	= quiet,	" ти̏шӣ
су̑х } су̑в }	= dry	" су̏шӣ " су̏вљӣ

*In these cases soft stem adjectives substitute -e- for -o- (with the same quantity) in the endings. See paragraph on soft stems above, p. 271.

љ̑ут	= angry, hot,	Comp.	љу̑ћӣ
жу̑т	= yellow,	"	жу̑ћӣ
бле̑д	= pale,	"	бле̑ђӣ
мла̑д	= young,	"	мла̑ђӣ
тврд̑	= hard,	"	тврђ̑ӣ
бр̑з	= quick,	"	бр̑жӣ
бе̑о	= white,	"	бе̑љӣ
цр̑н	= black,	"	цр̑њӣ
глу̑п	= silly,	"	глу̑пљӣ
гру̑б	= rough,	"	гру̑бљӣ
глу̑в } глу̑х }	= deaf,	"	глу̑вљӣ глу̑шӣ
гу̑ст	= dense,	"	гу̑шћӣ
чврс̑т	= firm,	"	чвр̑шћӣ
бе̑сан	= furious,	"	бе̑шњӣ or бе̑сниjӣ

Adjectives ending in a palatal consonant absorb the j of the ending into the final consonant of their stem, hence, e.g.:—

вру̑ћ	= hot,	Comp.	вру̑ћӣ
ри̑ђ	= red-haired,	"	ри̑ђӣ

Many adjectives ending in the Positive degree in -ок, -ак and -ек drop this syllable in the formation of their Comparatives. The same yotations occur with the final consonant of the stem remaining, e.g.:—

кра́так	= short,	Comp.	кра̀ћӣ
пли́так	= shallow,	"	плѝћӣ
ре́дак	= rare,	"	ре̂ђӣ
сла̀дак	= sweet,	"	сла̀ђӣ
вѝсок	= high,	"	ви̏шӣ
нѝзак	= low,	"	ни̏жӣ
да̀лек	= distant,	"	да̀љӣ
та̀нак	= thin,	"	та̀њӣ
шѝрок	= broad,	"	ши̏рӣ
ду̀бок	= deep,	"	ду̀бљӣ
же̏сток	= fierce,	"	же̏шћӣ

and with absorption of the -j-:—

тежак	= heavy,	"	те̂жӣ

For the vast majority of adjectives the third set of endings (c) with -иjӣ, etc., are used. This includes many monosyllabic and disyllabic adjectives and all adjectives of three or more syllables, i.e. in their masc. Indefinite Nom. sing. form. E.g.:—

пу̑ст	= empty,	Comp.	пу̑стиjӣ
све̑т	= holy,	"	свѐтиjӣ
сла̑н	= salty,	"	сла̀ниjӣ or сла̀њӣ
чи̏ст	= clean,	"	чи̏стиjӣ

мȕо	= beloved, dear,	Comp.	мȉлијӣ
пу̑н	= full,	"	пу̀нијӣ
лȏш	= bad,	"	лȍшијӣ
но̑в	= new,	"	но̀вијӣ
ста̑р	= old,	"	ста̀ријӣ
здра̑в	= healthy,	"	здра̀вијӣ
сла̑б	= weak,	"	сла̀бијӣ
зре̑о	= ripe,	"	зрѐлијӣ
крȍтак	= meek,	"	крȍткијӣ
крȅпак	= firm,	"	крȅпкијӣ, крȅпчӣ
гȉбак	= flexible,	"	гȉпкијӣ
бȉстар	= clear,	"	бȉстријӣ
јȁсан	= bright, clear,	"	јȁснијӣ
же́дан	= thirsty,	"	жѐднијӣ
сту́ден	= cold,	"	студѐнијӣ
спȍсобан	= capable,	"	спосо̀бнијӣ
сирȍмашан	= poor,	"	сирома̀шнијӣ
незадово̀љан	= discontented,	"	незадово̀љнијӣ
далеко̀видан	= far-seeing,	"	далековѝднијӣ

Notice the irregular Comparatives: —

дѐбео	= fat,	Comp.	дȅбљӣ
прȅтио	= stout, corpulent,	"	прȅтљӣ
нȁопа̄к	= reversed, wrong,	"	наопа̀чнијӣ
дȍбар	= good,	"	бȍљӣ
р̀ђав ⎱ зȁо ⎰	= bad,	"	го̀рӣ
вѐлик(ӣ)	= big, great,	"	вѐћӣ
ма̑лӣ ⎱ ма̀лен ⎰	= small,	"	ма̀њӣ

It will be observed that all disyllabic Comparatives (i.e. with (b) endings) have the short falling tone ˋ, while all Comparatives of three or more syllables with -ијӣ, etc. endings (c), have the short rising tone ˋ on the third syllable from the end.

Superlative adjectives are formed by prefixing на̑ј- to the Comparative degree. Only when they are formed from disyllabic Comparatives with ˋ, the Superlative forms *may* have only the one accent on the на̑ј-. In other instances both the prefix на̑ј- and the following adjective, comparative in form, have their own accents (tones), like compound words.

Thus: на̑јбољӣ = best, or на̑јбо̏љӣ, but *only*: на̑јспосо̀бнији = the most capable.

Than = нȅго, or од + Genitive, e.g.:—

о̑н је де̏бљи нȅго ја̑ or од мȅне = He is fatter than I.
Rather better = нȅшто бо̏ље; but: rather good = до̏ста до̏бар.
Less than = ма̏ње нȅго; more than = вӣ̏ше нȅго.
The bigger, *the* better = што̏ (or чи̑м) вȅће, то̑ (or ти̑м) бо̏ље.
As big *as* = и̏сто̄ та̏ко вȅлик ка̏о ...
As fast as possible = што̏ бр̏же; as soon as possible = што̏ пре̑.
The best of all = на̑јбољӣ од свӣ̑х.
The same as = и̏стӣ ка̏о ...
Too (much) = сӯ̏више̄, о̏двећ(е)
In the same way as = и̏сто та̏ко ка̏о ...

ADVERBS

These are regularly formed from adjectives by using the form for the Nom. Acc. neuter singular, e.g.:—

до̏бар = good, до̏бро = well

except in the case of adjectives ending in -скӣ, which have corresponding adverbs in -ски, e.g.:—

пријатељски = in a friendly way

There are a few special adverbial endings, such as -це, -ке, e.g.:—

нȅхотице̄ = unwillingly
пȅшке̄ (or пȅшице̄) = on foot

The Instr. sing. of nouns is also used, as in other Slavonic languages, e.g.:—

већи̏но̄м = for the most part

The Comparison of Adverbs

Comparative adverbs, formed from adverbs of adjectival origin, have the same form as the Nom./Acc. neuter sing. of the corresponding Comparative adjective. The final -e can be either short or long. E.g.:—

бр̏же	= quicker	ти̏ше = more quietly
јефти̏није	= more cheaply	бо̏ље = better
ла̏кше	= more easily	

Superlative adverbs are formed by prefixing нȃј- to the Comparative adverbs, as in the comparison of adjectives. E.g.:—

нȃјбрже	= most quickly	нȃјлакше	= most easily
нȃјјефтѝније	= most cheaply	нȃјбоље	= best

The only irregular Comparative and Superlative adverbs are:—

мно̀го	= much	вȉше	= more	нȃјвише	= most
мȁло	= little	мȁње	= less	нȃјмање	= least

Temporal, local and other adverbs can have a great variety of endings owing to their various derivations. The commonest are:—

Place:—

о̀вде	= here	(од)о̀зго̄	= from above
тŷ	= there	(од)о̀здо̄	= from below
тȁмо	= there, thither	нȁпољу	= out of doors, outside
о̀нде	= yonder	нȁпоље	= out
сву̀да	= everywhere	спо̀ља	= from outside
о̀вамо	= hither	нȁпред	= forward
о̀намо	= thither	нȁтра̄г	= backwards
о̀да̄вде̄	= hence	о̀стра̄г	= from behind
о̀туд	= thence	поза́ди	= behind
о̀вуда̄	= this way	уну́тра	= inside
о̀нуда̄	= that way	чȁк	= right up to
нȉгде	= nowhere	прȁво	= straight on
блȋзу	= near	ȅво }	= look, here, Fr. *voici*
далѐко	= far	ȅто } + Gen.	= look, there
го̀ре	= above, upstairs	ȅно }	= look, over there } Fr. *voilà*
до̀ле	= below, downstairs	нȉзбрдо	= downhill

Time:—

сȁда or сȁд	= now	ста̑лно	= constantly, permanently
тȁд(а)	= then		
дȁнас	= to-day	нȉкада	= never
јỳче	= yesterday	да́вно	= long ago
су̀тра	= to-morrow	мȁлоча̄с	= just recently
вȅћ	= already	до̀цкан } кȁсно }	= late
јо̏ш	= still		
у̀век } свȁгда } вȁзда }	= always	рȁно	= early
		ла́не, ла́ни	= last year
		зȋми	= in winter

Time, *cont.*: —

лȅти	= in summer	прȇ	= formerly
да̏њу,[1]		си̏ноћ	= last night
о̏бда̄н	= by day	но̏ћас	= to-night
ма̏хом	= mostly	у̏вече	= in the evening
међу̀тим	= meanwhile	у̏јутру	= in the morning
на̏јзад	= at last	у̏скоро ⎫	
о̏дма̄х	= immediately	скȍро ⎬	= soon
онȍма̄д ⎫		у̏брзо ⎭	
онома́дне ⎭	= the other day	та̀ма̄н	= only just
ȍпет	= again	тȅк	= only (also of degree)
пȍсле ⎫		ба̏ш	= just (" " ")
пȍто̄м ⎭	= afterwards		

Manner: —

та̀кō	= so, thus	и̏знена́да ⎫	= suddenly
ова̀кō	= like this	одједа̀нпут ⎭	
она̀кō	= in that way	кра̑дом	= stealthily
и̏наче	= otherwise	о̏бично	= usually
ни̏ка̄ко	= in no way	та̀чно	= exactly, punctually
бр̑зо	= quickly	бада̀ва	= in vain, gratis
(по)лага́но ⎫		(у̑)за́лӯд	= in vain
пȍла̄ко ⎬	= slowly	нȅмилице	= mercilessly
спȍро ⎭		к(а)оба̀јаги ⎫	
дру̀кчије	= differently	то̏бож(е) ⎬	= making out that, allegedly
за̀једно ⎫		на́водно ⎭	
ску̏па ⎭	= together	на̏паме̄т	= by heart

Degree: —

вр̏ло ⎫		поту̏пно	= completely
веȍма ⎭	= very	са̀свим	= quite
мнȍго ⎫		на́равно ⎫	
пу̏но ⎭	= much	сва̀како ⎬	= of course
ма̏ло	= little, a little	да̀како ⎭	
ви̏ше	= more	са̏мо	= only
ма̏ње	= less	и̏сто	= equally
до̏ста	= enough	јȅдино	= solely
не̏колико	= some	ма̀кар ⎫	
прили́чно	= fairly	ба̑р(ем) ⎭	= at least
су̏више ⎫		скȍро ⎫	
о̏двећ(е) ⎭	= too much	го̏тово ⎭	= almost
толи̏кō	= so much	јȅдва	= hardly
ни̏мало	= not in the least	на́рочито ⎫	
прȍсечно	= on an average	ȍсобито ⎭	= especially

[1] Irregularly formed from да̄н = day, on the analogy of the regular нȍћу (Instr. sing.) = by night.

Degree, *cont.*:—

доиста }	= truly, indeed	ваљда	= probably
заиста }		сигурно	= surely, for certain, probably
донекле	= to a certain extent	уопште	= in general
збиља	= really	баш }	= just
јамачно	= surely	управо }	
можда	= perhaps	чак	= even

Interrogative:—

  кад or када? = when?
  где? = where?
  куд, кудā? = whither?(Eastern); which way? (Western)
        ><камо? = whither? where to?
  откуд(ā)? } = whence?
  одāкле? }
  докле? = how far?
  зашто? = why?
  како? = how?
  колико? = how much?
  ...ли...? enclitic interrogative particle
  да ли...? interrogative particle used initially
  зар...? interrogative particle expressing surprise
  ...јел'те? = is that not so? Fr. *N'est-ce pas?*

Not = не no = не yes = да, јест of course = дабоме, свакако

CONJUNCTIONS

 Neither coördinating nor subordinating conjunctions in Serbocroätian have any special forms.

Coördinating:

и	= and	међутим	= however, on the other hand
а	= and, but (adversative)		
али }	= but	ни(ти)... ни(ти)	= neither...nor
но }			
или	= or	него, већ	= but (after a negative)
ипāк	= however		
као	= as	дакле	= and so, then
ни	= not even	те	= and so
такође }	= also	па	= and then
такођер }		та	= then (urging), but (emphatic exclamatory)
пāк	= however, on the contrary		
само	= only	ала...!	(exclamatory) = my word...!

Subordinating:

а̀ко	= if	пре̑ него што̀	
ка̀д(а)	= when, if	пре̑ но̑ што	} = before
до̀к(ле̄)	= while, до̀к не = until	о̀ткако о̀ткад	} = ever since
је̏р за̀то̄ што збо̀г то̀га што	} = because	чи̏м те̏к што	} = as soon as
		ка̏о што	= as
да	= that, in order that, so that, if	и̏ако ма̀да пре̏мда	} = although
што	= that (referring to a fact)	ма̀кар да а да не	= even though = without (doing)
по̏што = after; since (causal)		ка̏ко би	= so that
бу̀дӯћи да	= seeing that	а̏ко и	= even if
ка̏о да	= as if		
са̏мо да	= only that, provided that		

PREPOSITIONS

These can govern any case except the Nom. or Voc., of course, and largely agree with the usage in other Slav languages.

With Gen.:

без	= without	у̀место, место	= instead of
из	= out of	о̀ко	= round
с(а)	= off	по̏сле̄	= after
о̀сим, се̏м	= except	ра̀ди	= for the sake of
од	= from, made of	спра̀м	= in front of
ко̀д у (less common)	} = by, near	пут	= towards
		врх	= on top of
због	= because of	подно	= below, at the bottom of
по̏ред	= beside		
пре	= before (of time)	чело	= at, by
пре̏ко	= across	широ̄м	= all over
про̀тӣв	= against	ниже	= below
за	= in the time of	више	= above, over
бли́зу	= near	сред	= in the middle of
ва̏н	= outside, beyond	ду̏ж кра̏ј	} = alongside
до	= as far as, until, before, close to		

and all compound prepositions such as испод = below, испред = in front of, изнад = above, изван = outside, и̏змеђу = among, и̏за = from behind, на̏спрам = opposite, по̏крај = alongside, besides, накрај = at the end of, на̀кон = after, in, по̏пӯт = like (*sic*), у̀здуж = along,

SERBOCROATIAN

ỳсред, нàсред = in the middle of.

With Dat.:

к(а)   = towards
супрот
насу̏прот   = against (also with Gen.)

ỳ(с)пркос = despite
унàточ   = in spite of, for all...

With Acc.:

у   = into
на   = on to
кроз = through
за   = for, (to) behind
мèђу = between (motion)
пред = (to) before (motion)
под   = under (motion)

над   = over (motion)
уз   = up, with, beside
нѝз   = down
мѝмо = past, beyond, apart from
о   = on, against
по   = for, to fetch

With Instr.:

с(а) = with
пред = before (rest)
мèђу = between

за   = behind (rest)
над   = over (rest)
под   = under (rest)

With Loc.:

у   = in
на   = on
о   = about

при   = near, by
прèма = towards, according to
по   = about, by

    The prefixes раз- and про- do not occur as prepositions, but пре occurs as a temporal preposition governing the Gen. As in all the other South Slav languages, there is no prefix corresponding etymologically to the Russian вы-, W. Slav. *vy- (wy-)*, for which из- is used in Serbocroãtian.
    The accent may shift from monosyllabic and disyllabic words with *falling* accents (only) on to a preceding preposition in the form of either ` or ". E.g. кȍд ста̄рца = at the old man's, ỳ књизи = in the book, ѝз гра̄да = from the city, нȁ воду = on to the water.
    Some original (non-compound) prepositions consisting of, or ending in, a consonant take a euphonic fill-vowel -a before words beginning with the same or similar consonants when the combination would otherwise be difficult to pronounce, e.g.: са стра̂хом = with fear, са ше̑вом = with a lark, са зе̑мљом = with the earth, са же̑ном = with his wife, безȁ зла = without evil, кȁ гра̄ду = towards the city, са псȍм = with a dog, нѝза стра̄ну = down the side, уза зи̑д = up the wall.

This is particularly common before short personal pronouns, e.g. cа̀ мно̄м = with me, на̀да̄ се = above oneself, прѐда мно̄м = before me, по̀да̄ њ = (to) under him, кро̀за̄ њ = through it, him.

THE CONJUGATION OF VERBS

Voices and Tenses

The conjugations in Serbocroätian are, on the whole, nearer to the original Old Slavonic models than those of modern Russian, for instance. Here, too, the Dual Number has completely disappeared. The Passive Voice is expressed by the verb "to be" + the Past Participle Passive, or by the 3rd person plural of the verb used impersonally, or by the reflexive verb, i.e. the Active verb + ce written separately, for subjects mostly in the 3rd person, e.g.:—

        Зо̀вӯ се = they are called
        О̑н би̂ва̄ хва̂љен or Хва̂ле̄ га = he is praised
        О̑н је хва̂љен = he has been praised

Tenses

Only the Present, Aorist, and Imperfect are simple tenses, while the Future, Past or Perfect, Pluperfect and the Future Perfect are compound tenses. It should be specially noted that the Present of perfective verbs in Sbcr. does *not* have a future meaning, as it has in E. and W. Slav languages; this is a characteristic of S. Slav languages, though the usage of Slovenian is peculiar. In Sbcr. the Perfective Present is used in main clauses in narratives and descriptions as a kind of Historic Present in order to give vividness. In conversation it is used almost exclusively in subordinate clauses introduced by да = that, ако = if, etc. The (compound) Future is formed from verbs of *both* aspects.

The Conditional Mood is also expressed by a compound form. The only other surviving *Mood* is the Imperative.

Present and Past Active (indeclinable) *Gerunds* (or verbal adverbs) also exist, but of the Participles (declinable verbal adjectives)—in contrast to Russian—only the Past Participle Active in -*l* and the Past Participle Passive are still used.

The use of the Aorist and Imperfect tenses is now largely confined to the literary (written) language, and is seldom heard in conversation.

Classification of Serbocroätian Verbs according to their Presents, with Subdivisions according to their Infinitives.

In Sbcr. the Present tense is characterized by one of three vowels: е, а, и, to which is added, where necessary, the final consonant or syllable indicating the person. (See p. 284.)

As in O.S., the first three classes have the same endings, but in the second class these are preceded by н while in the third class they are preceded by j. These are subdivided according to the Infinitive ending.

	3rd Pers.Sing. Pres.	Infinitive	
I. A.	тре́сē	тре́сти[1]	= shake. Same stem in the Pres. and Infin., consonantal stem.
also	по̀чнē	по̀чети	= begin (Pfve.). Infin. in -ети, from -ᴧти.
	у̏мрē	у̏мрети	= die (Pfve.). Infin. in -рети, from *-erti*.
B.	бе̏рē	бра̏ти	= gather. Infin. in. -ати, cons. stem.
II.	ди̏гнē	ди̏гнути (ди̏ћи)	= lift (Pfve.). *n*-stem.
	ле̏гнē	ле̏ћи	= lie down (Pfve.). *n*-stem.

III. *j*-verbs.
  1. Primary verbs:

A.a.	чу̏jē	чу̏ти	= hear. Same vowel stem in Pres. and Infin.
b.	ме̏љē	мле̏ти (from *melti*)	= grind. Same consonant stem in Pres. and Infin.
c.	пе̏њē се	пе̏ти се (from пᴧти)	= climb. Same nasal stem in Pres. and Infin.
B.a.	бри̏jē	бри̏jати	= shave. Vowel stem, Infin. in -ати.
b.	пи̏шē	пи̏сати	= write. Consonant stem, Infin. in -ати (yotation in present!)

[1] So also—
With velar stem:— пѐчē, 3rd p. pl. пѐкӯ пѐћи = to bake,
" dental " :— плѐтē, " " " плѐтӯ плѐсти = to knit,
" labial " :— грѐбē, " " " грѐбӯ грѐпсти = to scratch.

2. Derived verbs: (Categories III.2.A.a and b of
O.S. have contracted their endings, III.2.A.a giving
the new Sbcr. category No. IV below).

  ку̏пује̄ купо̀вати = buy. -у- Pres. stem, -ова-
            Infin. stem.
  пока̏зује̄ пока́зивати = show. -у- Pres. stem, -ива-
            Infin. stem.
  во̏јује̄ воје̏вати = make war. -у- Pres. stem,
           -ева- Infin. stem.

Here also really belong the few former -*eje*-
verbs, now contracted to -*e*:

  у̏ме у̏мети = know how to
  3rd pers. pl. у̏мејӯ

IV. New category, contracted from -*aje*- in Present,
including verbs with Infin. in -авати.

  чу̏ва̄ чу̏вати = keep
  и̏ма̄ и̏мати = have
  пове̏ћа̄ва̄ пове̏ћавати = increase

V. A. хва̑лӣ хва́лити = praise. *i*-stem throughout.
  B. ви̏дӣ ви̏дети = see. Pres. stem -и-,
          Infin. -ети<ѣти
   држӣ држати = hold. Pres. stem -и-,
          Infin. -ати, derived from
          -ѣти.

   бо̏јӣ се бо̏јати се = fear. Pres. stem -и-, In-
          fin. -ати<ѣти.

The few former "*m*" (athematic) verbs survive in
Sbcr. only in the Present of би̏ти (= to be), and
да̏ти (= to give, Pfve.); see Irregular Verbs below.
But it should be noted that the characteristic -м of
the 1st pers. sing. of this class has become generalized in Sbcr. for all the five modern categories of
verbs.

Tense and Mood Endings and Formation.

       Sing.   *Plur.*
     1st 2nd 3rd 1st 2nd 3rd
Present: тре́се̄ ⎫
    и̏ма̄ ⎬ -м, -ш — -мо, -те, ⎰-ӯ[1]
    ви̏дӣ ⎭   (*t* lost),   ⎨-ајӯ[1] (*t*
                     ⎩-е̄[1] lost)

[1]These endings are added direct to the final *consonant*
of the Present stem.

SERBOCROATIAN

	Sing.	Plur.	
	2nd.	1st.	2nd.

Imperative: трéс ⎫
    пи̑ш ⎬ -и   -имо, -ите consonantal stems
    др̀ж ⎭
    чу̑ ⎫
    и̑ма̄ ⎬ -j   -jмо, -jте vowel stems

  Formed from the *Present* stem. The 3rd pers. sing. and plur. are formed with не̏ка + Present.

Velar stems undergo the Second Palatalization, e.g. пѐци! = bake (stem пек-). Prohibitions are regularly expressed by нѐмо̄j, -мо, -те + Infinitive of either aspect:—нѐмо̄jте ви̏кати! = do not shout!.

	Sing.			Plur.		
	1st	2nd	3rd	1st	2nd	3rd

Aorist: Infin. stem + -x, -(-е), -(-е), -смо, -сте, -ше: зва̏х, зва̏, etc. = I called (*o* fill-vowel for consonant stems of Cl. I (and II), e.g. трéсох, трȇсе, etc. = I shook). This tense can be formed from verbs of either aspect but is most usually used for Perfective verbs. For velar stems of Cl. I 1st Palatalization occurs in 2nd and 3rd pers. sing., e.g. рѐкох, рѐче or рѐче.

	Sing.			Plur.		
	1st	2nd	3rd	1st	2nd	3rd

Imperfect: -иj ⎫
     -j ⎭ -а̄х, -а̄ше, -а̄ше, -а̄смо, -а̄сте, -а̄ху:

  This tense is formed from either the Present or the Infinitive stem of *Imperfective verbs only.*
  All verbs with Infinitive in -ати, have Imperfects in -а̄х, -а̄ше, etc., not preceded by j or -иj, e.g.:—

  бра̂х   = I was taking чу̑ва̄х = I was keeping
  пи̂са̄х = I was writing др̀жа̄х = I was holding
  пока̀зӣва̄х = I was showing

Other vowel stem verbs of Class III have the endings preceded by j, viz. -jа̄х, -jа̄ше, etc., e.g.:—

  чу̑jа̄х = I was hearing у̀меjа̄х = I used to know how to

  All verbs of Classes II and V have the endings -а̄х, -а̄ше, etc., with yotation of the preceding consonant of the *Present* stem, e.g.:—

то̀нēм = I sink, Infin. то̀нути Imperfect то̀ња̄х
но̀си̑м = I carry, "   но̀сити   "   но̀ша̄х

ви̏дӣм = I see, Infin. ви̏дети Imperfect ви̏ђа̄х
ми̏слӣм = I think   "   ми̏слити   "   ми̏шља̄х

Verbs of Cl. I with consonantal stems and with Infinitives *not* in -ати, have the endings -ија̄х, -ија̄ше, etc., or -а̄х, -а̄ше, etc., added to the Infinitive stem. Before the endings -ија̄х, etc. velar stems undergo the Second Palatalization. E.g.:—

тре́сија̄х or тре́са̄х = I was shaking
ве́зија̄х   " ве́за̄х = I was embroidering
 (from ве́зе̄м, Infin. ве́сти)
пѐција̄х   = I was baking

бе̏ре̄м, бра̏ти = to take, can also have: бе̏рија̄х as an alternative to бра̄х.

Past[1]: Past Part. Active in -о (masc. sing.), -ла (fem. sing.), -ло (neut. sing.), -ли (masc. plur.), -ле (fem. plur.), -ла (neut. plur.) added to the Infinitive stem + enclitics сам, си, је, смо, сте, су, or with the Personal Pronouns preceding the enclitic followed by the P.P.A., ја̑ сам би̏о, etc. = I was, have been. The enclitics can be omitted from the forms of the 3rd persons sing. and pl. in reports, etc., and are regularly omitted in the 3rd persons with reflexive verbs. Negative form: ни́сам био = I have not been, was not (See p. 290, footnote 5).

Pluperfect: Imperfect of би̏ти (бе̏ја̄х) + Past Part. Active: ја̑ бе̏ја̄х би̏о = I had been, or (Compound) Past of би̏ти + Past Part. Active: ја̑ сам би̏о и̏мао, би̏о сам и̏мао = I had had. (Rare; used only in complex sentences.)

Future: Infin. less -ти, + -ћу, -ћеш, -ће, -ћемо, -ћете, -ће̄: и̏маћу[2], or with Pers. Pron. preceding enclitic and full Infin.: ја̑ ћу и̏мати = I shall have. (Infinitives in -ћи preserved in full and written separately: ре̏ћи ћу = I shall say (Pfve).) Negative form: не́ћу и̏мати = I shall not have. (See p. 291, footnote 1.)

Future Perfect (Exact Future): бу̏де̄м, бу̏де̄ш, бу̏де̄, бу̏де̄мо, бу̏де̄те, бу̏дӯ, + Past Part. Active: (ка̏д) бу̏де̄м пи́тао = (when) I shall have asked (rare). Used

---

[1]Also called: Compound Past or Perfect,—the normal tense for past time.

[2]In the western tradition this is written: ȉmat ću, but pronounced ȉmaću.

Notice the assimilation of consonant с to ш in тре́шћу, etc. = I shall shake.

only in complex sentences. In the Perfective aspect usually replaced by the Perfective Present: кȁд до̑ђеш = when you come, for кȁд бу̏де̄ш до̏шао,...

Conditional: Past Part. Active + enclitics бих, би, би, бисмо, бисте, би: ѝмао бих, ѝмали би, or in the reverse order preceded by the Pers. Pron. or other subject: jȃ бих ѝмао = I would have. (Formed from verbs of *both* aspects.)

Past Conditional: Formed from the Conditional of би̏ти + Past Participle Active: би̏о бих пи́тао = I would have asked.

Infinitive termination: -ти; -ћи for velar stems of Cl. I.

Present Gerund Active: 3rd pers. plur. Pres. + -ћи: ѝмајӯћӣ, тре́сӯћӣ, но̀се̄ћи = having, shaking, carrying. (Formed from Impfve. verbs only!)

Past Gerund Active: Infinitive stem plus -в(ши): ѝма̄вши = having had. (Formed from verbs of either aspect, but mostly from Perfective verbs.) Fill-vowel a is used for cons. stem verbs of Cl. I, e.g. рѐка̄вши = having said.

Past Participle Active: Infin. stem + -о (masc.), -ла (fem.), -ло (neut.); plur. -ли (masc.), -ле (fem.), -ла (neut.). (Formed from verbs of either aspect.) Consonant stem verbs of Cl. I use fill-vowel a in the masc. sing., e.g. мо̀гао =(was)able.

Past Participle Passive: This is formed (for transitive verbs only) in four different ways from the Infinitive stem of verbs of both aspects with the endings:—

	Sing. m.	f.	n.	Pl. m.	f.	n.
(a)	-н	-на	-но	-ни	-не	-на
or (b)	-т	-та	-то	-ти	-те	-та

1. All verbs with Infinitive in -ати add endings *(a)* to the Infinitive stem in -a, e.g.:—

бра̑н = taken   пи́са̄н = written
ку̀пова̄н = bought   пе̏ва̄н = sung
др̀жа̄н = held

2. Endings *(a)* preceded by e are used for

(i) consonant stem verbs of Cl. I (velar stems undergo the 1st Palatalization):—

тре́сен = shaken   пѐчен = baked

(ii) vowel stem verbs of Cl. III 1 A a, which develop a ј or в before these endings to avoid hiatus:—

добѝјен or добѝвен = obtained
чу̏вен = heard
испѝјен (or ѝспӣт) = drunk up

3. Endings *(a)* preceded by e are also used for verbs of Cl. V, the stem of which undergoes yotation, e.g.:—

но̏шен = carried   вѝђен = seen

4. Endings *(b)* are used for all verbs of Cl. II, being added to the Infinitive stem in -ну, and for a few other verbs with monosyllabic roots:—

дѝгнут = lifted   препо̏знāт = recognized
до̏нēт = brought   у̏сӯт = strewn
про̏др̄т = pierced   по̏чēт = begun
да̏т = given

The participles can be used adjectivally and declined, either as Definite or as Indefinite adjectives.

Verbal Nouns. These can be formed by adding -је to the Past Participle Passive, most commonly of Imperfective verbs. e.g. пи́сање = writing, пу̏шење = smoking, зна́чење = meaning. Verbal nouns from Perfective verbs usually have a purely substantival meaning, e.g. створе́ње = creature, свану́ће = dawn, ослобође́ње = liberation.

SERBOCROATIAN

Examples of the Conjugation of the Simple Tenses of Verbs

1. *e*-type   трѐсти = to shake

	Present.	*Imperative.*	*Imperfect.*	*Aorist.*
Sing. 1	трéсе̄м [1]	—	трéс(иј)а̄х [2]	трéсох [3]
2	трéсе̄ш	трéси	трéс(иј)а̄ше	трȇсе
3	трéсе̄	—	трéс(иј)а̄ше	трȇсе
Plur. 1	трéсе̄мо	трéсимо	трéс(иј)а̄смо	трéсосмо
2	трéсе̄те	трéсите	трéс(иј)а̄сте	трéсосте
3	трéсӯ	—	трéс(иј)а̄ху	трéсоше

Gerunds: Present, трéсӯћи; Past, трéсавши.
Past Participles: Active, трȇсао, трéсла, трéсло; Passive, трéсен.

2. *a*-type   ѝмати = to have

	Present.	*Imperative.*	*Imperfect.*	*Aorist.*
Sing. 1	ѝма̄м [4]	—	ѝма̄х	ѝмах
2	ѝма̄ш	ѝма̄ј	ѝма̄ше	ѝма
3	ѝма̄	—	ѝма̄ше	ѝма
Plur. 1	ѝма̄мо	ѝма̄јмо	ѝма̄смо	ѝмасмо
2	ѝма̄те	ѝма̄јте	ѝма̄сте	ѝмасте
3	ѝма̄јӯ	—	ѝма̄ху	ѝмаше

Gerunds: Present, ѝма̄јӯћи; Past, ѝма̄вши.
Past Participles: Active, ѝмао, ѝмала, ѝмало; Passive (чѝта̄н = read).

---

[1] With change of accent in 1st and 2nd pers. Pl. Pres.: плѐте̄м = I weave, плете́мо, -е́те; мре̑м = I die, мре́мо.

[2] Cf. то̀њах, чу̏јах, пи́сах, вѐровах = I was sinking, hearing, writing, believing.

[3] Cf. ди̏гох, мѐтнух, чу̏х, пѝсах, вѐровах = I lifted, put, heard, wrote, believed.

[4] With change of accent in 1st and 2nd pers. pl. Pres.: вѐнча̄м = I marry (trans.), венча́мо, -а́те.

3. *i*-type   хва́лити = to praise

	Present.	*Imperative.*	*Imperfect.*	*Aorist.*
Sing. 1	хва̂ли̂м[1]	—	хва̂ља̄х[2]	хва̂лих[3]
2	хва̂ли̂ш	хва́ли	хва̂ља̄ше	хва̂ли
3	хва̂ли̂	—	хва̂ља̄ше	хва̂ли
Plur. 1	хва̂ли̂мо	хва́лимо	хва̂ља̄смо	хва́лисмо
2	хва̂ли̂те	хва́лите	хва̂ља̄сте	хва́листе
3	хва̂ле̄	—	хва̂ља̄ху	хва́лише

Gerunds: Present, хва́ле̄ћи; Past, хва́ли̂вши.
Past Participles: Active, хва́лио, хва́лила, хва́лило; Passive, хва̂љен.

Conjugation of Irregular Verbs in Serbocroätian.
The old Athematic Verbs.

би̏ти = to be

	Present.	*Imperative.*	*Imperfect.*	*Aorist.*
Sing. 1	је̏сам, сам[4],[5]	—	бе̏ја̄х	бе̂х[6]
2	је̏си, си	бу̏ди	(reg.)	бе́ше	би̂
3	је̏ст(е),[4] је	—	бе́ше	би̂
Plur. 1	је̏смо, смо	бу̏димо	бе́смо	би̏смо
2	је̏сте, сте	бу̏дите	бе́сте	би̏сте
3	је̏су, су	—	бе́ху	би̏ше

Gerunds: Present, бу̏дӯћи; Past, би̏в(ши) (As an adj. = former).
Past Participle: би̏о, би̏ла, би̏ло.

  The tense: бу̏де̄м, бу̏де̄ш, бу̏де̄, бу̏де̄мо, бу̏де̄те, бу̏дӯ, is used for "to be" in subordinate clauses not

---

[1] With change of accent in 1st and 2nd pers. pl. Pres.: го̀ри̂м = I burn (intrans.), гори́мо; спи̂м = I sleep, спи́мо.
[2] Cf. у̑ча̄х, ви̑ђа̄х, др̏жа̄х = I was teaching, seeing, holding.
[3] Cf. ви̏дех, *je*-dialect ви̏дјех; др̏жах = I saw, held.
[4] The forms without je- for 1st, 2nd p. sing. and 1st, 2nd, 3rd p. plur. and "je" for 3rd p. sing. are the enclitic and auxiliary forms. A form је̏сте = it is (so), is used in answer.
[5] Special negative form, also used with neg. Past tense; ни́сам, ни́си, ни́је, ни́смо, ни́сте, ни́су.
[6] The *je*-dialect has the vowel је̑ throughout in all persons: бје̑х, бје̑ше, etc.; also би̏ја̄х, etc.

dealing with facts: мо̑ра да бу̏де̄ = he should be, but мо̑ра̄ да је = he must (surely) be. It is also used to form the Future Perfect.

је̏сти = to eat

Pres. је̏де̄м (reg. Class I) or и̏је̄м (reg.)

Imperative је̏ди

Gerunds: Present је̏дӯћи

Past (по̏)једа̄вши

Past Partic. Act. је̏о, је̏ла or и̏о

Aor. је̏дох

Imperf. је̏ђа̄х or је̏да̄х

Past Partic. Pass. је̏ден

да̏ти = to give (Pfvę.)

Present

Sing. 1 да̏м or да́дем   Imperative: да̑ј
2 да̑ш   (reg.)   Past Gerund: да̏вши
3 да̏   Past Part. Act.: да̏о, да́ла
Plur. 1 да́мо   Aorist: да̏х or да̏дох (more common)
2 да́те   Past Part. Pass.: да̑н or да̑т
3 да̏јӯ or да́дӯ

Other Verbs.

хте̏ти = to want

	Present.	*Imperat.(rare)*	*Imperfect.*	*Aorist.*
Sing. 1	хо̏ћу[1]	—	хо̏ћа̄х, хо̏тија̄х,	хте̏дох or
2	хо̏ћеш	(хте̏дни)	or хти̏ја̄х	хте̏х (rare)
3	хо̏ће	—	(regular)	(regular)
Plur. 1	хо̏ћемо	(хте̏днимо)		
2	хо̏ћете	(хте̏дните)		
3	хо̏ће̄	—		

Gerunds: Present, хо̏те̄ћи or х(о)те̏ћи; Past, хте̏вши or хо̏те̏вши.

Past Participle Active: (eastern) хте̏о, хте̏ла, хте̏ло

---

[1]Special negative form, also used with neg. Future tense; не́ћу, не́ћеш, не́ће, не́ћемо, не́ћете, не́ће̄.

хтѐло, (western) хтио̀, хтјѐла, хтјѐло.

мо̀ћи = to be able

	Present.	*Imperfect.*	*Aorist.*
Sing. 1	мо̀гу	мо̀га̄х	мо̀гох
2	мо̀жē̄ш	(reg.)	мо̀же or мо̏же
3	мо̀жē̄		мо̀же or мо̏же
Plur. 1	мо̀жē̄мо		мо̀госмо
2	мо̀жē̄те		мо̀госте
3	мо̀гӯ		мо̀гоше

Gerund, Present: мо̀гӯћи, Past: мо̀га̄вши
Past Participle Active: мо̀гао, мо̀гла, мо̀гло

зна̀ти (= to know), ѝмати (= to have) have Presents зна́дē̄м, има́дē̄м besides зна̑м, ѝмам*

Notice also:—

Infinitive Class I.	*Present.*	*Past Part.Act.*	*Past Part. Pass.*
ра́сти = to grow	ра́стē̄м	ра̑стао, ра́сла	—
сѐсти = to sit down (Pfve.)	сѐднē̄м	сѐо, сѐла (So also па̀сти = to fall, Pfve., etc.)	—
бо̀сти = to prick	бо̀дē̄м	бо̀, бо̀ла	бо̀ден
грѐпсти = to scratch	грѐбē̄м	грѐбао, грѐбла	грѐбен, гребѐна
		(So all labial stems.)	
по̀мо̀ћи = to help (Pfve.)	по̀могнē̄м	по̀могао, по̀мо̀гла (Imperative по̀мо̀зи)	—
на̀сӯти = to pour out (Pfve.)	на̀спē̄м	на̀суо, на̀сула	на̀сӯт
клѐти = to curse	кӯ́нē̄м	клѐо, клѐла	клѐт
у̀зѐти = to take (Pfve.)	у̀змē̄м	у̀зео, у̀зела	у̀зē̄т
на̀дути се = to swell (Pfve.)	на̀дмē̄м се	на̀дуо, на̀дула	на̀дӯт or наду̀вен

*Special negative form: нȇмати, Pres. нȇма̄м = I have not, нȇма̄ш, нȇма̄, нȇма̄мо, нȇма̄те, нȇмајӯ; нȇма = there is (are) no(t)....

у̀мре̄ти = to die   у̀пре̄м   у̀мр̏о, у̀мрла   —
   (Pfve.)   (So also other verbs with *r*-root.)
тр̏ти = to rub   тр̑е̄м or   тр̏о, тр̏ла   тр̏т or
                      та̀ре̄м   (Aor. тр̏х, тр̏)   тр̀ен or
                                                             тр̀вен
тка̀ти = to weave   че̑м, че̑мо,   тка̀о, тка̀ла   тка̑н
                      чу̑ or тке̑м
                      or тка̑м
гна̀ти = to drive   жѐне̄м or   гна̀о, гна̀ла   гна̑н or
                      гна̑м   (Imperf. гна̏х)   гна̑т

Class II.

ста̀ти = to stop   ста̀не̄м   ста̀о, Aor.
   (Pfve., intrans.)   ста̏х or ста̀дох
дѐнути or
   дѐсти = to   дѐне̄м or   де̏о, де̏ла,   дѐвен or
   put (Pfve.)   дѐде̄м   Aor. де̏х or   де̏т
                                        де̏дох
      (Many verbs of Class II can drop the syllable -ну in
      the Past Part. Active and Aorist.)
пр̏снути¹ = to   пр̏сне̄м   пр̏скао, пр̏сла   —
   burst, spirt   or   пр̏снуо
   (Pfve.)   (Aor. пр̏скох,
                                          пр̏ште or пр̏снух)

Class III.

млѐти = to grind   мѐље̄м   мле̏о   млѐвен,
                                                              млевѐна
сла̀ти = to send   ша̀ље̄м   сла̏о
по̀слати = to
   send (Pfve.)   по̀шаље̄м or   по̀слао   по̀сла̄н or
                     по̀шље̄м   по̀сла̄т
кла̀ти = to
   slaughter   ко̀ље̄м   кла̏о   кла̑н or
                                                              кла̑т
жѐти or њѐти
   = to reap   ње̑м or   же̏о or   же̑т or
                     жа̑ње̄м   ње̏о   њѐвен,
                                                              њевѐна
пе̏ти = to raise   пѐње̄м   пе̏о, пе́ла   пе̏т
кљу̀вати = to peck   кљу̀је̄м   кљу̀вао   кљу̀ва̄н
                                        (Imperf. кљу̀ва̄х)

¹So also сти̏снути = to squeeze, пра̏снути = to explode.

да̀вати = to give
(Impfve.)   да̑је̄м or   да́вао   да̄ва̄н
             да̑ва̄м   (Imperf. да̑ва̄х)
             Imperative: да́ји (see Class V below)
             or да̑ва̄j

Class IV

тре̏бати = to be
  necessary   тре̏ба   тре̏бало
  (impers.)

Class V

Verbs with long root vowels in the Infinitive before a j, have Imperatives in -ји:—
   So: та́јити = to conceal, Imperat. та́ји
       га́јити = to cultivate,   "   га́ји
   благосло̀вити = to bless, regular except Past Part. Pass.: благосло̏вен, благословѐна

ве̏лӣм (rarely ве̏љу) = I say, has only a Present, Pres. Ger. ве̏лѣћи or велѣ́ћи, Imperf. ве̏љӑх.

Infinitive.   *Present.*   *Past Part. Act.*

вре̏ти = to boil, врӣ̏м, 3rd p. pl. вру̑, Pres. Ger.
               вру̑ћи, otherwise regular.
    So also зре̏ти = to ripen (rare).
спа̏ти = to sleep   спӣ̏м   спа̏о
       (usually спа́вати, спа̑ва̄м, regular Cl. IV)
ста̏јати = to stand сто̏јӣм   ста̏јао, ста̏ја̄ла
                                  (Imperat. сто̑j)
ћу́тати = to be
  silent   ћу́тӣм, otherwise regular
  but
ћу́тети = to feel   ћу́тӣм (quite regular)

Verbs of Going and Conveying

и̏ћи (= to go—on foot or conveyed, Impfve., Pfve. and Freq.) has Pres. и̏де̄м or и̏де̑м; Past Participle и̏шао or и̏шао, и̏шла; Past Gerund и̏ша̄вши, Aor. и̏дох, Imperfect и̏ђа̄х.
   до́ћи (= to come, Pfve.) has Pres. до̑ђе̄м; Past Part. до̀шао, до̀шла, Aor. до́ђох; Impfve. до̀лазити.
   о̀тићи[1] (= to go away, Pfve.) has Pres. о̀тӣде̄м or о̀тӣђе̄м or о̀де̄м; Past Part. о̀тишао,[1] Aor. о̀тӣдох[1] or отӣ̀ђох or о̀дох; Impfve. о̀длазити.

[1] Alternative possible accents are given.

и̏зи̏ћи[1] (= to go out, Pfve.) or и̏за̑ћи[1] has Pres. и̏зи̑ђе̄м or и̏за̄ђе̄м or и̏зи̑де̄м; Past. Part. и̏зи̏шао[1] or и̏за̀шао,[1] Aor. изи̏ђох, иза̑ђох or изи̑дох; Impfve. и̏злазити.

Notice also:—

- хо̀дити (Impfve. and Freq.) = to go (on foot), Pres. хо̏ди̑м; Imperat. хо̏ди = come here!
- хо̀дати (Impfve. and Freq.) = to walk, pace, Pres. хо̑да̄м
- сти̏ћи (Pfve.) = to arrive, Pres. сти̏гне̄м, P.P.A. сти̏гао, сти̏гла
- сти̏зати (Impfve.) = to arrive, Pres. сти̏же̄м
- ја̀хати " = to ride, Pres. ја̏ше̄м
- поха́ђати " = to visit, " по̏ха̄ђа̄м
- по́ћи (Pfve.) = to start out, (like до́ћи); по̀лазити (Impfve.)
- на́ћи " = to find, (like до́ћи), P.P.P. на̀ђен; на̀лазити (Impfve.)

To carry = но̀сити (Impfve. and Freq.), Pres. но̀си̑м[2]
по̀не̄ти (Pfve.), Pres. понѐсе̄м, понѐсе́мо[1]
Past Part. Act. по̀нео (masc.), по̀не̄ла (fem.)
Aor. понѐсо̄х or по̀не̄х
Past Part. Pass. по̀несен or по̀не̄т

To bring (carrying) = доно̀сити (Impfve.), Pres. до̀носи̑м; до̀не̄ти (Pfve.), Pres. донѐсе̄м

To lead = во̀дити (Impfve. and Freq.), Pres. во̀ди̑м.[3]
по̀вести[1] (Pfve.), Pres. повѐде̄м, Past Part. Active по̀вео (masc.), по̀вела (fem.)

To bring (a person) = дово̀дити (Impfve.), Pres. до̀води̑м.
до̀вести[1] (Pfve.), Pres. довѐде̄м.

To convey = во̀зити (Impfve. and Freq.), Pres. во̀зи̑м.[4]
по̀вести[1] (Pfve.), Pres. повѐзе̄м, Past Part. Act. по̀везао (masc.), по̀ве̄зла[1] (fem.)

To bring (conveyed) = дово̀зити (Impfve.), Pres. до̀вози̑м; до̀вести[1] (Pfve.), Pres. довѐзе̄м.

[1] Alternative possible accents are given.
[2] но̏сати, Pres. но̑са̄м = to carry to and fro.
[3] во̏дати, Pres. во̑да̄м = to conduct, accompany, walk (a horse).
[4] во̏зати, Pres. во̑за̄м = to drive, trundle, to and fro.

The Formation of Aspects.

Aspects in Serbocroätian are formed, as in other Slavonic languages, in four main ways:—

1. The Perfective from the (simple) Imperfective by adding a prepositional prefix, e.g.:—

пи́сати	= to write	написати
мо̀лити	= to request	замо́лити
пѝти	= to drink	по̀пити

2. The Imperfective from the (simple or compound) Perfective by lengthening phonetically or by adding a syllable, e.g.:—

одгово̀рити	= to answer	одгова́рати
помо̀ћи	= to help	пома́гати
у̀мре̄ти	= to die	у̀мирати
ку́пити	= to buy	купо̀вати
по̀стати	= to become	по̀стајати
да̏ти	= to give	да́вати
у̀бити	= to kill	уби́јати

3. The Impfve. from the Pfve., by changing the Infinitive ending:—

пу̀стити	= to let, allow	пу́штати
дѝгнути, дѝћи	= to lift	дѝзати
у̀дарити	= to hit	у̀дарати
ле̏ћи	= to lie down	ле́гати

4. Sometimes different forms of the same root are used for the two aspects or entirely different roots:—

у̀зети	Pfve.	= to take	у̀зимати	Impfve.
по̀че̄ти	"	= to begin	по̀чињати	"
до̀не̄ти	"	= to bring	доно̀сити	"
до̀ћи	"	= to come	до̀лазити	"

Only wide experience and reading can guide the student as to usage on this point, as there are no absolute rules for any class of verbs, as in other Slavonic languages.

WORD ORDER WITH ENCLITICS

The word order in a sentence is very free in Slavonic languages owing to the inflections, which themselves indicate the relation of words one to another in a clause. This gives greater scope for emphasizing different words of a phrase to express emotion, excitement, contrast, etc. than in uninflected languages.

The general rule is that all *clauses* must start with a strong (non-enclitic) word. But when a clause includes enclitics, certain rules are generally adhered to in conversation and in good writing. The rules in Serbocroätian are more elaborate than in any other Slavonic language owing to the greater frequency of enclitics.

The word order in both main and subordinate clauses follows the following formula[1]:—

1. Usually only one non-enclitic word to start the clause (this may be a noun, main verb, conjunction, adverb, adjective—even separated from its noun, a strong pronoun, numeral, or a preposition + its noun or pronoun);
2. enclitic auxiliary verb;
3. Dative (or Genitive) encl. Personal Pronoun;
4. Accusative encl. Personal Pronoun, e.g.:—

    Jâ сам му се вѐћ (би̏о) прѐдставио.
    = I had already introduced myself to him.

The aux. verb when negative does not count as an enclitic, and therefore follows the true enclitics, e.g.:—

    Jâ му се jо̑ш ни̏сам прѐдставио.
    = I have not introduced myself to him yet.

Only the 3rd pers. sing. Past enclitic aux. verb "je" does not conform to this order; it *follows* the encl. Pers. Pronouns, e.g.:—

    О̑н ми их је вѐћ да̏о.
    = He has already given them to me.

In Serbocroätian, in contrast to Slovenian, "ce je" is usually reduced to just "ce", e.g.:—

    То̑ им се са̏мо та̏ко чѝнило.
    = This only seemed to them like that.

With the Future tense either the Infinitive (usually merged with the aux. verb), or the subject (noun or Nominative Pers. Pronoun) ordinarily comes first. e.g.:—

---

[1]It can be observed in modern writing that when only *one* enclitic, particularly ce or je, occurs in a clause, it is often put *after* the main verb, e.g. Мла̏ди Пѐтар сти̏гао је у Бео̀град = Young Peter has arrived in Belgrade. Стра̏на валу́та ме̑ња̄ се о̏вде = Foreign currency is exchanged here.

Ка̑заћу му то̑ or Jа̑ ћу му то̑ ка́зати.
= I shall tell that to him.

With the Past and Conditional, either the Past Participle or the subject start the clause; the *strong* form of the Past or Future aux. verb *may* start the clause to express emphasis, e.g.:—

Ка́зао сам му то̑ or Jа̑ сам му то̑ ка́зао.
= I have said that to him.

Ка́зао бих му то̑ or Jа̑ бих му то̑ ка́зао.
= I would say that to him.

Jѐсам му то̑ ка́зао.
= I *have* said that to him.

Хо̀ћу му то̑ ка́зати.
= I shall indeed say that to him.

N.B.—Neither the Nominative Pers. Pronouns, as in the examples above, nor any cases of the Demonstrative pronouns, even if monosyllabic, e.g. то̑, are enclitic. (But the Reflexive pronoun "се" counts as an Accusative enclitic—see examples above). E.g.:—

Ти̑ му нѐћеш ка́зати то̑!
= You won't tell him *that*!

The long accented forms of the Personal Pronouns are used only for emphasis, and may then come anywhere in the sentence, e.g.:—

Ње̏га нѐћу ни̏када во̏лети!
= Him I shall never like!

In questions it is safest for the foreigner to start with да̏ ли, after which the identical order as above is preserved, e.g.:—

Да̏ ли сте га ви̏дели?
= Have you seen him?

If only ли (itself an enclitic interrogative particle, taking precedence over all other enclitics) is used with a compound tense, then a non-enclitic word (either the Past Part. or the *full* form of the aux. verb) must start the sentence, except that "је", the 3rd pers. sing. Past enclitic aux. verb, may regularly start a question, e.g.:—

Да̏о ли би му то̑ ти̑?
= Would *you* give that to him?

Jѐси ли му је ве̏ћ да̏о?
= Have you already given it (fem.) to him?

Хо̀ћеш ли му то̂ ре̏ћи?
= Will you say that to him?

Је̏ ли о̑н ве̏ћ та̏мо?[1]
= Is he already there?

Questions starting with Interrogative pronouns or adverbs follow the general rules above, e.g.:—

Гдѐ си му их (ти̑) прѐдао?
= Where did you hand them over to him?

The negative particle не is a *proclitic* capable of starting a sentence and always preceding the verb or other word it negatives; it is fused with the aux. verb in the Past and Future tenses, and takes the accent off words with a falling intonation, e.g.:—

Ни́сам га та̏мо ви̏део.   = I have not seen him there.
Не́ћу га ви̏дети.   = I shall not see him.
Не ва̄ља̄   = One should not
Нѐ може̄(><мо̏же̄)   = One cannot, it is impossible

"Jу" replaces "je" for the Accusative sing. fem. 3rd pers. Personal Pronoun in cases where two "je's" would otherwise follow or in any other doubtful case (cf. footnote 3, p. 264), e.g.:—

О̑н jу jе во̏лео.
= He liked her, or loved her.

TEXTS

I. Свето Јеванђеље по Луци, глава 8.

ПРИЧА О СИЈАЧУ

5. Изиђе сијач да сије сјеме своје; и кад сијаше, једно паде покрај пута, и погази се, и птице небеске позобаше га. 6. А друго паде на камен, и изникавши осуши се, јер немаше влаге. 7. И друго паде у трње, и узрасте трње, и удави га. 8. А друго паде на земљу добру, и изникавши донесе род сто пута онолико. Говорећи овако повика: ко има уши да чује нека чује.

---

[1] је̏ ли, when added at the end of a question, means 'isn't it so?' (French n'est-ce pas?), e.g.: То је пра̑ва̄ и̏стина, је̏ ли? = That's the real truth, is it?

II. *Sveto Jevanđelje po Luci*, glava 8.

PRIČA O SIJAČU

5. Iziđe sijač da sije sjeme svoje; i kad sijaše, jedno pade pokraj puta, a pogazi se, i ptice nebeske pozobaše ga. 6. A drugo pade na kamen, i iznikavši osuši se, jer nemaše vlage. 7. I drugo pade u trnje, i uzraste trnje, i udavi ga. 8. A drugo pade na zemlju dobru, i iznikavši donese rod sto puta onoliko. Govoreći ovako povika: ko ima uši da čuje neka čuje.

III. *From the collection of folk tales*: В. Караџић, Српске народне приповетке.

ОЛЕС АЈНС, КАО ШВАБИ ТРАЛАЛА

Приповиједа се како су ђаво и Швабо погодили да један другога носи, докле онај који се носи не испјева једну пјесму. Тако најприје узјаше ђаво на Шваба и започевши најдужу пјесму коју је знао, стане пјевати, а кад је сврши, онда Швабо узјаше на ђавола, али мјесто каке праве пјесме заинтачи пјевати *тралала*, и тако Швабо преварио ђавола, те га је морао носити читав дан, а пјесми ни краја ни конца.

IV. *From the collection of folk tales*: V. Karadžić, Srpske narodne pripovetke.

OLES AJNS (ALLES EINS), KAO ŠVABI TRALALA

Pripovijeda se kako su đavo i Švabo pogodili da jedan drugoga nosi, dokle onaj koji se nosi ne ispjeva jednu pjesmu. Tako najprije uzjaše đavo na Švaba i započevši najdužu pjesmu koju je znao, stane pjevati, a kad se svrši, onda Švabo uzjaše na đavola, ali mjesto kake prave pjesme zaintači pjevati *tralala*, a tako Švabo prevario đavola, te ga morao nositi čitav dan, a pjesmi ni kraja ni konca.

V. *Passage from a Serbian folk ballad* (народна песма).

СМРТ МАЈКЕ ЈУГОВИЋА

Мили Боже, чуда великога,
Кад се слеже на Косово војска
У тој војсци девет Југовића
И десети стар Јуже Богдане.
5 Бога моли Југовића мајка,
Да јој Бог да̂ очи соколове
И бијела крила лабудова
Да одлети на Косово равно
И да види девет Југовића
10 И десетог стар-Југа Богдана.

Што молила, Бога домолила:
Бог јој дао очи соколове
И бијела крила лабудова.
Она лети на Косово равно,
15 Мртвих нађе девет Југовића
И десетог стар-Југа Богдана,
И више њих девет бојних копља,
На копљима девет соколова,
Око копља девет добрих коња,
20 А поред њих девет љутих лава.
Тад завришта девет добрих коња,
И залаја девет љутих лава,
А закликта девет соколова.
И ту мајка тврда срца била,
25 Да од срца сузе не пустила,
Већ узима девет добрих коња,
И узима девет љутих лава,
И узима девет соколова,
Пак се врати двору бијеломе.
30 Далеко је снахе угледале,
Мало ближе пред њу ишетале:
Закукало девет удовица,
Заплакало девет сиротица,
Завриштало девет добрих коња,
35 Залајало девет љутих лава,
Закликтало девет соколова.
И ту мајка тврда срца била,
Да од срца сузе не пустила.
Кад је било ноћи у поноћи,
40 Ал' завришта Дамјанов Зеленко.
Пита мајка Дамјанове љубе:
"Снахо моја, љубо Дамјанова,
Што нам вришти Дамјањов Зеленко?
Ал' је гладан шенице бјелице,
45 Али жедан воде са Звечана?"
Проговара љуба Дамјанова:
"Свекрвице, мајко Дамјанова,
Нит' је гладан шенице бјелице,
Нити је жедан воде са Звечана.
50 Већ је њега Дамјан научио
До поноћи ситну зоб зобати,
Од поноћи на друм путовати;
Пак он жали свога господара,
Што га није на себи донио."
55 И ту мајка тврда срца била,
Да од срца сузе не пустила.
Кад у јутру данак освануо,
Али лете два врана гаврана;
Крвава им крила до рамена,
60 На кљунове б'јела пјена тргла:

```
           Они носе руку од јунака,
           И на руци бурма позлаћена;
           Бацају је у криоце мајци.
           Узе руку Југовића мајка,
      65   Окретала, превртала с њоме,
           Па дозивље Дамјанову љубу:
           "Снахо моја, љубо Дамјанова,
           Би л' познала чија ј' ово рука?"
           Проговара љуба Дамјанова:
      70   "Свекрвице, мајко Дамјанова,
           Ово ј' рука нашега Дамјана,
           Јера бурму ја познајем, мајко,
           Бурма са мном на вјенчању била."
           Узе мајка руку Дамјанову,
      75   Окретала, превртала с њоме,
           Пак је руци тихо бесједила:
           "Моја руко, зелена јабуко,
           Гдје си расла, гдје л' си устргнута!
           А расла си на криоцу моме,
      80   Устргнута на Косову равном."

           То изусти, лаку душу пусти.
```

VI. В. Петровић.

ВЕРУЈТЕ ПРВО

Прво је: сваки нека зна шта хоће!
О маглу копља никад се не ломе.
Слободе? Добро! Ал' то није воће
Што зрело пада у шешир ма коме.
Верујте прво! и стисните пести,
Па онда трести, трести!

Господин, сељак, богат и сирома',
У успех борбе верујте—и доста.
И ваша снага биће снага грома,
И замршена питања сва проста.
Верујте прво, и стисните пести,
Па онда трести, трести!

Велика дела ишту тврду шију.
Зачеп'те уста мудрих грошићара!
Дигните срца! Згаз'те сумње змију,
И бор'те се за успех без шићара.
Верујте прво, и стисните пести,
Па онда трести, трести!

Вера у успех, успеха је пола.
Слободе прстен ко на руци носи,
Тај већ је јачи него сила хола,
И церов лист му већ цвета у коси.

Верујте прво, и стисните пести,
Па онда трести, трести!

—Ми сви сад знамо: хоћемо слободе,
И да смо своји у рођеној кући;—
И пре но што нам мач срца прободе
О вољу нашу он ће крто пући.
Ми верујемо! И стиснутих пести,
Са руку наших ланце ћемо стрести!

VII. J. Дучић.

ЈАБЛАНОВИ

Зашто ноћас тако шуме јабланови,
Тако страсно, чудно? Зашто тако шуме?
Жут је месец давно зашао за хуме,
Далеке и црне к'о слутње, и снови

У тој мртвој ноћи пали су на воду,
К'о олово мирну и сиву, у мраку.
Јабланови само високо у зраку
Шуме, шуме чудно, и дркћу у своду.

...Сâм крај мирне воде, у ноћи ја стојим,
К'о потоњи човек. Земљом, према мени,
Лежи моја сенка. Ја се ноћас бојим
Себе, и ја стрепим сâм од своје сени.

VIII. J. Dučić.

JABLANOVI

Zašto noćas tako šume jablanovi,
Tako strasno, čudno? Zašto tako šume?
Žut je mesec davno zašao za hume,
Daleke i crne k'o slutnje, i snovi

U toj mrtvoj noći pali su na vodu,
K'o olovo mirnu i sivu, u mraku.
Jablanovi samo visoko u zraku
Šume, šume čudno, i drkću u svodu.

...Sâm kraj mirne vode, u noći ja stojim,
K'o potonji čovek. Zemljom, prema meni,
Leži moja senka. Ja se noćas bojim
Sebe, i ja strepim sâm od svoje seni.

IX. Р. Домановић.

From ПЕВАЧЕВ УСКРС

Он је у овоме месту, где сада живи, тек од пре три месеца. Никоме није причао од куда је дошао, а бесумње га нико за порекло није ни питао. У осталом, ко ће га и питати? Он лепо пева и удара у тамбуру, а то је главно. Весело друштво се искупи и зове Перу. Тамбура зазвечи, а он запева, рецимо: "Од севдаха горег јада нема, ал' севдах се са севдахом вида!" или ма шта тако, и коме би онда крај вина и такве песме пало на ум, да припита Перу одакле је и што је амо дошао.

Не верујем да би и теби, читаоче, стало до његова порекла, па чак и до ове моје приче, само кад би чуо звук његове тамбуре и онај његов и сладак и силан глас. Та кад он запева коју песму што у срце дира, заборавиш и сâм ко си и шта си, већ се сав предаш звуцима, који те опијају час слатком тугом и чежњом, час бујном веселошћу, те се душа, устрептала, опијена од таква осећања, предаје валима звука на милост и немилост, да је носе собом куда хоће.

Е, али кад њега нема да запева, онда можете допустити да бар ја о њему причам.

Није он случајно дошао у ово место, где га нико није познавао. То је тако морало бити. Пера је син доста имућних родитеља, без којих остаде још у осамнаестој својој години. Кад је постао пунолетан ожени се, прими наслеђе и отпочне трговати. Он млад, наиван, невешт, добра срца и поверљив према сваком, а друштво рђаво, те злоупотреби те његове добре стране, и онда није никакво чудо, што му се, кад је узео тридесету годину, продало све за дуг, а он остао сиромашак са женом и четворо ситне деце. Пријатељи и познаници га напустише и он бејаше остављен себи самом.

Заната никаква није знао, а породицу је требало хранити. Једино што је могао и умео, то је да вешто удара у тамбуру и лепо пева. Недаће живота уплетоше јад и тугу у његов, иначе ведар и весео дух, а баш та туга, чиста и искрена, даваше необичне дражи гласу његову.

. . . .

Он остави место свога рођења и пође у свет, да тугом својом људе весели. Неколико година већ живи од те горке зараде, идући тако по местима, где га нико не познаје.

SERBOCROATIAN

X. V. Nazor

VARKE SUTONA

Vi, što suton volite i veče,
Čuvajte se varke prvog mraka:
U njoj raste i stvar mrtva svaka,
I kretnje su svečanije, veče.

Onda, kad je vrelo dnevnih zraka
Na zenitu, neka zebnje vaše
Promatraju sve čega se plaše:
Dô, močvaru, lava i divljaka.

Naš je život put kroz cvetne grane.
Smrt je samo taman savijutak,
A na kraju jedne svetle pruge.

Sve su staze suncem obasjane.
Dan je dug, a suton tek trenutak.
Ne verujte Anđelima Tuge!

XI. D. Cesarić.

MRTVA LUKA

Znam: ima jedna mrtva luka,
I ko se u njoj nađe
Čuti će ujutro pjevanje ćuka
I vidjet će umorne lađe.

Brodovi u njoj vječito snivaju
Kako se brodi,
Al njihova sidra mirno počivaju
U plitkoj vodi.

I tako u snovima gledaju sreću,
A plovit se boje,
Na jarbole šarene zastave meću
I—stoje.

XII. Д. Максимовић.

ПОЂИМО У ШУМЕ

Пођимо у шуме.
Ноћас сам рада
да гледам, како јесен бела
цвета и пада
и на равни пут.
Пођимо у шуме:
из свију врела
гледа по један месец жут.

Пођимо у старе
искусне шуме;
ноћас се храшћа уморне гране
спокојно сломиле.
Пођимо у шуме;
на све стране
тужно миришу
пролећа̂ увелих гомиле.

Пођимо кроз болни
осмех честа̂:
ноћас су букве витке и беле,
и сенке бреста
тихо се плаве.
Пођимо у шуме;
уз пут ће јеле
држати небо врх наше главе.

Пођимо у шуме:
ноћас ће траком
свију се река сребро осути.
Пођимо у шуме, —
под звездом сваком
сањају мирно листови жути
стазом и мостом, брдом и долом.
Пођимо у шуме: —
ноћас би хтела,
да ме се увек сетиш с болом.

XIII. Д. Максимовић.

БАЛКАНАЦ

Не стидим се што сам,
како ви велите,
варварин са Балкана,
тла прљавштине и буре.
Чућете сад,
и код нас има неке
вама непознате културе.

Ви прво испитујете и сумњате,
далеки сте и од Рођених синова,
за трпезу своју
не посадите сваког туђина;
ви можете да пијете,
а да сваком не пружите
чаше вина.

А код нас су још стари обичаји груби:
ми пуштамо свакога под своје слеме,
код нас се још и с намерником љуби,
код нас се подвизи због гостољубља чине;
код нас сваки човек има
читаво племе
пријатеља и родбине.

Ви, доиста, имате
неколико милиона Христових кипова,
на сваког човека по једнога,
имају га друмови и поља, апсане и школе;
а код нас, кад људи верују у Бога,
у себи га носе,
и тихо му се,
скоро у сну, моле.

Ви, истина, за сваки кут живота
имате справа и машина,
све сте срачунали и све знате,
изуми ваши су за дивљење;
а ми још имамо старинске алате,
али све је код нас још здраво
и природно као глина;
и умирање, и рађање, и живљење.

Ви имате читаве збирке
правила и наука о слободи,
о свему се код вас пише и приповеда;
али ми и по неписаним законима
слободно живимо
и неког природног држимо се реда,
слично огњу, ветру, и води.

Код вас је, збиља, све тачно прописано,
како се једе, говори, облачи;
а ми, кад говоримо, вичемо
и машемо рукама,
и чорбу гласно срчемо,
и у рукавицама смо
као на мукама.

Све је код нас заиста просто;
обућу носимо од свињске коже,
пуно је код нас сељачких
навика и ствари;
и краљевски преци наши
доиста су били говедари.

Народ наш, збиља, у гневу може да коље,
руши и пали;
али ми нисмо они што смишљено тлаче,
ми не сматрамо да је свет цели
наше поље;
ми не бисмо поднели
ни урођеник прашумски да због нас плаче;
душа је наша пространа,
иако смо бројем мали.

XIV. Ч. Миндеровић.

АНТЕНЕ

Та тужна клавирска етида са оне стране
    зида,
Како упорно зове, како носталгично мами...
Ако се гласно не плаче онда се нечујно
    рида,
И за последњи поход се расте
У пустошној полутами.

И теку широке реке, широке реке из вена,
Крај градова у агонији,
Крај оборених антена.

SECTION 5. SLOVENIAN

INTRODUCTION

The Slovenes, a people at present numbering in their homeland rather less than two million, settled in the mountainous north-west corner of Yugoslavia at the time of the Slav migrations about A.D. 600. The centre of this small and unique Alpine Slav civilization is Ljubljána, a delightful and most civilized, though small, capital city standing in a small plain bounded by high mountains. Slovenia is a land of small individual farms and small industrial centres such as mines and foundries, connected by railways along most of the valleys. Beyond the Rivers Dráva and Múra the hills melt into the Pannonian Plain. The people are mainly of the Roman Catholic faith. Literacy in Slovenia reaches almost 100 per cent of the population; and the general level of urban, rural, and domestic culture is high even by West European standards. Thanks to this happy position the Slovenes have always enjoyed as a nation the respect of other Yugoslavs and have been regarded as hardworking, intelligent, reliable, and honest, rather like the Scots in England, or the Czechs. All who know the Slovenes regret the fact that even after the 1939-45 war, this small people was far from entirely united within the frontiers of Yugoslavia, 44 per cent of their total number remaining outside. However, the remainder live in a compact area in the Socialist Republic of Slovenia, in which the Slovenian language was, and is, regularly used as the official language. This separate existence within the Yugoslav state seemed to point to the possibility of an extension of this system of national existence within a broader federation, such as has now been introduced in the Socialist Federal Republic of Yugoslavia. The history of their language, as we shall see, also shows those qualities of steadiness and perseverance in the people, while their beautiful literature is often characterized by a gentle melancholy or a positive and constructive optimism which reflect further sides of the Slovene's character.

Their language, which must have become separate from Serbocroätian between the seventh and ninth centuries A.D., is in many ways an archaic form of Slavonic—it preserves the Dual number, for instance. Owing to the geographical nature of the country (many valleys separated by high mountains) it is split up into as many as nine main dialects.

Slovenian is the language of one of the oldest

documents written in any Slav language, the Freising
Leaves (Brižínski spomeníki), a MS. written in Latin
characters and containing prayers, confessions, and
homilies, believed to date from the eleventh century.
   The Slovenes early lost their political independence to their more powerful German and Italian
neighbours. Hence from the earliest times the languages of culture in Slovenia were Latin, German, and
Italian. It was not until the Reformation that the
Slovenian language came into its own, when the Protestant reformers insisted on writing their message of
salvation for their people in their own tongue, as
was the practice in many countries at the time. The
first was Prímož Trûbar (1508-86), who was banished
from his country for a long time and wrote most of
his works in Tübingen and elsewhere in Germany. Among
other things he translated the New Testament. Soon
after him came Júrij Dâlmatin (born c 1546), who
translated the Old Testament. Both these writers
were from the central province of Dolénjsko (Lower
Carniola), on the dialect of which they based their
language. This was a fact of decisive importance for
the subsequent development of literary Slovenian
which was based mainly on their language, with an admixture of the sounds and forms of the neighbouring
dialect of Gorénjsko (Upper Carniola). (Ljubljána
lies in Gorénjsko, near the border of the two dialects.)
   No less important was Ádam Bǫhorič, the author of
the first grammar of the Slovenian language. Sebástian Krêlj was another of Trûbar's important followers.
   As in other countries, the Reformation in Slovenia was followed by a vigorous Roman Catholic
counter-reformation in which Protestant writers were
persecuted and their books burnt. But the Protestants
won the day in at least one respect: they convinced
everyone of the importance of writing in the native
tongue. Thus it was that the most important Catholic
writers of the subsequent two centuries wrote much of
their work in Slovenian. Such were the ambitious
Tomâž Hrèn (1560-1630) and Matîja Kastêlic (1620-88),
both of them religious writers.
   It was not until the eighteenth century that
there appeared nationally conscious writers on lay
subjects. The first of these was Márko Pohlîn (1735-1801), who wrote a grammar of Slovenian, in which he
confidently asserted that the people need not be in
the least ashamed of their comparatively undeveloped
and much neglected language. Another such writer was
Léopold Wólkmer (1741-1815), who wrote lyric poems

and fables. Antôn Lȋnhart (1757-95) created the first dramas in Slovenian and translated a comedy of Beaumarchais.

Among the most notable ecclesiastical writers of the eighteenth century was Júrij Jápelj, the Jansenist writer who edited Dâlmatin's translation of the New Testament and himself translated the Old with the help of his colleagues. He used the sixteenth-century writers as his model, and introduced a consistent orthography with some modernizations. This helped to establish the historical character of Slovenian spelling, e.g. dâl (= gave) for what is pronounced dau̯, gládka (= smooth) for a pronunciation glátka.

In 1758 was born, in Šiška near Ljubljána, the herald of the modern era of the Slovenian language, the poet Válentin Vôdnik, who died in 1819. He was sixteen when he wrote his first published work. He went to school at a Franciscan monastery in Ljubljána, and worked as a priest in Slovenia and was liberally helped by the rich Baron Côjz (Zois), who was a patron of Slovenian letters at this time and also died in 1819, at the age of 72. Vôdnik's first published work was *Prátika*, a "national calendar," containing poems and other amusing and instructive material; this was followed by a more topical journal about contemporary important events, called *Novȋce*. From 1798 he worked in Ljubljána, teaching divinity and publishing elementary readers, a grammar, a dictionary, and handbooks on divinity and archaeology. When Napoleon established his province of Illyria, Vôdnik was one of its most ardent supporters, and was appointed head of the "gimnázija" and inspector of elementary schools, and held other important posts. This was a time of great cultural and creative activity for him, and some of his happiest patriotic poems date from this period. When Illyria fell and Austrian domination was reëstablished, Vôdnik did not leave his beloved Slovenia, though he was advised to do so; he ceased to work as a public figure, but continued his efforts for his people in the cultural field till his death, writing a history of the Slovenes and a Slovenian-German dictionary.

His successor in the field of poetry was the Pushkin of Slovenia, Dr. Francè Prešéren (1800-49), whose poetry can truly be compared to that of his great Slav contemporaries, such as Pushkin, Mickiewicz, Kollár, and Mácha. Like Pushkin, Prešéren finally moulded the Slovenian poetical language, on the basis of the main dialects, being a staunch opponent of the Illyrian movement which stood for fusion with Serbocroätian. In doing so, he created classical masterpieces, such as his sonnets, which were also widely translated and so known abroad.

Meantime, while Prešéren and other writers were developing the expressive and literary powers of the language, the scholar and censor for the Austrian government, Jérnej Kopîtar (1780-1844), another staunch opponent of the Illyrian movement, wrote the first scientific grammar of Slovenian, publishing it in 1808. He it was who encouraged Vûk Kàradžić in his work of reform of the Serbocroätian literary language.

Kopîtar, like other "Romantics" of his time, paid serious attention to questions of length (i.e. quantity) in pronunciation in his writings (1809), as did Vǫdnik in his *Pîsmenost* (1811) and Prešéren in his carefully accented edition of his poems and Frànc Metélko in his scientific grammar of Slovenian (1825). His pupil, Matîja Čǒp, who was also Prešéren's close friend, wrote only eight years later that the Slovenes had no accepted literary pronunciation, but that each spoke in his own dialect. He held up as an ideal that the literary language should be a compromise in pronunciation and spelling between the various main dialects.

Stânko Vráz (1810-51), a successful poet in Serbocroätian, was on the other hand an enthusiastic supporter of the Illyrian movement, and believed in the abandonment of the Slovenian language and the complete linguistic fusion of his people with the Croäts.

The need for a common literary language was, however, coming to be ever more strongly felt as the use of Slovenian spread more and more in public life in Slovenia. Some writers even proposed the adoption of a pronunciation exactly according to the spelling, so difficult was it for them to believe that the common people spoke better Slovenian than the semi-denationalized townspeople of the time.

It was not until 1839-46 that Jánez Bleiweis (1808-81) in his *Novîce*, succeeded in striking a true balance when he adopted Gâj's orthography (*gâjica*) for his paper, while preserving the Slovenian language phonologically, grammatically and lexically. Modern Slovenian, such as we read to-day, with its simple spelling and its three accented consonants modelled on Czech: č, š, and ž—really dates from this great and decisive reform. After 1848, the unity of the literary language was more and more strongly advocated, and a wider basis, founded on all the dialects, was adopted. The writings of Trûbar, Vǫdnik, Kopîtar and Prešéren were taken as the chief models. This movement was greatly helped by Matèj Cigalè and Lúka Svętec, who formed a progressive group among the Slovenes in Vienna. Basing himself on pan-Slovenian and pan-Slavonic criteria, Cigalè among other things translated the Austrian Law Code into Slovenian. He was also a journalist, editing the paper *Slovénija*, and had great influence on the Slovenian school books of his time.

One of the most important reformers and creators of the modern Slovenian prose language was the scholar, writer, and poet, Fràn Lẹ́vstik (1831-87). As a young man he suffered from his poverty and also for his liberal convictions. He wrote some successful poetry which was popular among the younger generation, but condemned by the priests. He managed to study for a while in Vienna under Míklošič, and was misled by the latter's belief that Old Slavonic was Old Slovenian. His enthusiasm for the old language caused him later rather to over-favour archaisms. He was a great admirer of the creator of modern Serbocroätian, Vûk Kàradžić, and of his pupil and follower, Đúro Dàničić, whose dictionary he regarded as a model of pure language and good syntax.

Lẹ́vstik tried to restore the Slavonic character of Slovenian, regarding the language of the Národne pèsme collected by Vûk Kàradžić as examples of superb purity. But he did not try to identify Slovenian with Serbocroätian, though he believed that they would ultimately flow together like two neighbouring streams. In his *Napâke slovẹ́nskega pisânja* (= Errors in written Slovenian), he pointed to the German basis in thought and construction of contemporary Slovenian ("we write Slovenian words, but think in German"), and advocated a restriction of the use of the Infinitive and Passive constructions, the placing of the negative always before the verb and not after as in German, the freer use of Possessive adjectives instead of Genitives of nouns, the use of "môči" instead of "znâti" for "to be able," etc.

In 1862, he was editor of the short-lived paper *Naprẹ́j*, run by the poet Vîlhar, to whose children he was also tutor for a time. This paper stood for the introduction of the general use of Slovenian in public life and as a language of instruction in the schools in Slovenia, for the unification of the Slovenes administratively, and even showed wide Yugoslav sympathies. After a short while it was suppressed, and Vîlhar was imprisoned. In 1868 Lẹ́vstik started writing poetry again under the influence of a hopeless and unhappy love.

He later wrote a grammar of Slovenian in German

and collaborated for a while on Wolf's Slovenian-
German dictionary, but lost his post through trying
to make the dictionary scientific, while his col-
laborators were for making it "practical." He in-
curred, too, the jealousy of Jánez Bleiweis, who was
regarded as the chief authority on the language at
that time. He also edited many works by other writers, including Prešéren, and by the time he died was
one of the most influential men in the literature and
thought of his countrymen and a prophet of the future
Yugoslavia.

The last great reformer of Slovenian was really
Father Stânislav Škrábec (1844-1918), who devoted his
life to careful criticism and scholarship. He taught
that the basis of the literary language was the dialect of Dolénjsko and the writings of the Protestant
writers of the sixteenth century, especially as regards morphology. He believed that, for models, the
sixteenth century should be regarded as the oldest
limit in time. The sound system, according to
Škrábec, should be based on features common to most
dialects, and where these differ, those features
nearest the basic system should be chosen, often
those also nearer Old Slavonic and Serbocroätian, but
in keeping with the general Slovenian sound system.
Other dialects would thus contribute mainly in vocabulary. The distinctive Slovenian vocabulary should
be preserved; but no deliberate differentiation from
Serbocroätian or Slavonic generally should be forced
through, but rather borrowings, where necessary, from
other Slavonic languages should be made. He was an
opponent of Lévstik's archaisms and believed in a
"realistic" approach, basing his norms on the language as actually spoken. He believed that the
orthography should be an "exact and beautiful photo-
graph" of the pronunciation, but in certain cases
supported Lévec's (see below) compromises with history.

The appearance in 1894-5 of the big Slovenian-
German dictionary by Màks Pletéršnik, now no longer
covering the whole modern vocabulary but still very
useful, and in 1899 of the *Pravopis* (= orthography)
by Fràn Lévec, based on Pletéršnik's dictionary,
slowed down the process of fixing the literary language, as they did not follow Škrábec's principles,
but introduced a system of compromise between historical and phonetic spelling. Among other things
Lévec also advocated the pronunciation of all l's as
a clear l (and not w) contrary to the practice in
most dialects, and thereby caused a long and heated
controversy.

In 1912, the periodical *Vęda* (= Science) carried out an inquiry as to whether the Slovenian language should be altogether dropped in favour of Serbocroätian under the pressure of the general movement for Yugoslav political unity. The answer proved to be, from all evidence, an emphatic "no"; and this was even confirmed in 1918 by Dr. F. Ílešič, regarded till then as a "neo-Illyrian," and also by Dr. Glǫ́nar and Dr. Brȩznik.

A further important step in consolidation was made by the founding of the university of Ljubljána after the 1914-18 war.

Professor Béličz, from the Serbian side, wisely said that in Slovenia Serbocroätian merely had value as a further medium of spreading knowledge and culture.

The real heir of Škrábec's teachings was Dr. Antôn Brȩznik, whose grammar of Slovenian for schools first appeared in 1916, and whose *Pṛavopı̃s* was first published in 1920, being based on the modern, pure, living language. This book he subsequently thoroughly revised, together with the authoritative scholar, Professor Fràn Ramôvš, and republished it under their joint names as *Slovęnski Pravopı̃s* in 1935, after long preparatory studies by them and their distinguished colleagues, Dr. Ívan Gráfenauer, Dr. F. Kîdrič, Professor R. Náhtigal, and Dr. Ívan Prijâtelj. They were all members of a special orthographical commission set up by the Znânstveno drûštvo in Ljubljána, and they based their work on Slovenian writers since 1870.

It was after the 1914-18 war that the poet and dramatist, Óton Županči̥č, finally won through with his contention that actors on the stage should speak naturally, in particular using the *w* (ʯ) sound for the written *l* as in colloquial Slovenian. Previously this had only been admitted in lighter pieces, thereby leaving the stage as the disseminator of an artificial pronunciation.

In 1935 there appeared Dr. Jóža Glónar's important dictionary of the language (unaccented), which contained certain criticisms of the new *Pravopı̃s*. But it can safely be said that Brȩznik's grammar and the 1935 edition of the *Pravopı̃s* finally decided not only the orthography but also the pronunciation of the literary language.

This language can be stated to be more distinct from its regional dialects than is the Serbocroätian literary language. The scholars Tomînšek and Bezják have even pointed out that the *conversational* language of educated Slovenes differs from both the literary language and the dialects. They also show that the Slovenes are well aware that the real developers of a language are the constant stream of writers, poets, and journalists, and this can also be inferred from the statements and examples in Brêznik's grammar. The ultimate ideal is that the language should be expressive, accurate in differentiation and definition, and flexible.

Ever since Prešéren, throughout the nineteenth century and to our own day, there has been a steady stream of exceedingly interesting writers of prose and poetry in Slovenian, who followed the main trends of European literature of the time. Such were, to mention only a very few: Sîmon Gregǫ̂rčič, the gentle priest-poet; Antǫ̂n Âškerc, the balladist and lyric poet; and the "naturalist" woman novelist, Zófka Kvéder (1878-1926). The moving writings of Îvan Cánkar (1876-1918), and the really lovely, delicate poetry of Óton Župânčič formed a fitting climax to the steady stream of development and careful hard work, deep patriotic loyalty and sensitive self-development which we can find in abundance in all the greater works of Slovenian literature. This literature and its carefully tended literary language is a true reflection of a people, though small in numbers, yet great in spirit.

New school grammars appeared in 1947, 1956 (Bajec, Kolarič, Rupel) and 1966-68 (Toporišič), and an excellent and much expanded new *Slovénski Pravopis* in 1950 and again in 1962. The first volume of *Slovar slovenskega knjižnega jezika* appeared in 1970, the second in 1975.

THE SLOVENIAN ALPHABET

Slovenian		Approx. English equivalent
A	a	(more open and forward than) *ah*
B	b	*b*
C	c	*ts* pronounced together as in "bits"
Č	č	*ch* in "church"*
D	d	*d* (dental)
E	e	*e* in "bet", *a* in "day", or *e* in "opera" (phonetic ə)
F	f	*f*
G	g	*g* in "go"
H	h	*ch* in "loch"

SLOVENIAN

Slovenian		Approx. English equivalent
I	i	*ee, i* in "machine"
J	j	*y* in "yes" or in "boy", as in Serbocr. and West Slav
K	k	*k*
L	l	*l* in "last" or *w*†
M	m	*m*
N	n	*n* (dental)‡
O	o	*o* in "for"; French *ô* in "hôte"
P	p	*p*
R	r	*r* (rolled)§
S	s	*s* in "so"
Š	š	*sh**
T	t	*t* (dental)
U	u	*oo* in "boot"
V	v	*v* or *w*†
Z	z	*z*
Ž	ž	*s* in "pleasure"*
Qu		is rendered by *kv*
X		is rendered by *ks*
W, Y		are not ordinarily used

*The combination šč is quite frequent, = *shch* in "Ashchurch". See also below parts thus marked.

†See below, section on pronunciation, parts thus marked.

‡See below, section on pronunciation, parts thus marked.

§r can be syllabic and is then pronounced ər in educated conversational language, e.g.:—

between two consonants: vr̂h = summit
grmẹ́ti = to thunder.

or initially when accented: r̂že = neighs.

Initially before a consonant when unaccented it is also pronounced ər, e.g.:—

rzáti (= to neigh)—three syllables!
rdèč (= red)—two syllables!

(This is much rarer in Serbocr. which has a true vocalic r: р̥зати (= to neigh), but ржа̀ница (= rye bread).)

In dictionaries the digraphs *lj* and *nj* are not treated as separate letters, as they are in Serbocr., but follow words beginning with "li" and "ni". *lj* is very rarely pronounced soft as in Serbocroätian. It is usually pronounced the same as *medium* (not dark) *l*.

The digraph *dž* is also regarded as two letters (pronounced like English *j*).

The *ć* and *đ* (ћ and ђ) of Serbocroätian are totally absent from Slovenian.

The palatal consonants of Czech and Slovak: *tʼ*, *dʼ*, *ň*, *ř* (Czech only), *lʼ* (Slovak only), and Polish: *ć*, *ś*, *ń*, *ź* do not occur in Slovenian. Neither do the vowels *ě* and *ů* (Czech), *ô* and *ä* (Slovak), and *y* (West Slav generally).

Long vowels are not as a rule marked in ordinary printing or writing.

h represents West Slav *ch*, the Czech and Slovak sound of *h* corresponding to *g* in Slovenian.

The Polish *ą* and *ę* (nasal vowels), *ó* (= *u*) and *ł*, *ż* are also absent in Slovenian spelling, though *l* is pronounced like *ł* in certain positions.

v corresponds to Polish *w*.
ž corresponds to Polish *ż*.

THE SYSTEM OF ACCENTUATION

The system of accentuation used in the following pages is the modern one used for the tonemic variety of the language in the new Academy dictionary, the first volume of which appeared in 1970. It distinguishes the three different intonations (tonemes), as did Pletéršnik, by the following three accents *over* the vowels (including vocalic *r*):

    ` short falling
    ´ long rising
    ^ long falling.

With the pointed *circumflex* accent ^ the Academy dictionary indicates the *open varieties* of *e* and *o* in each entry in the dictionary containing such a vowel. In the tonemic indications in brackets that follow, these open vowels have no accent *below* the letter, while the *close* varieties have a subscript dot, thus ế, ố and ệ, ộ.

The accent ¯ over a vowel indicates that *either* of the long intonations is admissible.

Pletéršnik also distinguished the open *e* and *o* from the closed *ę*, *ę*, and *ǫ*, *ǫ*, i.e. the *open* vowel *quality* by the *absence* of a mark *below* these vowels. (The other vowels do not vary in this way.)

Pletéršnik further distinguished the closed *e*'s and *o*'s by their origin and by their regular variations of pronunciation in certain central dialects (see section on the Slovenian dialects) with marks *below* these vowels. He used:—

ẹ for the *e* derived from C.S. ѣ(=ě), and
ę for the *e* derived from C.S. e or ѧ(= ę).

Similarly he used:

ọ for the *o* derived from C.S. o (formerly written *u* in Slovenian), and
ǫ for the *o* derived from C.S. ѫ(= ǫ), or from an original C.S. o (always spelt with *o* in Slovenian).

For comparative purposes this was the most informative and complete system.]

Many modern works on Slovenian such as the grammars of 1947, 1956 and 1966-68 and the *Pravopis* of 1935, 1950 and 1962 ignore the difference between the rising and falling intonations in long syllables, accenting both ´. They use ê and ô to distinguish the open varieties of these vowels from the closed varieties which are indicated by é and ó. (For the foreign student this gives less information.) The grave accent ` is retained for *short* (falling) accented vowels.

In normal literary texts the accents are not indicated except in words where the accent has importance for meaning or for metre in poetry.

(See also "The Accent in Slovenian.")

PRONUNCIATION

Slovenian spelling is a compromise between "phonetic" and historical spelling. The "phonetic" features are embodied in the principle of one letter per sound, largely followed by the orthography, in the writing of ц, ч, ſ, з, as *c*, *č*, *š*, and *ž* (copied from the Croat orthography of Gâj by Bleiweis), and in the (rather oversimplified) rendering of the vowels (see below).

The historical features are to be found mainly in the preservation (in writing) of unvoiced consonants before voiced, though both within words *and* in word groups they are voiced in pronunciation, and *vice versa*, in contrast to the practice in the Serbocroätian spelling of words. (As in other Slavonic languages, there is no assimilation of consonants before *v* and the continuants *n*, *m*, *r*, *l*, e.g.: tvój (= thine) keeps *t*.) Likewise final voiced consonants which, as in all Slavonic languages except Serbocroätian and Ukrainian, become unvoiced, are preserved in writing as voiced in Slovenian. Thus:—

hríb (= a hill)   pron. xríp,

grâd (= castle) pron. grât, etc.

Toporišič recommends such a pronunciation in word juncture also when the following word begins with a voiced consonant or even with a vowel, e.g.

mlâd mûc = a young pussy, pron. mlaːt muːts
mlâd órel = a young eagle,   "   mlaːt 'ɔːrəu

But he explicitly *excludes* prepositions and verbal prefixes, e.g.

od mûca = from the pussy, pron. od 'muːtsa
od órla = from the eagle, pron. od 'ɔːrla
odnésti = to carry away, pron. od'nɛːsti

The ·Consonants

The pronunciation of the consonants is straightforward, with the exception of the assimilations just mentioned. Regressive assimilation is the rule (i.e. the second consonant decides whether a group is voiced or unvoiced).

j plays the same rôle as *j* in Serbocroätian and West Slav.
r is rolled and can be syllabic, pronounced ər (see above).
‡*n* before the velars *k* and *g*, as in other South and West Slav languages, is pronounced ŋ, i.e. as *ng* in English "sing," e.g. ángel = angel.
**č, š*, and *ž* are palatalized and pronounced with the tip of the tongue fairly well forward, allowing žîv (= alive) to sound ʒîᵾ, for instance (in contrast to Russian жив pron. ʒɨf) and šíti (= to sew) to sound ˑʃíti.
Only *l* and *v* present difficulties.
†*l* before vowels is a clear "medium" *l* as in English "lend"; and *lj* can usually be similarly pronounced finally or before other consonants. Before vowels, as in the Instrumental singular of feminine nouns of the *i*-declension, e.g.:—

živâljo = animal,

adjectives such as—

kobîlji = mare's (adj.),

nouns in -*lje*, e.g.:—

povélje = command,

(all going back to *lьj*), *lj* are pronounced as ļi. Colloquially, however, in e.g. Ljubljana, one often hears [lu'blana] with medium l's. Finally and before consonants a palatalized *l* [ḷ], as in Russian, is pronounced, e.g. pọ̑lj = of fields, pọ̑ljski = field (adj.).

but *l* finally, e.g. in

bȋl (je) = he was, and
umȓl (je) = he died

or usually before other consonants, e.g.:—

pọ́ln = full
budȋlnik = alarm clock

is pronounced as u̯, like a weak English *w*, e.g.:—

bȋl, pron. beew (phon.: bȋu̯)
umȓl phon. u'məȓu (three syllables), etc.

‡*n* + *j* are similarly pronounced as ni̯ before vowels, as in— e.g. sánjati̯ = to dream the Instr. sing. of fem. *i*-stems ending in *nj*, e.g.:—

z dlanjọ́ = palm of the hand,

the Nom. plur. of nouns such as

tržánje = inhabitants of a small town,

and adjectives such as

jelẹ́nji = deer's (adj.)

Finally and before consonants -*nj* represents a single sound, palatalized *n*, (phon. ɲ), e.g.:—

kònj = horse
kọ́njski = horse's

Before the velars *k* and *g* nj is pronounced ŋ: mânjka, pron. mâŋka = is lacking

†*v* is pronounced as a labio-dental *v*, as in English, initially and medially before a vowel, as in—

vóda = water,
sevệda = of course

and before *r* and (initial) *l*:—

vrábec = sparrow
vlâda = government

also between *r* and *j*:—

črvjệ = worms

Before other consonants and finally after a vowel (including vocalic r) it also, like l, is pronounced bilabially: ṷ (English w), e.g.:—

vsàk (= every), pron. ṷsâk or wsâk (w *un-voiced*!)
óvca (= sheep), pron. óṷtsa
pràv (= just, right), pron. pràṷ (like English "prow")
čŕv (= worm), pron. čəŕṷ!

(This w sound can develop further into a vocalic u before agglomerations of consonants and between consonants (also of separate words), as in:—

vzpostáviti = to restore, pron. uspostáviti, predvsèm = above all, pron. predusèm.)

Thus words ending in a vowel + l can rhyme with those ending in a vowel + v, e.g. in Župančič: zdràv, znàl; bẹ́l, cẹ́v.

The pronunciation of the preposition v follows the above rules:—

v ústa (= into the mouth), pron. vústa
v róki (= in the hand), pron. vróki

but

grẹ́m v šọ̑lo (= I am going to school), pron. grẹ́m u šọ̑lo,

as opposed to

tjà v šọ̑lo (= there to school), pron. tjà ṷ šọ̑lo

Exactly the same rules of pronunciation are are applied to all initial u's except before v, l and before vowels, e.g. ulomíti = to break off, pron. ul- (See "Features characteristic of Slovenian," No. 18.)

Double consonants in writing, also in word juncture, should be pronounced as single but long consonants. E.g.:—

oddáti = to give away
izzváti = to challenge
pollẹ́tje = half-yèar
tî boš šə̀l = you will go
jàz sam míslil = I thought
òn nọ́če = he does not want to

SLOVENIAN

The Vowels

The vowels are not difficult to pronounce in the case of *a* (open, as in other Slav languages), *u* (closed and with lip-rounding, as in other Slav languages), and *i* (like French *i* in "ici," or English *i* in "machine"). The latter two vowels are pronounced less clearly when not stressed. (There is no *i̵/y* (ы) sound in Slovenian.)

The letters *o* and *e*, however, require a choice of alternatives which embarrass the foreign learner, even if he is a Slav.

- *o* can be pronounced open or closed. It is pronounced *open* and *long* where the accent has shifted on to it from the subsequent syllable, cf.:—

    Russian: конéц,   окнó,   водá
    Slovenian: kónǝc,   ókno,   vóda

    This open *o* is indicated in modern grammars and dictionaries by an *ô*.

    Short open ò occurs only in final syllables and monosyllables, e.g.:—

    otròk = child
    nòž   = knife

- *o* is pronounced *long closed*, as in French *hôte* or as in German *rot* (a pure vowel) when derived from Common Slav ǫ (Old Slavonic ѫ), corresponding to y in Russian, Ukrainian, and Serbocroätian (and in this case was marked ǫ in Pletéršnik's dictionary), or when derived from a Common Slav o when the accent has *not* shifted (marked *ọ* and *ǫ* in Pletéršnik's dictionary), e.g.:—

    pǫ́t, now pọ́t   = road
    mǫ́ka, now mọ́ka   = flour
    (na)rǫ̂kǫ, now rǫ̂kǫ   = hand (Acc. sing.)
    gospộd   = master, Mr.
    ǫ̂ni   = they

    ǫ and *o* therefore have the same phonetic value, but indicate a different origin, interesting for comparative purposes. (See also above, "The System of Accentuation.") In modern works on Slovenian they are indicated by *ó* (and *ô*).

    Short closed ọ̀ occurs only before final *l*, e.g.:—

vǫ̏l (= ox), pron. vǫ̏u̯

Unstressed *o* is usually a little more closed than in Serbocroatian.

e is pronounced *open* and *long* (like *ê* in French "tête") in words where the accent has shifted on to it from the subsequent syllable, cf.:—

    Russian: сестрá, женá
    Slovenian: séstra, žéna

It is also pronounced *open* and *short* in some monosyllables, e.g.:—

    mèč = sword
    lèv = lion

Long open *e* is indicated in modern Slovenian grammars and dictionaries as *ê*.

e is pronounced *closed* and *long* (as *é* in French *été* or the first *e* in German *sehen*) when derived from—

    Common Slav *e* (with no accent shift), or
    Common Slav *ę* (Old Slav. ᴀ), or
    Common Slav *ě* (Old Sl. ѣ).

See "The System of Accentuation" above.
    E.g.:—

    from *e*—
        mêd   = honey
        šêst   = six
    from *ę*—
        rêd   = order
        desêt = ten
        vzéti = to take
    from *ě*—
        dél   = part
        lês   = wood
        léto   = year
        hlêbec = small loaf

Before *r* this *e* sounds particularly closed, almost like *i*, e.g.:—

    večêr = evening
    véra = faith
    Prešéren poet's name

Pletéršnik distinguishes *e* derived from *ě* by marking it *e*, as opposed to *ę* for *e* from *e* or *ę*. Some modern works on Slovenian indicate all three, irrespective of intonation, by *ê*.

As with ǫ and ọ, there is no phonetic difference in literary Slovenian between ẹ and ę; but they indicate a different origin.

Short closed e occurs only before *j*:—

imẹ̀j! = have...! (Imperative)

e, however, is also used to represent a sixth vowel sound, totally absent from Serbocroätion, but common enough in English, French, German, Russian, and Bulgarian—namely, the so-called "neutral vowel," rendered in phonetics ə or in Bulgarian ъ, the sound of "er" in Southern English "butter," or of the second *e* in German "seh*e*n," or of the second *a* in Russian лápa.

This *e* (printed in Pletéršnik's dictionary as an italic *e*) generally represents in Slovenian the semi-vowels ъ and ь of Common Sl. and Old Sl., e.g.:—

vèn	= outside	— O.S. вънъ	= out
pès	= dog	— O.S. пьсъ	
vès	= all	— O.S. вьсь	
sestáviti	= to compose	— O.S. съставити	
sláven	= glorious	— O.S. славьнъ	

But old stressed semi-vowels, when long, develop into full vowels in Slovenian, e.g.:—

dân = day—O.S. дьнь
vâs = village—O.S. вьсь (cf. вьсь = all, above!)

Unstressed *e* is pronounced either ə, or ɛ (short *e* as in English "yet"), according to its derivation, e.g.:—

sláven (from славьнъ), pron. 'slávən (= glorious), but

veselí (from веселитъ), pron. vɛsɛ'lí (= pleases)

Only a knowledge of Slavonic etymology can be a guide as to the three main alternative pronunciations of *e* in Slovenian.

N.B.—In the examples throughout this section we print ə for Slovenian *e* when pronounced as the neutral vowel to remind the student of the correct pronunciation. He should bear in mind, however, that this ə is never used in ordinary Slovenian print.

C.S. vocalic ŗ, ŗ̄ (O.S. ръ) are generally preserved as Slovenian vocalic *r* (usually pronounced ər) e.g.:—

vȓh (= summit) — O.S. връхъ

while C.S. vocalic l̥, l̥' (O.S. лъ, ль) become -ol- in Slovenian, e.g.:—

vȏlk = wolf (pron. voᵘk)
pȏln = full — C.Sl. pl̥'nъ, O.S. плънъ, etc.

C.S. rъ, rь also become Slovenian vocalic r:—

krvȋ = blood, Gen. sing.
kȓst = baptism

C.S. lъ, lь likewise become ol, like l̥, l̥':—

pȏlt = complexion
sȏlza = tear

All the vowels can form diphthongs with j (i) or ᵘ (spelt l or v), except ə (spelt e) with j, e.g.:—

zdàj	= now	dȃl	= gave	pràv	= just (adv.)
precèj	= rather	bẹ̑l	= white	cȇv	= pipe
		vídel*	= saw		
krȋj	= cover!	bȋl	= was (m.)	sȋv	= grey
		nósil*	= carried, wore (m.)		
pókoj	= peace	vȍl	= ox	duhȏv	= of spirits
				rȃkov	= of crayfish)pl.)
váruj	= guard! (Imperat.)	obȗl	= he put on (footwear)	--	

pósel (-əᵘ) = business, molitev (-əᵘ) = prayer
tópel (-əᵘ) = warm (m.)
nẹ́sel*(-əᵘ) = carried (m.)

* In the masc. sing. Past Participle Active, spelt with final -l, the diphthongs [eᵘ, iᵘ, əᵘ] can be reduced to [u] in colloquial speech.

(See also above paragraphs on the pronunciation of l and v.)

The Accents (Intonations) in Slovenian.

Slovenian is considered to have a musical accent, as is Serbocroatian, but its system is different and in fact more archaic. This makes the *position* of the accent in Slovenian agree somewhat more closely with that of Russian and East Slav generally and Bulgarian, especially in finally stressed verbs, in contradistinction to Serbocroatian in which the accent has generally shifted by one syllable nearer the beginning of the word. *Any* syllable in the word may be stressed, as in Russian and Bulgarian, e.g.:—

svèt = world, Gen. sing. svetȁ
grȁd = castle, " " grȁda or gradù

králj = king, Gen. sing. králja

and may be rising or falling, except final *short* syllables which always have ˋ (short *falling*).

Literary Slovenian, unlike Serbocroätian, has only the *one* short accent, the short falling marked ˋ (in contrast to Serbocr. ˝), mostly occurring on final syllables (never accented in Serbocr.), e.g.:—

        brȁt = brother
        bȍb = bean
        məglȁ = mist
        dəskȁ = plank

It is really a short *rise-fall* and is noticeably longer and less abrupt than ˝ in Serbocr.

Thus it can be inferred that, except in the case of final syllables, the choice of accent is usually only between the two *long* ones: long rising marked ´, or long falling marked ˆ. This makes Slovenian more similar in accent system to English, German, and Russian, which generally associate length with stress. There are also no unaccented ("subsequent") long syllables in literary Slovenian in contrast to Serbocroätian, Czech, and Slovak.

´ usually represents a shifted accent as compared with Russian (e.g. séstra = sister, vóda = water), while ˆ represents an original accent preserved (e.g. gospôd = Mr., Russian: госпóдь) usually on monosyllables or on the second syllable of polysyllables. Monosyllabic prepositions and prepositional prefixes, when preceding words with ˆ, cause this accent to shift by one syllable nearer the beginning of the word, e.g.:—

        vo̯dô = water (Acc.) but na vô̯do,
        dobı̑l = got   but pridô̯bil = won

It should also be pointed out that the differences between long and short vowels and rising and falling intonations are less clearly preserved and audible in the Slovenian literary language than in Serbocroätian.

While the long falling accent ˆ in Slovenian is similar to that in Serbocr., though it has a smaller range of fall and is shorter, the Slovenian long rising accent ´ is *noticeably* shorter and of smaller range than ´ in Serbocr. But, as in the latter language, the syllable after a *rising* accent usually remains on a *high* pitch, while after a *falling* accent it is usually on a *low* pitch. The syllable *before* a falling accent, on the other hand, is as a rule pronounced with *high* pitch. (The intonations, however, are confined to the central dialects and are therefore not demanded as essential in any schools.)

Only compound words, felt as such, can have *two* accents, e.g. pòdpredsẹ̑dnik = vice-president; nèprijẹ́ten = unpleasant, prábábica = great grandmother; pẹ̀tindvâjseti = twentyfifth.

COMPARISON OF SLOVENIAN AND SERBOCROATIAN ACCENTS

The correspondence of the Slovenian accents to those of Serbocroätian is worth noting:—

I. Original Common Slav ´ (long rising) is preserved in position in Slovenian medially, and finally when it becomes `, while in Serbocroätian it is preserved in position (as ˝) only medially, but if originally final, shifts one syllable back, e.g.:—

Slovenian: mẹ́ra = to measure Serbocr.: м(ј)ѐра
Slovenian: gíniti = to disappear Serbocr.: гѝнути = to perish
Finally: Slovenian: bràt = brother   Serbocr.: бра̀т

Medially ´ becomes ^ in Slovenian in certain cases, viz.:—

in closed syllables, e.g.:—

Slovenian: bȋtka = battle Serbocr.: бѝтка

before suffixes, e.g.:—

Slovenian: gǫ́ba = sponge   but gǫ̑bec = snout

in the Present tense >< the Infinitive, e.g.:—

Slovenian: vȋdeti = to see but vȋdim = I see
cf. Serbocr. вѝдети, вѝдим

and in certain participles, e.g.:—

Slovenian: vȋden = seen   Serbocr.: вѝђен

In terminations Slovenian preserves original Common Slav ´, while Serbocroatian shifts it one syllable nearer the beginning of the word, making it into ` if the syllable is short, keeping it ´ if the syllable is long, e.g.:—

Slovenian: lisíca = fox   Serbocr.: лѝсица
          "   želím   I wish   "   жѐлим
but   "   hvalíti = to praise "   хва́лити

II. Original Common Slav final (short) ` may be preserved in Slovenian or may be shifted on to the preceding syllable, when it is preserved as ` only on the semi-vowel ə or on ę (from ѣ) in dialects—otherwise it becomes ´. In Serbocroätian it always shifts on to the preceding syllable, becoming ` on short

SLOVENIAN

syllables and ´ on long syllables, e.g.:—

	Common Slav	mьglà
	Russian	. мгла = (heavy) mist, darkness
	Slovenian	. mẹglà, or (dial.) mȅgla = mist
	Serbocr.	. мȁгла

| | Slovenian | . svẹ̀təl, or (dial.) svȅtəl = bright |
| | Serbocr. | . свȅтла (but masc. sing. only свȇтао) |

but Slovenian . plášen, or plášen = shy
                     trpí, or tŕpi = suffer

cf. Russian . головá
    Slovenian . gláva
    Serbocr. . глáва

but Czech . hlava (short *a*)

    Russian . душá
    Slovenian . dúša
    Serbocr. . дýша

but Czech . duše (short *u*)

    Russian . молокó
    Slovenian . mlẹ́ko
    Serbocr. . млéко
and Czech . mléko

This is the origin of the open *e* and *o* in Slovenian.

    Cf. Russian . селó = village
        Slovenian . sẹ́lo = settlement
        Serbocr. . сȅло = village

        Russian . окнó = window
        Slovenian . ókno = window

Some verbal forms preserve final `: e.g.:—

Slovenian: kipèl (je) = was boiling cf. Serbocr.: кипео (je)
   "   puščèn = released, let go   "   пуштен
   "   iskàl (je) = was seeking   "   искао (je)

III. Original Common Slav ˆ (long falling) is preserved in Slovenian on monosyllables and on the second syllable of polysyllables. (This always corresponds to a falling accent in Serbocroatian, either ˋ or ˆ—on the *preceding* syllable in the case of polysyllables.) E.g.:—

Slovenian: grȃd = castle   Serbocr.: грȃд = town
        Gen. sg. gradȗ   Gen. sg. грȃда
   "   nȏč = night   "   нȏћ
        Gen. sg. nočȋ   Gen. sg. нȍћи

Slovenian: gospôd = master   Serbocr.: го́спо̄д = the Lord
"   mesô̧ = meat   "   ме̑со

(For the shift of this accent in Slovenian after prepositions, etc., see p. 327.)

THE SLOVENIAN DIALECTS

As will be seen from the Introduction, the Slovenian literary language is based mainly on the dialect of Dolénjsko (Lower Carniola, Unterkrain in German), with a borrowing of the pure vowels of the dialect of Gorénjsko (Upper Carniola), its northern neighbour. Ljubljána is situated just within the borders of Gorénjsko.

The most important feature of these central (and some western) dialects is the so-called Modern Vowel Reduction, which spread there in the seventeenth century. Unstressed and short vowels began to weaken and even disappear in pronunciation, and dark l ($ł$) came to be pronounced as u. This we can hear in the dialect of Ljubljána to the present day: mèš for mìš (= mouse), nèč for nìč (= nothing), pálca for pálica (= stick), dau for dȧł (= he gave). One of the features peculiar to the Dolénjsko dialect is the Infinitive without the final -i. The dialects of Dolenjsko and Nótranjsko also pronounce accented long ẹ as ^ie but e as e^i, and accented long ọ as ^uo, but o almost as u. But Gorénjsko does not know these distinctions.

The other dialects, though interesting to the specialist in Slavonic, have not played so important a part in the formation of the Slovenian literary language, except to contribute vocabulary.

Perhaps the most interesting of the other dialects is that of Carinthia (Koróško), which has certain features such as the preservation, in certain regions, of the groups -tl-, -dl-, and the ending -e for adjectives in the neut. sing., e.g. dobre mleko (= good milk), which seem to point to its being a transition stage to West Slav. But in the dialect of Rôž, in Carinthia, the archaic final stresses such as are preserved in Russian жена́, земля́, etc., also survive, and can be compared to the accents in Serbocr. čakavština, e.g. ženȁ.

Very curious, too, is the dialect of Prekmŭrje with its strangely distorted vowels, ö and ü, e.g. in šürki, völki for široki (= broad), veliki (= great), tüji for tihi! (= quiet), and consonants, as in gêtra for jétra (= liver), graj for gràh (= pea), and vŭra for ura (= hour). In other respects it is a transition to Croätian.

The dialects of Slovenian are far more difficult to understand when spoken than the dialects of the plain-dwelling Slavs, such as the Russians or the Poles, or even those of the Serbs and Croäts. This is doubtless due to the geographical barriers in Slovenian territory, which have tended to keep the dialects apart and encourage differences to arise.

VOWEL GRADATION AND VOWEL LENGTHENING

In common with the other Slavonic languages, Slovenian possesses the familiar Indo-European feature of vowel gradation or Ablaut:—
Examples:—

dûh = spirit—dəhníti = to breathe
bérem—bráti = I collect, read—to collect, read, Infin.
nésem—nosíti = I am carrying—to carry, Frequentative Infin.
víti —vénec or vénec = to weave—wreath
lęzem—láziti = I creep—Freq. Infin.

Lengthening of vowels is also a common feature in Slovenian:—
Examples:—

vózim—prevâžati = I convey—to transport
mrèm (from mьrem)—umírati = I die—to die
dəhníti—díhati (from dyxati) = to breathe, Pfve.—Impfve.
napôj—napâjati = watering (of cattle)—to water

SLAVONIC CHARACTERISTICS

1. Metathesis of Indo-European syllables with *e* or *o* + liquid (*r* or *l*), as in other South Slav languages. Cf.:—

C.S. *golva   Slovenian: gláva = head
Germ. Bart   "   bráda = beard
C.S. *mel-ti   "   mléti = to grind
Germ. Berg   "   brég = bank, mountain slope

2. The 1st Palatalization is also common in Slovenian, *k, g, h*, changing to *č, ž, š* before *i, e*, and *ə*. E.g.:—

róka—ročíca = hand—little hand
drûg—družína = companion—family, household
gréh—grešíti—grešən = sin—to sin—sinful

pekǫ́ (3rd pers. plur. Pres.) = they bake,—
  pę́čem = I bake
uhǫ́ = ear—ušę́sa (Gen. sing.)

c also changes to č before i and e. E.g.:—
resníca = truth—uresníčiti = to realize
pę́vec = singer—pę́včev = singer's (adj.)

3. The 2nd Palatalization survives only in the Imperative of certain verbs, but has been lost in declensions through analogy with other cases in nearly all nouns with stem ending in a velar. Thus k, g, (h) change to c, z, (s) (h>s only in dialects):—

pę́či   = to bake (root pek-)—pécí!
vrę́či   = to throw (root vrg-)—vŕzi!
(dial. trę́buh = belly—Nom. plur. trebúsi)
otròk   = child—Nom. plur. otróci is an
           exception, cf. the regular
           gręšnik = sinner, Nom plur.
           gręšniki.
vǫ́lk   = wolf, has Nom. plur. volcję̂ as
           well as volkôvi

(The forms drûzega, drûzih from drûg = another, are false colloquial forms and should not be used.)

4. *Yotation*, or the influence of j on consonants. The velars k, g, h change to č, ž, š, as in other Slavonic languages. E.g.:—

plákati = weep   —pláčeš (2nd pers. sg.
                     Pres., from *plakješ)
lagáti = to tell lies—lážeš (2nd pers. sg.
                     Pres.)
dûh   = spirit   —dúša = soul (<duhja)
píhati = to blow   —píšeš (2nd pers. sg.
                     Pres.) or píhaš

The dentals t and d change to č and j—the latter a *feature peculiar* to Slovenian. E.g.:—

svétiti   = to shine—svę́ča   = candle
požlatíti = to gild —pozlačen = gilded
rodíti   = to bear —rójen   = born

C.S. *medja, Slovenian méja = fontier.

The siblants s and z change to š and ž:—

tesáti = to hew —tèšeš (2nd pers. sing. Pres.)
kázati = to show—kážeš (2nd pers. sing. Pres.)
bŕzo   = quickly—bŕže = more quickly

SLOVENIAN

The liquids *l* and *r* and *n* take *j* (see above on *l+j* and *n+j* under "Pronunciation—The Consonants"). E.g.:—

    volíti = to chose, wish—vólja = will
    hraníti = to preserve, feed—hránjen (Past Part. Pass.)
    oráti = to plough—órjem (as well as: orâm) = I plough

The labials *b*, *p*, *m*, *v*, add *lj*. E.g.:—

ljubíti	= love	ljúbljen	= loved
kápati	= drip	káplja	= a drop
lomíti	= break	lómljen	= broken
pozdráviti	= to greet	pozdrâvljen	= greeted

c changes to *č*:—
    klícati = to call—klîčem = I call

st, *zd* + *j* become *šč*, *ž* respectively—the latter another peculiarity of Slovenian, e.g.:—

krstíti	= christen	kŕščen	= christened
zagozdíti	= to fasten with a wedge	zagožèn	= wedged tight

sk + *j* also becomes *šč*, e.g.:—
    iskáti = to seek   íščem = I seek

5. The loss of consonants in Slovenian is illustrated in many peculiarly Slovenian examples, as well as in those common to all Slavonic languages.

    Beside—
sèn	= sleep	from	*sъpnъ
šèl	= went	"	*šьdlъ
vréme	= weather	"	*vertmę

we have—
čèz	= through	"	*črez
storíti	= to do	"	*stvoriti
tŕd	= hard	"	*tvrd
všêč	= to one's liking, pleasing	"	*voščeč
lâs	= a hair	"	*vlas
zlâsti	= especially	"	*izvlasti

6. Epenthesis. Consonants are inserted in certain cases only:—

    nj in the full forms of the 3rd pers. Personal Pronoun: njéga = him.
    An initial *v* is occasionally added to words beginning with a vowel, as in East and West Slav, e.g.:—

vǫgəl = 1. corner, 2. coal
vǒzəl = knot
vǫhati = to smell (transitive)

FEATURES CHARACTERISTIC OF SLOVENIAN
*(Those marked * are peculiarly Slovenian)*

*1. C.S. *tj*, *dj* become *č*, *j* respectively:

svę́ča = candle
rǒjen = born
méja = boundary

2. C.S. *kt*, *gt* + *i* or ь both become *č* (cf. Russian):

nǫ̑č = night, Gen. sing. nočî
mǫ̑č = strength

3. *t* and *d* are dropped before *l*:—

plèl = wove (as well as plę́tel)
šəl = went
pàl = fell (as well as pâdel)
krílo = wing
molíti = to pray

Plę́tel, pâdel are later forms, formed by analogy with the Present plétem, pádem; also to be met with in the Carinthian dialect (see above—"Slovenian Dialects").

4. Metathesis only—*no* "polnoglasie" as in Russian—see above "Slavonic Characteristics."

5. As in other South and East Slav languages, original C.S. *kv*, *gv* become *cv*, *zv*:—

cvę̂t = flower
zvę̂zda = star

6. Labials + *j* have *lj*, as in East Slav (see "Slavonic Characteristics," No. 4), e.g.:—

zémlja = earth

*7. The nasal vowels, O.S. ѧ and ѫ, develop into *e* and *o* (both may be closed) respectively:—

rê̜d = order
pǫ̑t = way

8. C.S. *y* (O.S. ы) develops into *i*, as in Serbocroatian, Macedonian and Bulgarian:—

SLOVENIAN

                    mîsəl = thought
                    bíti = to be

*9. Both ъ and ь develop into ə, or sometimes—when long under stress—into a:—

                    vès = all
                    vèn = outside
but—
    vâs   = village
    dân   = day
    dáhnem = I breathe (Infin. dəhníti)

10. C.S. ě (O.S. ѣ) becomes ẹ, as in Serbocr. *ekavština*:—

                    cvệt

11. C.S. vocalic *l* and *r* (*l̥*, *r̥*), O.S. лъ,ль, ръ,рь become *ol*, *r* (vocalic) respectively:—

                    vọ̑lk = wolf
                    pȓst = finger

12. Regressive assimilation of consonants (i.e. the *second* deciding whether a group is voiced or unvoiced). This is the general rule of pronunciation, as in other Slav languages, but is not much shown in Slovenian spelling, e.g.:—

z besệdo = with a word   but—s prijâteljem = with a friend
  grízem = I bite   but grísti = to bite

but—
    kdọ̑ (pron. gdọ̑)   = who?
    gládko (pron. glátko)   = smoothly
    dolọ̑čba (pron. dolọ̑džba) = appointment, decision
    glâsba (pron. glâzba)   = music (cf. p. 319-20)

13. Infinitives with velar roots, e.g. C.S. *pekti, *mogti, have *č* in Slovenian (as in Russian—cf. No. 2):—

                    péči = to bake
                    móči = to be able

14. Contraction of vowels. In Slovenian the stressed vowel predominates, e.g.:—

              gospá, from gospojà = lady
also—
    igrâš se, from *igráješ se = you play
    nọ̑čem   "   *nehọ̑čem (but = I do not want
                        also nẹ̑čem)
    nîmam,   "   *neîmam   = I have not
    báti se,   "   *bojáti se   = to fear

*15. e (pron. ə) used as "fill-vowel" between consonants:—

óge̦nj (Gen. sing. ognja) = fire
séste̦r (Gen. plur. of séstra) = of sisters
vẹ̑te̦r (Gen. sing. vẹ̑tra) = wind
ískе̦r (Gen. plur. of. ískra) = of sparks
dẹ̑kе̦l (Gen. plur. of dẹ̑kla) = of girls

16. The palatalized consonants j, lj, nj, c, $č$, $š$, $ž$ must generally be followed by front vowels:—

králjem; kónjem (Instr. sg.) >< sélom, méstom
= king; horse   = site, settlement; place, town

but not in the Instr. sing. of a-stem nouns:—

z vódo, s postâjo = with water; with the station

But Slovenian, like Russian and Serbocroatian, changes original ъ to a after the *chuintantes*: č, š, ž, e.g.:—

bežáti from *běžěti = to flee

*17. Original palatalized r becomes rj (pronounced separately):—

morjẹ̑ (O.S. мор ѥ) = sea

18 v and l at the end of words and syllables, and v and u^1 before consonants initially, especially after a word ending in a vowel, are pronounced u̯ (= w), as in Ukrainian (cf. Polish ł, also Lusatian, Slovak and Byelorussian):—

dẹ̑lal   pron. dẹ̑lau̯   = worked
rápav   "   rápau̯   = wrinkled
vstáti   "   u̯státi   = to get up
tâ účе̦ne̦c "   ta u̯čе̦ne̦c = this pupil

19. Initial je is preserved as a general rule, e.g.:—

jẹ̑zero = lake

éden, before nouns èn, (= one) forms an exception.

20. Partial loss of 2nd Palatalization (see "Slavonic Characteristics," No. 3).

21. Free accent (see "The Accents in Slovenian," p. 326).

---

[1]But u before r, l, as before vowels, is pronounced as a full vowel. See p. 322.

*22 Closed *e* and *o* (see above—"Pronunciation")— peculiar closed vowel quality unknown in other Slavonic literary languages.

23. Freer use of the Infinitive than in Serbocroatian and Bulgarian.

24. Pronunciation of *lj* and *nj* as ļi and ņi before vowels, e.g. in the Instr. sing. of feminine *i*-stems, adjectives formed from the names of animals, and Nom. plur in *-je* of certain masculine nouns. (See "Pronunciation"—the consonants.)

25. Assimilation of *šs* to *š*, as in Serbocroatian:—

   čệški (for češski) = Czech

*26. Reduction of *dn* to *n*, cf. Byelorussian:—

   brézno = abyss
   èn, for éden = one

*27. Simplification of *ts* to *s*:—

  bogâstvo (for bogatstvo) = riches
  posệstvo (for posedstvo) = possession, property

28. The modern change of *kt, gt* to *ht* (cf. Russian pronunciation of кто as хто):—

  lahtî, Dual and Plur. of lâket   = elbow
  nộhta, Gen. sing. of nộht,[1] from nog- = nail
  nihčè, from nikъtože   = no one

29. Dissimilation of *k* and *g* before *k* (cf. Russian мягкий, pron. мяхкий):—

lâhka (fem. sing.) = light hence masculine lâhǝk, cf. Pol lekki
méhka " " = soft "   " méhǝk
pléhka " " = insipid " " pléhǝk (also plígek)
hkráti, for k kráti = at the same time

30. Assimilation of *nb* to *mb*:—

  braníti = to defend obrâmba = defence
  premeníti = to change spremệmba = a change

*31. Change of *d* to *j* before *s* and *š*:—

  grâd = castle   adjective: grâjski
  Blèd (place-name) "   blệjski
  enâjst = eleven } Cf. Bulgarian
  dvâjset = twenty

---

[1]Formerly nộhǝt.

hûd = angry, Comparative: hûjši
mlâd = young   "   mlâjši

32. Change of ž to r (cf. Serbocr. jèp for јеже):—

mȏrem, for možem = I can
kdǫ̂r, for kdož   = who (Relative)

MORPHOLOGY

The morphology of Slovenian is distinctive in that, in contrast to all the other living Slavonic languages except Lusatian,[1] it has preserved the Dual number throughout its declensions and conjugations. This, of course, greatly increases the number of cases that the foreign learner has to memorize in the declensions, even though the Genitive and Locative Dual are now the same as the Genitive and Locative Plural for all nouns, adjectives and pronouns, except the 1st and 2nd person Personal Pronouns. In the verbs the 2nd and 3rd person Dual are now identical, in contrast to Old Slavonic; but a new distinction has arisen: the endings in -a (-va for 1st pers. Dual, and -ta for the 2nd and 3rd pers. Dual) are used for masculine subjects and those in -e (-ve for 1st and -te for 2nd and 3rd pers. Dual) are used for feminine and neuter. To the latter there are special corresponding feminine and neuter forms of the 1st and 2nd pers. Personal Pronoun—$m\hat{\imath}dve$ = we two (fem.), as opposed to $m\hat{\imath}dva$ (masc. or mixed genders); $v\hat{\imath}dve$ = you two (fem. and neut.), in contrast to $v\hat{\imath}dva$ (masc. or mixed genders). In the plural, too, Slovenian also has the peculiar forms $m\stackrel{?}{e}$ for "we" (fem.) as opposed to $m\hat{\imath}$ (masc.), and correspondingly $v\stackrel{?}{e}$ for "you" (fem.) as opposed to $v\hat{\imath}$ (masc.).

The use of the Dual number is fully alive in modern literary Slovenian—it is used quite naturally when referring to two words taking a certain ending, for example—and once the habit of thinking in it is acquired (especially easy for married people), it seems quite easy and natural; and the grammatical cases answering this need provide the corresponding forms so required. (Use of the plural instead *may* cause misunderstandings.)

The Instrumental case, like the Locative, is only used with prepositions, as in Lusatian. To express the plain instrument by which something is done, the preposition s/z is used. Cf. Z aviȏnom = by plane (air mail), with Serbocr. Aviȏnom.

---

[1] and Kashubian (Polish dialect).

(In the following tables the full accentuation is given wherever I have been able to find it indicated, as it is advisable for the foreign learner at least to *know* of the existence of the intonational distinctions, if not to reproduce them. I am grateful to Professor F. Ramôvš for his valuable assistance on accents.)

THE DECLENSION OF NOUNS

As in Russian and Serbocroåtian, owing to the disappearance of the *ŭ-* and *ū-*stems, four main types of declension exist in Slovenian:—

*i-*stems	all feminine,
consonant stems	neuter, except for two—with the endings, however, of neuter *o-*stems,
*a-*stems	largely feminine,
*o-*stems	masculine (ending in a consonant) and neuter (ending in *-o* or *-e*)

The three genders are thus preserved, but, as in Russian and Slovak, special forms for the Vocative (sing.) case have been lost. The Dual, as already mentioned, has the same endings for nouns in the Gen. and Loc. as the Plural, but endings of its own for the Nom. and Acc. (identical to each other) and the Dat. and Instr. (also identical to each other).

In the plural all the cases of fem. and neut. nouns have different endings except the Nom. and Acc. (as in Russian and West Slav); but in masc. nouns (as in Serbocr.) the Nom. and Acc. are distinguished by preserving distinct (originally soft stem) endings.

1. *i-*stems, all feminine. Those accented in most of the cases on the last syllable have different endings in the Dat., Inṣtr. and Loc., Dual and Plural from those not so accented. Therefore cf.:—

nìt = thread   kộst = bone

	Singular		Dual		Plural	
Nom.	nìt	kộst	nîti	kostî	nîti	kostî
Gen.	nîti	kostî	nîti	kostî	nîti	kostí̧
Dat.	nîti	kósti	nîtma	kostẹ́ma	nîtim	kostẹ́m
Acc.	nìt	kộst	nîti	kostî	nîti	kostî
Instr.	nîtjo	kostjǫ́	nîtma	kostẹ́ma	nîtmi	kostmî
Loc.	nîti	kósti	nîtih	kostẹ́h	nîtih	kostẹ́h

The many nouns in *-ost* follows nìt, e.g. rádóst = joy.

Nouns such as mîsel (mîsəu̯) = thought, bolêzən = illness, which have the neutral vowel in their final syllable in the Nom. sing., have the endings -*ijo* in the Instr. sing., -*ima* in Dat. and Instr. Dual and -*imi* in Instr. plur., e.g.:—

  ·Instr. sing. mîslijo, bolêznijo
  Dat., Instr. Dual mîslima, bolêznima
  Instr. plur. mîslimi, bolêznimi

But those ending in -*ev* (əu̯) only follow this rule in the Instr. sing., e.g.:—

  s cêrkvijo = with the church

Their Gen. sing. ends in -ve: cêrkve, a survival from the old long *ū*-stems. In the Dual and Plural they follow the *a*-stems (see below).
 Note also: krî (from *kry, cf. Latin cruor = blood), which has an irregular Nom. sing.—Gen. sing. krvî, Dat. Loc. s. kȓvi. It is declined like kôst.
 The old masc. *i*-stems have only left their trace in certain masc. Nom. plurals -*je*:—

  gospôdje = gentlemen
  golôbje = pigeons
  (otherwise *o*-stems, see below).

 Ljudjê (= people) has alone preserved the original masc. plur. endings:—

  Nom. ljudjê   Acc. ljudî
  Gen. ljudî   Instr. ljudmí
  Dat. ljudém (and -êm) Loc. ljudéh

 Pót = (road) is now either masc., when it has Gen. sing. pôta, or fem., when it has Gen. sing. pôti. In the plural it is either neuter—pôta, or fem. potî.

Accentuation
 The general rule to follow is to keep the accent the same as in the Nom. sing. throughout the declension, but to note the exceptions and changes that occur. Here, of course, only the main ones are noted.
 Monosyllables or nouns with final syllable accented ˋ (short falling) change this accent to one of the long ones in the oblique cases. So nìt (above), and ràk and kònj (below).
 In the *i*-declension monosyllables accented ˆ in the Nom. sing. have the accent on the last syllable in the oblique cases, except in the Dat. and Loc. sing., as kôst (above). But this ˆ accent shifts to the first syllable after a preposition in *all* declensions, also in disyllables, e.g.:—

Gen. sing. noči = night, but do nǫ̀či = till night
" " jesę̑n = autumn, " na jęsen = for the autumn

2. Consonant stems, in -n-, -t- and -s-, all neuter. These all now have o-stem endings, as in Serbocr., see p. 346-48, e.g.:—

N. jâgnje = lamb or žrebę̀ = foal   brême = burden   drevô = tree
G. jâgnjeta   žrebę́ta   bremę́na   drevę̑sa
D. jâgnjetu   žrebę́tu   bremę́nu   drevę̑su
   etc.   etc.   etc.   etc.

The two surviving r-stems, feminine, are to be regarded as irregular. We give them below, in the singular, as they are important nouns. In the Dual and Plur. they are declined like a-stems (see lípa, below).

Nom.   máti = mother   hčî = daughter
Gen.   mátere   hčę̑re
Dat.   máteri   hčę̑ri
Acc.   máter   hčę̑r
Instr. mâterjo   hčę̑rjo
Loc.   máteri   hčę̑ri

The important noun dân (= day) is really an irregular n-stem, and is now declined as follows:—

	SING.	DUAL.	PLURAL
Nom.	dân	dnę̑va	dnę̑vi
Gen.	dnę̑, dnę̑va	dnî	dnî
Dat.	dnę̑vu	dnę̑ma, dnę̑voma	dnę́m, dnę̑vom
Acc.	dân	dnî, dnę̑va	dnî, dnę̑ve
Instr.	dnę̑m, dnę̑vom	dnę̑ma, dnę̑voma	dnę̑mi, dnę̑vi
Loc.	dnę̑, dnę̑vu	dnę̑h, dnę̑vih	dnę̑h, dnę̑vih

3. a-stems, mostly feminine. Here, as in Serbocr., the old ja-stems have predominated in the Gen., Dat., and Loc. sing., and in the Nom. and Acc. Dual and Plural.

lípa = lime tree   góra = mountain

	SING.		DUAL		PLURAL	
Nom.	lípa	góra	lípi	góri, gorę̑	lípe	gorę̑
Gen.	lípe	gorę̑(góre)	lîp	gôr, gorá	lîp	gôr, gorá
Dat.	lípi	góri	lípama	gorâma	lípam	gorâm(góram)
Acc.	lípo	gorǫ̑(góro)	lípi	góri, gorę̑	lípe	gorę̑
Instr.	lîpo	gorǫ̑(góro)	lípama	gorâma	lípami	gorâmi
Loc.	lípi	góri	lípah	gorâh(górah)	lípah	gorâh(górah)

Masculine nouns and names in -a are similarly declined, e.g. vǫ́dja (= leader), Míha = Mike or else they can have the terminations of masculine o-stems.

In the Gen. plur. ə is the regular fill-vowel,
e.g.:—

    séstra = sister,   Gen. plur. séstər

But *i* occurs before *j* and *c*, as in

    ládja = boat   Gen. plur. ládij
    klǫ́pca = bench   Gen. plur. klǫ́pic

and -*a* appears when the final syllable is stressed,
e.g.:—

    óvca = sheep   Gen. plur. ovâc

In this (Gen. plur.) case the *ending* -*á* (accented), instead of no ending, may be an alternative (reminding one of Serbocr.), e.g.:—

    stəzá (as well as stə̀z) = of paths
    sestrá
    gorá

Notice also the Gen. plurals like—

    hrûšk, from hrûška = pear
    drûžb   = of companies
    bîtk   = of battles
    gǫ̂db   = of bands, etc.

where a fill-vowel is not considered necessary. So also with some neuters.

(There is *no* 2nd palatalization in Slovenian, e.g. rę́ka = river, has Dat. Loc. sing. rę́ki.)

The noun gospá (= lady, Mrs.) is irregular and declines as follows:—

	SING.	DUAL	PLUR.
Nom.	gospá	gospę́	gospę́
Gen.	gospę́	gospá	gospá
Dat.	gospę́	gospę́ma	gospę́m
Acc.	gospǫ́	gospę́	gospę́
Instr.	gospǫ́	gospę́ma	gospę́mi
Loc.	gospę́	gospę́h	gospę́h

Accentuation

The accent position of the Nom. sing. is preserved throughout the declension, except in the case of nouns with an open *e* or *o* (i.e. *e* or *o* with no accent written below) in the root (corresponding to nouns accented on the last syllable in Russian). These accent the first syllable of the ending in all cases but the Nom., Dat., Loc. sing. and the Nom., Acc. Dual.

Those accenting the last syllable, such as stəzà

SLOVENIAN

(= path), retain the accent on the last syllable throughout. In this word and in all others where the ending is stressed, in Nom., Acc. Dual the ending is -ê (not -i).

4a. *o*-stems, masculine. As in Serbocr., the old hard *o*-stems predominate in the singular except in the Instr., where soft stems are distinguished, but in the Dual and Plural the distinction between the old hard and soft declensions is more generally preserved. In the plural more of the old case terminations survive than in Serbocr., viz. in the Dat., Loc. and Instr. plural.

The soft consonants in Slovenian are the *chuintantes* č, š, ž, — *j* and its combinations, mainly *lj* and *nj*, and *c*. After these the *o* in hard terminations is changed to *e*.

As in other Slavonic languages, the Acc. sing. of masc. nouns has the same form as the Gen. sing. for animate nouns, and that of the Nom. sing. for inanimate nouns. In the Loc. sing. the ending is always -*u*, as in Serbocr.

ràk = crawfish, cancer   kònj = horse
kràj = locality, edge,
otherwise declined like kònj

SINGULAR

Nom.	ràk[1]	kònj		kràj
Gen.	ráka	kónja		
Dat.	ráku	kónju		
Acc.	ráka	kónja	but	kràj
Instr.	rákom	kónjem		
Loc.	ráku	kónju		

DUAL

Nom.	ráka	kónja
Gen.	rȃkov	kǫ́nj
Dat.	rákoma	kónjema
Acc.	ráka	kónja
Instr.	rákoma	kónjema
Loc.	rȃkih	kǫ́njih

PLURAL

Nom.	ráki	kónji		
Gen.	rȃkov	kǫ́nj	but	krājev
Dat.	rákom	kónjem		
Acc.	ráke	kónje		
Instr.	ráki	kǫ́nji		
Loc.	rȃkih	kǫ́njih		

[1]Proper names in -*o* follow this type of declension, e.g.: Jânko, Gen. s. Jânka, Dat. s. Jânku; Márko, Gen. s. Márka, etc.

Most polysyllabic nouns in -*ar*, -*ir*, -*or*, and -*ur* insert *j* before the endings, e.g.:—

  cēsar = emperor, Gen. sing. cesárja

  Dəž̀ (= rain) also has Gen. sing. dəžjà.

-*ov* (-*ev* for soft stems) (from the old *ŭ*-stems) is the general ending for the Gen. dual and plural. The exceptions are:—

		Gen. du. and pl.	
kònj			kǫ́nj
lâs	= hair		lâs
môž	= man		mǫ́ž
otròk	= child		otrók
vôz	= carriage, waggon		vǫ́z or vozǫ́v
zǫ̂b	= tooth		zǫ́b or zobǫ́v

which have or can have *no* termination in the Gen. plur.; but note the change of accent!

The syllable -*ǫv*- (-*ęv*- after *j*) is also inserted before the terminations of the Dual and Plural of most monosyllabic nouns, as in Serbocr. e.g.:—

  svę̂t = world, Gen. sing. svętâ

Nom. dual	svetǫ̂va
Nom. plur.	svetǫ̂vi
Gen. plur.	svetǫ́v
Dat. plur.	svetǫ̂vom
Acc. plur.	svetǫ̂ve
Instr. plur.	svetǫ̂vi
Loc. plur.	svetǫ̂vih

The old *ŭ*-stems have also left traces in the Gen. sing. of certain nouns, e.g.:—

mę̂d	= honey	Gen. sing.	medû *or* mę̂da
grâd	= castle	" "	gradû *or* grâda
strâh	= fear	" "	strahû *or* strâha

and also, of course, in the general termination -*u* of the Loc. sing.

Notice also:—

ǒče	= father	Gen. sing. očę́ta[1]	Nom. plur. očę́tje[2]
sînko	= sonny	" " sînka	
nágəlj	= carnation	" " nágəljna	

[1]Proper names in -*e* follow this type, e.g. Jǫ̂že = Joseph, Gen. s. Jǫ́žeta.

[2]Cf. p. 340, Nom. plurals in -je. Further common examples: brátje = brothers, fántje = boys, góstje = guests, sosę́dje = neighbours, meščánje = townsmen (Nom. s. meščàn).

E = ə as well as ordinary e are the fill-vowels:—

    vêtər = wind   Gen. sing. vêtra
    ógenj = fire   "   " ógnja

ə from the semivowels ъ and ь is similarly dropped in declension, unless it follows two consonants, e.g.:

	pósəl = business	Gen. sing.	póslà,
	dogǫ́dək = event	"	"	dogǫ́dka
	vrábəc = sparrow	"	"	vrábca
	kášəlj = cough	"	"	kášlja
	sə̀n = sleep	"	"	snà
	pə̀s = dog	"	"	psà
but	jȇzdəc = rider,	"	"	jȇzdəca

Accentuation

    For the foreign learner it is safest to retain the accent of the Nom. sing. throughout the declension, except that all ` (short falling accents) must either be changed to ´, e.g.:—

    ràk   Gen. sing. ráka (above)

or else move to the termination, e.g.:—

    də̀ž   Gen. sing. dəžjà (above)

    Nouns with an open *e* or *o* in the root, indicating a shift of stress, follow the model of kònj.

    Certain monosyllables may stress the ending of the Gen. sing., as:—

    svȩ̑t - svȩtâ
    grȃd - gradû

These generally stress the termination in the Dual and Plural.

    Polysyllables bearing ˆ on any syllable retain it on that syllable throughout the declension, e.g.:—

    prijâtelj (= friend), prijâtelja

while those that have ´ often shift it one syllable nearer the end, e.g.:—

    jézik (= tongue), jezíka

We give below three further examples:—

stebər = pillar   dȗh = spirit   mȏž = man (irreg.)

SINGULAR

Nom.	stebər	dȗh	mȏž
Gen.	stebrà	duhȃ (dȗha)	možȃ
Dat.	stebrù	dȗhu	možȗ
Acc.	stebər	dȗh (duhȃ)	možȃ
Instr.	stebròm	dȗhom	možèm
Loc.	stebrù	dȗhu	možȗ

DUAL

Nom.	stebrà	duhȏva	možȃ
Gen.	stebrǫ́v	duhǫ́v	mǫ́ž
Dat.	stèbromà	duhȏvoma	možę́ma
Acc.	stebrà	duhȏva	možȃ
Instr.	stèbromà	duhȏvoma	možę́ma
Loc.	stebrę́h	duhȏvih	možę́h

PLURAL

Nom.	stebrí	duhȏvi	možjȇ [1]
Gen.	stebrǫ́v	duhǫ́v	mǫ́ž
Dat.	stebròm	duhȏvom	možę́m
Acc.	stebrè	duhȏve	možè
Instr.	stebrí	duhȏvi	možmí [2]
Loc.	stebrę́h [3]	duhȏvih	možę́h [3]

After prepositions the accent can sometimes shift on to the preceding syllable: e.g., primȇr = example, but na prímer = for example; večȇr = evening, na vȇčer = towards evening.

4b. *o*-stems, neuter. As in the masc. *o*-stems, the difference between the hard and soft[4] neut. *o*-stems appears only in those cases where there is an -*o*- in the ending of the hard stems, which is replaced by an -*e*- in the soft stems,[4] i.e. Nom., Acc., Instr. sing.; Dat., Instr., Dual; Dat. Plur.

---

[1]Further Nominatives plural in -jȇ: zobjȇ = teeth, lasjȇ = hair, vozjȇ, more commonly vozȏvi = carts.

[2]So also: *z* - volmí (= with oxen), lasmí (hairs), vozmí (carts), zobmí (teeth).

[3]About thirty nouns, mostly monosyllabic or with ə in their second syllable, *can* have a Loc. pl. (and dual!) in -ę́h, e.g. kónəc = end, Loc. du., pl. koncę́h or kóncih.

[4]See p. 343, No. 4a, second paragraph, for definition.

SLOVENIAN

lẹ́to = year   poljẽ, or põlje = field

	SINGULAR			DUAL	
Nom.	lẹ́to	poljẽ, or põlje	Nom.	lẹ́tį	põljį
Gen.	lẹ́ta	poljá̧	Gen.	lẽt	põlj
Dat.	lẹ́tu	põlju	Dat.	lẹ́toma	põljema
Acc.	lẹ́to	poljẽ, or põlje	Acc.	lẹ́tį	põljį
Instr.	lẹ́tom	põljem	Instr.	lẹ́toma	põljema
Loc.	lẹ́tu	põlju	Loc.	lẹ́tįh	põljįh

	PLURAL	
Nom.	lẽta	põlja
Gen.	lẽt	põlj
Dat.	lẹ́tom	põljem
Acc.	lẽta	põlja
Instr.	lẽtį	põljį
Loc.	lẽtįh	põljįh

In the Gen. plur. ə is the fill-vowel, except before *j* when it is *i*, e.g.:—

ókno	= window	Gen. plur.	ókən
kõpje	= lance	" "	kõpij
kraljẽstvo	= kingdom	" "	kraljẽstəv
dẽjstvo	= fact	" "	dẽjstəv
morjẽ or mõrje	= sea	" "	mõrij
písmo	= letter	" "	pîsəm
védro	= pail	" "	vêdər
sédlo	= saddle	" "	sêdəl

Irregular are:—

drvà (neut. plur.) = firewood   tlà = floor

Nom.	drvà	Nom.	tlà
Gen.	dŕv	Gen.	tál
Dat.	drvòm	Dat.	tlòm
Acc.	drvà	Acc.	tlà
Instr.	drvmí	Instr.	tlí or tlẹ̃mi
Loc.	drvẹ̃h (also dŕvih)	Loc.	tlẹ̃h

dnò = bottom, has Gen. Plur. dnòv or dán.

Okõ (= eye) Gen. sing. očẹ̃sa, has the original Nom. dual očî (declined like kostî, above) used as a plural, as well as Nom. plur. očẹ̃sa and óka for other than human eyes.

Ušẹ̃sa (= ears) from uhõ, like nógẹ̃ (=legs) (either accent!), rokẹ̃ (= hands) and kolẹ̃na (= knees!), are usually used in the plural, not in the dual as one might expect.

Notice also: igõ, Gen. sing. ižẹ̃sa = yoke; ojẽ, Gen. s. ojẹ̃sa = shaft, and uljẽ, Gen. s. uljẹ̃sa = ulcer. Nebõ = sky, has *s*-stem only in the plural: nebẹ̃sa; čûdo or čúdo = marvel, wonder, has plural either čúda or čudêsa. Kolǫ̑ with the meaning 'wheel' has the plural kolệsa, but kǫ́la (Nom., Acc. plur.) = carriage, cart. Kǫ̑lo, with initial accent, is the well-known Yugoslav round dance, as in Serbocr. (Cf. p. 341, No. 2.)

Accentuation

Those nouns that accent a non-final syllable usually retain the position of the accent throughout the declension, though not necessarily the intonation, e.g.:—

   písmo = letter Nom. plur. pîsma
   síto = sieve " " sîta
 cf. Russian:—

    письмо́, пи́сьма
    си́то,   си́та

Those with open *e* and *o*, with accent shifted in Nom. sing. in Slovenian from the original final position in Common Slav, usually retain, in the plural, the intonation but not the vowel quality of the Nom. sing., e.g.:—

 lệto with non-shifted accent (= year)
   Nom. plur. lệta
but—
ókno with shifted accent (= window)
   Nom. plur. ǫ́kna or ókna
 cf. Russian:—

    окно́,   о́кна
    ле́то (= summer) лета́ (= years)

Those nouns, on the other hand, that have ̑ on the final syllable in the Nom., Acc. sing. in Slovenian, e.g. poljê̑ or mesǫ̑ (= meat), shift this accent to the first syllable in Dat., Loc. and Instr. sing. and throughout the dual and plural.

Those nouns that have the final short stress ˋ in the Nom., have ´ (on the final syllable) in the Gen., Instr., and Loc. plur., e.g.—

  drvà Gen. plur. dŕv Instr. plur drvmí
      Loc. plur. drvệh

DECLENSION OF THE INDEFINITE ADJECTIVES

 The Indefinite Adjectives have the same endings in all cases, except the Nom. sing. masc., as the Definite Adjectives. The reader is therefore referred to the section below dealing with the latter.
 Slovenian (not Russian) names in -ov, -ev follow this type, e.g. Prệžihov, Gen. s. Prệžihovega;

Matâjev, etc. Cf. p. 361, Possessive Adjectives.

THE NUMERALS

Cardinal: 1 is declined and treated as an adjective when it qualifies a noun: èn, énega. When used alone, the Nom. sing. masc. has the special form édən. Similarly: nobèn, nobédən (none). (The indefinite article should not be rendered by èn, but with nệki = some, when necessary.)

2 dvâ (masc.), dvệ (fem. and neut.) is an adjective taking, of course, the dual (as does also obâ, obệ = both).

3 trîjệ (masc.), tri (fem. and neut.) and 4 štîrje (masc.), štîri (fem. and neut.) are adjectives with the noun in the plural.

5 onwards are treated as nouns, taking the Gen. plur. in the Nom. and Acc. and governing a verb in the (neuter) singular; in the other cases they are adjectival, agreeing with their noun in case.

All simple numerals may decline[1] (from 5 onwards all in the same way), including (occasionally) —

    stô   = hundred   (declined like pệt - sic!)
    tîsoč(m.) = a thousand } ("   " masc. -o-stem nouns)
    milijôn   = a million }

E.g. ob trệh = at 3 o'clock.

Compounds of 1-4 generally have the verb in the neuter singular owing to the usual form ending in the tens, i.e. "twenty-three" is more usually in the form "three and twenty" in the spoken language.

	NOM.			GEN.			DAT.		
	Masc.	Fem.	Neut.	Masc. Neut.		Fem.	Masc. Neut.		Fem.
1	èn (édən)	éna	éno	énega		éne	énemu		éni,
				etc., like lẹ́pi below, p. 360.					

	NOM./ACC.			GEN./LOC.	DAT.	INSTR.
	Masc.	Fem.	Neut.	All Genders	All Genders	All Genders
2	dvâ		dvệ	dvẹ́h	dvẹ́ma	dvẹ́ma
3	trîjệ [2]	tri		trẹ́h	trệm	trệmi
4	štîrje [2]	štîri		štîrih	štîrim	štîrimi

[1] The modern tendency is *not* to decline numerals (cf. Serbocr.) especially when used as attributes, e.g. âvtobus 7 (sédəm) = bus No 7, after prepositions: z devệt prijâtelji = with nine friends, and in mathematical expressions: ộsəm množẹ́no z dvẹ̀ = eight multiplied by two.

[2] Nominative only.

	NOM./ACC.	GEN./LOC.	DAT.	INSTR.
	All Genders			
5	pêt	pétih[1]	pétim[1]	pétimi[1]
6	šêst—declined like pêt			
7	sédəm " " "			
8	ósəm " " "			
9	devêt " " "			
10	desêt etc.			
11	enájst			
12	dvánájst (either accent)			
13	trínájst " "			
14	štírinájst " "			
15	pêtnájst " "			
16	šêstnájst " "			
17	sêdəmnájst " "			
18	ósəmnájst " "			
19	devêtnájst " "			
20	dvâjset (dvájsti)			
21	édən in dvâjset (dvâjset édən)			
22	dvâ in dvâjset (dvâjset dvâ)			
30	trîdeset			
40	štírideset			
50	pêtdeset			
60	šêstdeset			
70	sédəmdeset			
80	ósəmdeset			
90	devêtdeset			
100	stô (*sometimes* declined like pêt)			
101	stô édən[2]			
102	stô dvâ[2]			
200	dvêstô			
300	trîstô			
400	štíristô			
500	pêtstô			
600	šêststô			
700	sédəmstô, etc.			
1,000	tîsoč			
2,000	dvâ tîsoč			
3,000	trî tîsoč			
10,000	desêt tîsoč			
100,000	stô tîsoč			
1,000,000	milijôn			

sto is here almost an enclitic, unstressed, and is not usually declined. (for 400–700)

The *Ordinal* Numerals are declined like Definite Adjectives. Trêtji = (third) and tîsoči (= 1,000th) have soft stems, hence neut. Nom./Acc sing. *-e*. From

[1] These forms are identical with the corresponding plural cases of the (adjectival) ordinal numerals below.

[2] In compound numerals, only the last figure *may* be declined.

five onwards they are formed by adding -*i* to the Cardinal (and dropping ə where it occurs, in sę́dəm, ǫ́səm). Compound Ordinals have only the last part in the ordinal form. Ordinals are always used for indicating dates:—

dnę̑ trę́tjega aprîla (lę́ta) tîsoč devę̑t stǫ̑ sę́dəm
 in štírideseteɡa = (on) 3rd April, 1947

 1st pŕvi   -a   -o
 2nd drúgi -a   -o
 3rd trę́tji -a   -e
 4th četŕti
 5th pę́ti
 6th šésti
 7th sédmi
 8th ósmi
 9th devéti
 10th deséti
 11th enájsti
 12th dvanájsti
 20th dvâjseti
 21th enaindvâjseti (dvâjset pŕvi only in dictation)
 25th pę̑tindvâjseti (dvâjset péti only in dictation)
 30th trîdeseti
 100th stóti
 101st stǫ̑ in pŕvi or stopŕvi
 1,000th tîsoči
1,000,000th milijǫ̑nski

There are two kinds of *Collective Numerals* (cf. Serbocr.). After dvǫ̑j, -a, -e (= 2), trǫ̑j (= 3), četvę́r (= 4), these are formed by adding -ę́r, -ę́ra, -ę́ro to the Cardinals:—

1. Plural Collective Numerals, varying in gender, used with nouns in the plural only, or to indicate a group:—

 dvǫ̑je gráblje   = two rakes
 trǫ̑ja vráta   = three doors
 petę́re Mǫ̑jzesove búkve = the five Books of Moses
 dvanajstę́ri apǫ̑stoli   = the twelve apostles

These are also used with abstract nouns to indicate "double," etc., otherwise expressed by adjectives in -*ən*:—

 dvǫ̑jne dúri   = double doors
   but
 dvǫ̑ja, *or* dvǫ̑jna, krivíca = a double wrong

2. Neuter singular Collective Numerals, indicating a group of varied people or things which follow in the sing. or Gen. plur.:—

dvóje písmo = two kinds of writing, alphabets
četvęro živínčet = four (different) head of cattle
petęro víno = five kinds of wine
sedmęro ljudí = seven people (men, women, and children)

These are also used for a number of unspecified things:—

na četvęro razdelíti = to divide into four

Po + the Cardinal in the Nom. (or Acc.) is used for *Distributives*:—

po èn = one each

-krat = times:—

dvâkrat = twice
mnǫ́gokrat = many times

-č is added to the Ordinals to form adverbs:—

drúgič (*or* drúgikrat) = for the second time

THE PRONOMINAL DECLENSION

As in other Slavonic languages, the Personal Pronouns of 1st and 2nd person have a declension peculiar to themselves. The other Pronouns all have similar declensions based on two main types:—

tâ = this   Gen. sing. tȩ̂ga Gen. plur. tȩ̂h

representing the hard type;

òn = he   Gen. sing. njéga Gen. plur. njîh

representing the soft type. (tîsti = that, forms a third, mixed type.)

The two *main* types in Slovenian, in contrast to Serbocr., differ more in the dual and plural than in the singular, in which the soft endings have largely predominated. The other pronouns, with vès (= all) as the sole exception, even though hard, follow the soft model in the plural, like tîsti.

The usual categories figure in Slovenian:—

Personal:—

jàz = I
tî = thou
òn = he
mî = we

Demonstrative:—

tâ, also tâle or le-tâ (masc. and fem.!) = this
ǫ̑ni = that (yonder)
tîsti = that (near you)

SLOVENIAN

Interrogative:—

    kdó? = who? (pronounced gdo)
    káj? = what?

Indefinite:—

    nękdǫ́ = someone
    nęki = some

Negative:—

    nîhčè } = no-one
    nîkdo

Possessive (pronoun-adjectives):—

    mǫ́j   = my, mine
    nàš   = our(s)

Relative:—

    ki   = that
    kdǫ́r   = (he) who
    čîgar = whose (indeclinable, referring
                to masc. nouns only)

Definitive:—

    vès   = all
    sâm   = -self
    îsti   = the same
    slę̂herni = every
    màrsikdo = many a (person)
    màrsikaj = many a (thing), much

HARD

    tâ = this

SING.	Masc.	Neut.	Fem.
Nom.	tâ	tǫ̂	tâ
Gen.	tę̂ga, *encl.* tegà		tę̂
Dat.	tę̂mu, *encl.* temù		tę̂j (tî)
Acc.	tę̂ga, tâ	tǫ̂	tǫ̂
Instr.	tę̂m		tǫ̂
Loc.	tę̂m		tę̂j (tî)

DUAL

Nom.	tâ	tî, tę̂	tî, tę̂
Gen.		tę̂h	
Dat.		tę̂ma	
Acc.	tâ	tî, tę̂	tî, tę̂
Instr.		tę̂ma	
Loc.		tę̂h	

PLURAL
Nom.   tî   tâ   tê̦
Gen.   tê̦h
Dat.   tê̦m
Acc.   tê̦   tâ   tê̦
Instr.   tê̦mi
Loc.   tê̦h

SOFT
        ȯn = he, óna = she, ónǫ̂ = it
        Masc.   Neut.   Fem.
                (encl.)   (encl.)
Nom.   ȯn   óno or   óna
                        onǫ̂
Gen.   njéga   ga   njé̦   je
Dat.   njému   mu   njé̦j (njî)   ji
Acc.   njéga   ga   njǫ́   jǫ
Instr. njîm   njǫ́
Loc.   njém   njé̦j (njî)

DUAL
Nom.   óná (dva)   { óni(dve)   óni(dve)
                       oné̦(dve)   oné̦(dve)
                                      (encl.)
Gen.   njîju,njû,njîh;   ju, jih
Dat.   njîma;   jima
Acc.   njîju,njû,njîh;   ju, jih
Instr. njîma
Loc.   njîju,njîma,njîh

PLURAL
Nom.   oní̦   óná   óné̦
Gen.   njîh; jih
Dat.   njîm; jim
Acc.   njîh *or* njé̦; jih
Instr. njîmi
Loc.   njîh

1. The enclitic forms of ȯn are used in sentences where the pronoun in the oblique case is not stressed. (See also note on "Word Order with Enclitics" at the end of this Section.) The full forms are used after prepositions and when the pronoun is emphasized. The Nom. Pers. Pronouns are not used with verbs unless there is contrast or emphasis on them.

2. For the *masc.* Acc. sing. after prepositions the form -*nj* is suffixed to the preposition as an alternative to the full form njéga after the preposition, thus—

        zânj = za njéga = for him
        prêdənj   = (to) before him

For the *neut.* Acc. sing. after prepositions the old form *je* has survived; it is joined to the preposition by an epenthetic *n*, and thus we have—

zânje = for it, or zânj (as in masc.)

Similarly for the *fem.* Acc. sing. we have: zânjo = for her.

In the Acc. plur. after prepositions the older form *je* is used for all genders, e.g.:—

grệm pǫ̂nje = I am going for (to fetch) them

Nje can also be used without a preposition for an emphatic "them," e.g.:—

samǫ̂ njệ = only them

For the Acc. dual we have -nju: zânju = for them two.

3. On, óna, ónǫ̂ should only be used when the 3rd p. Pers. Pronoun bears emphasis, or to express contrast. When a pronoun is required merely by the logical requirements of a clause, tâ or le-tâ (= this) should be used in the appropriate gender. In the following example, if tâ was not used, tudi (= also) would qualify the wrong word, i.e. the verb instead of the pronoun referring to the noun in the previous clause, e.g.:—

... vǫ̂sǝk (= wax); tudi tâ obstojí ... (= *it* also consists ...)

MIXED TYPE

tîsti = that

	Masc.		Neut.	Fem.
SING.				
Nom.	tîsti		tîsto	tîsta
Gen.		tîstega		tîste
Dat.		tîstemu		tîsti
Acc.	tîstega, -i		tîsto	tîsto
Instr.		tîstim		tîsto
Loc.		tîstem		tîsti
DUAL				
Nom.	tîsta		tîstj	tîsti
Gen.		tîstih		
Dat.		tîstima		
Acc.	tîsta		tîsti	tîsti
Instr.		tîstima		
Loc.		tîstih		
PLURAL				
Nom.	tîsti		tîsta	tîste
Gen.		tîstih		
Dat.		tîstim		
Acc.	tîste		tîsta	tîste
Instr.		tîstimi		
Loc.		tîstih		

SLOVENIAN

Only vès (masc.), vsà (fem.), vsè (neut.) (= all)

Gen. sing.	vsègà (masc. and neut.),	vsè	(fem.)
Dat. sing.	vsèmù "	" vsèj(vsì)	"
Instr. sing.	vsèm "	" vsò	"
Loc. sing.	vsèm "	" vsèj(vsì)	"
Instr. plur.	vsèmi (masc. and neut. and fem.)		

follows the declension of tâ in all cases. It has the ` accent in all cases. In the dual it is only used with adjectives: vsà tǫ́žna prišlà = they (two) came all sad ...

According to the soft model of "òn" are declined:—

the Possessives, with fem. Gen. sing. in -e, fem. Dat., Loc. s. in -i, and Gen., Loc. du. in -ih.

mǫ́j (masc.),	mǫ́ja (fem.),	mǫ́je (neut.)	= my
tvǫ́j	tvǫ́ja	tvǫ́je	= thine, your (fam.)
svǫ́j	svǫ́ja	svǫ́je	= own, belonging to the subject of the sentence (any person).
nàš	náša	náše	= our(s)
vàš	váša	váše	= your(s)

The other pronouns, except for the few irregular ones given below in full, are declined like the compromise model tîsti above, which also represents the declension of all adjectives (in all degrees of comparison) in Slovenian (see below). Like tîsti are declined:—

ǫ̀ni	ǫ̀na	ǫ̀no	= that
nèki			= some
sâm	sáma	sámo	= -self
îsti			= the same
slę̀herni, slę̀dnji			= every
vsàk			= every
tâk (-šən)	(-šna	-šno)	= such
tǫ̀lik (-šən)	"	"	= so great
katéri			= which? (of several), who, which (Rel.).
màrsikatéri			= many a(nother)
kàkršən			= of which kind (Rel.)
čigáv?			= whose?
kâk (-šən)?	"	"	= what kind of?
kǫ́lik (-šən)?	"	"	= how great?

njegǫ́v¹   njegǫ́va   = his
njẹ́n¹   = her
njûn¹   = of them two, their
njîhov¹   = their (of more than two)
nâjin   = of us two, our
vâjin   = of you two, your
oné (finally stressed oná   onó = someone not (to be) named
   throughout)

The Gen. sing. masc., neut. onẹ́gá is sometimes used for the Nom., Acc. s. masc. Note the fem. Dat., Loc. s. onẹ́, cf. gospá, p. 342.

     kdǫ́? (= who?) and káj? (= what?), and their corresponding Relatives kdǫ́r and kàr, are irregular, and are declined as follows:—

Nom.	kdo̥	káj	kdǫ́r	kàr
Gen.	kǫ́ga	čẹ́sa	kǫ́gar	čẹ́sar
Dat.	kǫ́mu	čẹ́mu	kǫ́mur	čẹ́mur
Acc.	kǫ́ga	káj	kǫ́gar	kàr
Instr.	kǫ́m	čím	kǫ́mər	čímər
Loc.	kǫ́m	čẹ́m	kǫ́mər	čẹ́mər

     All compounds of the above, e.g. nẹ́kdǫ́, Gen. sing. nẹ́koga (= someone); nîkdo, Gen. sing. nikǫ́gar (= no one); màrsikdǫ̀, Gen. sing. màrsikoga (= many a man); nẹ́kaj, Gen. sing. nečẹ́sa (= something); vsâkdo, Gen. sing. vsâkogar (= anybody, everybody), are declined as above, having the appropriate prefix.

     The declension of nìč (= nothing) should also be noted:—

Nom.	nìč
Gen.	ničẹ́sar
Dat.	ničẹ́mur
Acc.	nìč
Instr.	ničîmər
Loc.	ničẹ́mər

(Sometimes it is not declined).

     Nîhčè (< nikьtože), Gen. sing. nikǫ̀gar, is an alternative Nom. to nîkdo, declined like kdǫ́r.

     Ki is the "general Relative," referring to someone known, and does not decline. If not used as a Nom. Relative it must be amplified by the Personal Pronoun in the case required by the verb of the relative clause (the *enclitic* form is required if used

---

[1] The Possessive Adjectives of the 3rd pers. are often replaced by the corresponding Genitives of the Pers. Pronoun: njéga, njẹ́, njú, njîh:—

         njéga ǒče = his father

without a preposition), e.g.:—

Mǫ̂ž, ki nas je vídel ... = the man who (Nom.) saw us
but—   ...
Môž, ki smo ga vídeli... = the man whom (Acc.) we
                             saw ...
Ràd bi dó tébe ki te
  ne mǫ́rem pozábiti   = I would gladly (come) to
                           you whom I cannot forget.

The preposition, if required, is put before the *full* form of the 3rd pers. Personal Pronoun. After a preposition katȩ́ri may be used as an alternative, e.g.:—

Prijâtelji, ki smo pri
  njȋh bilȋ ...   =⎫
or—   ⎬ the friends with whom we were ...
Prijâtelji, pri katȩ́rih⎪
  smo bilȋ ...   =⎭

The *Personal Pronouns* of the 1st and 2nd person are declined as follows:—

	jàz = I		tȋ = thou	
SING	*Full form*	*Encl.*	*Full form*	*Encl.*
Nom.	jàz		tȋ	
Gen.	méne	me	tébe	te
Dat.	méni	mi	tébi	ti
Acc.	méne	me	tébe	te
Instr.	menój (mâno)		tebój (tâbo)	
Loc.	méni		tébi	

	mȋdva = we two		vȋdva = you two	
DUAL	*masc.*	*fem. and neut.*	*masc.*	*fem. and neut.*
Nom.	mȋdva,	mȋdve	vȋdva,	vȋdve
		(mȩ̂dve)		(vȩ̂dve)
Gen.	nâju	naju	vâju	vaju
Dat.	nâma	nama	vâma	vama
Acc.	nâju	naju	vâju	vaju
Instr.	nâma		vâma	
Loc.	nâju *or*		vâju *or*	
	nâma		vâma	

	mȋ = we		vȋ = you	
PLURAL	*masc.*	*fem.*	*masc.*	*fem.*
Nom.	mȋ	mȩ̂	vȋ	vȩ̂
Gen.	nàs		nas	vàs	vas
Dat.	nàm		nam	vàm	vam
Acc.	nàs		nas	vàs	vas
Instr.	nâmi			vâmi	
Loc.	nàs			vàs	

sébe (= self) is declined exactly like tébe. It

has Gen. and Acc. enclitic se, Dat. enclitic si (frequently used, as in Czech).

The enclitic forms, as in the case of ȍn, are used in sentences where the Pronoun in the oblique cases is not stressed. (The Nom. Pers. Pronoun is usually omitted altogether if not stressed.) (See also note on "Word Order with Enclitics.")

Notice the use of the enclitic forms compounded with prepositions: zâme = for me, nâte = on to you, zâse = for oneself, vâme = into me (note the -â-!).

THE DECLENSION OF ADJECTIVES

The hard and soft stems differ from each other only in the Nom. and Acc. sing. neut.: lȩ́po (= beautiful), but rdȩ́če (= red). In the other cases of the masc. and neut. sing., the *e* vowel has become generalized at the expense of the *o* (in contrast to Serbocr.).

In the Dat. and Loc. sing. fem. the ending is -*i*, as in the *a*-stem fem. nouns—this also is a difference as compared with Serbocr.

As in Serbocr., Definite and Indefinite Adjectives exist (corresponding to an adjective qualifying a noun preceded by the definite or the indefinite article respectively in English), but these differ in form *only* in the Nom. and (inanimate) Acc. sing. masc., their endings being otherwise identical. Most adjectives distinguish the definite from the indefinite form by intonation. The accent of the definite form in all cases is usually the same as that in the Nom. sing. fem. of the indefinite form. The foreign learner should note the position and intonation of the accent in the Nom. sing. masc. and fem. indef. (as given in some dictionaries), and apply this rule, preserving the correct length and intonation (and quality too, if possible) of the vowel—i.e. of the Nom. sing. fem.—in all other cases. (See also "Accentuation" below.) As in Serbocr., the Indefinite Adjective is tending to be used mainly predicatively, where it is essential in the masc. sing. It is also used after vsȃk = every.

The rule about the Acc. sing. masc. being like the Gen. sing. masc. for animate nouns and like the Nom. sing. masc. for inanimate nouns, applies in Slovenian too, when the adj. is used *with* a noun. But in the literary language, when an adj. referring to an inanimate masc. noun is used by itself in the Acc., it takes the *Gen.* form, e.g.:—

Vȩ̑liki zvǫ̑n smȍ žȩ̑ prelîli, srȩ̑dnjega pȁ šȅ lȩ̑ bǫ̑mo. = The big bell we have already recast, but the medium one we still have to do.

We give below a specimen declension for clarity's sake:—

Hard: lêp = beautiful   Soft: rdèč, fem. rdéča = red

SING. *Masculine*   *Neuter*   *Femine*
Nom. lêp, lépi (def.)   lépo (rdéče)   lépa
Gen.   lépega   lépe
Dat.   lépemu   lépi
Acc. lépega, lép(i)   lépo (rdéče)   lépo (rdéčo!)
Instr.   lépim   lépo (rdéčo!)
Loc.   lépem   lépi

DUAL
Nom. lépa   lépi   lépi
Gen.   lépih
Dat.   lépima
Acc. lépa   lépi   lépi
Instr.   lépima
Loc.   lépih

PLURAL
Nom. lépi   lépa   lépe
Gen.   lépih
Dat.   lépim
Acc. lépe   lépa   lépe
Instr.   lépimi
Loc.   lépih

Adjectives in -*nji*, e.g.:—

srêdnji = middle

and Possessive Adjectives in -*ji*, -*ski*, -*ški*, -*čki*, e.g.:—

krâvji   = cow's
brátovski = brother's, brotherly
móški   = men's, manly

and all Comparative and Superlative adjectives (see below) have no indefinite or predicative, form; also—

mâli   = small
óbči   = common
prâvi   = right, real
záli, zála (fem.)   = pretty
râjni   = the late
umŕli   = the deceased

The predicative form of mâli is mâjhən.

Some adjectives are used as nouns, but decline like adjectives, e.g.:—

blîžnji   = one's neighbour
mâla (déklica)   = little girl

gospǫ́ska (oblȃst) = the authorities
Štȃjerska (dežéla) = Štȃjersko = Styria.

On the other hand Possessive Adjectives in *-ov* (*-ev*) and *-in*, e.g.:—

brȃtov = brother's
sȇstrin = sister's

never have the definite (*-i*) ending in the Nom. sing. masc.

Rȁd (masc.), rȃda (fem.) = glad(ly), is confined to the Nom. of all genders and numbers, while its Comparative rȃjši usually remains in the masc. sing. form.

A few adjectives, such as—

nȃpak = wrong (way round)
pȇš = on foot
rȇs = true
všȇč = nice, welcome
kǫ́s = capable, equal to

and usually

tǝ̀šč = empty, unfed; and žȁl = offensive, angry are indeclinable.

Accentuation

Many adjectives retain throughout both the def. and indef. declension the same position (though not intonation) of the accent and the same vowel quality, e.g.:—

bȇl = white
mótǝn = troubled, dim

Adjectives with ˋ in Nom. sing. masc. change this to ´ in the Nom. sing. fem. and retain this ´ throughout the declension regardless of the number of syllables of the ending, e.g.:—

bogàt = rich   Nom.sing.fem. bogáta   Gen.sing.masc. bogátega
stàr = old   "   "   "   stára   "   "   "   stárega
nòv = new   "   "   "   nóva   "   "   "   nóvega

Some adjectives in their indefinite form *may* *stress* the ending (more usually only in the Nom. and Acc. sing. neut. and Nom. and Acc. du. and plur. of all genders). We give below the declension of mlȃd (= young) in full to show all the possibilities (two accents on a form indicate the two alternatives).

SLOVENIAN

	Sing.	Masculine	Neuter	Feminine
	Nom.	mlâd	mládô	mláda
	Gen.	mládega		mláde
	Dat.	mládemu		mládi
	Acc.	mlâd, mládega	mládô	mládô
	Instr.	mládim		mládô
	Loc.	mládem		mládi

	DUAL	Masculine	Neuter and Feminine
	Nom.	mládâ	mládi or mládê
	Gen.	mládih	
	Dat.	mládima	
	Acc.	mládâ	mládi or mládê
	Instr.	mládima	
	Loc.	mládih	

	PLURAL	Masculine	Neuter	Feminine
	Nom.	mládî	mládâ	mládê
	Gen.	mládih		
	Dat.	mládim		
	Acc.	mládê	mládâ	mládê
	Instr.	mládimi		
	Loc.	mládih		

The definite forms retain the accent of Nom. sing. masc. on the same syllable throughout the declension, e.g.:—

    lâhki = light Nom.sing.fem. lâhka Gen.sing.masc. lâhkega
    stâri = old   " " " stâra " " " stârega

So also—

        vệliki, vệlika = great

which has the indefinite forms—

        vélik, velíka.

Those adjectives that have ə in the termination of the Nom. sing. masc. indef. *may* stress the last syllable throughout (generally with ˋ), e.g. təmə̂n, or təmân (also tèmən) = dark:—

	Masc.	Neut.	Fem.
Nom. sing.	təmə̂n (təmân)	təmnô (or -ò)	təmnà
Gen. sing.	temnegà		təmnę́(or -è)
Nom. plur.	təmnì (or -î)	təmnà	təmnę̀, etc.

The Comparison of Adjectives

    The *Comparative adjectives* are formed with three alternative sets of endings:—

        -ši,   -ša, -še
        -ji,   -ja, -je
        -ęjši, -ęjša, -ęjše

The first set of endings is usually used with monosyllabic adjectives whose stem ends in b, p or d, e.g.:—

slȁb	= weak, bad	Comp.	slȃbši
lȇp	= beautiful	"	lȇpši
mlȃd	= young	"	mlȃjši
hûd, húda	= bad, angry	"	hûjši
tȓd	= hard	"	tȓši

The second set of endings is used for most adjectives with velar or sibilant stem, k, g, h changing before j to č, ž, š—according to the rules of yotation—and z, s to ž, š respectively (see "Slavonic Characteristics," No. 4,) e.g.:—

tȋh	= quiet	Comp.	tȋšji
jȃk	= strong	"	jȃčji
drȃg	= dear	"	drȃžji
glȗh	= deaf	"	glȗšji
visòk	= high	"	vȋšji (see below)

The third set of endings is used for many adjectives of two or more syllables, especially those ending in -r, -n, -an, -ak, -al, -iv, -it, e.g.:—

bístər	= bright	Comp.	bistrȇjši
prídən	= industrious	"	prídnęjši
drobân or dróbən	= small, fine	"	drobnȇjši
krępâk or krépək	= strong	"	krepkȇjši
šíbək	= slim, weak	"	šibkȇjši
ljuboznìv	= kind	"	ljuboznívęjši
bogàt	= rich	"	bogatȇjši
plemenît	= noble	"	plemenítęjši
débel, debȇla(fem.)	= fat	"	debelȇjši

and also with many monosyllabic adjectives, especially those ending in -st, e.g.:—

nòv	= new	Comp.	novȇjši
svȩ̑t	= holy	"	svetȇjši
mȋl	= gentle, kind	"	milȇjši
stàr	= old	"	starȇjši (stárši = parents)
čìst	= clean	"	čistȇjši

The ending -ęjši is accented with most monosyllabic and disyllabic adjectives. But adjectives of three or more syllables preserve the original position of the accent, lengthening ˋ, where it occurs, to ´, as with ljuboznìv above.

Adjectives ending in -ək (-ak) or -ok usually lose this ending in forming a Comparative, like visòk, vȋšji above, e.g.:—

SLOVENIAN

láhək	= light	Comp.	lážji
sládək	= sweet	"	slájši *or* sladkéjši
širòk	= broad	"	širši
tának *or* tənâk	= thin	"	tânjši
krátək	= short	"	krâjši *or* krâcji
nízək	= low	"	nîžji
težək *or* težâk	= heavy	"	težji
globòk	= deep	"	glôblji[1]
ózək	= narrow	"	ôžji

consonantal changes according to rules of yotation

but some keep the ending -*ək* (see šibkéjši and krepkéjši above), e.g.:—

górək = *warm* Comp. gorkéjši

The following important adjectives have irregular Comparatives:—

vélik, velîka	= big, great	Comp.	vêčji
mâjhən	= small	"	mânjši
dóbər, dóbra	= good	"	bôljši
dôlg	= long }	"	dâljši
dâlek	= far off		
cenên	= cheap	"	cenêjši

(or pocéni - indeclinable)

záli, zála (= bad, pretty) has zâlši *and* gôrši or gôrji. These last two forms can also be used as the Comparative of zəl (also pronounced zəṷ) = bad.

Periphrastic Comparatives, using the word bòlj (= more)+ the Positive degree, are formed mainly from—

1. Adjectives denoting colour, e.g.:—

bòlj črn = blacker

2. Pres. Participles in -*č* used as adjectives, e.g.:—

bòlj cvetóč = more flourishing

3. Adjectives ending in -*ski* or -*ji*, e.g.:—

bòlj slovénski = more Slovenian
bòlj dívji = more wild

4. Past Participles Passive in -(*e*)*n*, -*na*, -*no*, and -*t*, -*ta*, -*to*, and Past Participles Active in -*l*, -*la*, -*lo*, used adjectivally, e.g.:—

bòlj učèn = more learned
bòlj znàn = more well-known
bòlj vrèl = hotter, keener

---

[1] Also globokéjši and globôčji.

5. Adjectives in -av, -ast, -at and some in -en and -ən, and a few others, e.g.:—

zdràv	= healthy	Comp. bòlj zdràv, etc.
kràstav	= scabby	
gŕbast	= hunch-backed	Also: sûh = dry
tràvnat	= grassy	mókər = wet
jeklęn	= (of) steel	tûj = strange, foreign
ję́zən	= angry	sìt = sated

The *Superlative degree* is formed by prefixing *nàj-*, which bears its own accent, to the Comparative, e.g.:—

nàjčistę̄jši = the cleanest

The adjectives that form their Comparative with bòlj take nàjbolj—

nàjbolj znàn = the most well-known

Than	= kò, kòt, kàkor, *or* od (less commonly mimo) + Gen., e.g. Hûjša je žę́ja kò(t) glâd, *or* od gladû = Thirst is worse than hunger.
Rather better	= nękaj bǫ̀ljši, *but* rather good = precèj dóbər
Less than	= mànj kò(t); more than = bòlj kò(t)
The bigger, the better	= čìm vę́čji, tèm bǫ̂ljši
As beautiful as ...	= takǫ̀ lę̂p kàkor ...
As fast as possible	= čìm bř̀ž, čìm hitrę̂je, kàr nàjhitrę̂je, bř̀ž kò bǫ̀ mogǫ́če.
As soon as possible	= kàr nàjbř̀že, bř̀ž kò bř̀ž, prę̂j kò prę̂j, čimprę̂j
The dearest *of* all sons	= nàjljûbši iz—cf. Russian—(*or* od—cf. Serbocr., *or*—izmèd) vsèh sinǫ́v, *or* med (*or* nad) vsèmi sinǫ̀vi; *or* nàjljûbši sîn vsèh sinǫ́v, repeating the noun.

Pre- prefixed to an adjective express "too," e.g.:—

pretéžək = too heavy;

it expresses "very" only in certain expressions, e.g.:—

preljûbi sîn = (my) very dear (dearest) son!

ADVERBS

These are formed regularly from adjectives by using the neut. Nom. Acc. sing. form, e.g.:—

dǫ̀bər	= good	dóbro	= well
lę̂p	= beautiful	lepǫ̀	= fine

except in the case of adjectives in -*ski*, which have adverbs with the same ending, e.g.:—

  brâtski = in a brotherly manner

Nouns in the Instr. sing. or dual are also used as adverbs, e.g.:—

  mâhom(a) = at once, suddenly
  krížem(a) = crosswise
  mệstoma = in places, here and there
  dệloma = partly
  večínoma = mostly
  popộlnoma = completely

Comparative adverbs are formed from Comp. adjs. in -*ši* by dropping this ending and adding -(*ę*)*je*, e.g.:—

redkệje = more rarely   kasnệje *or* kášnje = later
slabệje = weaker, worse   hûje = worse, more angrily
bistrệje = more brightly, clearly   prostệje = more freely

but šîrše = more widely, krâjše = more briefly. Colloquially other comparatives in -*še* are frequently used.

  Comparative adjectives in -*ji* have corresponding adverbs in -*e* (or colloquially -*je*), e.g.:—

  blîže   = nearer
  drâže   = more dearly
  lâže *or* lâglje = more lightly
  mệče *or* mehkệje = more softly
  nîže   = lower
  vîše   = higher

Notice the irregular comparisons:

dáleč = far, Comp. dâlje
dộlgo = long, " dâlje, dàlj, or dljè
mâlo = little, " mànj = less
mnộgo } = much, many " vèč = more (of quantity, number)
velíko
zelộ = very, " bòlj = more (of degree)
dóbro = well, " bộlje
ràd, ráda, -o = gladly, " râje or râjši (for all three genders)
and the literary
čę̂sto = often " čệšče

The *Superlative degree* is formed by adding the prefix nàj- to the Comparative.

  A peculiarity of Slovenian is the use of the adverb lahkộ (lit. = lightly, easily) with verbs to indicate a potential action, e.g.:—

  lahkộ grẹ́š = you can go, you may go

SLOVENIAN

We give below a list of some of the commonest and most typical Slovenian adverbs, which give the language part of its characteristic colour. Many end in -*j*.

PLACE

tù, tûkaj	= here	tód	= this way
tàm, tàmkaj	= there	vèn(kaj)	= out
nękję́	= somewhere	nóter	= in
sèm	= here, hither	dáleč	= far
tjà (kaj)	= thither, there	zúnaj	= outside
ôndi	= over there	kvîšku }	
ondôd	= that way	(navz)gǫ̂r }	= up
zádaj	= behind	(navz)dǫ̂l	= down
nazâj	= back	blízu	= near
zgóraj	= above		
zdólaj }			
spódaj }	= below		

TIME

sədàj, zdàj	(often pron. zdej) = now	pràvkar	= just (now)
		včási(h)	= at times
tədàj	= then	spèt, zópet	= again
takòj, kòj }		rávnokar	= just
prècej }	= at once	màrsikdàj	= many a time
védno }		žè, or žę̂	= already
vsèkdar }	= always	šè	= still
vsèlej }		šelè	= (only) just
zmȇraj, }	= continuously,	dánəs	= to-day
zmȇrom }	always	nocój, }	= to-night, last
nîkdàr, }		drȇvi }	night
nikǫ́li }	= never	s(i)nǫ́či	= last night
zgǫ̂daj	= early	jútri	= tomorrow
hkráti }		včèraj	= yesterday
obênem }	= at the same time	láni	= last year
kmâlu	= soon	nè...vèč	= no more
skóro }		doslę̂j }	
skóraj }	= soon, nearly	dozdàj }	= till now
potèm, -têm	= after that, then	pótlej }	
pogóstoma	= often	poslę̂j }	= henceforward
dávi	= this morning	napǫ́sled	= finally
lętos	= this year	venomȇr }	
osorę̂j	= at this time	nenęhoma }	= continually
zvečèr	= in the evening	zdŕžema	= continuously
zjútraj	= in the morning	slę̂dnjič	= finally
zdávnaj	= long ago		
nękoč	= once		
prȩ̂j	= before		

MANNER

takọ̑	= so, thus	počẹ́ni }	= cheaply
nálašč	= purposely	cẹnọ̑ }	
skrivàj	= secretly	zastónj	= gratis, in vain
skûpaj } vrȅd }	= together	narávnost	= straight, plainly
		počási	= slowly
takísto	= likewise	narȏbe	= upside down
zapọ́red	= in succession	vnîc } vznȁk }	= on one's back
posẹ́bej } posámezno }	= separately	pokónci	= standing
začása	= in (good) time	zgȓda	= by force
tjavdȃn	= thoughtlessly, at random	nȃpak	= wrong
		skrátka	= briefly

DEGREE

zẹlọ̑	= very	rȇs	= really
tọ́likọ	= so much	gotọ́vo	= certainly, surely
precèj	= rather, considerably	pàč	= indeed, certainly (with negative)
zlásti	= especially	kȃjpa(da) } sevȇ(da) }	= of course
splòh	= in general, altogether		
		bajȇ	= they say, ostensibly
celọ̑	= even		
dósti } dovòlj }	= enough	morebíti } mordà }	= perhaps
pràv	= really, very, right	mendà	= possibly, supposedly
prevȅč	= too much		
kọ̑maj	= hardly	nemȃra	= perhaps
vsàj	= at least	rávno	= just, precisely
samọ̑ } lȩ̀ }	= only	málodane } tólikodane } domȃla } skóraj }	= almost
nikȃr	= on no account		
mnógo	= much		
právzaprav	= actually	kvȅčjemu	= at best
bȓžkone } bȓžda } bȓžčas } nȁjbrž }	= probably	povsȅ(m) } čísto }	= quite, entirely
		docȩ̑la	= wholly

čedálje + Comp. = ever, -er and -er, e.g.:—

čedálje bòlj = ever more, more and more.

CAUSAL

zatọ̑ } zatọ́rej } = for that reason   zatȇgadȩ̀lj = for that reason

INTERROGATIVE

kjȩ̑?	= where?	kọ́d?	= which way?
kám?	= whither?	kakọ́?	= how?
kdáj?	= when?	kọ́liko?	= how much, how many?
doklȩ̀j?	= till when?	zakáj?	= why?
		od kọ́d?	= whence?

```
ali ...?      ⎫
jêli          ⎬ = interrogative particle introducing a ques-
li?(encl. rare)⎭   tion, cf.:—

              Russ., Sbcr., Bulg. - ли
                             Pol. - czy
                             Ukr. - чи

kajnè(da)     ⎫
jèli(-ta, -te)⎭ = is that not so? Fr. n'est-ce pas?
màr...? = ... not ... really?  Russ. разве ...?
Not = nè; no = nè; yes = dà (colloquially: já).
'No' also = nàk(a) (rarer)
```

CONJUNCTIONS

These present no syntactical difficulties, but as Slovenian is far more fond of various modifying conjunctions and particles than English, they are often difficult to translate.

The commonest *coördinating* conjunctions are:—

```
in (enclitic)       = and
ter                 = and (weak), cf. Russian да, (also final)
                      so that
à                   = and, but (contrasting)
pà (often enclitic) = and, but, then (in questions), cf.
                      Russian же
tûdi                = also
kàkor               = as
kòlikor             = as much, as many
ozìroma             = or else
samò ⎫
lè   ⎭              = only
bòdisi              = either, or; even if, though
àli(... àli)        = either, or; but
nìti...nìti         = neither...nor
sàj                 = but, Rus. ведь, German doch
pàč                 = (but) yes, French si; indeed
sicèr               = it is true, otherwise, moreover
kàjti               = for
tòrej, zatòrej      = therefore
zatò                = therefore
takò                = thus
potemtákem          = therefore, thus
tedàj               = then
tòda                = yet
àmpak               = but, yet
tèmveč (colloq. ⎫
  temùč)        ⎬   = but (after a negative), Germ. sondern,
màrveč          ⎭     Serbocr. већ, Pol. lecz, Cz. nýbrž
vèndàr              = nevertheless, however
bajè                = they say (quoting)
```

češ = (quoting) as if, cf. Russ. дескать
námreč = namely

Many have ` on the penultimate syllable, otherwise rare.

The most important *subordinating* conjunctions are:—

dà (usually proclitic) = that (to introduce reported speech, purpose, consequence, conditional clauses, etc., but not usually to replace an Infinitive, which is more freely used in Slovenian than in Serbocr.)
čè = if (in indirect questions), whether (= àli)
čè, àko = if (in real conditions)
četûdi ⎫
čepràv ⎬ = although
dàsi (lit. lang.) ⎭
                                   dasirávno ⎫
                                   čerávno ⎬ = although
                                   akorávno ⎭
kò, ko = as, when; if (in unfulfilled conditions)
kèr, ker = because   zakàj = because
dòkler ⎫   dòkler...ne = until
medtèm ko ⎬ = while vtèm ko = while
kàdar = when(ever) kàkor da ⎫
kar ⎫   kòt bi ⎬ = as if
odkàr ⎭ = since   kò da bi ⎭
prêden ⎫   čèš da = as if, as
prêj kò ⎬ = before   though (quoting)
kàkor hítro ⎫   kômaj ⎫
brž kò ⎬   tóliko ⎬ = as soon as
(čim) ⎭ = as soon as
stêm da = by (doing kjèr = where
         something) kâmor = where to, whither
ne da bi ⎫ = without
da ne bi ⎭ (doing something)
namésto da bi = instead of (doing something)

PREPOSITIONS

On the whole the general use of prepositions in Slovenian follows the same lines as in Serbocr. and Russian, though peculiarly Slovenian uses exist, some of which we note below. A few prepositions govern two or three cases. Most monosyllabic prepositions are proclitic.

With Gen.:—
  brez = without
  iz = out of

SLOVENIAN

s (before voiceless consonants) z (before voiced consonants) (ž very rarely before *nj*)	= off, from
od	= from, by
do	= up to, till, to
za	= during (the time of)
izmèd	= (from) among
mímo	= beyond
blízu	= near
gledę̂	= regarding
(na)mę̂sto̧	= instead of
okô̧li (o)krô̧g	= round
poləg	= beside
prȩ̂ko or prèk	= across
rázən	= except
tîk	= just by, near
vpríčo spríčo	= in view of
vštric	= next to
zarâd(i) zbòg	= because of
zrâvən	= beside
iznad	= from above
izpod, spod	= from under
izpred	= from before
izza	= from behind, after
kónəc	= at the end of
kraj	= by the side of
vr̀h	= at the top of
povȓh(u)	= beside
srȩ́di	= in the middle of
ô̧nstran ô̧nkraj	= beyond
zastràn	= regarding
zavǫ́ljo	= for, because of

With Dat:—

k (h before *g* and *k*)	= to (*k* is also sometimes pronounced as *h* before *c, č, p* and *t*. *k* is pronounced as *g* before *b, d, z, ž,* and sometimes as phon. ɣ before *g*.
(v)kljùb (na)vzlîc	= despite
prǫ̂ti	= towards, against

With Acc.:—

v (pron. *v* before vowels, u̯ before consonants)	= into
na	= on to

skȏz(i)	= through
čèz	= across
raz	= off
ob	= against, near, by; during, at (of time); out of, short of
zȏper	= against
mèd	= (to) between, among
za	= for, (to) behind, in exchange for
pred	= (to) before
pod	= (to) under
nad	= (to) above, more than, over
po	= for, to fetch

With Instr.:—

s (before voiceless consonants) z (before vowels and voiced consonants) (ž very rarely before *nj*)	= with (also *always* of the instrument), e.g. píšem s perẹ̑som = I write with a pen, cf. Russ. пишу́ перо́м
med	= between (rest), during
za	= behind (rest), after, because of: za lákoto umrẹ́ti = to die of hunger
pred	= before (rest)
pod	= under (rest)
nad	= over (rest)

With Loc.:—

v (pron. as *v* or u̯— see Acc. above)	= in
na	= on
o	= about, concerning
pri	= at, near, with (Russ. у, Sbcr. код)
po	= over, according to, by, after: po obẹ́du = after dinner
ob, o	= by, at (of time): ob mȏrju = by the sea; o božı̑ču = at Christmas

Monosyllabic prepositions are often combined with enclitic pronouns into one word (cf. p. 359.) e.g.:—

prídi pȏme = come and fetch me
vsȃk zȃse = everyone for himself

The prefixes *pro-*, *pre-* and *vz-* (O.S. въz-, often reduced to *s*, *z* or *v*) are not used as prepositions.

iz- is used for West and East Slav *vy-* (вы-).

SLOVENIAN

THE CONJUGATION OF VERBS

The verbal conjugations in Slovenian are on the whole similar to those in Serbocr., but at the same time present a picture of transition, both in forms and use, to the conditions obtaining in West Slav languages.

Thus the main categories of verbs, divided according to their Present endings, agree fairly closely with those in Serbocr. But, as in West Slav languages, modern Slovenian knows no Aorist or Imperfect tenses, and its Future is formed with the Future of bîti (= to be): bǫ̂m, and the Past Participle Active in -*l*, as in Polish. The Supine also survives in Slovenian, as in Czech *spat* (= to sleep). The use of the Infinitive, as already mentioned (under "Features Characteristic of Slovenian" No. 23), is much wider in Slovenian than in Serbocr., and similar to its use in West and East Slav and West European languages. Like West Slav, too, Slovenian has a (declinable) Present Participle Active, as well as an (indeclinable) Present Gerund; but no declinable Past Participles Active (and very few Past Gerunds) are really alive any longer. The use of the Perfective Present is less restricted in Slovenian than in Serbocr. (see below), but it does not regularly acquire the meaning of a normal Future tense, as it has in West and East Slav.

Characteristically Slovenian is the rather frequent use of the Optative Mood which is formed by the Present tense of either aspect preceded by the invariable auxiliary nàj. Nàj + the *Past Conditional* is used to render the Past Optative.

Except for Lusatian, Slovenian is the only language which uses the Dual number throughout all the forms of the verb in agreement with nouns, etc., in the Dual. This adds a burden for the foreign learner, even though the 2nd and 3rd persons dual always have the same endings; but it is not difficult to acquire the use of the dual as a speech habit, and its use makes for greater clarity. For what "we two" want or do may be very different from what "we" do in the general plural! In the 2nd and 3rd pers. dual the ending -*te* is sometimes used to, or of, two feminine or neuter persons, creatures or things as opposed to -*ta* for masculine nouns.

In Slovenian, alone of the South Slav languages, the verb vę́dęti (= to know) still survives, as in West Slav.

The Passive voice is rendered by the same three periphrases as in most other Slav languages:—

the reflexive verb,[1] e.g.:—

　　　Imenûjejo se = they are called

the impersonal use of the 3rd pers. plur. Active with an object, e.g.:—

　　　Hválijo ga = he is praised

the verb "to be" + Past Participle Passive (usually of Perfective verbs), e.g.:—

　　　Òn je bîl pohváljen = he was praised

Tenses

　　The Present is the only surviving simple tense. The Future, the Past, for both aspects, and the Pluperfect, are compound tenses (see below). The Present Imperfective is used like the Present in other languages and offers no difficulties.

　　The use of the Perfective Present in Slovenian, however, should be specially noted, for while this tense does not acquire the meaning of a plain Future, as it does in West and East Slav, its use is far wider in Slovenian than in the other South Slav languages. It can be used—

(*a*) as an Historic Present in narration, after an introducing verb in the Past tense, as in Serbocr. It may then be followed by Imperfective Presents as well:—

　　Krîžman je bîl pisár pri nẹ́ki graščíni. Nêkdaj sta se
　　Križman was a clerk in a castle estate. Once they two

　　šlà òn in njegǫ́v gospǫ̂d izprehájat po hǫ́sti takǫ̂
　　went, he and his master, for a walk on a heath—so

　　dáleč, da žệ nísta vẹ́dela, kjệ sta.
　　far that they no longer knew where they were.

　　Gospǫ̂d se vŕne (Pfve. Pres.), Križman pa si urệže (Pfve.
　　　　　　　　　　　　　　　　　　　　　　　　　　　　　　　　　Pres.)
　　The master goes back, but Križman cuts for himself

　　v méji gŕčavko in hǫ́di (Impfve. Pres.) dálje
　　out of the hedge a knotted stick and walks further.

(*b*) to express a general truth without reference to any time—a gnomic use (cf. the "gnomic Aorist" in Ancient Greek). It is also used in science to state observed facts.—

　　Kàr ne príde iz sŕca, se ne príme srcâ.
　　What does not come from the heart does not grip (move)
　　　the heart.

[1] i.e. Active verb + the enclitic and separable Accusative Reflexive pronoun se.

Gosęnica se zabůbi, zaspí in spomládi izfrfotá metúlj.
The caterpillar changes into a chrysalis, goes to sleep,
and in the spring a butterfly flutters out.

(c) in negative questions with a pronoun, usually understood, as subject, asking for a reason:—

Zakáj ne prîdeš? = Why don't (won't) you come?

These questions do not refer to any particular time or occasion; they imply: "Why don't you *ever* come?—You *never* seem to be prepared to."

(d) The Perfective Present can be used with a *future* meaning mainly in conditional clauses, in both parts, and in conditional, time and relative clauses:—

Če se na glâvo postáviš, ti ne dovólim tęga
= (Even) If you stand on your head, I won't allow you this.

Jàz se ne vdám, doklèr me ne prepríčaš z dokázi.
= I won't give in until you convince me with proofs.

(e) Note the difference between:—

(i) Tô krávo prodám = I will sell this cow, i.e. I am ready to sell this cow (I expect I shall).

(ii) Tǫ krávo bǫm prodâl = I shall sell this cow, i.e. I am sure I shall.

Example (i) illustrates the use of the Perfective Present to express possibility, willingness, etc. Cf. (c).[1]

The Conditional mood is also expressed by a compound form consisting of the *invariable* auxiliary *bi* + Past Participle Active in -*l*. The Personal Pronoun is hence sometimes required for clarity. There is also a Past Conditional.

The other moods with forms of their own are the Imperative (formed from the Pres. stem), and the Optative. The Supine is used to express purpose after verbs of motion, as in Old Slavonic. (Note in example under (a) above: sta se šlà *izprehâjat*).

Of the (indeclinable) Gerunds (verbal adverbs) only the Present (Active) is alive. The Past Gerund

---

[1] The Perfective Present can also be used (f) in summaries, introductions, inscriptions, etc.; (g) in the 1st person singular with verbs of saying, denying, promising, ordering: réčem = I say; obljúbim = I promise.

in -(v)ši has remained genuinely alive for only a few Perfective verbs.

Of the Participles (declinable verbal adjectives) Slovenian has the Pres. Part. Active (usually formed from the Pres. stem), the Past Part. Active (ending in -*l*, -*la*, -*lo*) used to form the Future and Past tenses and also adjectivally from intransitive verbs, e.g.:—

    pretęklo lęto = the past year
    otękle rokę̇ = swollen hands

and the Past Part. Passive (usually formed from the Infinitive stem)—see above remarks on rendering the Passive voice.

As in the other Slav languages there are also Verbal Nouns in Slovenian ending in -*nje*, or -*tje*, formed from the Past Participle Passive.

Classification of Slovenian Verbs according to their Presents, with Subdivisions according to their Infinitives.

Most Slovenian grammars divide the verbs according to their Infinitive endings, on the model of Latin, etc., thereby obtaining six main headings and numerous sub-divisions according to the varying Presents, for the Infinitive in Slovenian is no clearer an indication of how to form the corresponding Present than it is in any other Slav language.

According to the endings of the Present, however, the same five main classes can be observed as in Serbocr., viz.:—

    (i) Present ending -*e* (3rd person sing.)
    (ii)   "   " -*ne*   "   "   "
    (iii) "   " -*je*   "   "   "
    (iv) "   " -*a*   "   "   "
    (v)   "   " -*i*   "   "   "

the personal endings being added to these vowels where required. The sub-divisions are according to the Infinitive ending:—

3rd pers. sing. Pres.   *Infinitive.*

I.A.a. nése   nésti[1] = carry. Same consonantal stem in Pres. and Infinitive.

    začnè   začę́ti = begin (Pfve.). Infin. in -*eti* from —ATH.

[1] So also with velar stem:—

    péče, 3rd p. pl. péčejo or pekǫ́ péči = to bake.
    Imperat. péci! Cf. vřžem vréči = to throw, p. 388.

SLOVENIAN

mrè or mrjè	mrę́ti	= die. Infin. -*reti* from *-erti*.
b. plóve (or plúje—III)	plúti	= swim, float. Same (originally) vowel stem in Pres. and Infin.
B.a. bére	bráti	= collect, read. Infin. in -*ati*.
II. dvȋgne	dvígniti	= lift (Pfve.). *n*-stem.

III. *j*-verbs.
1. Primary verbs:—

A.a. čúje	čúti	= hear. Same vowel stem in Pres. and Infin.
b.[1] mę́lje	mlę́ti(<*melti)	= grind. Same consonant stem in Pres. and Infin.
žánje	žę́ti	= reap. Cons. stem, Infin. in -*eti* from -ATH.

B. (Infinitives in -*ati*)

a. dáje (*also* dája)	dajáti	= give(Impfv.). ⎫ Vowel stem,
táje (*also* tája)	tájati	= melt. ⎬ Infin. in
rúje	r(u)váti	= tear out. ⎭ -*ati*
b. órje (*also* orȃ)	oráti	= plough. Cons. stem, Infin. in -*ati*.
píše	pisáti	= write. Cons. stem, Infin. in -*ati*, with change of stem through *yotation*.

2. Derived verbs (Imperfectives):—

kupúje	kupováti	= buy. -*u*- Pres. stem, -*ova*- Infin. stem.
vojúje	vojeváti	= make war. -*u*- Pres. stem, -*eva*- Infin. stem.
izpolnjúje	izpolnjeváti	= fulfil. -*u*- Pres. stem, -*jeva*- Infin. stem.
plačúje	plačeváti	= pay. -*u*- Pres. stem, -*jeva*- Infin. stem (with *yotation*).

The old stems in -*eje*- also belong to this category, e.g. umȇje still survives, as well as umȇ, Infin. umȇti (= understand, know how to).

IV. New class, as in Serbocr., contracted from verbs in -*aje*-.

dȇla	dę́lati	= work.
znȃ	znáti	= know (how to); also = French *connaître*

V. A. hváli hvalíti = praise. -*i*- stem throughout

---

[1] A rare class.

B. vîdi   vídeti   = see. *-i-* Pres. stem,
                   -ęti Infin.
   držî   držáti   = hold. *-i-* Pres. stem,
                   -ati Infin. from –ѣти after
                   chuintante
   stojî státi   = stand. *-i-* Pres. stem,
                   -ati Infin. (contracted).

All the four old athematic *-m* verbs have survived in Slovenian. They are given in full below, p. 387-8. The *-m* of the 1st pers. sing. Pres. has been generalized for literally all verbs, even hǫ́čem (= I want), mǫ́rem (= I can), as in Slovak (chcem, môžem)— (cf. Serbocr. xòħy, мòгу).

Tense and Mood endings and Formation.

Present:—

	SING.				DUAL	
1st	2nd	3rd		1st	2nd and 3rd	
konča̋- ⎫			(masc.[1])	-va	-ta	
nése- ⎬ -m	-š	—(*t* lost),	(fem. and neut.)			
vîdi- ⎭			occasionally also	-ve	-te	

                    PLURAL
  1st   2nd   3rd
                    stressed endings   *unstressed endings*
                    končájo (finish)   dę́lajo (work)
  -mo   -te   nesǫ́   (carry)   tré̜sejo (shake)
                    govoré̜, *or*   vîdijo (see)
                    govorîjo (speak)

Imperative—added to the Present stem:—

	SING	DUAL		PLURAL	
	2nd(and rarely 3rd)	1st	2nd	1st	2nd
vb. stems ending in a consonant: lę́z-	-i(climb)	-iva	-ita	-imo	-ite
nes-	-i(carry)	-îva	-îta	-îmo	-îte
cvat	-ì(flower)	-îva	-îta	-îmo	-îte
vb. stems ending in a vowel: dę́la- ⎫	(work)				
konča̋- ⎬ -j(finish)	(konča̋)-jva	-jta	-jmo	-jte	
kupû- ⎭	(buy)				

For the 3rd person of all three numbers the Optative form: naj + 3rd pers. Present, is usual, e.g. nàj nése = let him carry.

Past:—
Past Participle Active (varying in gender according to the subject) in:—

───────────
[1]Masc. endings also used for mixed genders.

SLOVENIAN

```
Sing.  -l (masc.)  -la(fem.)  -lo(neut.) ⎫  added to the
Dual   -la    "    -li    "   -li    "   ⎬  Infinitive
Plur.  -li    "    -le    "   -la    "   ⎭  stem (Infin.
                                             less -ti)
```
used with—

SING.			DUAL			PLURAL		
1st	*2nd*	*3rd*	*1st*	*2nd*	*3rd*	*1st*	*2nd*	*3rd*
səm	si	je	sva	sta	sta	smo	ste	so

(used as enclitic auxiliaries)

If this auxiliary precedes the Past Participle the noun subject or Nom. Pers. Pronoun or some other stressed word must precede both, e.g.:—

  jàz səm bȋl   = I was (masc.)
  Jánez je bȋl... = Janez was...

With Vȋ = you (polite) the Past Part. Act. is normally in the masc. plur.:

  Vȋ ste bilȋ = you were

Pluperfect:—

  Past Participle Active in -*l*, etc. (varying as above) + Past tense of bȋti (= to be), —formed from Perfective verbs only, e.g.:—

  pâdel səm bȋl   = I had fallen
  obljúbil si bȋl = you (sg.) had promised

or (as above)—

  jàz səm bȋl pâdel

or else—

  bȋl səm pâdel

Future:—

  Future tense of bȋti—

SING			DUAL			PLURAL		
1st	*2nd*	*3rd*	*1st*	*2nd and 3rd*		*1st*	*2nd*	*3rd*
bǫ́m	bǫ́s	bǫ́	bǫ́va	bǫ́sta		bǫ́mo	bǫ́ste	bǫ́do

(used as an enclitic auxiliary)

preceded by—

  Past Participle Active in -*l*, etc. (varying as above), or *vice versa* and preceded by the subject or stressed word:—

  dẹ̑lal bǫ́m, or (jàz) bǫ́m dẹ̑lal - I shall work

This formation of the Future applies to verbs of *both* aspects and is characteristic of Slovenian, e.g.:—

  napísal bǫ́m = I shall write (Pfve.)

Conditional:—

  Past Participle Active in -*l*, etc. (as above) + *bi* (usually enclitic) for all persons. A subject—

noun or Nom. Pers. Pronoun—is required in order to show which person is meant, e.g.:—

but—
    dę́lal bi = I, thou, or he would work
    jàz bi dę́lal (only) = *I* would work

Past Conditional:—
    Conditional of bíti: bȋl (etc.) bi + Past. Part. Active in -*l*, etc. (varying as above), or *vice versa:*—

or—
    (òn) bȋl bi dę́lal = (he) would have worked
    dę́lal bi bȋl = I, thou, or he would have worked
    The verb bíti = to be, has no Past Conditional.

Optative (usually only used in 1st and 3rd persons):—
    nàj + Pres. Pfve. or Impfve., e.g.:—
nàj dę̂la = let him work.   Káj nàj storím? = What
                                               should I do?
The Optative is also used for Indirect Commands: Òn je rę́kəl, naj mu dám knjígo = He told me to give him the book.

Past Optative (1st and 3rd persons only):—
    nàj + Conditional of bíti: bi bȋl (etc.) + Past Part. Act. in -*l*,[1] etc.:—
nàj bi bȋl vę́del = if only he had known! (would that
                                          he had known!)

Infinitive termination:—
    -*ti*; but -*či* for velar stems of Cl. I, (colloquially the final -i can be dropped) e.g.:—
    dę́lati = to work   pę́či = to bake

Supine termination:—
    -*t* (for Imperfective vbs. only); velar stems of Cl.I -*č*: pèč.
    The object of the Supine goes in the Genitive or the Accusative.
    E.g.: Grę́m júhe kúhat = I am going (off) to cook
                                                (the) soup

Present Gerund (Active):—
    (Some) intransitive Imperfective Present verb stems + ę́, e.g.:—
        grę́m   = I go; vb. stem gred-, gredę̀
        molčím = I am silent; molčę̀

[1]Equivalent to: nàj + Past Conditional.

Imperfective vbs. with Infinitives in -*ati* drop the -*ti* and add -*áje*, e.g.:—

    stopáje = stepping
    kupováje = buying

Past Gerund (Active)—rare:—
formed from the Infinitive stem of *some* Pfve. vbs.:—

consonantal verb stems add -*ši*: rękši = having said
vocalic verb stems add -*vši*: skrívši = having hidden

The accent always falls on the syllable before the -*(v)ši*.

Present Participle Active—(formed from Impfve. vbs.):—

  3rd pers. plur. Pres. (shorter forms)[1] + *č:*—
    gredǫ́č = going
    trpèč = suffering (3rd pers. plur. Pres. trpę́ or trpíjo)
    delajǫ́č = working
    kupujǫ́č = buying

Can be used in Nom. sing. masc. for Pres. Gerund:—

    Mîmo gredǫ́č səm pozdrávila tvójo máter
    = Going by, I (fem.) greeted your mother

The accent always falls on the *ending*.

Past Participle Active:—
  Infinitive stem (usually = Infin. less -*ti**) + -*l*, etc. (see Past tense above)—for verbs of either aspect; *ə* is the fill-vowel in the masc. sing.

*Exceptions are:—

  dental stems of Class I, e.g.:—
    pásti (stem pad-) = to fall; P.P.A. m. pâdəl, f. pádla, or m. pàl, f. pála.

  labial stems of Class I, e.g.:—
    tépsti (stem tep-) = to hit; P.P.A. m. tę́pəl, f. tépla.

  velar stems of Class I, e.g.:—
    péči (stem pek-) = to bake; P.P.A. m. pę́kəl, f. pékla.

  r-stems of Class I lose -*eti*, e.g.:—
    umrę́ti = to die; P.P.A. m. umȓl, f. umȓla.

[1] But from bósti = to prick - bodèč, from grébsti = to scratch, grebóč; note also from čúti = to hear, čujèč or čujǫ́č.

Past Participle Passive (formed mainly from transitive verbs, more often Perfectives):—
This is formed in four different ways from the Infinitive stem with the endings:—

	Sing. m.	f.	n.	Du. m.	f. and n.	Pl. m.	f.	n.
either (a)	-n,	-na,	-no	-na,	-ni	-ni,	-ne,	-na
or (b)	-t,	-ta,	-to	-ta,	-ti	-ti,	-te,	-ta

1. All verbs with Infinitive in -*ati* or of Class VB in -*eti* add endings (a) to the Infinitive stem:—

    zdę̆lan = finished   napísan = written
    kupován = bought   obrân = picked
    vîden = seen   zadržán = detained

2. Consonant stem verbs of Class IAa and many less common verbs with Infinitives in -*iti* of Class VA have endings (a) preceded by *e*:—

    pletèn = woven   zmǫ́ten = disturbed
    pečèn = baked (with 1st Palatalization!)

3. Verbs of Class II (Infin. in -*niti*) and the commoner verbs of Class VA have the endings (a) preceded by *je*, with yotation of the preceding consonant:—

    okrę́njen = turned   hváljen = praised
    izgùbljèn = lost   ponǫ́šen = worn out
    zapuščèn = neglected   zamujèn = missed

4. Nasal and *r*-stem verbs of Classes I and III and vowel and consonant stem verbs of Class III 1 A have endings (b) added to the Infinitive stem:—

začêt = begun   potŕt = depressed   požę̂t = reaped
skrît = covered   obût = shod   zmlę̂t = ground

Verbal Noun:—
Formed by adding -*je* to the (sometimes supposed) form of the Past Part. Passive of most Imperfective and many Perfective verbs. Verbal nouns from Perfective verbs express a result.

E.g.:— sedę̂nje = sitting But presenę́čenje = surprise
       pę̂tje   singing   zdrúženje   = union
       ležânje = lying   vzę̂tje   = capture

Examples of the Conjugation of the Regular Verbs, showing varieties of accentuation:—

    1. *e*-class

lésti = to climb trę́sti = to shake plésti = to weave začę́ti = to begin (Pfve.)

SLOVENIAN

SUPINE
	(lêst)	trêst		plêst	

PRESENT
Sing. 1	lêzem	trêsem		plétem	začném
2	lêzeš	trêseš		pléteš	začnéš
3	lêze	trêse		pléte	začné
Dual 1	lêzeva	trêseva		pléteva	začnéva
2 and 3	lêzeta	trêseta		pléteta	začnéta
Plur. 1	lêzemo	trêsemo		plétemo	začnémo
2	lêzete	trêsete		plétete	začnéte
3	lêzejo	trêsejo, tresó		pletó	začnéjo, začnó

IMPERATIVE
Sing. 2nd	lêzi	trêsi		pléti	začnî
Dual 1st	lêziva	tresîva		pletîva	začnîva
2nd	lêzita	tresîta		pletîta	začnîta
Plur. 1st	lêzimo	tresîmo		pletîmo	začnîmo
2nd	lêzite	tresîte		pletîte	začnîte

PRES. PART ACTIVE

                                          pletóč

PAST PART. ACTIVE
	lêzel	trêsel	plétel or plèl	začêl	Pl. začêli
	lêzla	trêsla	plétla " pléla	začêla	-e
	lêzlo	trêslo	plétlo " plélo	začêlo	-a
	etc.	etc.	etc. etc.		

PAST PART. PASSIVE
	—	raztrêsen	pletèn	začêt
		raztrêsena	pletêna	začêta
		raztrêseno	pletêno	začêto
		etc.	etc.	etc.

2. -*ne* class.

vêniti = to fade   krenîti = to turn (Pfve.)   páhniti = to push (Pfve.)

SUPINE   —   —   —

PRESENT
Sing. 1	vênem	krênem	páhnem
2	vêneš	krêneš	páhneš
3	vêne	krêne	páhne
Dual 1	vêneva	krêneva	páhneva
2 and 3	vêneta	krêneta	páhneta
Plur. 1	vênemo	krênemo	páhnemo
2	vênete	krênete	páhnete
3	vênejo	krênejo	páhnejo

IMPERATIVE
Sing. 1	vêni	krêni	pahnî
Dual 1	vêniva	krenîva	pahnîva
2	vênita	krenîta	pahnîta

Plur.	1	vę́nîmo	krenîmo	pahnîmo
	2	vę́nite	krenîte	pahnîto

PAST PART. ACTIVE

zvę́nil   krę́nil   pahnȋl
zvę́nila   krenȋla   pahnȋla
zvę́nilo   krenȋlo   pahnȋlo
etc.   etc.   etc.

PAST PART. PASSIVE

okrę́njen   páhnjen

Verbs of the type of kreníti can also have ´ on the first syllable in the Infinitive.

3. -je class

kríti = cover   ková́ti = to forge   písáti = to write   vę́rovati = to believe   kupováti = to buy

SUPINE

(svę́tovat = to advise)   kupovàt(kupóvat)

PRESENT

Sing.	1	krîjem	kûjem	píšem	vę́rujem	kupûjem
	2	krîješ	kûješ	píšeš	vę́ruješ	kupûješ
	3	krîje	kûje	píše	vę́ruje	kupûje
Dual	1	krîjeva	kûjeva	píševa	vę́rujeva	kupûjeva
	2 and 3	krîjeta	kûjeta	píšeta	vę́rujeta	kupûjeta
Plur.	1	krîjemo	kûjemo	píšemo	vę́rujemo	kupûjemo
	2	krîjete	kûjete	píšete	vę́rujete	kupûjete
	3	krîjejo	kûjejo	píšejo	vę́rujejo	kupûjejo

IMPERATIVE

Sing.	2	krîj	kûj	píši	vę́ruj	kupûj
Dual	1	krîjva	kûjva	píšiva	vę́rujva	kupûjva
	2	krîjta	kûjta	píšita	vę́rujta	kupûjta
Plur.	1	krîjmo	kûjmo	píšimo	vę́rujmo	kupûjmo
	2	krîjte	kûjte	píšite	vę́rujte	kupûjte

PRES. GERUND

kupováje

PRES. PART. ACTIVE

pišǭč   vę́rujǭč   kupujǭč

PAST PART. ACTIVE

krȋl   ková̂l   písal   vę́roval   kupová̀l(kupóval)
krȋla ková̂la pisála vę́rovala kupovála
krȋlo ková̂lo pisálo vę́rovalo kupová̂lo
etc.   etc.   etc.   etc.

PAST PART. PASSIVE

skrȋt   ková́n   písan[1]   zavę́rovan   kupován
skrȋta ková́na písana   zavę́rovana kupována

[1] As adjective, = variegated.

PAST PART. PASSIVE (contd.)
skrîto kováno písano zavérovano kupováno
etc.   etc.   etc.   etc.   etc.

Verbs with Infin. in -eváti follow kupováti,
e.g.:—
pla̋čeváti = pay

4. -a class.

dęlati = to work, do   jokáti or jǫkati = to weep   končáti = to finish (Pfve.)

SUPINE:
     dęlat   jǫkat

PRESENT
Sing. 1	dęlam	jǫkam or	jǫ́čem	konč́am
2	dęlaš	jǫkaš	jǫ́čes	konč́aš
3	dęla	jǫka	jǫ́če	konč́a
Dual 1	dęlava	jǫkava	jǫ́čeva	konč́ava
2 and 3	dęlata	jǫkata	jǫ́četa	konč́ata
Plur. 1	dęlamo	jǫkamo	jǫ́čemo	konč́amo
2	dęlate	jǫkate	jǫ́čete	konč́ate
3	dęlajo	jǫkajo	jǫ́čejo	konč́ajo

IMPERATIVE
Sing. 2	délaj	jǫkaj	or	jǫ́či	konč́aj
Dual 1	délajva	jǫkajva or	jokájva or	jǫ́čiva	konč́ajva
2	délajta	jǫkajta	jokájta	jǫ́čita	konč́ajta
Plur. 1	délajmo	jǫkajmo	jokájmo	jǫ́čimo	konč́ajmo
2	délajte	jǫkajte	jokájte	jǫ́čite	konč́ajte

PRES. GERUND
                      jokáje

PRES. PART. ACTIVE
    delajǫ́č   jokajǫ́č

PAST GERUND
    pridelávši

PAST PART. ACTIVE
    délal   jǫkal   konč́al
    délala   jokála   konč́ala
    délalo   jokálo   konč́alo
    etc.   plur. jokáli,-e,-a etc.

PAST PART. PASSIVE
    zdęlan   zjǫkan   konč́an
    zdęlana
    zdęlano
    etc.

Like dęlati in accent also verbs of Class III, e.g. mázati, mâžem = I smear.
Like jǫkáti in accent also verbs of Class III, e.g. pisáti (also písati), píšem = I write (cf. p. 384).

5. *i*-class.

vídeti = to see želéti = to wish motíti = to disturb
sedéti = to sit

SUPINE

                                mótit

PRESENT

Sing.	1	vîdim	želîm	mótim	sedím
	2	vîdiš	želîš	mótiš	sedíš
	3	vîdi	želî	móti	sedí
Dual	1	vîdiva	želîva	mótiva	sedíva
2 and 3		vîdita	želîta	mótita	sedíta
Plur.	1	vîdimo	želîmo	mótimo	sedímo
	2	vîdite	želîte	mótite	sedíte
	3	vîdijo	želé(želîjo)	mótijo	sedíjo, sedé

IMPERATIVE

Sing.	2	vísi	želi	móti	sédi
		(=hang)			
Dual	1	vísiva	želîva	motîva	sedîva
	2	vísita	želîta	motîta	sedîta
Plur.	1	vísimo	želîmo	motîmo	sedîmo
	2	vísite	želîte	motîte	sedîte

PRES. GERUND

                   želé   sedé

PRES. PART. ACTIVE
        videč   želeč   motèč   sedèč

PAST GERUND
                zaželévši   zmotîvši se

PAST PART. ACTIVE

vídel	želél	mótil	sedèl
vídela	želéla	motîla	sedéla
vídelo	želélo	motîlo	sedélo
etc.	etc.	etc.	etc.

PAST PART. PASSIVE

vîden	zaželèn	zmóten	vrtèn (=turned)
vîdena	zaželéna	zmótena	vrténa
vîdeno	zaželéno	zmóteno	vrténo
etc.	etc.	etc.	etc.

    Like vídeti in accent: mísliti = to think.
    Like želéti in accent: podíti—Supine podît! = to chase out.
    Verbs in -*im*, -*ati* behave like the above models, e.g. klečím, klečáti (= to kneel) follows želéti.
    Only reference to a fully accented dictionary or experience can give an indication as to which accent type a given verb of any class follows.

Conjugation of the most important Irregular Verbs in Slovenian

The Athematic (-m) verbs.

	dáti = to give (Pfv.)	vẹ́deti = to know	jẹ́sti = to eat	bíti = to be		
SUPINE			jêst			
PRESENT						FUTURE
Sing. 1	dâm	vém	jém	səm[1]	bọ̑m,[2]	bọ̄dem
2	dâš	vẹ́š	jẹ́š	sì	bọ̑š	bọ̑deš
3	dâ	vẹ́	jẹ́	jè	bọ̑	bọ̑de
Dual 1	dâva	vẹ́va	jẹ́va	svà, svè	bọ̑va	bọ̑deva
2 and 3	dâsta	vẹ́sta	jẹ́sta	stà, stè	bọ̑sta bọ̑ta	bọ̑deta
Plur: 1	dâmo	vẹ́mò	jẹ́mò	smò	bọ̑mo	bọ̑demo
2	dâste	vẹ́stè	jẹ́stè	stè	bọ̑ste bọ̑te	bọ̑dete
3	dadọ̑ dájò dadẹ̑	vedọ̑ vẹ́jo	jẹ́jo or jedọ̑	sò	bọ̑dọ (bọ̑jo dial.)	

IMPERATIVE

Sing. 2	dàj	vẹ́di (but: povẹ̑j = say)		jẹ̑j	bọ́di
Dual 1	dâjva	vẹ́diva (povẹ̑jva, etc.)		jẹ̑jva	bọ́dîva
2	dâjta	vẹ́dita		jẹ̑jta	bọ́dîta
Plur. 1	dâjmo	vẹ́dimo		jẹ̑jmo	bọ́dîmo
2	dâjte	vẹ́dite		jẹ̑jte	bọ́dîte

PRES. GERUND
    vedẹ́   jedẹ́

PRES. PART. ACTIVE
    vedọ́č   jedọ́č (bodọ́č, adj., =future)

PAST GERUND
  podâvši zvẹ́devši pojẹ̑dši (bívši, adj., =past, former)

PAST PART. ACTIVE

			sg.	du.	pl.
dâl	vẹ́del	jẹ̑del or jèl	bîl	bilà bilì or -î	
dâla	vẹ́dela	jẹ́dla	jẹ́la bilà	bilì bilè or -ê	
dâlo	vẹ́delo	jẹ́dlo	jẹ́lo bilọ́ (bilò)	bilì bilà	
etc.	etc.	etc.			

[1] Special negative form (with ni- prefixed in all persons except the 3rd p. sing.):—Sing. nísəm, nísi, 3rd p. s. ní, Du. nísva, nísta, Pl. nísmo, níste, níso.

[2] dobíti = to receive, get (Pfve.), follows either bíti, bọ̑m, or Cl. VA: Pres. (Fut.) dobọ̑m or dobím, Imperat. dobọ́di, or dóbi, P.P.A. dọ̑bîl, P.P.P. dobljèn, -éna.

PAST PART. PASSIVE
  dán   izvéden   pojéden
  dána   izvédena pojédena
  dáno   izvédeno pojédeno

Other Verbs
  hǫ́čem, 3rd pers. pl. hǫ́čejo, hotéti, hótel,
hotéla (= to want), has Imperat. hóti, Pres. P.A.
hotèč, Pres. Ger. hotę́. When negative, the Pres.
tense has the form nǫ́čem, nǫ́češ, etc. (or néčem,
néčeš).
  mǫ́rem, mǫ́reš, etc., mǫ́či, mǫ́gǝl, mǫ́gla (= to be
able) has Pres. P.A. mogǫ́č; also, like it: pomǫ́rem,
pomǫ́či, Imper. pomózi! pomozíva! (= to help, Pfve.),
and onemǫ́rem, o(b)nemǫ́či (= to grow weak).
  imám, imáš, imájo, imę́ti, imèl, imę́la, Imper.
imę̀j! (= to have), has negative Present nîmam, etc.
  (znâm, znâti, = to know, is regular.)
  Note also (* marks typical verb for consonant-
stem sub-groups of Cl. I)

	Present	Infin.	Past Part. Act.	Imperat.	
Class I	rástem *or* rásem	rásti	rástel, -tla *or* rásel, -sla		= to grow
	cvétèm *or* cvetîm *or* cvetę́ti(Cl.V)	cvèstì *or* cvésti	cvèl, cvelà¹ *or* cvéla	cvetî!	= to flower
	*plétem	plésti	plétel *or* plèl		= to weave
	*sę̂dem	sę́sti	sę̂del, sę́dla, *or* sèl, séla		= to sit down (Pfve.)
	*skûbem	skûbsti	oskûbel		= to pluck
	*lę̂žem	lę́či	lę̂gǝl, légla, -o	lę̂zi!	= to lie down (Pfve.)
	*réčem	réči	rę̂kǝl, rékla	réci!	= to say (Pfve.)
	*vr̂žem	vrę́či	vr̂gǝl	vr̂zi!	= to throw (Pfve.)
	*(u)mrèm *or* umrjem	(u)mrę́ti	(u)mr̂l		= to die (Pfve. with *u-*)
	tárem *or* trèm	tręti	tr̂l		= to rub, grind
	vrèm	vręti	vrèl	vrî!	= to boil (intrans.)
	vzámem	vzę́ti	vzę̂l	vzę́mi!	= to take (Pfve.)²

¹Also cvǝtèl, cvǝtlà or the newer forms cvétǝl, cvétla.
²So also posnámem posnę́ti = to take off, record (Pfve.)

SLOVENIAN

jámem	jéti	jèl		= to start, begin(Pfve.)
kólnem	kléti	klèl		= to curse
naspèm	nasúti	nasùl		= to pour out (Pfve.)
or nasûjem				
plévem	pléti	plèl	plévi!	= to weed
žénem	gnáti	gnàl,gnâla		= to drive
tkèm	tkáti	tkàl,tkâla		= to weave
or tkâm				
žgèm	žgáti	žgàl		= to burn, distil, roast (coffee)
pšém	pháti	phàl		= to stamp, pound
or phâm				

Past Part. Pass. phân or pšèn, pšéna

bérem	bráti	brâl,brála	= to collect, to read
zóvem	zváti	zvàl,zvála	= to call

Class II
utégnem	utégniti (regular)		= to have time to (Pfve.)
stânem	státi	stâl	= to cost
dénem(Pfve.)			= to put, do, say
dêm	déti	dèl,déla	
déjem	dejáti	dejâl	

Class III
pǫ́šljem	posláti	poslàl,-slála pòšlji!	= to send (Pfve.)
postéljem	postláti	postlàl,-ála postélji!	= to spread (Pfve.)
pǫ́ljem	pláti	plàl,plála pólji!	= to winnow, swirl
kǫ́ljem	kláti	klàl,klála kólji!	= to slaughter
žánjem	žéti	žèl,žéla žnjì *or* žánji!	= to harvest
dájem (dájam sg. only) dajèm	dajáti	dajàl,dajâla dájàj!	= to give (Impfve.)
pójem	péti	pèl,péla	= to sing
štéjem	štéti	štèl,štéla	= to count
umèm	uméti	umèl uméla uméj!	= to know how to
or umèjem			
spèm	spéti	spèl spéla	= to hasten
or spèjem			
smějem se,	smějati se,	smejàl se, smêj se!	= to laugh
or smějam se		*or* smějaj se!	
or smejím se			

Class IV
glêdam	glédati	glêdal,-a glêj!	= to look

	mǫ́ram	mǫ́rati	quite regular,		= to have to
			used with Infinitive		(must)
			following		
Class V	spím	spáti	spȃl,-a	spı̏!	= to sleep
	stojím	státi	stȃl	stǫ́j!	= to stand
	bojím se	báti se	bȃl se	bǫ́j se	= to fear

Verbs of Going and Conveying

Grẹ́m, grẹ́š, grẹ́, grẹ́va,[1] grẹ́sta,[1] grẹ́mo,[1] grẹ́ste;[1] 3rd pl. gredǫ́ (or grẹ́jo[1]), also accented ` (on last syllable): grȅm, grevȁ, etc. Infin. íti, P.P.A. šə̏l, šlȁ, šlȍ, Imper. pǫ́jdi! = to go (Impfve.), Fut. pǫ́jdem[2] or bǫ̑m šə̏l, Pres. Ger. gredẹ́, Pres. Part. gredǫ́č.

hǫ́dim	Infin.	P.P.A.		Imperat. hǫ́di!
= to walk, go	hodíti	hódil, hodíla		hodíte!
(Freq.)				
prídem,	príti,	prišə̏l, prišlȁ,		Impfve. prihȃjati
= to come				
(Pfve.)				
odídem,	odíti,	odšə̏l, etc.		Impfve. odhȃjati
= to go away				
(Pfve.)				
izídem,	izíti,	izšə̏l,		Impfve. izhȃjati
= to go out				
(Pfve.)				
nájdem,	nájti,	nášəl, nášla,		Impfve. nahȃjati
= to find		*or* našə̏l, našlȁ		
(Pfve.)		Imper. nájdi!		
		Past Part. Pass. nájden, nájdena		
doídem,	doíti,	P.P.A. došə̏l,		Impfve. dohȃjati
= to reach				

              Present   *Infin.*   *Past Part.Act.*   *Past Part.Pass.*
To carry = nésem   nésti(Impfve.)   nə́səl,[3] nésla   nesèn, neséna
           nǫ́sim   nosíti(Freq.)   nósil, nosíla   (po)nǫ́šen, -a
           ponésem   ponésti(Pfve.)
  To bring (carrying) = Impfve. prinȃšati Pfve. prinésti
  To lead = védem   vésti(Impfve.)   vę́dəl, védla   (od)vedèn, -éna
            vǫ́dim   vodíti(Freq.)   vódil, vodíla   vǫ́jen, -a
            povédem   povésti(Pfve.)
  To bring (a person) = Impfve. privȃjati Pfv. privésti
  To convey = pę́ljem   peljáti(Impfve.) *also* = to drive
     also   peljȃm
              vǫ́zim   vozíti(Freq.)   vózil, vozíla   (po)vǫ́žen, -a
              popę́ljem   popeljáti(Pfve.)
  To bring (conveyed) = Impfve. dovȃžati Pfve. pripę́ljati

[1]Or else with ẹ́ (open).
[2]poíde, poíti, pošə̏l, pošlȁ = to come to an end, run out.
[3]Colloquially pronounced nę́su.

The Formation of Aspects

Aspects in Slovenian are largely used and formed in the same way as in other Slavonic languages. (For the various uses of the Perfective Present, see above pp. 374-375). They are formed:—

1. The Perfective from the (simple) Imperfective by adding a prepositional prefix, e.g.:—

písáti	= to write	napísáti
prosíti	= to request	poprosíti
píti	= to drink	popíti, izpíti

2. The Imperfective from the (simple or compound) Perfective by lengthening a root vowel or inserting a syllable, e.g.:—

odgovoríti	= to answer	odgovârjati
umréti	= to die	umírati
pomóči	= to help	pomágati
kupíti	= to buy	kupováti
postáti	= to become	postâjati
dâti	= to give	dajáti
ubíti	= to kill	ubíjati
prejéti	= to receive	prejêmati
pláčati (Pfve.)><Sbcr. плáћати (Impfve.)		
	= to pay	plačeváti
oplodíti	= to fertilize	oplájati
spoznáti	= to recognize	spoznávati
réšíti	= to save, solve	reševáti

3. The Imperfective from the Perfective by changing the Infinitive ending, e.g.:—

pustíti	= to let, allow	púščati
dvígniti	= to lift	dvígati
udáriti	= to strike	udárjati
léči	= to lie down	légati
kreníti	= to turn, start	krétati

4. By using different forms of the same root or two entirely different roots, e.g.:—

Pfve.		Impfve.
vzéti (Pres. vzámem)	= to take	jemáti (Pres. jémljem)
príti	= to come	prihâjati
začéti	= to begin	začênjati
prinêsti	= to bring	prinâšati (not *prinositi!)
vréči	= to throw	metáti
réči	= to say	govoríti, práviti
storíti } naredíti }	= to do	{ délati { narêjati

One cannot tell only from the form of a verb to which aspect it belongs, except in the case of verbs with Infinitives in -ávati, -eváti and -ováti, which are Imperfective. As in other Slavonic languages, *compound* Perfective verbs acquire Imperfective aspects mostly by method No. 2 above, e.g.:—

vzdígniti (Pfve.) = to pick up   vzdigováti
podpísáti   " = to sign   podpisováti
potopíti   " = to drown (trans.) potâpljati

WORD ORDER WITH ENCLITICS

Slovenian, like Serbocroätian, has both freedom of word order like other Slavonic languages and certain rules with regard to the obligatory position of enclitic words in a written or spoken sentence. These rules are different in some respects from those in Serbocroätian.

The enclitics in Slovenian are:—

1. The auxiliary verbs (*a*) of the Past tense: səm, si, je, sva, sta, smo, ste, so. (No accents!).
    (*b*) usually also of the Conditional mood: bi.
    (*c*) the shorter form of the Future tense auxiliaries (which are the usual ones to use): bǫm, bǫš, bǫ, bǫva, bǫsta, bǫmo, bǫste, bǫdǫ.

2. The shorter forms of the Personal and Reflexive Pronouns: .Gen./Acc. me, te,se, ga; Gen. fem. je (= of her); Acc. fem. jo; Gen./Acc. naju, vaju, nas, vas, ju, jih; Dat. mi (= to me), ti (= to you, sg.), si, mu, ji, nama, vama, nam, vam, jima, jim.

The rule is that the *sentence* must start with a strong, i.e. non-enclitic accented word, except when—

(*a*) the interrogative particle "àli" is left out, or
(*b*) answering a question or referring explicitly to something in the preceding question or sentence and therefore implying a certain amount of emphasis on the pronoun. (Both these cases are rare in practice.)

After this accented word *and* any words closely associated with it and together expressing one idea, the enclitics must follow in the following order:—
1. The auxiliary verb—any of the above *except* je and the Future auxiliaries.
2. The Reflexive Pronoun, either Acc. or Dat., if present.
3. The Dat. Personal Pronoun.
4. The Gen. or Acc. Personal Pronoun.
5. je or the Future auxiliaries, bǫm, bǫš, etc.

E.g.:—

With auxiliary verb and pronouns:—

Jàz səm ga vídel, *or*
  Vídel səm ga   = I have seen him.
but—
  Jánez ga je vídel   = Janez has seen him.
likewise—
  Lépi Jánez ga je vídel = Handsome Janez has seen him.
  Jánez bi ga vídel   = Janez would see him.
  Ljudjẹ̑ so jo vídeli   = People saw her.
  Jàz səm mu ga dâl   = I gave it to him.
  Jánez ji ga je dâl   = Janez gave it to her.

With Reflexive Pronoun, as well as auxiliary verb and other pronoun:—

Jàz səm si jih kúpil, *or*
 Kúpil səm si jih   = I have bought them for myself.
Ti si si ju kúpil   = You have bought them (two) for yourself
    but—
Marîja si ga *je* kupîla = Mary has bought it for herself.

    Again—
Marîja *bi* si ga kupîla = Mary would buy it for herself.

Ljudjẹ̑ so si jih vzẹ́li = People have taken them for themselves.

Jàz səm se kǫ́pal, *or*
 Kǫ́pal səm se
Jàz səm se mu pokázal   = I showed myself (appeared) to him.

Pokázali so se mu   = They showed themselves to him.

    but—
Jánez se mi *je* pokázal = Janez showed himself to me.

Jánez se nam ga *je* iznẹ̑bil = Janez has got rid of it for us.

(Note that Slovenian, like western Sbcr., but not

eastern, preserves je with se.)
With Future auxiliary and pronoun:—

Jàz ga bǫ̑m vídel, *or*	= I shall see him.
Vídel ga bǫ̑m	
Marîja jo bǫ̑ vídela	= Mary will see her.
Ti se ga bǫ̑s bâl	= You will be afraid of him.

But when the *negative* is introduced, the Past auxiliaries, which are then prefixed by *ni-* (except in the 3rd pers. sing. which *becomes ni*)—cease to be enclitics, e.g.:—

Jàz ga nísəm vídel	= I have not seen him.
Jânez ga ní vídel	= Janez has not seen him.
Jàz mu ga nísəm dâl	= I have not given it to him.
Marîja si ga ní kupîla	= Mary has not bought it (for herself).
Jânez se mi ní pokázal	= Janez has not shown himself to me.

Note also the usual order with negative Future and Conditional with enclitics, e.g.:—

  Marîja je ne bǫ̑ vídela = Mary will not see her.
and—
  Marîja je ne bi vídela = Mary would not see her.

But note:—
Sentences starting with enclitics under the conditions explained above (p. 392, last paragraph).

(a) Si ga vídel? *for* Àli si = Have you seen him?
    ga vídel?
    Si se ga žę̑ navelîčal? = Have you already got tired of it?
(b) (Àli si mǫ́j prijâtelj? = Are you my friend?)
    Answer: Səm tvǫ́j = I *am* your friend.
      prijâtelj
    (Àli ga poznâ? = Does he know him?)
    Answer: Ga ne poznâ = He does not know him.

The other important difference, in comparison with Serbocr., is that in Slovenian, when a sentence has once started with a subordinate clause, that clause is treated as the initial strong word or word group for the main clause, and the main clause may then follow, even after a comma, *starting* with the enclitics (in the usual order). Compare:—

  Ǫ́če slovę́nskega slǫ̑vstva = The father of Slovenian
    je Prímož Trûbar   literature is Primož
                                 Trubar.

Dêcək z objókanimi očmî se mi je v srcệ smílil = The boy with his tearful eyes moved me to pity.

Kò je Lávdon oblệgal Béograd, se je Vệga pȓvič odlikovàl v vójski = When Lavdon was besieging Belgrade, Vega first distinguished himself in the war

Strâst, kì ga je imę́la v oblàsti, se mu je poznála pri vsâki besẹ̣di = The passion which held him in its power, was recognizable in his every word.

As in Serbocr., the same auxiliary is not repeated with successive verbs if they are closely connected by sense, e.g.:—

Ozŕla sta se na jokajǫ́čo mâter in obstála srẹdi sôbe = They (two) looked round at the sobbing mother and stopped in the middle of the room.

Prišəl səm, vídel in zmâgal = I came, I saw, I conquered.

The longer forms of the Personal Pronouns are used for emphasis only, as in other South and West Slav languages:—

Njéga se ne bǫm bál = Of him I won't be afraid!

The interrogative particle àli (like other interrogatives—adverbial or pronominal) should always *start* a question. After àli the enclitics follow in the usual order:—

Àli si mu ga dâl? = Have you given it to him?
Àli je Jánez bîl v Ljubljáni? = Has Janez been to Ljubljana?

cf.:—
Kjẹ́ jih je Jánez vídel? = Where has Janez seen them?

But the less frequent interrogative particle "li" stands second word in a question:—

Jè li rẹ̑s? = Is it true?

TEXTS

I
Sv. LUKEŽ, pogl. VIII.

5. Sejalec je šel sejat seme svoje. In ko seje, pade nekatero poleg ceste, in ga pogazijo, in ptice nebeške ga pozobljejo.

6. In drugo pade na skalo, in bržko vzraste, usahne, ker nima vlage.

7. In drugo pade sredi trnja, in trnje zraste ž njim vred in ga uduši.

8. In drugo pade na dobro zemljo, in ko zraste, prinese stoteren sad. Ko to pravi, zakliče: Kdor ima ušesa, da sliši, naj sliši!

II. F. PREŠEREN.

MEMENTO MORI

Dolgóst življenja našega je kratka.
  Kaj znancev je zasula že lopáta!
  Odprta noč in dan so grôba vrata;
al' dneva ne pove nobena prat'ka.

Pred smrtjo ne obvár'je koža gladka,
  od nje nas ne odkup'jo kupi zlata,
  ne odpodí od nas življenja tata
vesêlja hrup, ne pevcev pesem sladka.

Naj zmisli, kdor slepôto ljubi svéta
  in od veselja do veselja leta,
  da smrtna žetva vsak dan bolj dozóri.

Znabiti, da kdor zdaj vesel prepeva,
  v mrtváškem prtu nam pred koncem dneva
  molčé trobéntal bo: "Memento mori!"

III. IVAN CANKAR.

DESETICA

Dvanajst ali trinajst let mi je bilo; hodil sem v tretji razred realke. Ob desetih, ob uri počitka so vstali vsi, da bi si šli kupit malice k vratarju ali prebegat se po dvorišču. Grabilo me je za srce, da sem sam, čisto sam. Prišel je tovariš in rekel: "Ti, zate je pismo!"

Res je bilo na deski napisano moje ime. Šel sem k vratarju. Ko sem pismo dobil, so se mi roke tresle in skril sem se k oknu, da bi ne videlo tega svetega pisma nobeno nevredno oko. Odpiral sem počasi in čisto čudno, veselo in težko mi je bilo pri srcu. Tam so bile tiste velike, težke, neokretne črke: "Ljubi sin!" Zakaj mati se je bila šele od nas otrok naučila pisati, zato da bi je ne bilo sram. Ko sem razgrnil pismo, je zaklenketalo po tleh. Sklonil sem se in sem pobral: desetica je bila.

Tista tenka, ogoljena srebrna desetica, ki jih že zdavnaj ni več. Ko sem jo vzel v roko, me je obšlo kakor milost božja. Vse je vztrepetalo, vzplapolalo v meni, vzdignilo me kvišku kakor v plamenu ljubezni. Videl sem tisto ljubo, velo, trepetajočo roko, ki je držala med prsti poslednjo desetico ter jo naposled spustila v pismo. Zakaj desetica je bila poslednja, to sem vedel, kakor da je bilo na njej sami to napisano.

Skril sem se čisto v kot, da bi me nihče ne

videl. Iz srca, iz prsi, iz vsega telesa mi je
planil jok, stresal me kakor v vročici. Ali ko sem
se vračal po stopnicah v šolsko izbo, je bilo v meni
svetlo, svetlo. Iz daljave je videla mati mojo bolest
in se je smehljaje ozrla name, kakor se ozre samo
ljubo sonce.

IV. ALOJZ GRADNIK.

PRIČAKOVANJE

Kakó te čakam, o kakó te čakam!
Ko pride v hišo gost moj, črni mrak,
poslušam, ali čujem tvoj korak.

in vprašam: „Sam?"—„Sam, sam," mi tiho reče.
O, da bi vedel ti, kako me peče
in grize me beseda ta vso noč.

Vso dolgo noč je póstelj moja prazna
in vso, vso noč premolim, kakor blazna
ime presladko tvoje jecljajoč.

V. OTON ŽUPANČIČ.

MENI SE HOČE...

Meni se hoče širokih ravnin
in svobodnega obzorja,
meni se hoče mogočnih višin,
vladajočih zemljé in morja.

Meni se hoče čarobnih noči
in neba, ki se koplje v zarji,
in goščav, kjer hrupa človeškega ni,
in v vrhovih vale se viharji.

In viharjem bi dal svoje črne strasti
in v morjé bi potopil bolesti,
da mi duša očiščena v soncu živi,
polna jasne, ponosne zavesti!

VI. OTON ŽUPANČIČ. (Accented by Professor FRAN
RAMOVŠ.)

Z VLÂKOM

Odhòd. In zažvížgal je vlâk skozi mrâk.
O devộjka tî, ob óknu slonệ,
si-li čúla ta vrísk, plakajộč skozi nộč:
o zbộgom, domovína!?
In kakor ovíje se vâl okrog skâl,
ob Grâdu se líje Ljubljâna,
vsà z mệsecem posejána;
bojệče se strệhe stískajo,
po vr̂sti mi kríži blískajo
poslệdnji, zlât pozdrâv
in gâsnejo v mrâku daljâv.

Pošástno sopihajǫ́č
kot dêmon vlâk grè v nǫ̂č.

Mejíca têče ob tîru,
za njǫ̂ v polnôčnem mîru
gubíjo se pôlja, s stezâmi prepę̂ta,
tàm brę́za samótna, kraljîčna zaklę́ta,
glèj, mę̂secu kâže srebŕni nakît.
Z gorę́ razgledûje se Mâti Marîja,
sijâjna, pokǫ̂jna zrè svę̂t pod sebǫ́j,
sijâjna, pokǫ̂jna razlíva svît...
Vasíca med dŕevjem... in tàm domačîja
gozdârja na sâmem... in vsè za menǫ́j.

Pošástno sopihajǫ́č
kot dêmon vlâk grè v nǫ̂č.

Skrîj mę̂sec, za oblâk se skrîj,
nàj je ne vîdim, kakǫ́ bežî,
kakǫ́ ostâja za mâno
domovína...

S sîlo neznâno
si sę́gla mi do dúše globîn:
dozdàj nísem vę́del, kakǫ́ sem tvǫ́j sîn,
kakǫ́ te ljúbim globóko...
Domovîna, dàj mi rôko,
ne bę́ži, ostâni pri mę́ni,
tesnǫ̂, tesnǫ̂ me oklę́ni,
in pę̂l ti bom pę̂sem visóko,
pę̂l mâteri čęščę́ni,
kot ní ti šé nihčè pę̂l...
Sŕc milijǫ̂n bom razvnę̂l,
uklónil jih tvôji oblâsti,
raznę́til v dúšah strastî
bom plemeníte, mlâde,
da radovǫ́ljno zaklâde
nàjdrâžje pred-tę̂ položę̂.

Zvę́zde, stopîte z zenîta
stŕmih višîn!
Klîče vas sîn,
ki vsè predǫ́lgo v sŕcu mu spîta
tŕpka bolę̂st in ljubę̂zen, šè nę́ma...
V vênec sklenîte se, njǫ̂ naj obję̂ma,
njǫ̂, za vekǫ̂ve bolečîn.

Dàj svôjo glǫ́rijo, jútranja zârja!
Klîčem tè srę́di pǫ̂lnočî,
klîčem tè z glâsom stražârja,
ki štêje ûre, ko nǫ̂č ležî.
Dàj svoj škrlât,
njǫ́ ž njîm ogŕni,

ki žalovâla v oblęki je čŕni
dǫ́lge nočî brez nâd.

Ne bę́ži, ostâni pri méni,
domovîna, tesnǫ̑ me oklêni!

Pošástno sopihajǫ́č
kot dêmon vlâk grè v nǫ̑č.

Bežî... vse bežî... Le v dâlji planîne!
Tàm zémlja je nâša zakipę́la,
zahrepenę́la, v nebǫ̑ je hotę́la,
v višîno pognâla se kot vâl,
a v nalę́tu pod zvę́zdami vâl je obstâl...
Takó strmî zdaj sŕedi višîne
okamenę́li zanòs domovîne:
blestę̑ se v daljâvi razdŕti grebę̑ni,
nad njîmi, glèj, zvę̑zde, čuję́čni plamę̑ni:
ko spî naša zémlja, le ǫ̑ne nad njǫ̑
skrbę̑ z menǫ̑j, bedę̑ nad nočjǫ̑...
In glèj: planîne in zvę́zde gredǫ́ z menǫ̑j,
vse drûgo gubî se za mâno v pokòj.

Z menǫ̑j, ve zvę́zde, z menǫ̑j, ve planîne!
Razšîri, raztę́gni se, krǫ̑g domovîne,
razpnì se kot mǫ̑rje
v brezbrę́žno obzǫ̑rje,
dǫ̑m mǫ̑j!
Kàmor stǫ̑pi mi nóga—na tvójih sem tlę̑h...
kàmor nése me jâdro—na tvójih valę̑h...
kàmor hǫ́če srcę̑—pri svójih ljudę̑h...

Kám, mîsel? Stǫ́j!

Pošástno sopihajǫ́č
kot dêmon vlâk z menǫ́j grè v nǫ̑č,
in še dânes v tûji slâvi
nèznânca me tûja zârja pozdrâvi...

FOR NOTES

FOR NOTES

FOR NOTES

FOR NOTES

FOR NOTES

FOR NOTES

FOR NOTES

OTHER BOOKS FROM SLAVICA PUBLISHERS

American Contributions to the Eighth International Congress of Slavists. Zagreb and Ljubljana, Sept. 3-9, 1978. Vol. I: Linguistics and Poetics, ed. by Henrik Birnbaum, 818 p., 1978; *Vol. 2: Literature*, ed. by Victor Terras, 799 p., 1978.

Balkanistica: Occasional Papers in Southeast European Studies, ed. by Kenneth E. Naylor, I(1974), 189p., 1975; II(1975), 153p., 1976; III(1976), 154p., 1978.

Henrik Birnbaum: *Common Slavic Progress and Problems in Its Reconstruction*, xii + 436 p., 1975.

Henrik Birnbaum and Thomas Eekman, eds.: *Fiction and Drama in Eastern and Southeastern Europe Evolution and Experiment in the Postwar Period*, ix + 463 p., 1980.

Malcolm H. Brown, ed.: *Papers of the Yugoslav-American Seminar on Music*, 208 p., 1970.

Ellen B. Chances: *Conformity's Children: An Approach to the Superfluous Man in Russian Literature*, iv + 210 p., 1978.

Catherine V. Chvany: *On the Syntax of Be-Sentences in Russian*, viii + 311 p., 1975.

Frederick Columbus: *Introductory Workbook in Historical Phonology*, 39 p., 1974.

Dina B. Crockett: *Agreement in Contemporary Standard Russian*, iv + 456 p., 1976.

R.G.A. de Bray: *Guide to the Slavonic Languages. Third Edition, Revised and Expanded*, in three parts: *Guide to the South Slavonic Languages*, 399 p., 1980; *Guide to the West Slavonic Languages*, 483 p., 1980; *Guide to the East Slavonic Languages*, 254 p., 1980.

Paul Debreczeny and Thomas Eekman, eds.: *Chekhov's Art of Writing A Collection of Critical Essays*, 199 p., 1977.

Bruce L. Derwing and Tom M.S. Priestly: *Reading Rules for Russian A Systematic Approach to Russian Spelling and Pronunciation With Notes on Dialectical and Stylistic Variation*, vi + 247 p., 1980.

OTHER BOOKS FROM SLAVICA PUBLISHERS

Dorothy Disterheft: *The Syntactic Development of the Infinitive in Indo-European*, 220 p., 1980.

Ralph Carter Elwood, ed.: *Reconsiderations on the Russian Revolution*, x + 278 p., 1976.

Folia Slavica, a journal of Slavic and East European Linguistics. Vol. 1: 1977-78; Vol. 2: 1978; Vol. 3: 1979; Vol. 4: 1980-81.

Richard Freeborn & others, eds.: *Russian and Slavic Literature*, xii + 466 p., 1976.

Victor A. Friedman: *The Grammatical Categories of the Macedonian Indicative*, 210 p., 1977.

Charles E. Gribble, ed.: *Medieval Slavic Texts, Vol. I, Old and Middle Russian Texts*, 320 p., 1973.

Charles E. Gribble: *Russian Root List with a Sketch of Word Formation*, 55 p., 1973.

Charles E. Gribble: Словарик русского языка 18-го века/ *A Short Dictionary of 18th-Century Russian*, 103 p., 1976.

Charles E. Gribble, ed.: *Studies Presented to Professor Roman Jakobson by His Students*, 333, p. 1968.

William S. Hamilton: *Introduction to Russian Phonology and Word Structure*, 187 p., 1980.

Pierre R. Hart: *G. R. Derzhavin: A Poet's Progress*, iv + 164 p., 1978.

Raina Katzarova-Kukudova & Kiril Djenev: *Bulgarian Folk Dances*, 174 p., 1976.

Andrej Kodjak: *Pushkin's I. P. Belkin*, 112 p., 1979.

Demetrius J. Koubourlis, ed.: *Topics in Slavic Phonology*, viii + 270 p., 1974.

Michael K. Launer: *Elementary Russian Syntax*, xi + 140 p., 1974.

Jules F. Levin & Others: *Reading Modern Russian*, vi + 321 p., 1979.

Maurice I. Levin: *Russian Declension and Conjugation: a structural sketch with exercises*, x + 160 p., 1978.

OTHER BOOKS FROM SLAVICA PUBLISHERS

Alexander Lipson: *A Russian Course*, xiv + 612 p., 1977.

Thomas F. Magner, ed.: *Slavic Linguistics and Language Teaching*, x + 309 p., 1976.

Mateja Matejić & Dragan Milivojević: *An Anthology of Medieval Serbian Literature in English*, 205 p., 1978.

Vasa D. Mihailovich and Mateja Matejić: *Yugoslav Literature in English A Bibliography of Translations and Criticism(1821-1975)*, ix + 328 p., 1976.

Alexander D. Nakhimovsky and Richard L. Leed: *Advanced Russian*, xvi + 380 p., 1980.

Felix J. Oinas, ed.: *Folklore Nationalism & Politics*, 190 p., 1977.

Hongor Oulanoff: *The Prose Fiction of Veniamin A. Kaverin*, v + 203 p., 1976.

Jan L. Perkowski: *Vampires of the Slavs* (a collection of readings), 294 p., 1976.

Lester A. Rice: *Hungarian Morphological Irregularities*, 80 p., 1970.

Midhat Ridjanović: *A Synchronic Study of Verbal Aspect in English and Serbo-Croatian*, ix + 147 p., 1976.

David F. Robinson: *Lithuanian Reverse Dictionary*, ix + 209 p., 1976.

Don K. Rowney & G. Edward Orchard, eds.: *Russian and Slavic History*, viii + 311 p., 1977.

Ernest A. Scatton: *Bulgarian Phonology*, 224 p., 1975.

William R. Schmalstieg: *Introduction to Old Church Slavic*, 290 p., 1976.

Michael Shapiro: *Aspects of Russian Morphology. A Semiotic Investigation*, 62 p., 1969.

Rudolph M. Susel, ed.: *Papers in Slovene Studies, 1977*, 127 p., 1978.

Charles E. Townsend: *Russian Word-Formation, corrected reprint*, xviii + 272 p., 1975 (1980).

OTHER BOOKS FROM SLAVICA PUBLISHERS

Charles E. Townsend: *The Memoirs of Princess Natal'ja Borisovna Dolgorukaja*, viii + 146 p., 1977.

Daniel C. Waugh: *The Great Turkes Defiance On the History of the Apocryphal Correspondence of the Ottoman Sultan in its Muscovite and Russian Variants*, ix + 354 p., 1978.

Susan Wobst: *Russian Readings & Grammar Terminology*, 88 p., 1978.

Dean S. Worth: *A Bibliography of Russian Word-Formation*, xliv + 317 p., 1977.